Timothy Green Beckley's

STRANGE SAGA

UPDATED EDITION

A Life-Long Hunt For:
UFOS & ALIENS
UNKNOWN CREATURES
THE TRUTH ABOUT
GOVERNMENT COVER-UPS

"MR. UFO"
TIMOTHY GREEN BECKLEY

ONE OF THE MOST POWERFUL AND CONTROVERSIAL FIGURES IN UFOLOGY AND THE PARANORMAL SPILLS HIS GUTS!

The CIA used water-boarding techniques on him yet he never broke his code of silence.

The MIB stalked him and yet he didn't bat an eye (not any one of his three!)

The Dero set up an underground tunnel system in his basement and he uses it to go to work every day.

Tim Beckley - dubbed "Mr. UFO" because only he knows the TRUTH -- has been saving the world from aliens for fifty years. He is the reason they haven't landed on the White House lawn and why you remain safe in your homes.

At the age of ten, Beckley had his first of three UFO sightings. The event stunned him so much that he took out every book on the subject that he could find in the library. He wrote to the local media questioning the policy of silence he was convinced was taking place worldwide.

At fourteen, he was already appearing on national radio and TV, proclaiming the existence of the aliens (whom he now believes to be inter-dimensional to some extent and, as another likely possibility, the product of Nazi wartime technology.)

His bio is so extensive that he would have to run it in several parts.

Beckley started his writing/publishing career in his youth. At age 14, he purchased a mimeograph machine and started putting out "The Interplanetary News Service Report." Over the years, he has written over 50 books on everything from rock music to the MJ-12 documents. He has been a stringer for the national tabloids, such as the Enquirer, the Star and the Globe, and the editor of over 30 different magazines (most of which never lasted more than a couple of issues). His longest running effort was the newsstand publication UFO UNIVERSE, which went for 11 years. Today he is the president of Inner Light/Global Communications and editor of "The Conspiracy Journal" and "Bizarre Bazaar." He has been a regular contributor to "Fate Magazine" for over 40 years and more recently to "Open Minds Magazine."

He is one of the few Americans ever to be invited to speak before closed-door meetings on UFOs presided over by the late Earl of Clancarty at the House of Lords in England. He visited Loch Ness in Scotland while in the UK and went home with the belief that Nessie was somehow connected with the dragons of mythology as well as strange discs engraved on cathedrals and ghostly phenomena. He is also a recognizable figure on the pop culture scene, having produced and starred in several movies under the moniker of Mr. Creepo. He has hung out with the counterculture's greatest names and promoted rock shows and New Age festivals.

Though his time in the trenches is by no means over yet.

This book, for the most part, contains his early writings. Samples of his column On The Trail Of The Flying Saucers for Ray Palmer's "Flying Saucers From Other Worlds Magazine"

Timothy Green Beckley's Strange Saga
UPDATED EDITION
By Timothy Green Beckley

This edition Copyright 2013
by Global Communications/Conspiracy Journal

Published in the United States of America By
Global Communications/Conspiracy Journal
Box 753 · New Brunswick, NJ 08903

Staff Members
Timothy G. Beckley, Publisher
Carol Ann Rodriguez, Assistant to the Publisher
Sean Casteel, General Associate Editor
Tim R. Swartz, Graphics and Editorial Consultant
William Kern, Typesetting, Formatting and Cover Art

Sign Up On The Web For Our Free Weekly Newsletter
and Mail Order Version of Conspiracy Journal
www.ConspiracyJournal.com

Order Hot Line: 1-732-602-3407
PayPal: MrUFO8@hotmail.com

WHAT A LONG, STRANGE TRIP IT'S BEEN! 50 YEARS IN THE MAKING!

The Amazing And Bizarre Lifetime Journey Of Conspiracy Journal Editor And Publisher Timothy Green Beckley

STRANGE SAGA

CONTENTS

MR. UFO

GLOBAL COMMUNICATIONS

MR. E.T.

UFO REVIEW

MAX FYFIELD - 83

ADMIRAL BECKLEY

I had the weirdest dream!

GLOBAL COMMUNICATIONS

EX LIBRIS

POST OFFICE BOX 753
NEW BRUNSWICK, NJ 08903

Tim Beckley on William Shatner's
"Weird Or What"

UFOS AND THE IMMORTALITY FACTOR

By Timothy Green Beckley

Preface

As I sat in my hospital room recently attached to a medical contraption that looked like it was part of the main frame of the Enterprise, I couldn't help but think of my own mortality versus that of the UFO phenomena. I was filled with anxiety as I waited for them to put me on a stretcher and wheel me to the third floor of Bellevue for a Pacemaker to be put in.

Here I am in my sixties, but with the spirit (and perhaps mind some would say) of someone in their twenties or thirties.

I am not prone to think about death unless I am writing on electronic voice phenomena or séances and mediums, topics I have discussed widely in both my books and on shows like Coast to Coast AM. In fact, if you type my name and George Noory's into the search bar on You Tube you will come up with several of the shows I did for Coast on these very same topics.

Normally, my mind tackles topics like local hot spots to dine and un-wind, places to visit where bikini's are the norm at least nine months out of the year, and where the sidewalks are not rolled up before 10 PM. Basically, it's a hard knock life but someone has to live it.

So being in the hospital threw me for a loop, especially when my condition of not being able to breath so that I could walk down the block, hit me like a ton of bricks. At least, for a few days, I thought my life might be on the back burner, and I started to relive some of the good and the bad days of my humble existence.

Believe it or not, I thought about UFOs and how a subject considered so nutty five or six decades ago, has endured after all this time— time enough to possibly outlast me.

I reminisced about how I had my first of three sightings in 1957 around the same time I had read Major Donald Keyhoe's best seller ***Flying Saucers From Outer Space***. Everyone thought in those days the subject would either go away or the mystery would be unraveled in no time.

WRONG!

Here we are these many years later and the topic still remains one of great fascination and wonderment to a larger percentage of the world's population than ever before.

I thought of all the articles and books under my belt and the great times I had with fellow researchers trying to get to the bottom of what in hell's bells was going on up in the clouds and under our very feet.

Truth is UFOs/flying saucers/whirling discs – call them what you will – have been with us long before I was born, and will stay around long after I am a footnote in paranormal history.

Because this is the riddle that persists and will not go away, because it is part of our environment, always has been and always will be. Some may equate UFOs with extraterrestrials and of course there is a chance we could be dealing with space aliens, but there is something much more perplexing we have to live with that may always remain part of the unknown.

So let me tip my space antenna to those who have come before. The Ray Palmers, the Richard Shavers, the Donald Keyhoes the Jim Moseleys and on and on. They never got to know the full truth – because there is none my dear friends; though I will try finding out the solution to this mystery right down to the very end. Here in a nutshell is what I learned so far over fifty years of chasing down those buggers known as UFOs.

My best,

Timothy Green Beckley

November 2013

WHAT A LONG, STRANGE TRIP IT'S BEEN
TIMOTHY BECKLEY'S STRANGE SAGA:
AN INTRODUCTION

By Sean Casteel

In telling the story of Timothy Green Beckley, one wonders where to begin. There has been so much water under so many bridges that time is hard to grasp and truly lay hold on. But we can at least approach the telling of Beckley's personal odyssey by beginning at the beginning, when he was a child growing up in New Jersey.

"I don't know how many people know this," Beckley began, "but the house I grew up in in New Jersey was 'possessed' or 'haunted.' There were all sorts of poltergeist type manifestations. We had lights going on and off and we had doors opening and closing.

"I remember one time," he continued, "being seated at the kitchen table with my parents and there was a nice-size plate, chinaware, that just kind of scooted across the tabletop and dropped onto the floor but didn't break."

There were further events around the Beckley home that made it difficult for Beckley to sleep the peaceful sleep of childhood.

"When you're that age," he said, "certainly talk of ghosts and spooks will send a chill up your spine."

There was another incident that Beckley witnessed while with his mother, who was herself interested in the paranormal and had read some of the literature available at that time, the mid to late 1950s.

"She was interested in all these things," Beckley said, "and maybe

1

even brought on a little of the phenomenon. One time, in the middle of the night, she woke me up and told me to listen and see if I could hear anything. I can recall hearing the sound of a baby crying somewhere, but it didn't seem to be coming from inside the house, but from outdoors somewhere."

Beckley and his mother followed the sound to the back door. It was midwinter, and there was snow on the ground.

"We opened the door and there were what appeared to be baby foot-prints or booty prints in the snow. My mother followed them out to the gate and she said that they just disappeared."

There was also a later incident, this time involving Beckley's god-mother, who was a devout Catholic with little or no belief in the paranonnal.

"She had the fright of her life," Beckley said. "She described this to me later, about how she had been [visiting there] one night and heard this sound of the baby crying. She opened the door that led from our apartment to the apartment upstairs, and she said there was a woman standing there with a baby in her arms, trying to get the baby to stop crying. She knew it wasn't 'real.' There was nobody like that living there."

Beckley explained further that the woman his godmother saw was dressed in clothes from a much earlier period in history. His godmother crossed herself and closed the door. When she summoned up the courage to take another look, there was nobody there.

"Later on, we did find out that apparently back about 1910, 1912, dur-ing one of the big epidemics, someone had died in the house and their child had died at the same time or shortly thereafter. They had a wake with an open coffin with the baby in the woman's arms. Perhaps this was what was responsible for spooking me out.

BECKLEY'S HIGH STRANGENESS CONTINUES

Beginning around that same time, Beckley began to have what he feels were genuine "out-of-body-experiences," which may have been related to the ghostly happenings described earlier.

"The best way I could describe it," he said, "was that I was in a cold sweat and I woke up. I guess 'woke up' isn't the right word. I 'rose' up, and I could feel myself kind of floating in midair. The room had vanished, or seemed to have vanished, and had changed colors or dimensions. I could feel myself floating toward the ceiling.

"Now I didn't see any of this ectoplasm or the umbilical cord that's supposed to tie the body to the spirit or anything along that line, but I do remember hearing distinctly what I guess would be described as celestial sounds or celestial music."

Beckley admits to having had more than just one experience of this kind, but doesn't put himself in the same category as those who claim to be professional remote viewers.

MR. UFO SEES HIS FIRST SHIP

As a child of ten, Beckley witnessed his first UFO on a warm summer evening.

"In those days," he said, "we didn't have any air conditioning, so we just sat on the front stoop of the house until it got a little bit cooler indoors. It was probably around twilight. As I recall, someone came rushing up to the front porch where I was seated with my parents and maybe a couple of friends and pointed out two objects in the sky. One was across the street, hovering over an abandoned factory building, and the other was almost directly over the house."

Beckley and the rest of the group watched as the two objects changed position in tile sky in a very slow sweeping motion, with one of the ships again coming to a stop almost directly overhead.

"I can't claim that I saw any windows or landing gear," he said. "There were no Martians waving at us or anything like that. The oddest thing was that they appeared to be just right above the cloud layer, so you couldn't make out a lot of detail. But the one across the street, it looked like someone pulled a light switch and it just disappeared. The other one stayed up in the sky there for a little while afterwards, until, to be honest with you, we lost interest and went indoors."

The next day, the sighting was reported in the local newspaper, with the authorities attempting to put the matter to rest by using the old standby cover story of weather balloons to explain what so many people in Beckley's New Jersey hometown had seen.

"'Well, even at the tender age of ten," Beckley said, I had enough in-

3

telligence to realize that these things seemed to be under some sort of intelligent control. They weren't weather balloons bobbing and weaving in the air current or anything along that line. So I guess I was pretentious enough to write a letter to the local newspaper. In those days, people seemed to do that more than they do today."

Beckley said his local paper printed his letter in its entirety and he received a couple of phone calls from people who had more to say about the local UFO sighting. All of which was the beginning of a lifelong devotion to researching and writing about what for him has been an endlessly fascinating subject.

CONTACT OF THE PUBLISHING K[ND

Beckley began to read everything he could get his hands on about UFOs and the mysterious occupants who flew them. From pulp magazines that sold for a quarter to the more upscale magazines of maverick paranonnal publisher Ray Palmer, Beckley's voracious reading on the subject led him to try writing and publishing himself.

By his mid-teens, Beckley had started putting out his first UFO publication. It was mimeographed on his own home press and was called *The Interplanetary News Service Report*. He built the circulation to around 1500 copies—quite a challenge in those days considering he had to collate and staple every copy by hand. In 1968, famed author/researcher/publisher Gray Barker gave Beckley his first big break when Gray's *Saucerian Press* published Beckley's first book of major consequence, *The Shaver Mystery and the Inner Earth*, followed up a year later by *The Book of Space Brothers*. With these credentials under his belt, Beckley contacted his hero, publisher Ray Palmer, and offered to do a regular column for Palmer's *Flying Saucers From Other Worlds* magazine in exchange for some ad space so Beckley could sell his books.

Some of those early columns are featured in this volume.

"If you could find the actual magazines that published these columns," Beckley said, "including those from *Saga* and its spin-off *UFO Report*, which are also in the volume, you'd probably have to pay hundreds of dollars. I'm not even sure you could [find them] because I've looked around for copies and haven't been able to locate them. So basically, what I've decided to do in the *Strange Saga* book is combine all this early writing of mine—and some of it was really good—because in those days we actually did field trips. I mean we went to spots where all sorts of weird things were happening. Or we spent hours on the telephone investigating all kinds of concepts and different ideas, trying to pin down as much material and prove its accuracy as we could."

THE SAGA OF SAGA

"Now *Saga Magazine*," Beckley recalled, "was a newsstand publication. It was known in those days, I guess, as a men's adventure book. There were a couple of other competing publications. One was *Argosy*, which had been published for about 80 years, and the other one was *True*, which had published some of the original flying saucer stories by Major Donald Keyhoe in the early to mid-1950s. These publications—this was pre-*Playboy*—might have had a cheesecake photo or two, but basically they were adventure books and had tremendous circulations. I think that *True* had about maybe a million, *Argosy* was around 900,000, and *Saga* was third on the totem pole with maybe a 500,000 circulation or something like that. They had some really good investigative articles, and they paid. What a concept!

Sometime in the mid-1960s, Beckley made the acquaintance of a writer, researcher and promoter named Harold Salkin. Salkin had been on the scene when NICAP (the National Investigating Committee on Aerial Phenomena) was started and had been responsible for booking people like M. K. Jessup and George Adamski, as well as other early contactees on radio and television shows in the Washington, D.C. area so that people could hear these rather fantastic stories about flying saucers and beings from other planets. Salkin also booked a lecture date for Beckley in the nation's capital near the end of the Vietnam era.

"I was on a stage lecturing at the large YWCA," Beckley recalled, "and the street had been blocked off. But while I was onstage, I could see through a large picture window that there were hundreds of protestors running from the police in the street where they were lobbing tear gas. There were only five or six people watching my slide lecture—though I always suspected that some of those people running around in the street were trying to get in to hear my talk."

But back to Beckley's relationship with Harold Salkin.

"Harold was kind of the man behind the scenes," Beckley said. "He had graduated from Rutgers University and he was a great journalist. Of course, I was just starting out, and I had never been really good at English.

5

Most people are kind of shocked to find out that I just about squeaked through English in high school. It was never one of my better subjects, but after a while it kind of grows on you, and you just kind of learn.

"Anyway, Harold showed me a lot about writing and we worked on an article which is in the *Strange Saga* book. I do believe it's probably one of the most important in my career as a paranormal and UFO writer."

Working alongside Salkin, Beckley made one of the numerous fieldtrips that were to give his writings their firsthand authority and depth. Their first article together was called "***Apollo 12: Mysterious Encounters With Flying Saucers***," and appeared in the May 1970 issue of ***Saga***.

"We went to Washington, and spent about a week at NASA headquarters. We went through almost every transcript that we would possibly find trying to cull out reports of sightings of UFOs by our astronauts in space. Now there are some skeptics and those with un-open minds who will not do any of the research on their own but who insist that no astronaut has ever seen a UFO in space, with the possible exception of James McDivett. Well, this just ain't true. In fact in this very lengthy article that's reprinted word for word in the *Strange Saga* book, we go through almost all the transcripts and I would say there's probably at least 12 to 15 references to UFOs, some of which even followed some of our early space voyagers."

Beckley said it was revisiting articles like that that made publishing this book so exciting for him. He looks back especially fondly on a magazine called **UFO Report**, which was put out by the publishers of **Saga**, which had itself been published for over 40 years. In the mid-1960s, **Saga** started printing UFO articles on a regular basis. They eventually put together what is known in the trade as a "oneshot," which was a "pickup" special called **Saga's UFO Annual**, consisting of articles originally published in **Saga**. After several annuals, they decided to go quarterly, due to interest in the UFO phenomenon, and called it **UFO Report**. Eventually, it became a bimonthly with a circulation of around 60,000 before it was killed in the early 1980s due to dwindling newsstand sales. **UFO Report** published the early writings of Jerry Clark, as well as stories by Jacques Vallee, Otto Binder, Brinsley Le Poer Trench, John Keel, and of course, Beckley himself, some of whose efforts from that earlier era are reprinted in these pages.

"Looking back over them," he said, "I just think that there's some really worthwhile contributions here, and I don't think anything like this is being presented in the field today. One of the greatest stories here is my investigation into the kidnapping or space hijacking of a hunter by the name of Carl Higdon. I describe in really minute detail all the evidence that proves that this gentleman actually had some horrific experience. And I believe this is one of the few actual cases of people being taken onboard a UFO—being abducted and taken to somewhere else."

BECKLEY TAKES THE SHOW ON THE ROAD

Another early and profound influence on Beckley was radio talk show host Long John Nebel.

"Now Long John was a pitchman," Beckley said. "I mean this guy was good. He could sell you anything. He started out as a pitchman on Times Square, on the street corners of New York selling ice to Eskimos, as they say. Long John was the first all night radio talk show host. He started out at midnight and went until five 0 'clock in the morning, six or seven days a week. He had a clear channel in those days, 50,000 watts, and was heard in some thirty states. He had a massive audience.

"And one of his favorite subjects was UFOs. He brought on some of the most sensationalistic people you would ever want to hear. He brought on George Adaniski, Howard Menger, Dan Fry—people who claimed not just to have sighted UFOs,, but these people claimed that they had actually met people from other planets and had been taken on trips onboard UFOs. The stories went on and on. And even though Long John would say he didn't buy it, he presented the stories in quite a believable fashion. People actually got into it. Even if you didn't believe it, you were anxious to hear the next story, say, that George Adamski had to tell."

Beckley would stay up all night, hiding under the covers with his transistor radio and listening to Long John and company tell their incredible stories. Beckley would often be late for school after an all-nighter with Long John.

"I was much more interested in Alpha Centauri than I was in algebra, I'll tell you that," Beckley quipped.

Later, as a young adult Beckley took to the road; as he says he was fed up with the ignorance of the masses—and the media in particular—when it came to the reality of the vast UFO situation. He covered a good many states, at his own expense, in order to promote UFOs and bring up the public's awareness level.

"I tried not to come off as a fanatic," he recounted. "I touted myself as a journalist who had an open-minded interest in the subject and could see its relevance in a lot of different ways. After all, by that time, I had written probably six or seven books on related matters, and had become a stringer for such national publications as the *Enquirer*."

As can be seen from the various press clippings included in this volume, the reaction he generated was a mixed bag. Some are sympathetic to the "cause," while others are written with tongue in Beckley's cheek.

"This was long before Budd Hopkins or Ray Fowler or Whitley Strieber were out there," he said. "And later on, when they came along, I kind of handed them the torch so to speak because I got tired of doing it year after year."

Before passing the torch, however, Beckley managed to become a regular feature on many a radio talk show.

"Pepper-tongued Barry Farber and the arch conservative Bob Grant thought they could chew me up and spit me out, but they found out I wasn't an easy mark for their UFO stupidity. I even became something of a regular on the Long John Show, although more so with his wife Candy Jones, after John became sick with cancer and finally passed. Candy would have me on just about every Sunday night to talk about Bigfoot, Loch Ness, Mothman, and anything else her vast audience wanted to delve into."

Harold Salkin was still helping to book Beckley, and even set him up with Major Wayne Aho out of Seattle to give a press conference and lecture at the famed Space Needle in a little known small auditorium in the structure's base.

"Some of the hosts would take it seriously," he said, "and were very glad to have me on their programs, and others just thought it was totally unacceptable. But I did manage to collect quite a scrapbook from my travels. In fact, in the *Strange Saga* book that accompanies this interview, I'm actually going to reprint some of these old magazine and newspaper articles from around the country. Take them for what they're worth, with a grain of salt."

In the course of his travels, Beckley would find himself knocking on farmer's doors in the middle of the night to investigate reported UFO sightings in the rural settings in which they so often happen. Quickly, he discovered that when one anomalous event was reported, it was quickly followed by a whole slew of other paranormal happenings, as if a window had been opened to another dimension or time zone.

"So I was out there," he said, "huffing and puffing and promoting UFOs, and this was back in the days when there was actually a little bit of legwork to be done, field investigations. Today most researchers seem content to stay in front of their computer and exchange emails and sightings reports, and there are very few people who are actually seriously investigating the phenomenon anymore, with the possible exception of MUFON (The Mutual UFO Network). I do give them credit for staying in there all this time and doing the best they can to come to some kind of rationale about UFOs.

AN INVITATION FROM THE HOUSE OF LORDS

Beckley said that from his early days, beginning in his teens when he published his own mimeographed UFO newsletter, he had established contact with some 125 organizations around the world that researched the subject and put out their own publications. Beckley and the other groups exchanged newsletters and research information and formed a formidable network.

One of those informed associates happened to be an Englishman named Brinsley Le Poer Trench, who, long before Erich von Daniken, was writing books about ancient astronauts.

"His book called *Sky People* was absolutely tremendous," Beckley enthused. "It's a rare book now, but if you can, try to find it and read it. It's just a fabulous read, and he was long, long before his time. Anyway, Brinsley was also the Earl of Clancarty, and of course he sat in the House of Lords, and he was responsible for trying to get the Crown, the British government, to try to open their UFO files. Being in bed with the U.S. military, they kept to the skeptical party line and said, well, there's nothing to these UFOs.

It's called kissing international political ass," Beckley reminds us.

Beckley's friend Brinsley had set up a private group at the House of Lords, which hoped to bring pressure on the Crown to release their information on the subject. There were about 40 members, meeting every couple of months and listening to UFO researchers and authorities from around the world that would come to address the minority gathering of believers.

"It was just something you did on your own," Beckley said. "It wasn't a paid appearance or anything like that. In fact, you even had to get there on your own. I kind of combined it with a couple of lectures while I was in the U.K., and then later on I went up to Loch Ness and did a little bit of investigation there, into the Loch Ness Monster and some poltergeist experiences, so that my expenses would be covered. But I managed to meet people like Lord Hill Norton, a retired admiral from the British fleet, who passed away recently. Lord Hill Norton had a tremendous interest in UFOs, as did other members of the House of Lords. Some of them had actually had sightings of their own. But that was the pinnacle of my traveling experiences, to be able to speak at the House of Lords."

AND A FEW ROCK STARS ALONG THE WAY

While it is inarguably difficult to cram even a small portion of Beckley's adventures over the years into the small amount of space available here, it must at least be mentioned that Beckley has met a few rock stars and other celebrities on his strange path to the present. Beckley at one time worked as a concert and dance promoter in New York, often tying things together with paranormal themes and futuristic alien costumes that fit together neatly with the glam rock of the 1970s.

Beckley at one point befriended John Lennon's former girlfriend, May Pang, who told Beckley about the multifaceted UFO she and the much-loved Beatle had seen from Lennon's balcony overlooking the Manhattan skyline. Beckley also spoke with David Bowie and other rockers who have an alien tie-in.

"Most people don't realize," Beckley said, "that when David Bowie was a kid, he was the editor of his own little UFO newsletter over in England. So I went through my pop star days, and I still keep in touch with some of the people in the music business. There is a definite connection between UFOs and celebrities and rock and roll music and so forth."

As for a way to put it all in a nutshell, the years of writing and researching and slogging through fields in the wee hours of the morning, Beckley said, "I do know that whatever these [UFOs] are, and of course we've discussed this before, I'm not necessarily sure they're all occupied by aliens from outer space, but they do seem to be intelligently controlled and they can read our minds. So that's the thing that really freaks you out after awhile, when you realize that they're one step ahead of us. But maybe that's what they're trying to show us, that we haven't reached our full potential yet, but that we might not have far to go if we clean up our act."

And if Beckley is right in that estimation of the situation, then maybe catching up on your reading with the book you hold in your hands is a smart way to respond to the challenge presented by UFOs and their mysterious occupants, a challenge Beckley has been facing up to for more than forty years. It is impossible to list all of Beckley's achievements across that span of time. There is, for instance, the "high traffic" *School of Occult Arts and Sciences* that Beckley ran in New York and which offered lectures by many of the biggest names in the field.

He also edited about 30 different magazines over the years, with titles such as *UFO Universe, Angels and Aliens, Prophecies and Predictions, Front Page Disasters, Super Bowl Classics, Soap Opera Today, Moped Action, Future Fantasy* and *Joe Franklin's Memory Lane News*. There was also the world's only flying saucer newspaper, *UFO Review*, which Beckley published for over a decade and which is now combined with the *Conspiracy Journal*, a quarterly publication read both online at ConspiracyJournal.com and in a snail mail edition.

And we haven't even touched on Beckley's career as a B movie producer and horror movie host (i.e. Mr. Creepo) as it's really not related to our current subject matter.)

The CD that accompanies this book contains an interview I did with Beckley that casts an even fuller shadow of the man, who is a true journeyman of popular culture. But closest to his heart is his coverage of UFOs and the paranormal, and what is contained herein is ample proof of his devotion to finding the truth behind innumerable mysteries. While the tone and meaning of the articles collected here changes from year to year, from one experience to the next, the reader can begin to piece together a version of the truth from Beckley's writings that will stand the test of time with the best of them.

Charley Hickson and Calvin Parker

On the night of October 11, 1973 two very frightened men from Pascagoula, Mississippi presented themselves at the Jackson County Sheriff's department and told an incredible tale. Charley Hickson and Calvin Parker claimed that while they were fishing in a local river they were abducted by three bizarre robot-like creatures, taken aboard a UFO and physically examined.

FLYING SAUCERS
MYSTERIES OF THE SPACE AGE

MYSTERY ON THE MOHAWK

SPACEMEN IN HISTORY

A ROUND-UP ON THE BENDER MYSTERY

FLYING SAUCERS
DECEMBER, 1966 • • • Issue No. 50
50¢
MYSTERIES OF THE SPACE AGE

HOW EARTH "U.F.O." PILOTS WOULD APPEAR TO MARTIANS

ON THE TRAIL OF THE FLYING SAUCERS

FLYING SAUCERS
MYSTERIES OF THE SPACE AGE

MACACA NEMESTRINA—Captain of the Scout Ship Bios

TRACKING THE ASTRONAUTS IN APOLLO 8

100 YEARS BEHIND IN THE SPACE RACE

SPACE KINGS OF ANCIENT ROME

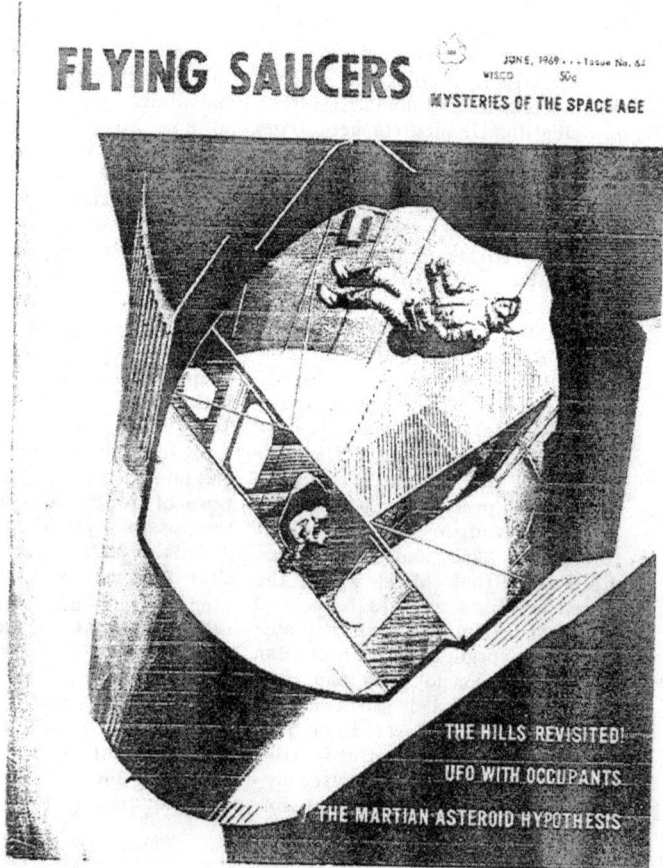

FLYING SAUCERS
JUNE, 1969 • • • Issue No. 64
WISCO   50¢
MYSTERIES OF THE SPACE AGE

THE HILLS REVISITED!

UFO WITH OCCUPANTS

THE MARTIAN ASTEROID HYPOTHESIS

Ray Palmer got me into this in a big way. He published some of my first works, including a regular column *On The Trail Of the Flying Saucers* which lasted for several years. We have lost most of the columns. Perhaps readers *can* help me located the missing **ones so** I *can* complete my files.

13

ON THE TRAIL OF THE FLYING SAUCERS

TIMOTHY GREEN BECKLEY
Director
Interplanetary News Service

Issue No. 50
Dec. 1966

Driving to **Cleveland** with Gray Barker (author **of** THEY KNEW TOO MUCH ABOUT FLYING SAUCERS) **we** couldn't help but get **the** feeling that this **was** to be a summer full of Flying Saucers. Because of the sightings throughout **the** country we knew that interest would be at an all-time high. And **we** were right!

Our **purpose** in going to Cleveland was to attend the 3rd annual Congress of Scientific UFOlogists held *from* June **23** to 26. The **Congress is a gathering** of *serious* **researchers** who meet each year TO discuss the **Current** status of flying **saucer** research and *to* debate **openly** what **new** ways can be found **to enlighten the** public about **UFOs.**

In our caravan **of cars we** *also* had James W. Moseley, editor **of** SAUCER NEWS; **John** and Mary Robinson of SEARCHLIGHT; Ray Barthowech **of** *the* New Jersey UFOlogical Society; Mel Ginsberg **and** Sol Lipsky long-time New York City **saucer** 'fans''; and pretty Pam Spelman.

We arrived **in** Cleveland about 10:30, **June 22nd, and checked** *into* the **Park Brook** Motel where the closed **sessions** were to be held. **1** had **just** finished signing the register when the Georgia delegation of Allen Greenfield, Donald **Cook and** Brad Cummings arrived. It had **been** some months since I had **last** seen my **good** friend and **close associate,** Allen Greenfield, **so** I **quickly** excused myself and pulled him **aside. I** im-

mediately **asked** him if he had heard anything more from **a** seemingly **serious** character who visited Greenfield's Atlanta home some months **ago** and was planning to *enter* a particular cave which he **knew to** be infested with **dero. Alien** said that he had not **and** hoped that **he** had not met his **fate in a pot of** boiling water as part **of** a dero stew. We both laughed and admitted that there **was** probably not much to the story anyway.

At **about this** time 1 was reintroduced to **Rick** Hilberg editor **of** UFO Magazine. **Ed** Beoble and the local **crowd** of **saucer** researchers from Cleveland **who have** set up *the* Congress each **of** its three **years.**

After **a quick interruption to** unpack, *eat* dinner and **freshen up** *from* she **12-hour drive** (marred by **frequent stops** at Howard Johnson) 1 **had a pre-planned** appointment with Tom Powell **who is** known widely as **a professional pickpocket,** comedian and television personality. The **purpose** of our **meeting was** *to* **discuss** the possibility of doing a special half-hour film on flying saucers for Video Star **Productions (Box** 12404, Cincinnati, Ohio 45212) which Tom **Powell** represents. We **talked** into the early **hours** of the morning about the nature **of** UFO research and **the material** which would **be needed for** such a program. Readers are **undoubtly familiar with** the difficulty involved **in** coming **up** with a **sensational pro-**UFO segment **of any** type. Regardless

Mr. Powell **informs m e** that **Video Star is** still "optimistic that **such a** show *can* be formulated." **He** makes a special **request of** all *saucer* **researchers** *to* come **up** with ideas **and suggestions. He believes, as does** this writer, that **if** UFO **groups are truly** founded "for the **purpose of** enlightening the public to the **presence** of these objects, which **you** are **so** confident **exists**; then **this** filmed *segment* should comprise **a** major project **on your** part."

The closed *sessions* ran smoothly for the **next** three days. Saucer groups were represented from ten different states.

But the big **event was yet to** come. **On** Saturday, June 25th, over 500 people jammed into the **new** Valley Forge high school auditorium to hear **talks by** Allan Manak, chairman **of** the **congress;** Elmer Schutt of the American UFO Committee; Pete Thompson, an independent UFO **researcher,** Lawrence Blazey, chairman of the Cleveland UFO Society; James W. Moseley, editor of SAUCER **NEWS;** John J. Robinson of SEARCHLIGHT; and this writer.

However, the main event **of** the evening was *a* lengthy illustrated slide lecture presented by Gray Barker. in **his** talk Gray **discussed** how **he** first became interested **in** Flying Saucers through his- **investigation** for FATE MAGAZINE of the Flatwoods **monster.** He went **on** to show how UFOs appeared over Washington in 1952, and why they **have gained considerable** acceptance over the **last** few years.

The large **turnout** at the **open** session **was** due to **advanced publicity on** several radio stations. Just the eve-

Some of the *delegates* present at the 3rd Congress of Scientific UFOlogists ic Cleveland.

Some of the crowd *that* turned out **for** this *year's* *convention* held **by** Buck Nelson.

ning **before,** from midnight to 5:30, Gary Short (of station WERE *in* downtown Cleveland) **had** as his **guests** Jim Moseley, **Gray Barker,** Allan Manak, Rick Hilberg and this columnist. During the **wee** hours **of** the morning **discussion** centered **around** recent **UFO** sightings in Michigan, **the** Shaver *mystery,* etc. **Hundreds** of phone calls **were** also **taken** from **listeners.**

It **was** decided unanimously that next **year's congress would be** held in New York City. Instead **of** merely having **one** main **session,** the *1967* gathering **will** be comprised of *a* 4-**day** convention *to* **celebrate** the 20th anniversary **of** Kenneth Arnold's sighting. Although nothing is definite as of **this** writing, **it is** hoped that guest **speakers** will include the editor of **this** magazine, Ray Palmer; Howard **Manger,** noted contactee; and **perhaps even** Ken Arnold **himself.** In any respect this convention will be the biggest and largest: *ever* held on the *east* coast. Visitors are *expected* to attend from almost **every stare** and perhaps *a representative or two* from some **of** the overseas groups. Readers **of** FLYING SAUCERS **will be kept posted** on **events** for this convention *as* time proceeds.

While the gathering **in** Cleveland **was** probably the **best,** there were other conventions **of** a slightly different nature. **These** *were* run by several of the better **known** contactees.

We sent *the* assistant director *of*

the Interplanetary **News** Service, long time **Fortean** expert Lucius Farish, out to Buck Nelson's **annual** convention **in** Mountain View, Missouri.

Buck Nelson is the **fellow who** claims that he **was** visited **in** *1954* **by** spacemen **and** later taken **for** *a* ride to **Mars,** Venus and **the** moon **in** a dome-shaped scout **ship.**

Lucius **reports that** although the turnout **was** rather poor, many **speakers** were **present to** tell why the space people **are being seen** in our atmosphere, **and** *what* we can learn from them.

A reporter **from the** Cape Giradeau, **Missouri** paper interviewed Lucius and *was* surprised to **learn** that all **those in** attendance did not believe every **speaker,**

Harry Fleenor **was** the **master of** ceremony and **introduced Lucius** on the speaker's platform before he could **turn** around.

But **probably** the largest of **all** gatherings took **place in** Reno, Nevada from July 8 to 10th. Head saucerite here **was** Gabriel Green, president **of** the Amalgamated Flying Saucer Clubs of America. The 3-day convention **was** held **at** the beautiful, **new** Centennial coliseum.

Harry Hoffman **of** the Interplanetary **News** Service was in attendance *and* said the program included some **twenty-one** different **contactees.** Among **these** were Michael "X" Barton, Dan Fry, Mel Noel, Howard Menger, Laura Mundo, Hope Troxell,

Carl Anderson, George Van **Tassel, Wayne S.** Aho and George King. All these tell similar stories **of** traveling, either in the **body or** by astral means, **in** flying **saucers,** meeting **space people** and visiting other planets. But, according to *Harry,* perhaps *the* favorite **of** the crowd **is** a pleasant and **charming** fellow **known** as Chief Frank B. Standing Horse from **Perris,** California. The chief claims he **has** made more than **a dozen** trips **in** flying **saucers** and **spent** Christmas day **of** *1962* **on** one of **the** planets **in** this **solar system.** Though not **everybody seemed** to **believe** his **various** accounts, they all seemed *to* agree *he* had a magnificent and **unusual** story **to tell.**

Recently **we** received a lengthy documented report from **the** SBEDV, which is a **large** civilian-led UFO society **in** Brazil. This **report** centered **around** the **story** which I *am* **about to** relate.

Chief Standing Horse, colorful **contactee pictured** here with **followers as he camps out on the grounds of** Buck Nelson's Convention. The Chief was the star of the **giant three day Reno**

It was *a* humid evening in late **August of** 1963. The **moon was** at its fullest and **was** brilliant. The stars twinkled with **an uncanny** eeriness. **Near the** town **of** Sagrada Famila live the Eustaguio family. Their home is modest **and** in a rural area. They have *not* heard of "Flying Saucers" **and** do not read science fiction. Their family **is** a religious one and so their children have been brought **up always** **to** tell the **truth.**

15

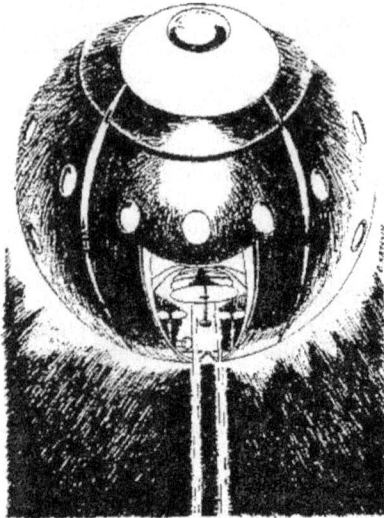

Illustration of the craft that hovered silently in the air over the single occupant that descended to the ground.

On this particular evening the two Eustaguio boys, Fernando 11, and Ronaldo 9, were told to go down to the well in the garden and clean the family coffee filter. The two went down the little stone stairs that led to the well. With them was Marcos, a neighbor boy. The night was so clear and so luminous they didn't immediately recognize the sphere that was floating in front of them at the well where they were standing turning the pulley to bring up a bucketful of water.

When they first saw the luminous sphere, it was above the trees, nearly touching some branches. Inside, the boys could make out people sitting about, one behind the other in four or five rows. Then suddenly the door shot open, making a humming noise. Two luminous parallel bands directed downward toward the ground near the flower bed. A slender being, about ten feet tall, glided on the two bands of light to the ground, landing near the foot of the stone stairway.

The being rode the beams down, his arms outstretched over the bands, floating down in a rather slow movement. Once he reached the ground he than walked about twenty feet in an odd fashion, by standing, his back stiff, his legs open, and arms stretched, balancing himself. He moved, swinging his body from left to right continuously until he reached a rock in the yard, and proceeded to sit down. All three boys agreed that the being wore a transparent helmet

over his head, and had only one visible eye of dark color situated in the middle of his forehead. The 'spaceman'' had on high boots, which had some sort of long thick triangular spikes sticking out from each. This spike made a strange impression in the soft earth, which could be seen during a period of several days following the incident.

The trousers which the being wore seemed to fasten itself to the boots in a ring fashion. The moment the being hit the ground, his suit seemed to inflate as if filling with air. His garment was similar to leather and was very shiny. Fernando said that the being had a copper-colored box on his back, and a square pack which covered part of his chest. He said this pack would give off flashes of light, and he got the impression it was either a camera or a flashlight.

The ship, still hovering in the air suspended above the boys and me single occupant who came out, seemed to have a framework of horizontal and vertical pieces which also had a ring-like effect. From the open door-way the boys could plainly see other occupants sitting behind control panels turning knobs and flicking switches.

Frozen in their tracks, the boys now say the being reached for one of them as if he meant to sweep him up in his giant hands and carry him away to the waiting craft. Fearing the worst, Fernando picked up a brick and was about to heave it at the spaceman, who was seated on the rock, when the being stood up and stared at the youth. Fernando was unable to move, or to throw the brick. It was if the being had control over his body and the movements which he made.

As if struck by the militant action of the boy, the ''spaceman'' moved away, moving his mouth in a vertical fashion, showing a row of nice white teeth with two big teeth at the corners of the mouth, one directed downward, die other up. The being proceeded to enter the ship, gliding up the beams of light emitted from the craft. This time, however, the ''spaceman'' floated skyward with his hands pressed against his body and not outstretched as before.

Looking through the door of the open ship the boys saw that all the crew members were of about the

same size and stature and wore the same transparent helmets. They also felt that one of the beings on board was a female, since it had long hair pulled tightly in a bun, while all the others appeared to be bald.

Somehow, as the beings left, the boys felt that the occupant who did descend to the ground was not really attempting to hurt them. They could not explain how they got this impression, but their fear was gone. They also were quite certain that he would return again. When asked how the boys knew this, they answered that it was just a feeling as if someone was talking to them. A local Brazilian UFO researcher said this was telepathy, and claimed that others in the vicinity had also reported strange objects in the sky that evening.

Last time 1 wrote 1 requested readers to send in reports of their personal sightings and also experiences that would tend to confirm the Shaver mystery. One of the most in-

Illustration of ''spaceman'' seen by members of the Eustaguio family in Brazil.

Buck Nelson, friendly master of ceremonies at annual convention in Mt. View, Missouri.

teresting responses I received came from **Mary** Chrietzberg of Tipton, Georgia. In her letter, which I am about to **quote,** she tells *of a* most **unusual** experience.

"I *am* not saying our house is, or ever has been, haunted. I simply don't know the explanation *for* what I'm about to **describe.** We moved here in *1960.* For the first 6 or 7 months we heard **all** sorts of peculiar and **unexplainable noises,** which **we** no longer hear.

"**We** discovered later that **the** man who lived here before we came was extremely fond of the place **and** he **passed away** while living **here. So** it could be possible that our house has been haunted. However, it could also **be** that what I am *going* to relate could **be** connected to the Shaver mystery. That **is** if there **is** a cave of dero **and** tero nearby.

"Anyway when **we first** arrived and **were busy** moving things **around, we** noticed **a radio could** be **heard** day and night. However, since we were **so** preoccupied, **we** paid little attention to it at first. One night after we had **been** here about a week I decided to discover which home played their radio **all** night and **all** day, **loud enough** *for* us to hear. So I **stood** *at* the window facing *the* **neighbor's house** toward the west. The noise became much softer. When I went **to a** window facing east, toward **the** neighbor on the other side of **our** house, the sound **almost** disappeared.

"I was *quite* mystified since I could hear the radio, **or** whatever **it** was, **quite** loudly while in my room,

"Having *a* natural *case* of noise trouble, I went **outside** and **kept walking** all **around** the house. Outdoor **no** noise could **be** heard anywhere. There **was** nothing **at** all wierd or frightening about all this. It **was**

simply puzzling. Being determined to find the source of this noise, I slowly **walked** over **every** inch of *the* house **in** order to discover at what point the noise **was** loudest. To my awe it was **best** heard while standing **over** the hall furnace! I could hear it more plainly in my **room,** but it was louder over the furnace.

"**At** first I figured that *our* furnace somehow picked up sounds from a radio *station.* The only factor which clashed with this *theory* was that it always sounded like a group of men in a serious discussion. There were never **any women's or** children's voices, **and never any music** or laughter. I've never heard of *a* radio station where nothing was heard but *a* group of men gossiping continually, day and night, for six months.

"And **it wasn't** me having hallucinations either. My parents also heard this, **as** did everyone who came visiting **during** that period."

Miss Chrietzberg *goes* on to **ex**plain that **this** reminded her of all the people who claim to hear voices which seem to come from nowhere.

I immediately wrote to the best source of information on *this* topic, Richard Shaver himself, and asked for his opinion. **In** his reply he mentioned the fact that many people he **has** talked with over the years **have** had similar **experiences.** Often these voices come through **such** things **as** bed **posts,** welders' **irons,** and similar everyday devices.

Shaver *also* replied that much **is** *to* be learned about the pre-deluge civilizations that populated the world and later hid in the **caves. These** an-

cient peoples, Shaver believes, were highly **skilled technicians** in art and optics *so* much **so** that they **made** 3-D paintings on rocks. Shaver **has** made a collection of these **rocks** and **has been able to** decode some of these ancient paintings. **We** quote **here** from **Dick:** "As you **study** these rocks **you** learn to distinguish early or more **ancient** races by the costumes and the surroundings, The earliest *are* all living underwater. Men **living** in crevices **and sea** caves **using a** highly developed camouflage technique to protect themselves from **such** unstoppable *creatures* as huge tiger sharks **and** killer whales. From the **rocks** I have **been** able to decode, it **seems** that these underwater people had a *steady* running battle with *a* long-legged creature very much like **the** Tyrannosaurus, but smaller. In *the* same way that the Indian **stalked** buffalo wearing a buffalo hide, there are pictures **of** early **undersea** men stalking herds **of** these **creatures.** The whole scene **is** underwater **and is very beautiful."**

Another reader, Lawrence **Rail** of **Alden,** N. Y., **reported** that while the current flap in Michigan was going on, **he on** several **occasions** saw mysterious objects in the sky. His **best look, however,** came **on** March *9,* 1966 at about 4:30 p.m. At **this** time he observed a huge odd-shaped object which **was hovering** silently at **about** 200 feet. **He** estimated it to be about 150 feet long, 100 **feet** wide and *20 feet* thick. **After** hanging silently for *a* few minutes, **it** moved **slowly** over a wooded area behind **his** home. From some **sort** of **window or** porthole **on**

Samples of the picture rocks uncovered. Richard Shaver appears in foreground.

the bottom he could see some sort of instrumentation as well as a red light that shone brightly. Some friends of Mr. Rail reported seeing an object which came to rest in a field about two miles outside Alden. It reportedly left a round and burned-out indention in the ground about 75 feet in diameter.

A peculiar light phenomenon appeared in the southern sky of Copenhagen, Denmark on May 16th, according to a newspaper clipping translated for us by John Prytz.

Kastrup Airport, the Copenhagen Meteorological Institute, and the Air Force were phoned by hundreds of persons who had seen the light and who wanted an explanation for its presence. In all cases the caller was told that no explanation could be offered.

The impression of the light varied quite a bit. People reported to have seen it over different locations, but they all agreed that it was a bright, strong light which disappeared at intervals, but was largely stationary.

In the control tower at Kastrup airport, the phenomenon was observed as early as 9 o'clock. They judged it to be someplace over East Germany. Airline pilots who observed it on their way to Copenhagen said the same.

On the radar screen at Kastrup airport a lot of flying activity could be observed over East Germany and it was thought that pursuit planes were sent aloft to investigate the light.

From the roof of the Berlingsky Times, also in Copenhagen, the light appeared simply as a brilliant star.

Just goes to show you that 'swamp gas" is a global phenomena.

Some time ago I received a most interesting manuscript from Henry R. Gallart who has done a great deal of research on the west coast into the various contact stories. Strangely enough, although he began as a skeptic, his investigation resulted in his

receiving some rather odd messages too. Mind you, Gallart is not a fanatic. Indeed, he is a very educated man with a degree from Columbia University.

After five years of research and talking to hundreds of saucer observers, Mr. Gallart believes he may have unlocked the door to how the UFOs manage to move through our atmosphere so quickly and without noise.

Through personal experience the author also came in contact with the Bender mystery and himself experienced the strange headaches and sensations which Albert K. Bender reportedly did. The author of this manuscript, which we titled FROM OTHER WORLDS, believes that the same beings who were in contact with Al Bender may also have been responsible for his condition.

Perhaps the most interesting incident related in this book was given to Gallart by Riley Crabb, director of the Boarderland Research Association (Box 548, Vista, Calif.). It centers around the alleged landing of several space ships at Edwards Air Force Base. This important event, if true, is said to have occurred in February of 1954. One of those persons at the base at the time said he had the distinct feeling that the world "had come to an end with fantastic realism."

Rumors also sprang up to the effect that President Eisenhower was spirited over to the base one night during a visit to Palm Springs. To

back up this rumor, and give it considerable weight, Riley Crabb did a little investigation of his own. He discovered that TIME MAGAZINE for March 1, 1954 carried a story which says that 75 news, radio, and TV reporters covering the President's trip to Palm Springs gave a demonstration of "mass hysteria" trying to discover what had become of the commander-in-chief. According to Crabb, "the Associated Press man flashed on his New York wire that Eisenhower had been assassinated." This was retracted a matter of seconds later.

This is only one of the unusual and important features of Mr. Gallart's manuscript. If readers feel they would like to read more about the above case and similar incidents (gathered from several sources) we have published this manuscript in booklet form and are distributing it privately. Copies are available for $1.50, which we believe to be very reasonable in today's high-priced book market.

In an attempt to illustrate this section of FLYING SAUCERS as much as possible we request that readers send in any photographs they might have of either flying saucers themselves or any personalities connected with the field. We also hope you will continue to mail us news clippings, magazine articles, and your own personal sightings and experiences.

Reporter at Small

by Robert Wolf

Saucer News sponsors lectures on the occult at Freedom House, which on a pleasant Friday night can attract at least 75 of the people in New York who'd believe anything and pay $2 to be told it. These are the people who send all the way to England for the international *Psychic News* (a feature in the current issue: "Can Spiritualism Help Homosexuals?"), and who speculate that the moon is simply a reflection of the earth. It's all done with mirrors.

Gathered around the book table (stacks of titles like *How to Meet Space People*), some of the early-comers heard a dramatic middle-aged man describe his meeting a few days ago with one of the 'ETB's' (extraterrestial beings) who are on earth to make contact with our intelligensia.

As he told the story and acted out the role of the space man, it became apparent that he'd been accosted by a fag. The limp-wristed, lisping "space man's" opening line: "Say, aren't you the truckdriver who banged into my rear the other day?"

The audience laughed. One man said, "Hey, buddy, that was a queer!"

"Oh, no," said the man, "that was just a *pose*. It's well known that they have to travel in disguises."

"So what happened?"

"Well, he stared at me for awhile, and I didn't say anything, so he left."

One of the evening's speakers was Tim Beckley, a young huckster who intends to find his future in the space age: since his teens, he's been working out an I-know-secrets-about-the-saucers pitch; as with most pitches, it barely disguises his contempt for the audience's intelligence. Program notes, which sounded like they were written by him, said that "Mr. Beckley's background in UFO research is such that he is already being compared to the late, great Charles Fort"—unfavorably, no doubt.

He was scheduled to give a slide lecture titled "Why the Space People Don't Want Us to Land on the Moon," but he allowed the slides to interfere as little as possible with what he intended to say. The program promised that if you listened carefully you'd "learn first-hand the *hidden* truth about what lies in store for the human race during the forthcoming era of interplanetary travel!" This would be assured because Beckley had "recently received startling 'inside' information from sources high in NASA and elsewhere" which would enable him to "predict that soon after the scheduled moon landing, terrible disasters will begin to occur on Earth—including inexplicable power failures, severe earthquakes, and other catastrophes such as Edgar Cayce predicted many years ago."

As Apollo-11 was zeroing in on the moon, Beckley told the audience that "UFOnauts" have used the moon as a

bas for at least 100 years. Their intention is to aid earthlings to acquire the scientific expertise which other celestial citizens already have, but at the same time their role is parental in that they're not about to let us use our newfound toys to disturb the universe. They have read that Edward Teller is already talking up the moon as a future bomb-testing site.

In a difference of opinion as to how to achieve their goals, the ETB's have split into two factions, "much like our Democratic and Republican parties," Beckley says. One faction thinks that it's wise to infiltrate our scientific community, and have done so. The other faction thinks that it's a good idea to remain at a distance and to intervene invisibly when necessary.

But both parties are adamant that the moon shall never be used as a missile base—especially since that's what the ETB's are using it for *now*. Not all those craters in the photographs, Beckley says, are craters: the ones with the smoothest edges are camouaged saucers.

He says that some sympathetic scientists in NASA (and you can guess who they are and what their motives are) have passed along to him, secretly, the information that astronauts reported having been followed by saucers while orbiting the moon: "According to secret government sources, one of the recent Apollo astronauts was overheard commenting in a Florida restaurant about the reality of UFO's and the fact that his spaceship had been followed closely by alien craft during its second orbit."

Of course, Nixon wouldn't want this information to get out—no telling what effect it would have on the stock market. In fact, he may be guarding the even-more-startling secret that he himself has been contacted by the ETB's or their agents.

If the ETB's (we're speaking of their fusion government now, presumably) see within 20 years that they've failed to sabotage the earthlings' plans to militarize the moon, they have something that'll make Montezuma's Revenge seem like nothing more than a cold. "Moon plague," infinitely more deadly than the Black Plague, will kill one quarter of the earth's inhabitants. America will not be a healthy place to be, though Canada and Mexico won't be so bad.

If you think this is alarming news, you'll understand why, says Beckley, that U Thant stated that "UFO's are the second most important problem facing mankind today, after the Vietnamese War."

The second speaker was Stewart Robb, billed as

The Realist was the leading radical chic anti-establishment zine of the 1960s edited by Paul Krassner. We took our first ribbing here. There would be many more to come. Nature of the beast I guess!

"America's leading psychic researcher." He said he had met Rosemary Brown, a journalist's widow who has become as famous in England as Jeane Dixon is here: BBC-TV has done two documentaries on her. A psychic all her life, he said, she can see and hear spirits without even going into a trance. Her specialty is what the program called "music from the 'other side.'"

It said that she is "the medium through which several of the greatest of the 19th Century European composers have 'come back,' and continued to write outstanding classical compositions!—new works, authenticated to be in the precise style of these famous deceased composers."

She was contacted by Franz Schubert, Robb says, who dictated a composition to her. A *London Times* music critic, on hearing it, wrote that he hoped that now there'd be some chance that Schubert would finish his Unfinished Symphony.

Once Rosemary Brown's stenographic reputation spread in the spirit world, she was utilized likewise by Beethoven, Chopin, Debussy, Bach and Liszt—transcribing to date about 400 works. Eleven of these have been recorded by a Scottish pianist, and the LP is available from Dr. George Firth, 3 Glenorchy Terrace, Edinburgh 9, Scotland.

Robb said he had asked Rosemary Brown if Liszt, a Hungarian, had transmitted in English, adding, "After all, he's had plenty of time to learn it." No, Rosemary said, the transmissions come to her through direct telepathy.

Next on Robb's agenda was what the program described as "a sensational tape recording, bound to make history in the psychic field." Robb had gotten it through Leslie Flint, a male English "medium" who had conducted a seance several years ago. The program said that the tape "contains about 20 minutes of what purports to be the *actual* posthumous voice of the world-famous Irish playwright George Bernard Shaw."

Robb admitted before playing the tape that authentication would be more probable if someone were to take the time to compare its "voiceprint" with a voiceprint of Shaw's recorded radio talks.

It began with automobile horns honking distantly in a silent setting. A voice faded in, and there were gratified murmurs among the participants. The voice made reference to the fact that the room was dark; it identified itself only as the writer "GBS." The participants recognized the initials (initials are popular among mediums), and Shaw seemed to have been flattered by the immediate recognition, commenting modestly on his "few" works. "But I could be Jesus Christ for all you know," he tested, and he muttered something about "people accepting too much on faith."

One of the women said, "You didn't believe in this when you were on earth, did you—how do you feel now that you're on the other side?"

Shaw was, he said, a fallen-away Catholic. "It was a very great surprise to me when I found that I was still alive, yet dead. And it was a great disappointment. I never could see any point to life after death. It seemed to me that if you'd lived a full life on earth, that was

enough. I'd have said that if God was a god of love, he'd not put me through this again."

"I'm told, though, that it's more fun there than on earth."

Shaw jested, "You seem to know more about it than I do."

"I feel like I'm there already."

Shaw laughed: "You don't look as if you were." This broke up the assemblage. "Seriously, it's been a revelation to me. I had very strong, fixed ideas about this death business, you know. Of course now I realize that I was more than just a body."

Someone asked who he'd met there. There was Sir so-and-so: "but of course *here* there are no 'Sirs.'" And his old acquaintance "Oscar" (Wilde). And he'd run into his parents: "Though I wasn't exactly elated."

"Do you ever go home—do you visit your home?" (It is now a museum.)

"I used to, but it just seems like an empty shell now. But I do like to look at the damn fools who go there." Why doesn't he appear to his friends, someone asked. "Because it would only frighten them."

They began to talk about the theater, and someone asked him what he spends his time doing: "Why, writing plays, of course."

I later asked Robb if this meant that Shaw was producing his new works in Heaven. Robb said, "Why, of course! Look at all the great actors he has to choose from."

The persistent woman kept trying to bring Shaw back to her favorite subject: "What's it like over there?"

"You know, I never met a woman before who was so anxious to know about death."

"It's interesting!"

"It's more interesting to know about life."

The Realist is published every other month by The Realist Association, a non-profit corporation. Publication office: 595 Broadway, New York 10012. Editor: Paul Krassner, Box 379, Stuyvesant Station, New York 10009. Subscription rates: $3 a year; $5 for two years. Second-class postage paid at New York, N. Y.

The Realist

ON THE TRAIL OF THE FLYING SAUCERS

TIMOTHY GREEN BECKLEY
Director
Interplanetary News Service

Issue No. 52
June 1967

Most saucer researchers are overly skeptical of contact stories. Those who fit the description of a "contactee" claim to have met beings from other planets at various spots on Earth or to have travelled to other planets (inhibited by intelligent beings identical to us in appearance) in this solar system (i.e. Mars, Venus, Jupiter).

It Is relatively easy to see why serious UFOlogists reject such extreme beliefs. The contact stories are more often than not totally lacking in supporting evidence. Occasionally a contactee will offer as proof a batch of fuzzy photographs, not totally impossible to duplicate in a home dark room, or a piece of supposed physical evidence.

This physical evidence can take many forms. Greasy pancakes, moon potatoes, parchment with strange writing on it, but to date no contactee has been able to produce any artifact that can truly be considered extraterrestrial.

Actually the lack of such evidence is not a total disproof of such encounters having occurred. We may find it to our amazement that other worlds throughout the cosmos are quite similar to ours both in make-up and social attitudes.

Despite these facts there has remained one contactee who has been more or less given considerable amounts of backing by more liberal saucer researchers. He is the late George Adamski.

Adamski was loved by some and despised by others. Yet no matter where he went on a lecture tour, Adamski would be met by hundreds of his devoted followers.

Adamski is the only contactee ever to have spoken with royalty; his audience with queen Juliana of the Netherlands made press copy all around the world.

A brief history of the Adamski legend might be in order.

We must go back to October 9th, 1946. On this evening residents of Sail Diego, California were startled to see a gigantic space ship hovering over a nearby mountain range. Among the observers was George Adamski. From that night on Adamski and his friends had their eyes continually glued to the heavens in a constant watch for any returning space ships. They were not disappointed. On several occasions they had the opportunity to view various unexplained aerial phenomena and photographed a number of them.

During this early period of sighting Adamski had heard that some of these ships were actually coming down in the desert not far from his Mount Palomar home. So on November 20th. 1952 Adamski invited a group of friends to accompany him to the desert for a picnic lunch and to look for saucers. Parking off the main highway, it was only about a half hour before their "saucer-watch"

drew positive results. Attracted first by the sounds of a plane's motors they "suddenly and simultaneously" saw close to the nearest mountain range "a gigantic cigar-shaped silvery ship, without wings or appendages of any kind". The craft seemed to drift in their direction, then stopped "and hovered motionless".

Adamski excitedly told those with him to stand where they were while he drove a distance off the highway to see if the ship wouldn't come in and land for him.

Setting up his camera equipment, Adamski saw a scout ship maneuver between nearby mountain peaks. The craft proceeded to land and a being got our. He was about: 5 feet 6 inches in height and looked to be about 150 pounds. Adamski described him as having "an extremely high forehead; large, bur calm, gray-green eyes, slightly aslant at the outer corners; with slightly higher cheek bones than an Occidental, but not as high as an Indian or am Oriental; a finely chiselled nose, not conspicuously large; and an average size mouth with beautiful white teeth".

Through the use of sign language and telepathy, Adamski was able to find our that this being came from the planet Venus. Although he had landed in the desert in a small scout ship, he indicated that all travel outside the atmosphere of Earth was done in a larger carrier or "mother ship". After a few more minutes, and a few more questions on Adamski's part, the space visitor climbed back into his parked ship and took off. Adamski then returned to the waiting party who later signed affidavits to the effect that such an encounter had actually transpired.

Throughout the years, Adamski had similar meetings with space people and also [ravelled into outer space in a scour ship which deposited him on the carrier craft hovering silently miles above the surface of the planet. Here Venusian men and women told him their philosophic concepts and scientific laws.

Probably the two elements which have placed Adamski in the limelight is his many photographs and the fact that prior to astronaut John H. Glenn, Jr.'s flight into space (in February of 1962) Adamski had already described in his book INSIDE THE SPACE SHIPS the much discussed firefly phenomena.

With the **passing** away of 'Mr. Adamski on **April** 23rd, 1965 many new facts about his supposed contacts have been brought **to** light, As well **as** a strange **story** sent to us recently **from** England by Jimmy Goddard, editor of SAUCER FORUM. In a lecture **given** for the British **UFO** Research Association information about a sighting which occurred **on** June **7,** 1965 came to light. The *title* *of* the lecture **was** "ADAMSKI - DID HE COME BACK?". The facts, *as* sent **to us** by Mr. Goddard, who attended the lecture; **are** as follows:

"A most **unusual** incident began on June 7th at **about** 10:30 p.m. **and** *the* witness, *a Mr.* Bryant, **was** just going to bed at his **home** In Scorriton (England) when he heard a sound like **that** of a **ship's** turbine. He looked outside and saw a pale blue light travelling west to east at **an** altitude of *300* to 400 feet. He **saw** This come down, then the light and *the* noise disappeared.

"**Next day** he looked over the **area and** found **strange** pieces of metal, some like turbines with curved blades, and some looking like more complicated pieces of machinery. Also there **was** a *glass* phial **with** some silver sand in it (later analysed **and** found with certainty to be **silver sand),** also in the phial **was** a message 'adelphos adelpho' (brother to **brother) in what appeared to** be classical Greek. There **was** also an evilsmelling patch of jelly-like **sub***stance* where the object had appeared to land, but this **quickly** evaporated.

"**Later** that same year (1965) Mr. Oliver, in his capacity **as** member**ship** secretary of BUFORA, sent a **questionnaire round to as** many interested people as possible, and one of the **questions was:** 'Have you ever had a sighting or contact?' **One** of these forms **was** sent: **to** Mr. Bryant **describing an** extraordinary contact claim **in** which the witness claimed, **on** April 24th, 1965, to have met **beings** from outer **space, spoken with** them and entered their **saucer.**

"**On** the day in question he **was** going for a **walk** *from* his home to Scorriton **Down,** and when he arrived there he turned **to look** back toward *the* village. He **saw** a large saucer **appear** OUT of thin air **over** the field, then descend to about three feet altitude and hover there. An opening **ap**peared **in** the middle of the saucer,

and a door appeared to slide upward. Three **beings, all dressed** in **'diving gear'** (complete with helmets) came **out,** and one **of** them beckoned wildly to Mr. Bryant."

Goddard continues **in** his communication to this writer by saying that Bryant went **over** to them, and **as** he did *so* they **took** off their hel**mets.** "Two *of* them were definitely not of **this** world – they had very long foreheads, blue *eyes,* (which reminded Mr. Bryant of cats' eyes), blond hair and squat noses. Their mouths appeared bluish, **but** Mr. Oliver said that this could be a reaction to our atmosphere. The **suits were** one-piece and silvery in color, **and** when the **beings** moved the sound suggested tinfoil. They had belts with a **strange 'sun'** or 'flower petal' symbol **on** them.

"The helmets had windows in them which appeared to **be** of a perspex-like substance, **and** at *a* place corresponding with *the* ears there were strange coils.

"The third occupant: **was** different from the other two, although dressed in a similar suit. He had the appearance of a 14 year old boy with black hair, and the suit appeared to be too big for him. He had what Mr. Bryant

described as 'a mid-European accent with a touch of American'."

Goddard then says that this third being is talked to Mr. Bryant and **this** is the gist of what he said: "One month from today we **will** bring **proof of** Mantell (Mr. Bryant had not heard of Mantell or Adamski **supposedly** at this time). Watch for the blue light in *the* evening. Danger of forces from Epsilon who take people from procreation purposes. These cause *what* you call poltergeists, which are only invisible **because** *of* **your** ignorance of the orbital plane. My name is Yamski."

When asked where he was from he said, "From Venus. If only Des or Les *were* here, he **would** understand." At this point it **is** worth noting that this contact occurred only about **12** hours after Adamski's death In Washington, D.C. Mr. Bryant then asked if he could *arrange for* "Des or Les" **to** see him, **and** Yamski replied, *"No,* **we** will arrange for them to *see* you".

Goddard continues with *his* communication by stating that after this "Mr. Bryant **was** helped up into the ship (*still* hovering at about **3** feet) **and** found inside that It **was** made of several identical compartments. **In**

The late Adamski and a Venusian **scout** ship illustrated **exclusively** for FLYING **SAUCERS** by Barry Hoffman.

22

each one there **was** a door leading in the floor **like the one** through which he had entered. There **was** a couch in each compartment, fitted **with** straps, and a large screen similar to a TV screen on which rainbow-colored **lights appeared to** be moving upward. **Mr.** Bryant **asked** how the craft was propelled, and he was told, 'Ideo motor movement'.

'Shortly after **this** he **was** taken out of the craft, which then ascended to about 40 feet, then vanished **in** the same manner in **which it** had arrived."

According to' Mr. Goddard as **soon as** this contact' **got** to **Mr.** Oliver of BUFORA he **went** along with a **Miss** Buckle to interview Mr. Bryant. "For the first *2* hours neither made mention of Adamski. During the interview they found Mr. Bryant to be about *50* years old, married with **3** children. He cold them that the **saucer** had the appearance of platinum, and that the sheep **in a** nearby field had seemed **unconcerned** during the lime the **ship** hovered, but when it left they turned their heads as if to follow the flight *of* the saucer which he could not see. He had apparently touched the craft with no ill effects, and **was** not warned not to do so by the occupants. All the compacements inside the saucer had appeared identical, except for one, which had a purple robe with a rose embroidered **on** it lying on The couch. He described **his** feeling when inside the ship to be 'as **if** I had just won

the **Pools.'** He claimed **to** have read no UFO books."

After giving him a word association rest, Mr. Oliver then told him everything about Adamski, **etc.** Mr. Bryant's first reaction to this was, "It couldn't be him, then."

Mr. Oliver later introduced Mr. Bryant **to** Adamski's **best** life long friend and associate Desmond Leslie co-author **of** Adamski's first **book,** FLYING SAUCERS HAVE LANDED. During **this** interview, and others which followed, more information **was** revealed.

"The craft had landing-pads, but it did not land, **but** simply hovered all the rime at a **3** foot altitude." Mr. Bryant was assisted **into** the craft by the occupants **who** could jump this height easily,

Yamski had **said,** "Karma really worked", referring **to** the **law of** Karma which **stales that** actions **of** any life bring **about consequences** in **succeeding** lives. Yamski also mentioned a particular family **who** were taken "for procreation purposes". Yamski **told Mr.** Bryant **that** if he went to the house he would find it empty '.'and that there would be *a* frying pan **on** the **stove,** to the left as one looked in the window." Goddard reports that the home **was** found later by an investigator, bur "**a** tin kettle **was on** the stove, not *a* frying **pan.**" The net curtains were **so** dirty That one could hardly *see* **in,** he said, and the door **was** padlocked.

Even more recent **is** the volume

entitled THE BOOK OF GEORGE ADAMSKI edited amply by **Mr.** Gray Barker. **In this** large 8 1/2 **x** 11 volume **Mr.** Barker (whose column *at* one time enhanced the pages **of** this publication instead of mine) **has** offered quite striking **evidence** that Adamski actually met the **space** people much earlier then his highly publicized *1952* desert encounter-Mr. Barker **has** asked me not to re**veal** this information but **has** offered to make **his book** available **to** readers of this column **at** a special price **of only** $3.00 (the **book** is clearly marked *$3.95)* if they request it immediately from this columnist, directly. We also have arranged **with** the publishers in **question** to stock Mr. Adamski's **two** other major **works.** They are FLYING SAUCERS **HAVE LANDED** which **goes** into his desert contact, detailed earlier, **and** how he made personal contact with *a* visitor from outer **space,** and took photographs **within** 100 *feet* **of** *a* flylag saucer. This **sells** for $3.50. And *also* again available, after being oat of print for *6* **years,** INSIDE THE SPACE SHIPS where George Adamski tells of meeting other **planetary** visitors; of being flown in **various** Venusian Scours to the great carrier **ships** where he **took** 16 photographs; of meeting men and women from other planets who openly **discussed** their philosophic and scientific laws. Price on this one $4.50. As American and Russian **astronauts** are going further out **into** space it will **be** interesting **to** see if their finds **agree** with **those** of Mr. Adamski **who** claims to have made the same trips - only years before. Already Mr. Bar**ker** believes that the photographs of the moon bear him **our.** The **address** from which **to order** the Adamski **books is** 3 Courtland Street, hew Brunswick, New Jersey, 08901 in care of this writer-

Dr. **Hynek mokes** known **his** belief in **UFOs**

Dr. J. Allen Hynek the Air **Force's** chief UFO consultant recently made known his opinions **about:** the subject and **it appeared,** at least according to NEWSWEEK, that Dr. Hynek "seemed to be defecting" to the side **of** the believers.

In a recent letter to the JOURNAL OF SCIENCE he made some points that he fell: were not **being** properly brought to the attention of the scientific community. Among them **was**

Photo taken *by* the late **George** Adamski on December 13th, 1952 through **his** *6* inch. telescope at Palomar Gardens, California,

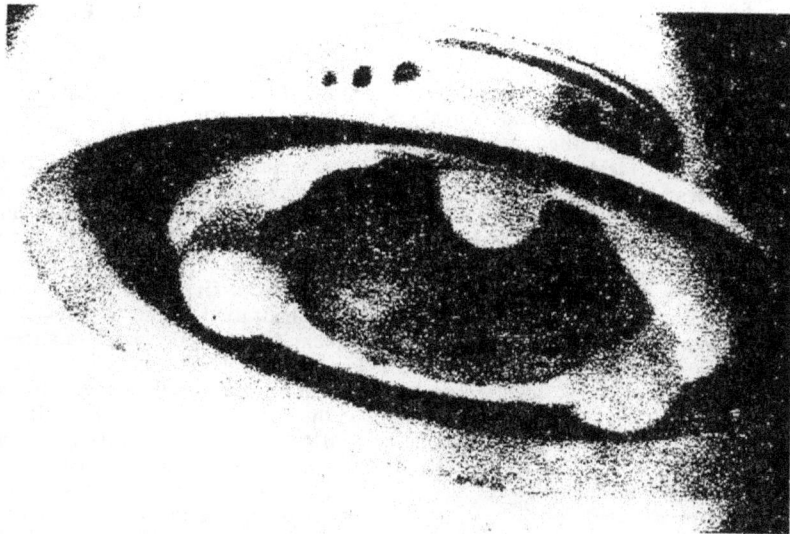

the fact that "it is inequivocally false TO say that UFOs are never reported by scientifically trained people. Some of the best, most coherent reports come from such witnesses. Four of the sightings on file with the Air Force were made by professional astronomers while on duty at their observatories, five sightings were made by technical specialists, including one report by *the* associate director of one of the nation's technical laboratories...all but *three* involved brilliantly illuminated craft maneuvering in the **air.**"

Although Hynek 'is the first to point out that there is no direct evidence that these objects are actually interplanetary ships he also states that ''As long as *there* are any 'unidentified' the question must obviously remain open.''

Hynek quite rightly points out that "In the past two years, UFO sighting -have reached a new high. Each wave of sightings adds to the accumulation of reports which defy analysis by present methods of attack.'' He further makes note of *the* fact that: ''No true scientific investigation of the UFO phenomenon has ever been undertaken, despite the great volume of hard data.''

" With this in mind I'm getting to the point where I'd like to say 'Let's put up or shut up' ..instead of having UFO a synonym for crackpots and ridicule, let's make it scientifically respectable. We should put as much effort on one of these puzzling cases -as we would on a Brinks robbery or kidnap *case.''*

Indeed during the late summer and early fall months it seemed that the ranks of the UFO believers were gaining many new supporters who previously had taken either a negative attitude toward the subject or had refused to make any sort of public comments.

One of these new supporters was Lt. Col. Charles Cooke, USAF, Ret. founder and editor of the Air Intelligence *Digest.*

In the August 7,1966 edition of the "Washington Star" Lt. Col. Cooke stated his belief that the UFOs are real and come from somewhere in outer space.

According to the current issue of SPACEVIEW (published in Henderson, New Zealand) Colonel Cooke's Air Force service record has been linked with UFOs. "In WORLD WAR II, while he was an intelligence officer in Europe, he heard first-hand reports from pilots who encountered the mysterious 'foo fighters'. While in the Pentagon, from **1948-1952, he became** founder and editor of 'Air Intelligence Digest' - the worldwide Air Force intelligence publication. Later, in Tokyo, he edited the 'Far East AF Intelligence Roundup'. During all this *time,* information copies of steadily increasing UFO reports flowed across his desk.''

During this early period he was connected with Project Blue Book. Often tie noted that many good reports were being poorly explained away. "No one *in* the USA Fassembly line down which the reports passed read and pondered them more absorbedly, more dedicatedly, than I.

I duly noted the myriad 'explanations' given out by the Blue Book staff - widely referred to as 'The Little Boy Blues' or 'The Little Blue Boys' - of sightings which they evaluated *as* mistakenly identified stars, planets, meteors, birds, reflected lights, mirages, marsh gas " *or as* delusions, hoaxes, publicity stunts, etc.''

In discussing the existing evidence for UFO reality Cooke corrects the widely held - but false - belief that UFO reports began with the now famous reports in 1947 made by Kenneth Arnold. Cooke comments '' Far from having begun in 1947 reported UFO sightings *go* way, way back.''

Weird saucer mystery from Brazil

The current edition of SAUCER NEWS **(Box 163,** Fort Lee, N.J.) contains one of the most puzzling and bazaar incidents that the editor of this column remembers having heard about during the some 7 years of his own personal UFO investigation.

According to information received by SAUCER NEWS editors from their staff of worldwide correspondents in the most fantastic case to come out of South America in many months, *two* electronics technicians were found dead on an almost inaccessible hillside near Rio de Janeiro, shortly after a woman living nearby had told police that she had seen a luminous object land in the vicinity. Police combing the area for the UFO found, instead, the two bodies, each with a lead mask over its face. The masks were of the kind used in electronics to protect the eyes and face from burns.

Strangest of all, an autopsy failed to reveal the cause of death! The bodies were found in a badly decomposed state on *August 17, 1966.* After 5 days of intensive investigation, during which they considered many theories, Rio police issued a statement admitting that they were still completely baffled by the case.

The technicians, named Miguel Jose Viana and Manuel Pereira da Cruz, had left home with **$2.200,** telling their families that they were going to buy electrical equipment in Rio. The **$2,200** was not found on either of the bodies, but each man still had the sum of $75.00 in his pockets - thus seemingly eliminating robbery as a motive for the killings.

Several letters in a still undeciphered code were also found on the bodies, as well as three electrical charts, bearing readable messages that made very little sense. One of the messages translates as: "At 4:30 p.m. we are in the determined place. At 6:30 we will take the capsules with orange. After the effect, protect half the face with lead masks, wait for agreed signal.''

Police at first theorized that the men had died from an electrical shock, but *the* post mortem showed no sign of shock, nor were any antennas or electrical apparatus found at the death scene. Poison, violence, and asphyxiation were also ruled out. Blood was found on a patch of ground nearby, but it was not from either of the two bodies! Also found were a lady's handkerchief, *a* raincoat:, sun-

Gray Barker editor of BOOK OF ADAMSKI is pictured here at the 1966 Congress of Scientific UFOlogists in Cleveland. Barker is scheduled to be one of *the* main speakers at the New York City "saucer" convention in June.

glasses, a toothbrush, and other apparently meaningless clues.

SAUCER NEWS editor James W. Moseley points out that "although the police tended to ridicule the flying saucer angle of the case, the original report by the woman living nearby was' later confirmed by several other people who telephoned police to tell of similar sightings they had made at exactly the samerime."

Plans for giant June convention continue

As of this writing *the* list of guest speakers planning to attend the *giant* **UFO convention at** the Hotel Commodore in New York City **continues to** grow, Dan **Fry** founder of Understanding, **Inc.** has accepted an invitation to attend **as has** Rev. **Richard** Basile **president of** Dynamic Living **Enterprises and Publications.** Dan Fry claims he went **in a** flying **saucer** from the White **Sands, New** Mexico **proving grounds** {in the summer of *1950)* to **New** York City and **back in** a half hour. Since then he claims to have **had** several **conversations** and **meetings with various** interplanetary **visitors.** Rev. Basile has **been an** ardent **UFO researcher** *since* 1951, as well **as a student of various** psychic phenomena, ESP **and** the occult.

Others present **will include Ray** Palmer, **Howard Menger,** Kenneth Arnold, Stuart Robb, **Long John Nebel, Art** Ford, **Gray Barker,** Gordon Evans, **Ivan T.** Sanderson, **the Amazing** Randi and **many others.** The dates for the **convention** are **June 22nd, 23rd, 24th and 25th.** The place **is the** Hotel Commodore located at Lexington **Avenue and 42nd**

Street **(opposite Grand Central** Station) **right** in the **heart of** midtown **New York** City **and only minutes** away from Times **Square.**

For' more *information* **on the** convention **you may write to this columnist** directly **or request** information from "1967 **Congress of** Scientific UFOlogists", **Box 163,** Fort Lee, N.J., *07024.* The **chairman of** the convention will be **James W.** Moseley, editor of SAUCER NEWS.

Whenever **possible we** attempt **to** use all **of the** material **that** is **passed** our way. If **not** in this column then in our monthly **newsletter** SEARCHLIGHT. **However, at** all times we **are** certain that material in both **these** publications differs **so** chat no duplication *exists.*

Readers are **asked to** continue sending material, newspaper **clippings** and personal experiences to our office at 3 Courtland Street, New Brunswick, New **Jersey,** *08901.* We promise **everyone who** writes *a* personal **reply.**

Reader response *at all* **time high**

Response from **the readers of** FLYING **SAUCERS** has been considerable **over the past few weeks. We continue** to **receive** information on **personal** sightings, tons of **news clippings, and all** sons **of odds and** ends *from* our many **faithful** readers. **We must send personal** thanks for material **we could** not **use** in this **issue** to Larry Lawrence of **National** Saucer Intelligence, **Ernest Givens, George** D. Fawcett, **Kenneth Larson,** Edgar Simons, **Donald Cook,** Lucius Parish, **etc.**

Chatting at *a* recent meeting of SAUCER NEWS is Otto Binder (left), editor of OUR SPACE AGE and Gordon Evans, UFO researcher and Mars expert. Mr. Evans will be among those addressing the convention at *the* Hotel Commodore in June.

ON THE TRAIL OF THE FLYING SAUCERS

TIMOTHY GREEN BECKLEY
Director
Interplanetary News Service

Issue No. 57
April 1968

It was a busier then usual summer for Flying Saucer students. UFO conventions and events of various types popping up all around the country. Also in a period of some three or four months over twenty different paperback books appeared on the newsstands pertaining to the mote than ever elusive flying disks. One of them was THE REAL UFO INVASION by Ray Palmer editor of the publication you are now reading.

UFO buffs will long remember what is certain to go down in saucer-dom annals *as* the biggest and "most important" saucer convention ever held. Indeed Montreal may boast about its Expo '67, but the Canadian fair was strictly limited to the planet Earth. New York, on the other hand, played host to a convention of interplanetary proportions known officially as the 1967 Congress of Scientific UFOlogists.

Held at the plush Hotel Commodore it was designed to be the most important and most exciting saucer gathering ever held. And it certainly was. Saucer "fans" and the general public crowded into the main ballroom to hear a host of speakers and see artifacts which those holding the convention claimed were from other worlds.

The purpose of this gathering, presided over by James W. Moseley editor of the popular SAUCER NEWS,

was "to present, in an entertaining manner, the latest news and views on flying saucers, so as to increase public awareness of this fascinating and important phenomenon. To commemorate the 20th anniversary of Kenneth Arnold's famous sighting of June 24th, 1947, which officially began *the* 'flying saucer era'. And finally to cooperate with an internationally set up network of UFO organizations which annually designate the week of June 21st to June 28th as 'flying saucer week', during which time sky watches are set up, and all sightings systematically reported."

The convention, which attracted over 8,000 people, examined every facet of the unidentified flying object phenomenon and traced the history of the UFOs from biblical times up to today's headline sightings.

Those speaking included Gray Barker, author of THEY KNEW TOO MUCH ABOUT FLYING SAUCERS who contended that mysterious men in dark clothing were visiting key saucer investigators and frightening them into silence- Barker hinted that these mysterious men were actually the pilots of the flying saucers who are trying to keep their identity unknown.

Another notable lecturer was Howard Menger who claims to have actually met and spoken to space people from Venus and Mars who landed on his farm in Highbridge,

New Jersey from 1954 to 1958. Menger, accompanied by his charming wife Connie, described in detail the civilization he claims has developed on the planets throughout this solar system and their way of life which he estimates is 10,000 years ahead of ours. He described his space contacts as being men and women who look exactly like Earth people except that *they are* much more beautiful.

Unfortunately all those present could not agree that the motivations of the Flying Saucers were totally friendly. According to Art Ford, the famous New York radio and TV personality, they have on a number of occasions actually kidnapped Navy and Air Force planes. In particular he cited the case of the mysterious disappearance of six Navy 'planes which vanished off the coast of Florida in 1945.

Other speakers included Ivan T. Sanderson the world famous naturalist, radio and TV personality, who is author of countless books including UNINVITED VISITORS and THE ABOMINABLE SNOWMAN; Stewart Robb, America's leading psychic researcher, and author of the forthcoming book REPORTS FROM BEYOND; James Randi, magician, escape artist who recently returned from Peru where he investigated reported landings of flying saucers.

Long John Nebel, the popular all night radio personality, presently with NBC introduced Vi-Venus to the 2,000 people present at the Sunday session. The attractive middle aged redhead told the rather amazed throng of people that she was actually born on Venus and had come to Earth in order to contact select people. Though even the true believers were quite skeptical of her story a murmer of silence fell over the hall as she related her experiences on another planet.

Two last minute guests were Dr. Edward U. Condon from Colorado university who was recently given a grant of some $300,000 (later increased by another $280,000) by the Air Force to set up a private research project that would not be motivated by any political or military officials. Condon sat rather poker faced throughout the proceedings, although an associate sitting next to him was busily taking notes. Condon was asked by this reporter what he thought of some of the stories being

26

On the left Long John Nebel of NBC radio tells saucer believers about his interest in the topic, At right is the chairman of the saucer gathering, James W. Moseley.

told. He commented, obviously not wanting to be questioned further! "Quire interesting - Quite interesting."

An added, and most welcome, attraction was Roy Thinnes, star of the TV series THE INVADERS who flew in from Hollywood just for the convention. He was prompted to get up in front of the crowd and tell of his own experiences In the field which include having viewed at close range a flying saucer back in 1964. Thinnes considers himself to be quite an authority on the topic and claims to do quire a bit of research for his TV series which deals with the topic in a rather serious vein despite the fact that the stories are fiction in content,

Thinnes, along with one or two other speakers, attacked the Air Force for their closed minded approach to the flying saucer enigma and questioned their policy of withholding vital information from the public. As Thinnes left the stage a mob of his fans followed him out of the hall seeking autographs. Despite this mobbing by his followers Thinnes was so engrossed in the convention that he returned the same evening to tell his story again.

Among the fascinating items on display in the outer lobby were a life size representation of a "humanoid" saucer creature; angle hair and space grass (the strange substance left behind when flying saucers land); a perpetual motion machine from outer space; a prototype of an actual

saucer now being constructed; an electronic flying saucer detector and to bring things down to Earth a plaster of parts cast of the footprints of an abominable snowman.

In addition, visitors saw a huge collection of startling flying saucer photos - many of them never publicly exhibited before.

At the closed sessions, which were open only to delegates of recognized saucer groups, John A. Keel (a well known writer for such magazines as TRUE and SAGA) gave an interesting talk on the three men in black and other mysterious aspects of the UFO field. Keel feels that we "should not be so concerned with sightings, but with the affairs that various UFO witnesses are having with these mysterious men."

Keel also talked of giant creatures which roam Earth and of the many disappearances of people who witness UFO activity. He stated that they are either kidnapped, their homes are destroyed or they are horribly burned, sometimes fatally.

According to Keel there has been much activity on the moon which cannot be ours. This indicates that there is either intelligent life on our nearest neighbor in space or else they (whoever the UFO pilots may be) are using it as a base for their operations.

As is to be expected with a convention of this scope, which was attended by all types of people, rumors flew rapidly. Allen Greenfield Chairman of the Closed Sessions and

editor of the popular ALTERNATE HORIZONS NEWSLETTER (free. sample copy by writing to Mr. Greenfield at 2875 Sequoyah Drive, Atlanta, Georgia 30327) listed some of these in his most recent publication:

"The stories ran from the bizarre to the intriguing. Like the one 1 heard that the late Ed Ruppelt was seen at the convention. Or the more credible story that a certain famous UFOlogy team, or part of it, was there, but apparently incognito.

"Then there is the weird business centering around Dr. Edward U. Condon, head of the government-sponsored UFO project. He was there, alright. He even stood when Chairman James W. Moseley identified him from the rostrum. But he was very much camera shy.

"O.K. Bur

"The story was around that everybody who took his picture got their picture taken as well by an unidentified individual or individuals.

"There were also little things of no probable importance. But still interesting. Like the call Timothy Green Beckley got from somebody who was supposed to be a government man (and at 5:30 in the morning too!). Or the funny business with the Library of Congress woman. Or the mix-up in one of the slide programs."

The list of mysterious events is still growing even at this late date as various saucer editors who attended the convention publish their reports. There were reportedly two men at the closed sessions with a concealed tape recorder or transmitter. One of

Roy Thinnes, star of the TV series THE INVADERS, speaks before 2,000 UFO fans at the Commodore Hotel in June.

the gentlemen **signed** the register as James M. Bond.

And the rooms of at least three UFOlogists were skillfully **broken** into. As Greenfield reports: "Here **is** one of those **funny** kind **of** stories where the intruder or intruders *seem* skilled yet leave distinct calling cards as if to leave a deliberate trail. Also, at this writing nothing appears to have been **takes**, although assuming for the moment *the* lack of a logical explanation, there is some reason to *believe* that some files *were* photographed. **This** too, of course, could be **part** of a *false* trail."

Indeed this saucer convention, the **first ever** held in New York, **and** certainly the largest of its **kind** anywhere, was attended **by** "experts" from every corner of the globe. And according to some of those present there might even have been a few from other places!

Editors *Vita* E. Miller of REAL *and* James W. Moseley of SAUCER NEWS stand posed in front of a *File* sized reproduction of a humanoid **saucer** pilot. The "**creature**" *was* the unofficial "**mascot**" of the **1967** Congress of **Scientific** UFOlogists. (Photo by August C. Roberts)

RUSSIANS SAY SAUCERS ARE REAL!

In a recent **news** story from Moscow two Soviet scientists, who *were* identified **as** F. Zieel and B.P. Konstantinov, went on record by declaring that the evidence gathered by them over a 5 year period showed that flying saucers could indeed be **spaces**hips from "an advanced civilization on another planet."

Dr. J. Allen Hynek in the December **issue** of PLAYBOY warned that the **Russians** may indeed be winning the race toward a solution to the UFO phenomena.

Another Russian scientist Prof. Agrest **has** *long* remarked in a number of scientific journals that the UFO problem was an ancient one which dated **back** to before biblical times.

Zigel, who was identified in the **Russian** news story as one of the editors of a **new** book INHABITED COSMOS, said that "the phenomena of the **UFO** today should be considered as global." He rejected *the* concepts being offered by *some* Soviet scientists that "birds, **insects or** plant **seeds** could **cause** reactions or radar **screens**" which were though; to be **interplanetary ships** by others-

The official English language Soviet monthly journal SPUTNIK for June carried a letter by **this** columnist pointing that the **"possibility of visitations** from other planets has been of **keen** interest to many persons . . . in the United States. Study has been made to date to report **and** analyze observations of unidentified **flying** objects known in our country **as** 'flying **saucers***. Thus may I make a *most* unusual request to your *large* readership . . . to send any information on **unexplained** sightings of UFOs **to our** international headquarters . . ." This letter brought amazing response (including reports, photographs **and** vital information) from a number *of* communist **countries** including Poland, Austria, Albania, etc.

Just another "proof" that the flying saucers, as scared by former United Nations aid Caiman Von Keviczky, "show no international boundaries."

MAN REPORTS STRANGE SUBSTANCE CAUSED ARM BURN

An Eastern Henrico, **Virginia** man told police **on June** 14th, 1967 he **was** burned **on** the arm by some substance which dropped from a searing bright light; which hovered briefly over his yard about 7:30 p.m.

Charles W. Fletcher told police he was sitting in a *chair* in the yard reading a newspaper when suddenly a bright light appeared from above

Colman Von Keviczky is shown in the convention foyer explaining how his organization plans to help solve the UFO mystery.

and *was* reflected on the newspaper.

The substance then dropped on *his* left arm near his elbow. He said it was like a liquid and he immediately wiped it off with the newspaper. At the same time Fletcher said the light burned him slightly on the right side of his face.

He then looked up and saw a shadow of an object he could not describe as it disappeared over the trees beyond his yard.

The substance on the newspaper was purple colored with what appeared to be metallic speckles. Fletcher went into the house and wiped his arm again with a wet rag. He said the rag, where it was stained by the substance, turned a purplish blue.

Police took both the newspaper and the rag and indicated the objects may be sent to a chemical laboratory for an analysis.

WASHINGTON BOYS STARTLED
BY FLYING SAUCERS

"I was just going to take his picture and he looked up and pointed and was sort of frantic.

"Then I saw them. They came out from behind the trees and seemed to be sort of spinning."

This is how Robert McNicol of Lynn Valley, **Washington** described his experience of taking *a* series of UFO photos on July 1st from his backyard.

"They seemed quite far away" observer Doug Miller told an unidentified reporter from THE CITI-ZEN - a local newspaper. "They were sort of metallic colored, and moved out from behind the trees and stopped as if they were watching us . . . then they seemed to spin away very fast; they just disappeared."

Robert claims that his father wrote to the Pentagon asking for an explanation of the sightings and an analysis of the photographs. As of this writing nothing in the way of an explanation has been given by the Air Force.

NEW EVIDENCE THAT M.K. JESSUP
MAY HAVE BEEN MURDERED

Many researchers may recall the tragic death of Dr. M.K. Jessup some years ago. The mystery of Dr. Jessup is one of the strangest in the history of UFOlogy. His death, officially labeled "suicide",

UFO over Woonsocket, Rhode Island by Harold A. Trudel on July 11th, 1967. (Courtesy PROBE MAGAZINE)

has been widely questioned by researchers who knew *the* noted astronomer and *UFO* investigator well.

There was, for example, the case of the strange annotated books, and the secret edition of one of Dr. Jessup's books titled THE VARO EDITION.

These annotations, together with letters from a mysterious Carlos Allende, told of an alleged *secret* Naval experiment and of disappearing ships and men.

Recently researcher Gray Barker has hinted that Jessup may be among the researchers to have been silenced by the mysterious men in black who have been reported off and on since the *days of* Albert K. Bender's *famed* International Flying Saucer Bureau. Another noted researcher, John A. Keel, has reported that many of these "men in black" or "silencers" have actually been dressing in the uniforms of Air Force officials. In England one of these "men" posed as a famous saucer investigator to gain entrance to *a* contactee's home. This *"con-*

tactee" was later found d.ad of an apparent heart attack.

These elusive "men in black" were reportedly busy again throughout the country this summer, and at least two of them fell into unexpected traps in the New York area. One is supposed to have been killed in the streets of the city, while the other was suddenly taken into custody by unidentified legal authorities.

According to a special report from John A. Keel to SAUCER NEWS (Box *163*, Fort Lee, New Jersey 07024) several teams of men in turtleneck sweaters visited eight separate communities in the *state of* Washington in April, allegedly warning UFO witnesses not to discuss what they had seen. They told some people that they represented Civil Defense and were trying to prevent a panic, but since most Civil Defense operations were disbanded two years ago, this seems unlikely.

Keel reported that "Citizens in Canada, Maine, New Jersey, California, and Long Island, N.Y. also told of being visited by 'government men' this spring. One of these witnesses says he was ordered to turn over some flying saucer pictures 'for the sake of yourself, your family and your world.'"

In West Virginia, Mr. Tad Jones, who observed a hovering globe in January of 1967, received two 'threatening notes warning him not to tell anyone what he had seen. These notes were crudely printed on cheap paper and cardboard and slipped under his door. . . The printing on these 'prank' warnings was identical to the printing on a note placed under the door of a UFO sighter in Middleport, Ohio. This girl. who had allegedly seen West Virginia's famous 'Moth Man' later escaped from *a* would-be kidnapper - a tanned young man who was driving an old car *'that* looked like new' . . . On Long Island, two men in Air Force uniforms harassed UFO witnesses. One *of these* men identified himself as Lt. Frank Davis and threatened two different people with a revolver warning them to 'watch out who you talk to.' . . . The Air Force denied that it knew anything about either *(case)*. . ."

According to Keel "Lt. Davis later turned up in a postman's uniform and was followed by me. Davis and another man were engaged in taking photographs of the homes of UFO sighters." While involved in this investigation, Keel had two encounters with a large black Cadillac in an isolated section of Long Island, In one of these encounters, the Cadillac, which contained two dark-skinned men, was parked and laying in wait on a deserted road, In the other incident, Keel did a turnabout and followed the Caddie for several miles.

On August 4th, a black Cadillac made a deliberate attempt to run over a UFO witness on the main street of a small Long Island town,

Keel reports that "One of the 'mystery men' known to be involved in the Long Island capers was reportedly killed in New York City by unknown assailants on July 28th. Lt. Davis was apprehended on August 5th by agents from an unidentified law agency. 'Davis' was in a public place when two well-dressed men approached him and forcibly removed him. All three men then drove away in a large black car, either a Cadillac or a Lincoln, according to the many witnesses."

These are only a few of the many strange cases which lead Barker to the conclusion that Dr. Jessup's death may not have been accidental as believed previously by many.

In a letter sent to a number of UFO buffs in early October, Barker related how "A strange series of telephone calls was the first of several recent puzzling matters to come to my attention. In a report to Mr. Moseley, John A. Keel reported having received a weird telephone call from me. This call was routine in some ways, reporting a sighting that had taken place in Pennsylvania. But John was disturbed. It sounded like my voice, but at the same time it didn't! The Southern accent was just a bit too pronounced. Certain other aspects of the conversation convinced Keel that it really hadn't been me on the other end of the line. A check made with me later confirmed his suspicions. 1 had made no call to John that night!

"But the really disturbing thing turned up when I checked my telephone bill. A telephone call to John Keel HAD been billed to my number on that date, and it had been a dialed call, seemingly impossible to originate from other than my telephone.

But according to the best of my recollection, I had been around the house all evening, and it seems impossible that an intruder could have slipped in if I had gone out briefly for some reason say to get the mail. And to think that somebody or something would take all this trouble for such a seemingly simple matter!

"An informant who has asked that his name not be used told me that during the first part of September his telephone rang, and when he picked up the receiver he heard a

Two objects hovered above Lynn Valley lads, and just after 'Robert McNicol snapped several photos, they sped off.

conversation between myself and Jim Moseley. The voices did not sound natural, but rather like "mechanical reproductions" of our voices. My informant spoke to them several times, but they did not reply to him, as if they were completely unaware of his overhearing their conversation. After a minute or so the voices faded to be replaced by weird noises and another voice mentioning the name of John Keel and something about tapes. Then the line went dead, and the party was unable to get the dial tone for the rest of the evening.

"The night after I checked out the above-mentioned situation, I received a telephone call from Dr. M. K. Jessup; but in this case I think we can safely say it was a hoax; for as most of you know, Dr. Jessup has been dead for several years!"

Did indeed Jessup and others "know too much"? Did Jessup take his own life rather than to face the terrifying truths he had learned? These are questions that need to be answered. Because of the importance of these NEW "Men in Black" cases, Gray Barker has decided to

put together a revised edition of his book THE STRANGE CASE OF DR. M.K. JESSUP and has offered it to dedicated UFO students since he doesn't wish to make any financial profit off the passing of this dedicated investigator. Thus please be advised that you can only order copies of this volume (printed in 8-1/2 x 11 format with various photos and documents) from this writer at 3 Courtland Street, New Brunswick, N.J. 08901. Price of this important volume is $3.95. A limited number of copies have been printed so order as soon as possible.

We hope to have more to report in our next column on these new "silence" cases. If the evidence holds out it seems that key UFO researchers and saucer observers will continue to be either "killed" or silenced. Let's hope that a rational explanation can be found for these cases. If anyone reading this knows of other cases (perhaps from personal experiences) we would appreciate learning about them even if we must keep them confidential. Also news reports of UFOs, photographs and material of all types are of course appreciated and acknowledged. Let us hear from you,

NIGHT OWL

SUNDAY NEWS
NEW YORK'S PICTURE NEWSPAPER

Vol. 49. No. 18   Copr. 1969 News Syndicate Co. Inc.   New York, N.Y. 10017, Sunday, August 31, 1969★

Saucer Expert: 'They're There'

By ALEX MICHELINI

Now that man has stepped foot on the moon and found no signs of life, can we safely write off all those tales about flying saucers as pure bunk?

"Not so fast," says Timothy *Green* Beckley of New Brunswick. He's one of the nation's leading authorities on Unidentified Flying Objects (UFO) and he insists it's too early to discount the existence of life on the moon.

"I don't really know how we could expect to find any signs of life when such *a* small portion of the surface of the moon was explored," says Beckley. "In fact, there is ample evidence to indicate *that* the lunar surface is being *used* as a base by alien beings."

Threats From Saucer Pilots

Beckley, who has received honorary certificates (if appreciation from Harvard and *the* Asia Foundation of New York for his work in *the* science field, *says* several persons who claim to have met with saucer pilots have warned that if earthlings attempt to colonize the moon there will be serious repercussions on earth.

"These will include earthquakes, explosions, fires and power failures," he explained.

Beckley noted *that* in recent weeks Japan, was hit by an earthquake and part of the U.S. was ravaged by Hurricane Camille. "So, perhaps some of these warnings are already coming about," he added.

If there are alien beings on the moon, what are they doing there?

Against Military Uses

"I have been informed that *those* who already have; bases on the moon *are* primarily concerned in preventing *us* from using" the moon for military purposes," he says. "The space people, I am told, want to show us they mean business. They are going to quarantine the earth until we learn to control our use of nuclear weapons."

Strange, unexplained signals from some U.S. satellites remain a mystery, the UFO expert pointed out.

"In *fact,* (TIT most recent Mariner probe to Mar's started sending back unscheduled trans-missions which have not been explained," he says.

And what about those reports of UFO sightings by some of our own astronauts? Beckley asked.

Cites Glenn Report

He referred *to* comments by Col. John Glenn *after* his 1962 flight in which he said he was convinced, "certain reports of flying saucers are legitimate." Glenn, according *to* Beckley, felt "the possibility of life in outer space most certainly is a possibility" sad *that* reports of UFOs could not be ruled out.

Thus, the moon landing doesn't disprove a thing, Beckley maintains.

"We take for granted now oar own explorations into outer space." he says. "80, who's to fay that someone from some other planet isn't hundreds, perhaps thousands, of years ahead of *us and* are now looking over, earth?"

Anybody got any more questions?

31

ON THE TRAIL OF THE FLYING SAUCERS

TIMOTHY GREEN BECKLEY
Director
Interplanetary News Service

Issue No. 61
December 1968

The last few months have been unusually void of UFO reports. Even the head of the Colorado University UFO Project, Edward U. Condon, reports that sightings have seemingly reached a low in number - at least compared to the peak periods of the past two or three years.

This is nor to say that no reports have been received. According to John A. Keel, a leading UFO investigator whose works have appeared frequently in **TRUE** and **SAGA** magazines, there is a vast amount of information which is just *not being* reported to the press and to so-called qualified officials. The reason being that reports of UFOs have become **so frequent in** certain **parts** of the country that citizens just *do* no;: deem it necessary to say **any**thing **about** them any longer. Indeed the Flying Saucers (from wherever they might be coming) have been generally accepted as being real hardware of **one** type or another.

Perhaps **then** this **should be** a time of soul searching **by** all dedi**cated** researchers. In what direction **should we** head? Has our investigation proven anything? What **can be** accomplished **by** remaining **in** "business"?

These were among the **questions** posed *at* the fifth annual **Congress** of Scientific UFOlogists held **in Cleveland,** Ohio during June. Some **35** UFO **organizations,** representing an **estimated** 60,000 UFO **enthusiasts and** researchers, attended the three day conference presided over by Allan Manak of UFO DIGEST.

However, the main topic of *discussion* **centered** around the "Silencers" or "Men in **Black**" who have been appearing to certain UFO **re**searchers with ominous warnings of **what** will occur if they do not get out of the flying **saucer field.**

A **typical** experience with the MIB **was** related **by** I.N.S. Ohio Director, **Robert Easley,** of Defiance **who** claims that after giving a lecture recently to a group of **approximately** 150 people he **was** shot at while attempting to gee into his auto parked in *a* church **parking** lot.

Also for **the** first time authentic **photographs** of at least one **of** these mysterious men were shown to those present and to the attending press. These photographs, which were taken jointly by James W. Moseley and this columnist outside of the home of New Jersey investigators Jack and Mary **Robinson** (**editors** with SAU-CER NEWS and SEARCHLIGHT) show what is (without a doubt?) **one** of **these** silencers who had **been** watching the Robinson **residence** for the **previous** period of **a week.** The **exclusive** story **on this** incredible incident, **along with** the photographs taken, **will** appear **in** the Fall **issue of** SAUCER NEWS **now** under the capable editorship **of** Gray Barker (**Box 2228,** Clarks-

burg, West Virginia). We hope to **be** able to present these photos to FLYING SAUCERS readers later on.

We also heard first hand reports on how the MIB are now attempting to *silence* researchers, **contactees and** UFO witnesses **on** a world-wide basis. Recent silence attempts have come from Germany, France and various South American countries. No matter where they are reported, however, **witnesses** describe these men as being human **in** appearance, but very **dark skin**ned and *often* with slanted eyes.

As in previous years there **was again a** number of interesting incidents which were quite apart from **the** official **business of** the Congress.

Alien Greenfield reporting In his ALTERNATE HORIZONS NEWS-LETTER (free sample copy **on** re-**quest** from *2875* Sequoyah Drive NW, Atlanta, Georgia 30327) discusses how this year the **telephone** seemed to **play** an unusual part in the convention. "It started off, **as** far as **I know,** with my checking in at the motel, well before the convention. One of the local people 1 got in touch with right away is Allan **Manak** of the UAPA.

"Shortly thereafter, Manak tried to phone me back. Figuring me to

John J. Robinson editor **of** SEARCHLIGHT **re**ported having his home watched by the MIB. (**Photo by August Roberts via** SAUCER NEWS)

be at the motel at which the delegates were **suppose** to stay (which sounds logical, and which is where I was), according to Manak, he called me there. He **was told that I wasn't** there or some such; the room I **was** in was empty.

"So Manak proceeded to call the other hotels **in** the **same** chain **in** town.

"No me.

"Finally, figuring still that I 'must' be In the place originally thought, Manak tried a more direct approach and came over; **knocked on** the door, whereupon I **opened** it. End of round one.

'Enter Tony Price, a sometimes reporter for underground news-**papers**. Price called **Rick Hilberg**, Congress **co-sponsor**. Getting Rick's wife instead, he left a number for Rick to call back- Rick called back. No trouble. Price wanted to talk. Click; Round two ended on **a** smooth note-

"Round three began **with** Rick, **in the** presence of this writer, trying to get in touch **with** Price again to nail **down** a time for us to get together with him. First, no answer, Then **a** *strange* signal **on** the phone - ringing followed by **a** busy signal - **a** couple of rimes indicated trouble. The operator **was** consulted. Opera-*tor* agreed: trouble.

"Later, we tried again. We got somebody **else** altogether. So, maybe Rick dialed wrong. Tried again. Same wrong number.

"I suggested **we** get **somebody in** another part of town to call. Somebody tried. They got through to what seemed to **be a local tavern.**

"Finally late at night: **another** try **was made** and **we** got through without a hitch. Later Tony told us, as I recall, something **about** the phone company **saying** things **would** be out **of** order or were **out** of order or something. Yeh, out of order."

Greenfield continued by saying that there were other problems with the phones of the **various** convention leaders during the **congress** which in Greenfield's mind, and the minds **of** others, "adds strain to the coincidence answer".

In the closed **sessions** one of the major resolutions passed was a praising of Dr. **Condon** by those in attendance. in **an** attempt: to **offset an attack** by John G. Fuller and the National Investigations Committee

on Aerial Phenomena in the May **14th** issue of **LOOK** MAGAZINE, on the University of Colorado UFO Project headed by Dr. Edward U. Condon, the congress unanimously adopted the following resolution:

(1) That Dr. Edward U. Condon **is** a **distinguished** scholar and distinguished American.

(2) That Dr. Condon has, **by** his unfailing **good** cheer and uniformly courteous consideration of those around him, made a valuable contribution to *the* **progress** of UFOlogy.

(3) That *it* **is** the **sense** of this Congress **that** Dr. Condon has been subjected **to** *the* unnecessarily and unmerited burden of **irresponsible** personal vilification, which has needlessly complicated the already impressive challenge of **his** office.

(4) That the leaders **of** the Congress **appreciate** Dr. Condon's apparent intention of full public disclosure in the conduct of his present investigation.

Therefore, *it* **is** the hope of the Congress that the close cooperation and mutually amicable relations between Dr. London **and** itself **will** remain **in** the **future, as** in the past, a source of constant encouragement - a bright light on the horizon of tomorrow's UFOlogy.

This award **was** presented on the **stage** of the open **session** of the 1968 Congress **of** Scientific UFOlogy **to** Capt. Robert Loftin (author **of** I-DENTIFIED FLYING SAUCERS) who accepted **on** behalf of **Dr.** Condon **who could** not attend at the last **minute because of** illness. Capt. Loftin **is** among those **who** have been **of** assistance to Dr. Condon in his investigation of select UFO reports.

In summing up the 1968 Congress of Scientific UFOlogists **we believe** Allen Greenfield's words will once **again** be fruitful. "While **we** didn't seem to anyone to solve the UFO-problem, as in years before, there **was again** the problem present of weird incidents which showed up again. It could be these conventions *are* **a** waste of time, but my droll other-self might have something to say about that worth mentioning. He might **say** that if the Congress **was** unimportant, the little **annoyances** might **be** a bit **less**. He might **say** that if the Congress **was** unimportant, the phone **would work."**

Countermeasures against the MIB

With the MIB or "Silencers" getting more involved in the UFO enigma every day, it would seem that there should indeed be a set of counter measures to use against these "aliens",

In the August issue of SAUCER SCOOP edited by Joan Whritenour (6464 **34th** Ave. No., St. Petersburg, Florida) SCOOP correspondent Richard S. Hack has given us a list of counter measures which we agree may **serve** a definite purpose **when** dealing **with** *these* MIBs. In this **issue** Mr. Hack has examined certain aspects of this most important problem and has suggested certain **active** or **passive** *measures* for the individual researcher and for the organization to **take** should they get involved in these matters.

THE CRANK CALL: The simpleat form of harrassment - and possibly **one of** the most complex is the use of the telephone. Most **UFO** researchers have reported numerous calls *from* crackpots and practical jokers. Some are just that - jokes. But others, such **as** the one reported by **John** Stuart are different. The callers may threaten, or simply perform meaningless acts such as reading off numbers into the phone. In fact, the call may **consist** of merely a **series** of **beeps or** no sound at all. In any case, it **is** clearly hard *to* tell with **whom you** are dealing - **a crank** - or the MIB. The MIB are unanimously reported to have **a monotone voice** and stilted speech patterns. This, then, **is** one clue. Another **is** *the* quality of the call: the line may sound hollow, *there* may be **no background sounds,** or perhaps the *voice* comes **across with** unusual volume. These are clues which suggest the involvement of the MIB. The frequency **of the calls** may be **a** factor. Practical jokers are NOT noted for their staying power-

Hack sells us correctly that "The most obvious defensive measure **is** an unlisted number. Unfortunately, for many people this **is** not practical, nor is leaving the **phone off** the hook. The most common solution **is** to call the police or the telephone company and attempt to have the calls traced. Other measures which **have been used** successfully include blowing a whistle into the instrument, inviting the caller to a meeting at which the police attend, and clicking the phone several times, then whispering; "This is the call I want traced, Officer!"

Richard Hack points out however, that the MIB are clever and that in these cases the above methods may not help. In this case the only thing to do is to threaten to tape the calls and inform other researchers "thus creating concrete evidence which the MIB will riot wish to have in existence". As a last resort, you may just have to take out your phone. In any case remember at all times 'Never give in to your caller by reacting emotionally or by giving out personal information. If you do, you are playing into the hands of the enemy, no matter who he is."

THE HOAX: Recently it has come to the attention of a number of researchers that attempts are being made to submit FALSE reports and manipulated UFO photos to various investigators and publications. This kind of thing can be very complicated, as witness recent cases in Texas, where hypnosis was employed to coach the witness. There are those who believe that such cases represent an attempt by SOMEONE to throw the entire UFO subject, including its investigators, into a bad light publicly. And it can happen to any of us, student and researchers!

The only defense is to investigate - and then investigate again! Investigate everything - and believe nothing! Careful interrogation and analysis is required in this field, perhaps more so than any other as there are parallels between UFO research and criminal investigation.

The mere recording of a witness' testimony is no longer enough. His account must be sifted through and the truth weeded from the falsehoods any story may contain. In the cases which give evidence of a "great deal of planning, expense and particularly cunning" we have proof that the MIB may well be backing it for some as yet unknown reason.

BREAKING AND ENTERING: As we all know on several occasions recently the MIB have gained entrance to the homes or offices of various researchers. In some cases material has been stolen, misfiled or even burned along with personal property, causing great loss. In a recent case such as this, George Smyth of Elizabeth, New Jersey reports that his home was broken into while he was out shopping. Files had been thrown about and the files of letters and articles written by this columnist had been stolen along with those of John A, Keel.

Automatic alarm systems linked to flood lights are an efficient, but expensive way of limiting these activities. There are systems which use sound waves in intricate patterns throughout the rooms which, when disturbed by a moving object, touch off alarms. There are systems that cannot be tampered with without tripping an alarm - providing the tampering is NORMAL, such as clipping the wires,

Because the MIB will go to any lengths to get their hands on important documents, Hack suggests that copies be made of important material and that these be scored in a safe place, such as a safe deposit box in a bank, Furthermore, avoid discussing the location and nature of your UFO material, as well as current investigations - THE GOVERNMENT IS NOT THE ONLY AGENCY WHICH CAN 'BUG' A CONVERSATION.

Indeed are all these MIB stories the work of deranged people and over imaginative researchers? In the December 1967 issue of PLAYBOY, Dr. J. Alien Hynek had this to say about the silencers: "I have on occasion been told what seemed to be a straightforward story, when suddenly the witness lapsed into a highly confidential mood and told me that he was sure that HIS PHONE WAS BEING TAPPED OR THAT HE WAS BEING WATCHED, sometimes on a regular schedule either fay the government or by 'occupants of the craft'."

Mr. Tad Jones, who witnessed a hovering sphere on a major highway on January 19th, 1967 received two threatening notes warning him not to tell anyone what he had seen. The printing on these "prank" warnings was identical to the printing on a note placed under the door of a UFO sighter in Middleport, Ohio, This girl, who had allegedly seen West Virginia's famous "Moth Man", later escaped from a would-be kidnapper - a tanned young man who was driving an old car "that looked like new".

MOTH-MAN. A girl who claims to have seen Moth Man later escaped from a would-be Kidnapper - a tanned young man who was driving an old car that "looked like new;".

Recently Jim Moseley, well-known UFO lecturer and investigator, received a most interesting letter from a contactee whose experiences have gained considerable publicity, but because of the nature of recent: writings felt it best not to give out his name. The letter is reproduced below in full:

Dear Jim (Moseley):

This is written in a rare and disquieting seriousness that could only be brought about by what I am to reveal below.

What I will relate here is to be considered in strictest confidence, and if any pan of it is in any way released to even a select audience, I request that I remain in total anonymiry as to its authorship.

You are, of course, aware of my contact work, to one degree or another, and unfortunately, with a most minute level of credence in what I claim. However, belief or disbelief is immaterial - the fact is that you are at least aware that I CLAIM to be in contact with extraterrestrials. THIS is cheerily IMPORTANT point.

I read your editorial in the Fall issue with a great deal of discomfort, and as you related the odd and frightening events that are even now transpiring within UFOlogical circles, I debated whether I should even reveal this at all, thinking maybe it would be preferable *to* simply let it remain under the hat, and continue on as *if* nothing had happened, with no one the wiser.

Whether my choice in telling you this is wise or foolhardy is a moot question, **and** only time **will** be the ultimate judge. But, for what it is worth to the total **understanding** of the unnerving phenomena that UFOlogy is now beseiged with, I open the doors unto you, content that your better judgement will conduct you properly with this information.

On the dace of 16 December 1967, at 0200 hours, I received a brief communication from my contacts - **a** normal, routine conversation that; lasted for perhaps twenty minutes. As we were about to close off, I detected on their end *a* good deal of agitation, and seconds later, the speaker informed me, "We are being monitored. Cease communication immediately. This station is clear." Everything went silent, for about a minute, and I was about to switch off the receiver when a tremendous burst of very-high-speed code rattled the **speaker** for ten seconds. When it left, there was nothing. Just dead air.

Having left my recorder running, I managed to copy the code transmission. I relate *it* here for what *it's* worth, because it is totally unintelligible to me.

RANSE DEMMA HYYPO LRATX CRWAW MMERM GRGAI HUUOF NIMRO XERCI TRIEO. COMPUTE 744-K. CL-5 OUT. CL-9 ACKNOWLEDGES. OUT.

That's it. Just those unbreakable five-letter code-groups, *and* that cryptic English tag on the end. The part, "CL-9 acknowledges. Out," **was** in a different tonal scale and slightly lower speed, and I assume that it **was** a second station replying to the first.

Continuing, I pored over this peculiar **exchange** for some three hours, trying a dozen types of substitution codes in an effort to break the message, to no avail. I believe it to be **an** alien language, or at least not English. The five-letter grouping is a standard technique of breaking down code messages, and **makes deciphering almost impossible.**

At 0600, I decided to hit the sack to catch a few winks. I slept very badly this particular morning. **As** soon as I drifted off, I **began** to dream - a most peculiarly horrifying dream, repeating **itself** over and over, in which I found myself thrust naked from the airlock of *some* unknown spacecraft into the black void of deep **space.** I awoke four times, and each time I went back to sleep, this distressing sequence repeated itself. After the last time, I decided **to** stay awake for a while, and hope that at a later time I could catch up on my needed **rest** without further repetition of this awesome and disconcerting dream.

I noticed soon after that I **was** beginning to develop a severe headache, especially acme in the form of shooting **pains** in the temples and **in** the center of the forehead. At **one** point, when it had become unbearable, I will swear that I heard **a** raucous, hollow laughter ringing in my head, interspersed with a mocking voice shouting, "Death to enemy". For fully two minutes, this torment continued. The sounds grew more intense, and I began to see things that weren't there - horrifying faces, grotesque masques twisted into disgusting semblances of **human** faces. Beastly apparitions, with bulging, pulsating red-streaked eyes that stared unblinkingly into my **very soul;** nostrils flared and emitting yellowish vapor; a slit mouth, with grisly green teeth, and an infested tongue slavering saliva downward, to **run** in a **slow** trickle from the monster's unshaven chin.

I managed to stagger over to my bed, or where it should have been if I could see beyond those phantasms from hell. **As** I fell back, clutching the sides of my head with my hands, a huge figure appeared beside the bed, a deformed, hairy creature like unto an ape, with **a** face so very much like the vacant insentience of a mongoloid idiot. In its bristly hand it weilded a most vicious-looking dagger **hewn** from scone, which it brought **up** above its head and thrust downward in *a* plunge right for my *chest.*

I believe I screamed - at least that's what my folks say. I can't recall for *sure.* In any event, **it** was over. Only a lingering trace of the head pains stayed on. The apparitions were *gone,* as were the haunting voices.

For an hour I simply lay **on** my bed, unmoving, trembling in uncontrollable spasms, breathing in quick, shallow breaths, fearing to open my eyes lest the *ghastly* demons be waiting to **start** anew their torment.

As the day **wore** on, the morning slipped into the afternoon, I had almost managed to forget the fearsome moments hours earlier. The family had gone into Pittsfield (the nearby large town to Washington), and I was alone in the house.

At **about** 1300, I went out to pick up the mail. a routine for me on Saturdays, The usual junk occupied the **box** - ads, bills, **and a** catalog. Tucked in amongst them **was** a strange envelope - a dark brown in color, almost black, to be sure - and of a size completely out of standard dimensions. **On** it **was** the single word, "Contactee!".

I brought it inside, and opened it carefully, not knowing what to expect. The second shock of the day came then. I have enclosed the 'letter' *that* was in the envelope, and would like to have it returned. Photocopy it **if** you so desire, but I'd **like** to have the original for my files.

Continuing, I placed this aside after a while, having become accustomed **to** nut mail by now, and thought no more of it. I didn't even **pay** attention to the fact that there **was** no stamp **on** the envelope, and that it **thus** must have been put in the **box** in person by the one who *sent it.*

At 1500, *the* events of the morning were just bad memories, am ' was settled down to a day of reading once more the various **saucer** mags in my file. I became deeply engrossed in one, and was unconscious to the entrance into my room of three men, until one spoke to me, saying, ". . . . , we would have words with **you."**

I think I jumped about three **feet** in the air, and when I had regained my composure, I stammered, "Who . . . who are **you?**" The one who **spoke** before replied, "Look closely. Do you not **know us** from your books?" I gave a cursory glance at the trio - that **was** all I needed. The **sudden** realization hit me **like a charge** of dynamite - BENDER'S THREE MEN IN BLACK.

"We are not of the same," he

corrected me, "bur a close union with them. Our purpose is similar."

I rook time to look *over* each one carefully. They looked like identical triplets, **about** thirty-five to forty years of age, with olive complexion, black, piercing **eyes** deep-set behind heavy **eyebrows**, Romanesque noses, and thin lips in what might **be** called a Mona Lisa smile. They were observing me in an **unblinking** stare.

They were **dressed** identically - black turtle-neck shirts, and **black** suits. The only variation was the charcoal-grey socks worn by *one*.

Since they seemed to be content to merely observe me, my fears abated somewhat, **and I asked** them what they wanted with me.

The leader of the group - or *so* I assumed, **as the** others seemed to let him have the run of the show - took a seat in one of my chairs, and while toying with a microphone **on** my work-bench, he said, "You are involved in flying saucer research. This is correct?" I could only answer, "Yes, of course. Why?"

"Here is where you receive your alleged communications from the space people. Is this correct?" he queried, ignoring my question. "Yes, but why . . ." He again avoided my interrogation, as he slowly swept his gaze over my charts and Playboy centerfolds hung about the room. For a moment, he stopped to look at one in particular, then nodded appreciatively, and with a half-smile, commerited, **"You have** most excellent taste in women."

Before I could acknowledge the compliment, he returned his attentions to me, **once** again toying unconsciously with the mike. "I am told that you had visitations this morning." I was abruptly aware that everything **was** beginning to fit. I had just opened my mouth **to ask** something, when he interrupted me. "Very unpleasant ones, they *say*." He seemed to be lost in thought, and allowed **his** voice to trail off as he said quietly, "A very effective weapon, indeed ... **but.. ."**

He came back *to* reality as quickly as he had left, and noticed the letter still lying on my desk. "I notice you have most strange correspondents, also."

By now I was **beginning** to become quite a little ticked off, and said

rather harshly, "Just what the hell do you want with. . ." A cutting glare from one of his companions shut me off instantly. He exhaled loudly, and admonished, "Belligerence will never do, ..."

He suddenly assumed a **very** serious composure, and riveted his stare into my *eyes*. I could feel his penetrating glare boring into my brain like a hundred little needles. "We are here to offer you *a* choice, You had a rather bad dream this morning, in which you were ejected into space quite unclothed."

"This is one alternative. The other **is** to cease your saucer work, refuse further communications from **your** alien contacts, and destroy all your files on the **subject**. When this is done, **you** will forget all you **know**. You will speak to no one, you will not discuss saucers, and you **will** terminate all related correspondence. In short, for *you*, flying saucers will cease to *exist*."

"That's impossible," I protested loudly. "How the hell am I supposed to just dump everything in **one** big bang, and not create a mess of suspicion? Tell me THAT." In reply he said, "Who has care about *the* **suspicions** of others? It **is** your life we discuss **now,** not theirs."

He stood and walked directly toward me, stopping three feet in front **of** me. "They who are suspicious will not be beside you *as* you are thrust into space." As he **spoke** he reached forward and pressed his ring against my head.

I **was** inside a space **ship**, in an airlock, **alone,** naked, terrified. I felt the cold hard metal beneath my feet, the draft of icy air as the pumps emptied the lock, the chill of space permeating every exposed inch of my **skin,** the irrational panic that precedes inevitable death.

I was **back** once more in my room. The three had regrouped, and the *leader* was saying to me, ". . . and this **is** as it must be **unless you** heed our warnings. Good day, ... You are **an** intelligent man. You will come to our **ways.**"

With that he and his partners spun on their heels and left the room. I followed them at a discreet distance, and watched as they boarded a red Volkswagen, and proceeded toward Becket. It **was perhaps** only the fact that I stood there a long moment just looking upward that enabled me to

catch a glimpse of *a* silvery disc streaking skyward, to disappear into the clouds.

And that **is** that. I have evidently defied [hem, and **as** yet nothing **has** happened. Whether they were bluffing remains to be seen. My contacts have told me that I **need** have no fear, but that feel of cold vacuum on *my* skin *doesn't* allow me to take very much comfort in the assurances my space friends have given me.

Again I *say*: IF ANY PART OF THIS IS USED, I WILL NOT ALLOW MY NAME TO BE USED WITH IT. YOU MAY SHOW THIS TO YOUR ASSOCIATES IF **YOU SEE** FIT, BUT I FULLY EXPECT THAT THIS WILL REMAIN **CONFIDENTIAL** WITHIN THE SAUCER NEWS OFFICE.

I request comments **as** soon as possible, else I might not **be** here when they come. If this fits in **with what** you've found **so** far, let me know, okay? Frankly, these men have me quivering in **my** shoes.

(Name Withheld)

● We have not **reproduced** the note for certain good reasons. Readers may be glad to know that the correspondent is continuing with his research despite this unpleasant experience and the threats by the three visitors. - Ed.

Recently even Jim Moseley has **been** acting **strangely.** He has sold out SAUCER NEWS, a magazine which he had been **editing** since 1954, to Gray Barker. He has moved - few people know his **new** address. And he remains strangely silent about a subject so dear to his heart, FLYING SAUCERS.

The Garden Island

Search is on for UFOs seen here

by Chris Cook

Hawaiian tales of menehunes, Madame Pele appearing as a phantom hitchhiker, the mo'o lizard and fireballs all have parallels in other cultures, says Timothy Beckley — aka Mr. UFO.

Beckley publishes UFO Review and Inner Light Magazine at his New York-based Global Communications office. He is currently touring Hawai'i collecting evidence of UFO sightings and Hawaiian psychic phenomena for a book on the Islands.

Kaua'i is the last stop for Beckley and Maria Carta, his clairvoyant companion, who also specializes in tarot cards. The pair has collected descriptions of UFO sightings on Maui and O'ahu, and even talked to an ex-military Honolulu man who claims to have been taken for a ride on a UFO in 1955.

A group of airline stewardesses witnessed the last major UFO sighting, in the late-1970s along

O'ahu's South Shore, Beckley says.

Beckley says his book will be marketed mostly on the Mainland, and feature kahuna chants, Hawaiian legends, information on Hawaiian herbal remedies, and ghost stories in addition to UFO tales. "The book will help draw visitors to Hawai'i from thousands of subscribers from all over the world on my mailing list," Beckley says.

Many of Hawai'i's hotels are haunted possibly because they are on the sites of ancient heiaus, Beckley claims. A sighting outside of a hotel on O'ahu happened about a month ago, he claims.

On the Mainland, a video called "Rainbow Bridge," a late 1960s movie featuring the late rock guitarist Jimi Hendrix filmed on Maui, was just released and has stirred up interest in the cosmic aspects of Hawai'i, Beckley says.

"Curtis Knight, a member of Hendrix's band in those days,

has told me that many of the events rumored to have happened during the movie's filming were real," Beckley says.

Claims of a UFO circling Hendrix's concert on the slopes of Haleakala spread throughout Hawai'i at the time, Maui surfer Leslie Potts' band "Space Patrol," based its music on the experience.

Beckley says Knight told him the UFOs continued to follow Hendrix around on the Mainland, saving the guitarist and his band when their van broke down on a remote road in a New England snowstorm.

Beckley says he has some other books in the works, including supernatural experiences of Country and Western music stars. Many of his books are available in the National Enquirer and other popular tabloids.

Beckley says he would appreciate receiving UFO reports from Kaua'i. He will be staying at the Plantation Hale in Waikua through Thursday. Those in-

terested can write to him at UFO Review, Box 753, New Brunswick, N.J. 08903.

UFO PUBLISHER Tim Beckley.

Democrat and Chronicle

People

At age 10, publisher Beckley had a sighting

'Two circular discs flying in circles'

By JIM MEMMOTT
Gannett News Service

Timothy Given Beckley has never seen an extraterrestrial being, but he believes they visit earth frequently.

Beckley, 31, is the author of several books and is the creator and the publisher of the monthly news-paper UFO Review.

"My main interest is cataloguing and collecting these creature sightings," says Beckley. In Rochester today and yesterday to promote "public awareness" of the phenomenon, Beckley's interest in unidentified

flying objects and their presumed pilots began in 1967 when, at age 10, living in New Brunswick, N.J., he saw "two circular discs flying in circles over the cloud layer," he recalls. The next day he told in the paper that government officials dismissed the sighting, reported by several citizens, as "marshlight."

"Impossible," he says now. "The beings would have had to travel from light where we were standing."

THERE ARE THREE possible explanations for sightings of extraterrestrial

beings, says Beckley.
1. The "witnesses" are lying.
2. They are hallucinating.
3. Extraterrestrial beings do exist.

And to maintain that sightings are too many and too well documented to rule out No. 3.

"I've talked to hundreds of these witnesses," he says. "Most of them are the reliable. I don't believe they're making this up story, and they're not hallucinating."

One recent and widely published sighting was filed by an Australian television news crew late last year. For

almost seven minutes the cameramen, on board a plane, recorded a bright light moving at seemingly incredible speeds.

The film later was analyzed by 20 top U.S. scientists, including Navy experts and Northwestern University's J. Allen Hynek, a former Project Blue Book consultant now considered one of the top UFO experts in the world.

Recorded in one frame — a time lapse of 1/50th of a second — the light, still unexplained, made a loop figure 8 loop at a distance of perhaps 10 miles

from the plane. That means the light must have been moving at more than 10,000 feet per second, Beckley says.

Furthermore, the brightness was compared to that of a 30,000-watt light bulb, which far exceeds the brightest possible neon made light bulb adds.

THEN THERE WAS the experience related to Beckley by country and western singer Johnny Sands. Sands was driving his car in the desert near Las Vegas when it began to stall, Beckley says. The singer got out to

Turn to Page 2C

Religion

ON THE TRAIL OF THE FLYING SAUCERS

TIMOTHY GREEN BECKLEY
Director
Interplanetary News Service

issue No. 64
June 1969

Finally **it's out**: The long awaited "Scientific Study of Unidentified Flying Objects" commissioned by the Air Force and **headed** by Dr. Edward U. Condon of Colorado University. And though its conclusions are negative, readers can be **assured** that a new project **will** soon be undertaken. Although nor public knowledge *as* yet, **we** are informed by "certain" unnamed parties that there **is** a considerable amount of unrest among the scientific college as to the unjustified results *of the* Condon Committee.

Reached by phone several days after **his** report was made public, Dr. Condon commented that his conclusions *were* final and that **as** far as he was concerned accusations **against** his findings **by** what he called "rebels" of the project were unfounded **and** unprecedented **in** science. He further frowned upon continued study of UFOs and said that in his opinion too much money, and *too* much time had already been spent. He also said that "nothing had come from the study of UFOs in the past **21** years char has added to scientific knowledge."

Condon also warned than high school and college Students were being misinformed in many cases about UFOs and **asked** that teachers no longer accept reports and projects about "flying Saucers" as proper subject matter.

The Committee itself studied several hundred sightings and came up with only a small handful of cases to which they **could** not attribute *a* scientific **explanation.**

Condon also disclosed that he had **been** offered **no** physical evidence which would tend to **prove** that UFOs **were** other than natural phenomena. 'No crashed saucers or crew members, not even a piece of hardware!"

And most of the photographs offered **fered** for evaluation were "easily" duplicated by members of **his** *staff.* The only real photos which Condon offers **no** explanation for **is** the historic photos taken by Paul Trent in the post Kenneth Arnold **days** of saucers.

Opinions on the results of the project have **varied.** It has been accepted in full by **the** National Academy of Sciences, and **New** York 'rimes science editor, Walter Sullivan, **has** called it **an** open minded report.

However, one of the Committee's ex-members, **Dr.** David **Saunders,** has blasted the project **in a** book which contains the findings of several of the project's investigators. Entitled UFOS? YES! (Signet), Saunders called the Condon report "unscientific, biased **with** preconcluded findings".

Major **Donald** E. Keyhoe, director of the unofficial Washington based organization NICAP called the report "full of holes", although those close to NICAP felt **that** the Major *was* overly critical because he had not been consulted by Condon on **key cases.** The report itself, according to the New York Post, had called Keyhoe "a sensationalist **who sparked** public interest in the bizarre **aspect of** UFOs and as an obstructionist".

Others, **such as** Coral and Jim Lorenzen of APRO (Tucson, Arizona) and James W. Moseley publisher of SAUCER NEWS (New **York,** New York) were commended for their **attitudes,** although like NICAP, Condon felt that they had dealt "lightly" with the truth in some **in**stances.

Civilian UFO *consultant* to the Air Force, Dr. J. Allen Hynek told reporters *in* confidence **that** he planned on continuing his own investigation and asked that other scientists have the foresight to **do** the same.

As this **goes** to press there *is* **even** serious talk *of* holding one or more scientific symposium's **under** Congressional **ties.**

What effects **has** the Condon Committee had **on** the **public's** attitude in believing **in** UFOs? It's probably too early to tell, although from. a sampling of opinion it seems *to* have had an adverse effect **on** squashing interest in the subject, Although **sightings** have nor been reported **in** any great numbers **in** recent months, we are still quite startled over the appearance **of books** on the subject (some **35** in paperback alone) which **have** been showing up on local newsstands around the country. Some new titles have included NEW UFO BREAKTHROUGH by Brad Steiger and Joan Whitenour (Award), MYSTERIOUS FIRES AND LIGHTS by Vincent Gaddis (Dell), also reprints of Frank Edward's **last** book FLYING SAUCERS: HERE AND NOW and FLYING SAUCERS AND THE THREE MEN by Albert K. Bender.

In fact, **as** this columnist has traveled **across** the country **in** recent weeks, we **have** never before noticed **so** many people **expressing** an interest in UFO and **New** Age subjects. In a period of less than **a** month, our travels took us a distance of almost 15,000 miles, **stopping** in **at least** a dozen scares. At each **stop we** were **surprised** to meet many readers of this publication who *took* **keen** interest **in** what **we** had been **able** *to* uncover in our recent investigations.

OUR INTERVIEW WITH JEANNE DIXON

In the nations capital we found Jeanne Dixon, the world's most famous and qualified prophetess, busy at **work** on a new foundation called CHILDREN TO CHILDREN, INC. Seen in a vision, it will be a means to "**alleviate** the suffering of children, and to assist them in attaining their true purpose in life".

Artist's conception of Jeanne Dixon's invisioned Children to Children hospital to be located near Washington.

Jeanne tells **us** that located close to the seat of government research 'it is motivated by a humanitarian concern for children and all **peoples,** in the hope of finding cures" to now incurable sicknesses. The hospital center, only one of *the* many com**plexes** to this vast foundation, "**will** contain all aspects of research, practical application, trends and treatment under one roof". This will, **as** Jeanne Dixon *says* herself, be "the **hospital** of the future".

Jeanne Dixon's psychic ability has long caused quite a rage in Washington. In effect, Mrs. Dixon *has* **been an** unofficial advisor to several presidents including Roosevelt, Truman and Kennedy. She **has** also advised prime ministers, congressmen and other notables. She has in reality become recognized as the **seeress** of **our** nation - a circumstance unique in American history.

So much does newly elected President Richard Nixon **think** of Jeanne Dixon (and *as* we learned, *so does* everyone else of importance near the Capital), that he **asked** her husband, James L. Dixon, to compose a **song** based **upon** his administration's slogan "Unite Us All Together".

We **asked** Mrs. **Dixon what she** foresaw for the next year or so **as far AS** Nixon **was** concerned. She, recalling a recent vision, warned that there would be "many troubled

times ahead. I *see* him openly criticized by the people - **but** he **will** stick *to his* task." She also warned that Nixon might be *in* danger and that full **protection** should **be** offered him by the secret service **in** the months ahead.

Although it is against the nature of **this** columnist to suggest worthwhile charities *for* readers to donate to, **we** have really been hit hard by Jeanne Dixon's visioned Children to Children foundation and hospital.

So those who would **like** *to* send a do ation or receive at least further information can do so by writing for **a** beautiful color pamphlet, which contains *a* personal message on the foundation by Mrs. Dixon, to Children to Children, Inc., 1144 18th Street, N. W., "Washington, D.C. 20036.

Also while in 'Washington we **talked with** our old friend Harold Salkin, who since the passing of the beloved **Clara** John, has **been** running THE LITTLE LISTENING POST (4811 Illinois Avenue) and ocher projects on his **own.** He has also promoted several lecturers in the area, including contactee Woody Derenberger, and **is** starring a syndicated radio program based on his interest **in** the offbeat.

Salkin recently, **while** visiting near this writer, saw seven unidentified flying objects in the space of little more than **four hours.** The New Brunswick Home News of December 9th **says** that the sightings **occurred** between *5* and 9:30 P.M. Salkin described them to this editor **as** being "red and white lights moving in different. **paths and** speeds in the *sky".* Several days later additional sightings were **reported** in the **New** Brunswick **area,** giving verifi**cation** *to* Salkin's report. Residents told reporters that the **UFOs "were** like moths around a flame... nothing like *a* **plane's** lights"+

THE BROWN MOUNTAIN LIGHTS

Accompanying **us** on our next investigation were James W. Moseley, long time publisher of SAUCER NEWS, who is now spending much of his rime **lecturing** to various universities across the country on the worldwide UFO problem. Also with us was Alien H. Greenfield **of** Atlanta, Georgia, editor of the UFO SIGHTER and originator **of** the Alternate Reality theory which has

been causing some excitement **in** saucer circles. Our point **of interest was** the mysterious Brown Mountain **located about** fifteen miles North of Morganton, North Carolina.

It *is* said that here for several hundred years, **perhaps** going back **as** far *as* 1200, long before the white man had reache.' the Shores of America, people have reported seeing **arrange** lights which appear **to** roam **about** the mountain peaks without any apparent source.

Various legends have sprung **up** about *the* origin of the lights. One **has** it that the lights are caused by the spirits of the Cherokee and Catawba braves searching the valley for their maiden lovers. It seems that the two tribes had a big battle hundreds **of** years ago which killed just **about** all the men of the two tubes. Apparently this legend does have some **basis in** fact. as most legends **do,** because within the last several years at least a half-dozen **Indian** graves have been found in the **area nearby.**

However, others who have *lived* **near** Brown Mountain for as many *as* 75 years seem to think that there **is** something even more odd and pe**culiar** than spirits ar work in the valley below.

According to **Paul** Rose, who accompanied us to a secret lookout point despite the 10 degree weather and the falling snow, they may he something from outer space.

Out **of** all the people living **in** the **area,** Rose, **and** another fellow whom we shall talk about in a minute, seems to have gotten closer to *the* lights than anyone else, His **first** sighting came when he **was** just a youth in **about** 1916. **At** the *time* it **was** thought that the lights might have been caused by the headlights on locomotives running through a nearby valley. However, during one rough spring all bridges were knocked out **and** roads were **too** muddy to enable **cars to pass.** Yet the Brown Moun*tain* lights **were** seen, in greater numbers **and** brighter than ever before, **weaving up** and down over the trees **on** Brown Mountain.

Rose *bases* **his** opinion that they **are** intelligently controlled **on** the fact that he has seen them fighting, burring into each ocher and bouncing like big **basket** balls. He has also tracked them at speeds of almost one hundred miles per hour.

He claims that on one particular night in the late 1950's, when excitement was at ah all time high, two of these lights appeared out of the valley, approached a rower he had built for the purpose of watching them over the trees and climbed to within feet of his position. The next day he, and a friend who had been with him, both became violently ill. This led Rose to the conclusion that these lights are highly radioactive.

Another old time resident of the Brown Mountain area is Ralph Lael, who was born in Alexander county on a small hillside farm in 1909. He ran for Congress in 1948 and lost by a few thousand votes. He now operates the "Outer Space Rock Shop Museum" on highway 181 just outside Morganton.

Lael claims not only to have seen the lights close up but to have communicated with them on numerous occasions as well.

Deciding that the only way to uncover the source of these lights was to go into the almost impassable mountain area itself, Lael started his own investigation. Shortly after midnight he got within one hundred feet of a light that had risen up from a large hole in the ground. Within 10 or 15 minutes the first light had been joined by as many as twenty more. Shortly after, they all took off into the timber and disappeared from Lael's view. A half - hour later others began popping up along the mountainside in a smaller valley below. One came so close, within ten feet, that Lael felt he could have read a book by it.

Several expeditions, and months later, Lael discovered that by asking the lights questions, they would answer by either moving up and down for yes or back and forth for no. After this form of communicating

had been established one of the lights led Ralph to a door which leads inside of Brown Mountain. (You just lost me! - Rap.)

Once inside he was led to a room about eight feet square, the walls made of crystal "as clear as glass", enabling him to see for what seemed to be miles. Suddenly a voice said: "Do not fear; there is no danger here." The voice continued by saying that Lael has been chosen to tell the people of Earth about their true history: that man was created on another planet named Pewam which our ancestors destroyed. Pewam is now the waste of the asteroids which lies between Mars and Jupiter.

The voices explained that they are not Earthbound beings and cannot ear or drink, but live on Pethine, a "gas we absorb from the light you see around us. We perish in your atmosphere or sunlight."

"We live on Venus which is a planer of pure crystal as you see surrounding you . . notice that the crystal is as clear as your air. Venus is completely surrounded by water vapor about one hundred and fifty miles above its surface."

In October of 1962 Lael returned to the rock, entered and was offered a ride to Venus - which he accepted. Arriving two days later on Earth's sister planet he was introduced to men who were said to have been direct descendants of the people from the planer Pewam. One is a rather attractive woman named Noma who is quite beautifully dressed in a bra and panties set.

While on Venus Lael is shown what appear to be newsreels of the destruction of Pewam as well as scenes going on back on Earth.

Although unbelievable as this story may seem, so are the Brown Mountain Lights. Ralph Lael told us that "there are many things I have seen and heard that I cannot reveal here because of my obligations to the Brown Mountain lights. Whether you believe or disbelieve what I have told is of no importance. You and others who have read these things should have more brotherly love for the people of Earth and those of the whole universe.

The entire story is in a small booklet entitled THE BROWN MOUNTAIN LIGHTS which Lael sells for $1.25. His address is Highway 181, Morganton, N.C. What a

story, is all we can say. (Readers: This ought to prove FLYING SAUCERS prints both sides of any story! - Rap)

This trip to Brown Mountain by no means ends our own interest. Our plans call for a return trip within several months. This time right into the valley where Ralph Lael and Paul Rose claim to have had their experiences. What are the Brown Mountain Lights? We don't know as yet, but are set on finding out.

THEHUNDREDYEARHAUNT

Our travels next took us to Maco, North Carolina a small community of some 150 people. Maco is about 15 miles northwest of Wilmington and the phenomena we are about to describe is there for everyone to see.

The legend goes that in 1868 Atlantic Coast Line conductor Joe Baldwin was beheaded in a railroad accident just outside Maco. Since then a pale yellowish light has been seen along the track in the exact spot where Joe met his death. Some people claim that they had gotten close enough to the light to determine that it is a lantern complete with guards around the lantern shades,

According to Jerry Tumberville, who owns a general store about 500 yards from the railroad track at Maco, a second light is said to have appeared in about 1873. This is thought by some to be Joe's head in search of his body.

The Ghost Light has gained credence in recent years when investigators from Washington failed to find any explanation for the light. Also an entire machine gun detachment from Fort Bragg visited Maco attempting to shoot at the light. The light seemed to bob and weave in front of them, making it impossible

Ralph Lael in his Rock Store near Brown Mt., N.C. Lael claims he was taken to Venus inside a space ship and has been inside the mountain itself- (Photo by Al Greenfield, Atlanta.)

Timothy Green Beckley points to spot on railroad track in Maco, N.C. where the ghost of Joe Baldwin has been seen for over 100 years. (Photo by James W. Moseley.)

to hit. Other men with scientific *training* and skilled analytical minds have tackled the problem, but no one **has** come forward *with* an explanation.

The only explanation offered is the light **is caused** by the reflection of *autos* along a nearby highway. However descriptions given by **various witnesses** and the *fact* that the light **was first seen** long before the highway **existed,** tend to discredit this theory. **Also on several** occasions traffic has been rerouted for several hours with no effect on the **"ghost"** light.

Another long time resident of North Carolina is Eugene B. Spooner. He tells us that at first the light is **seen** from some distance **down** the **track,** perhaps as much as a mile away. "It starts with a small flicker over the left rail and continues to grow larger and larger moving **up the** rail toward *you.* As it grows larger it also seems to pick up momentum. **Finally** it **dashes** forward **at** a high velocity, while swinging *from* right **to** left.

"When it gets to within 60 feet of you, it **seems to stop and stand still.** If you *try to* get closer, it will retrace its movements and **disappear** back down the track toward a **trestle** where **Joe is** said to have been killed."

Who has seen the light recently? **Just** about everyone from reporter Louise Lamica of the WILMINGTON STAR-NEWS to this columnist. In **fact we** managed to get a photograph **of the specter** with **our** German made Voigtlander. **Although** it shows only a bright yellowish light, it does indicate that something has been seen **along** this railroad **track** in Maco.

On several occasions since 1910, it has been reported that railroad **conductors passing through** Maco in the early morning **hours** have **seen Joe's** lantern light and have stopped their trains, thinking it is another stalled train. Since then, tram brakemen *in* the Maco district **have** used two lanterns - one green, one white - **so as** not **to** confuse **passing conductors.**

WESTWARD HO!

Our next lengthy **stop was** in Lawton, Oklahoma where **we spent several** weeks with our old friends William and Sandra **Ross.** Not: **far** from Fort Sill this area is ripe with UFO accounts and other weird stories. One **saucer** observer cold us how he **and** another **couple** had *witnessed a* doughnut *shaped object* nor unlike *the* **ones** reportedly observed during the controversial "Maury Island **Hoax".** (Fred L. Crisman was the hoaxer. - **Rap)**

We were also brought **up to date on** an old legend which **states** that over **five** million dollars **worth** of gold **was** hidden in the **area** by the Spanish several hundred years ago. Apparently they were **attacked by** Indians and forced **to bury** *the* heavy gold **in order to escape.** We talked to one **young** man who claims that **he** has found the location of the **gold,** but that *it* is hidden **in a cave on what is** now military land- Also the entrance of the cave is **now** guarded by a **number** of large and deadly rattlers.

During our **stay** Increased interest **in** the UFOs **was** caused by **the** syndication of Frank Edwards' book FLYING SAUCERS - SERIOUS BUSINESS as well *as* **the** release of the Condon report.

In nearby Oklahoma City **we** had an all too brief meeting with **long** rime saucer and Shaver buff Victor C. Johnston. From **Vic we** learned quite a bit about the mysterious **light** at SPOOKSVILLE near the Oklahoma - Missouri *stare* line. We **were** also **saddened** to hear the details of the late Capt. Robert Loftin's **passing.** FLYING SAUCERS readers **will** remember Loftin best **perhaps** for his **controversial book** IDENTIFIED FLYING SAUCERS **(David McKay)** which appeared **in** print **only** months before his passing.

Capt. Loftin had also been an Early Warning Coordinator for **the** Condon Committee and probably the **world's most** informed **authority** on the Spook light arrested to above. He died **of** an **apparent heart attack** while **on** the way to **a preview of** a **syndicated** TV series he had filmed only **weeks** before with Frank Stranges and contactee Carol **Watts** of Loco, Texas.

We also learned from **Vic** that he is planning to *start* publication devoted to the study of the "Inner Earth" theory. **We have** promised to keep **you** readers posted **on** this publication as it develops.

A good deal **of** our conversation was taken over in discussing the Shaver mystery. In particular the picture rocks which Dick claims to have discovered. For a good **explanation** of these rocks, which contain the written **history of the** pre-deluge days, it is suggested that readers **purchase** a **book** entitled THE SHAVER MYSTERY **AND** THE INNER **EARTH (\$4.95)** which **this** investigator *wrote* only *a* year ago. **Copies** can be obtained by writing directly to us **at** the **address** given at the **end of this** column-

MEET ME IN ST. LOUIS

In St. **Louis we** found a very enthusiastic group of readers lead by Warren and Nora Bartling whose interest *in* the UFOs **has** increased **over** the years. Warren, **known** as "Mr. Flying **Saucer"** in St. **Louis** along **with** his charming **wife,** Nora, have sponsored several **UFO** and New **Age** leaders in St. Louis. Lecturers have included **such** noted authorities **as** Wayne Aho, Dan Fry, **Buck** Nelson **and Mark** and Yolanda of the Mark-Age Center. Radio and TV coverage has been **very** good although the press **has** not been open to **such** events.

While in St. Louis we tried to locate the Mitchell Sisters (Helen and **Betty) who** were responsible for quite an unusual contact **story** which appeared *in* print several years ago.

It seems that **no one has** seen them for *at* least five years. As

Helen and Betty Mitchell claim to have been in contact with spacemen from Mars. They *have* since *vanished* despite many attempts to locate them. (Photo courtesy Nora Bartling.)

one long time saucer researcher told us "Since *the* space Brothers promised to take the girls on a trip to Mars, it is possible that they are there now; no one seems to be able to find them; their former Landlord said that they left without giving a forwarding address, but that he did see them in a supermarket area near St. Louis about five years ago," How such internationally know personalities can elude all of their many *former* friends is a mystery in the minds of many in St. Louis.

The Mitchell Sisters story is told in a small booklet entitled WE MET THE SPACE PEOPLE (available from this columnist at $1.10 per copy while the supply lasts). They claimed at one time to have the entire interplanetary language - which Helen had learned to speak.

One reader whom we talked with at great length commented that he had heard Helen use this strange tongue on a number of occasions. At one of her addresses for the Kansas City Saucer Club she gave a sample of the language which went something like this: "Mel Bez de Son. Ras, de ta ol de leon qua son twila urn bon-ta-bon Zabat dra um ta daga de tra-ce-te de ta io um bont. Zabat rma zabat ott ta rma qua zabat gavon-ta-bon um-quat que. Ban gav ban um ta ban ta zabat, nas qua pa qua zabat ta ol dat urn ta rama. Mel Bez de son,"

This translates as: "Peace be with you. Beloved, in the light of mind evolveness one chooses to serve, and so doing turns the forces of Love in this attraction toward him. When searching is difficult it proves advancement, for adversaries must work strongly to prevent evolvement. Let darkness fade to the nothingness it is, not potential or manifesting as is the light which takes its place. Peace be with you."

If anyone out there knows the whereabouts of the Mitchell Sisters we would certainly like to contact them. Their present whereabouts would be kept strictly confidential as we understand that they have two young children which they are busy raising.

Many readers of this magazine will also recall the controversy over the saucer ride promised by George Marlow of St. Louis to such personalities as Jack Parr, Jackie Gleason, Gray Barker, Ray Palmer and others. While in St. Louis we talked with Marlow over the phone and asked him what had happened to the planned trip. He informed us that the CIA had stepped in and stopped it at the last moment for reasons best known to themselves. He said, however, that he was still in contact with the Space people and that the trip would come off one of these days.

Marlow seemed quite hesitant over the phone and mentioned that he was afraid to get too envolved in the publicity aspects anymore. In his words he wanted to keep certain things under rapps. However, he promised when the right time came readers of this column would get *the* details first hand.

While in St. Louis we were also given the original full length manuscript that Dr. Raymond Bernard of Brazil "dared not to include in his *book* THE HOLLOW EARTH." Because, as our informant told us it "proves to a finality that neither Cook nor Peary ever reached the North Pole."

All in all St. Louis is certainly an active city - saucer *wise*.

BACK HOME AGAIN

Our trip to New York from St. Louis was uneventful with brief stops in Dayton, Ohio and Pittsburg, Pennsylvania. We arrived home shortly after to find our mail box filled with unopened mail. So those who have written recently and have not received a reply will understand why.

One of the most interesting letters received while we were gone came from saucer publisher Gray Barker who was excited over the response that my own book SPACE BROTHERS had received. Actually *Gray* and I both blamed this on the fact that it was being promoted along with Ted Owen's exciting new book HOW TO CONTACT SPACE PEOPLE.

Owens is the Philadelphia prophet who has foretold such things as the east *coast's* big blackout, the appearance of UFOs at specific times, strange disasters, weird storms and much much more. I had been responsible for first bringing Mr. Owens' contact experiences before the saucer public little more than a year ago. Since then between Gray and myself we must have re-

Ted Owens, author of HOW TO CONTACT SPACE PEOPLE claims to have predicted east coast black-out with help of space people.

ceived close to 10,000 letters from people all over the world telling us that Mr. Owens had cured them of various illnesses or brought them good fortune by putting them in contact with the SI's (short for space intelligence). At first we were skeptical, but after seeing all the evidence that Mr. Owens presents in his book, we just don't know.

We hope by the time this reaches the newsstands the book will be ready for delivery (this to all those that have ordered it already) but it may not since *it* is so large and will contain so many illustrations. In fact this volume will contain photographs of the space beings Mr. Owens claims to have contacted. They are like NOTHING ON EARTH.

Those who do not have copies will certainly want to get their orders in and have their name placed on a special SI Scroll which will be shown to *the* space entities and which already has brought many people who have signed good luck. Mr. Owens claims that the SI's will bestow good fortune on those that sign the scroll simply to show their well wishes to Earth people who believe in their existence.

Copies of HOW TO CONTACT SPACE PEOPLE by Ted Owens will be available through this column for only $4.95. Those who would like to have their name placed on the scroll must let us know immediately (we already have more *than 5,000 signers) so* that we can *take* care of this as soon as possible. Orders should be sent for the book to Timothy Green Beckley.

We still need your own personal *sighting* reports, news clippings, photos and theories. They should be sent to the above address. Until next time HAPPY SAUCERING!

42

ON THE TRAIL OF THE FLYING SAUCERS

TIMOTHY GREEN BECKLEY
Director
Interplanetary News Service

Issue No. 65
August 1969

Do alien visitors from outer worlds **walk** among us?

According to Philadelphia **re**searcher Milton L. Scott, at times the television **show**, "The Invaders", seems to he just "a bit more than a concoction **of** a science fiction writer's vivid imagination; the kidnappings, murders, and sabotage being done **by** David Vincent's adversaries **with** the **opposable** pinkies are the same **things** being **done by** their true-to-life counter-**pairs**." Or **so says** Mr. Scott.

Furthermore Scott points out that **the** difference between the television invaders and the real aliens **is** that there are **no** funny looking fingers **to make** them **easy** to **spot**. Thus in order to **carry on** their various acts while on Earth it **is** necessary for them "to resemble us as closely **as possible**". In order to do this they **need** not "involve **themselves** 'with **using** some fantastic hypno-screen that 'clouds' our minds to their true, gruesome appearance" because they are no more gruesome looking than Chinese, Japanese, Vietnamese, **or** Ainus.

Because of their Earth-like **ap**pearance they are able to carry on various acts of "espionage" **without** being **detected**,

How does a nation **wage** an undedared war with yet-to-be invented weapons against **an** enemy who **is not suppose** to exist? Milton Scott **says**: "You might start off by alerting the **nation's** power complexes to the ever-present: danger of sudden

black-outs, and **advising** those stations to close each **and every switch** within reach when they detect a gigantic **surge of** power racing down **the** lines from an unknown source."

Or: "You might also **make** noblesounding pronouncements of **peace** and friendship **to** the world — hoping that whoever **is** listening outside our civilization believes **it**, **You** could sign treaties among nations to ban wars **in** outer **space; clutching** at the powdery **straw** contactees **have** left to **us** in hopes that flying saucers invading **our** skies really **are** big-**brother** type angels who **she'd** tears **over our** savage nature,

"You could even build giant ra**die-telescopes'** to send **messages** beaming **across space**: 'We are really nice fellows. We can't hurt you, We only hare each other. Don't **hurt us.' "**

Scott asks: "Then **what do you do when the** blackouts 'keep occurring, and the **deaths and the** kidnappings continue **to** mount?

"You could **explode nuclear** bombs high **in** the atmosphere in *the* hope **that** the radiation will disrupt the machinery of *the* **saucers or even**. kill their occupants. **You** could even test your theory by having the bomb **explode** in the vicinity of a satellite - like the Transit 4-B satellite, **and when** the satellite suddenly **stops** sending **signals, you** could **congratulate** yourselves **on a** theory well proved. Then, what do you do when the satellite suddenly

comes back to life FIVE YEARS LATER - and starts rebroadcasting again?''

Obvious Scott is convinced that the UFOs are here on a non-peaceful mission. We asked him how he reached this important conclusion. His answer was as follows:

For over 20 years the public has been fed false information from both the government and newspapers who scoffed at anyone who dared report a flying saucer. It's gotten to the point that the air force and the CIA can expect more information from a Martian than they can from John Doe. Ol' John just won't tell anybody anything.

"That's where my tale begins: *the* first **stages** of the **war** that **the** flying **saucer** occupants have been **waging** against **us has been** psychological. They have **spread** confusion, **fear,** and **doubt** from one comer of the globe **to** the other **in** order to keep their movements **and** their **purpose** a secret until they are **ready to make** their move. *It's* a fantastic **tale** of **ghosts, ESP,** thought control, liars, **dupes** and **murder.**

"The **most important battle in** the war **of** the **worlds** *was* waged and **won** in the **minds of** the people. If *there* can be **one** glaring fault on **our** part that led **to** our defeat, it **was** the **view** that **we** were the supreme result **of** billions **of years** of a thing called **evolution** - that **we** were **the** only intelligent beings **in** the **universe**.

"Our **scientists,** philosophers and **clergy,** boosted **our egos** by telling **us, endlessly, what** great **works of** God **we** were - so complex **(and so stupid)** that there couldn't possibly be **anyone else as** grand and *as* wonderful as **we** were. It was a perfect **set-up** and the characters from the flying-saucers exploited it **to** the fullest extent: **they made a few** flights **over villages, countrysides,** swamps and **cities to shake up** the public **and** drive **a** wedge between belief **in** *what the government* says and what our **own** eyes say."

In order **to** keep their **mission** a *secret* **and make** UFOs look like *the* work of idiots, Scott **claims** that they **used ships** of varying **shapes,** *sizes*, colors, and methods of propulsion to spread confusion among the few investigators, and they even **used** an effect that produce a number of images from a few actual **saucers so that** the viewers would think there were whole fleets of saucers tooling about **the skies.** Thus the subject of flying saucers soon became a tiling for **disbelief** and tired old **jokes.**

Scott contends that the hundreds of little men, **gods,** beautiful space men, winged monsters, and **surplus** Atlantean **Biplanes** and talk of the UFOs being from the **bowels** of Earth, fifth -dimension, an anti-matter universe, etc., **was** nothing more than lies and false leads, implanted in gullible Earthly minds **by** the aliens.

In reality we were lulled to sleep while more land was taken. We nodded and dreamed while more men and materials from other worlds were flown in. We giggled *as* things **rushed** rapidly toward *a* point of no return. The government refused to believe the abundance of evidence before its eyes until it was too late.

Adamski, and all the other contactees, Scott tells us, **did** have real **enough experiences** but they were selected for their gullibility, and they wrote Books that were just **as** naive and **as** gullible *as* they were. The **books** got the large hee-haw from the public that the aliens had **expected,** and the case for flying saucers was laughed **into** obscurity for **ten** more years while the aliens went about their plans uninterrupted.

If, as Milton Scott says, the aliens **Purpose** for being here is other **than** peaceful- and they **look** almost exactly like us, how then **can** they be **identified?** The answer may lie **in** the **scientific analysis** of *a* "suspected" alien once he has been captured, "Perhaps the **answer** is in **the** chemical balances of the body **or in** the theory that the little DNA molecules only have *a* limited number of **types to choose from** among Earthlings."

Interesting theory? So much so that **upon** hearing **of** Mr. Scott's opinions many months ago, Dr. Edward U. Condon, of the ill-famed University of Colorado UFO study, **requested** that **we** send **reproductions** to him **of** several **newspaper** columns **which** had carried these **ideas.**

THE DIVERSIONS

In accord, with many **of** the opin-

ions expressed **by** Mr. Scott is another famed UFO investigator, John A. Keel. Besides being **one of** America's foremost authorities **on** flying **saucers,** Mr. Keel has long had **a** history **of** objective scientific study *of* ether phenomena. He **has** been a reporter for more than twenty **years** and has authored several *best* selling **books** dealing with both **off**-beat and more conservative topics.

Commenting *upon* the various diversions inherent in the UFO enigma, Keel **told us** recently that: "From 1897 **on** it has been a common practice for *the* UFOs to **leave** behind ordinary debris such *as* **newspapers,** pieces of metal, articles of ordinary clothing, mundane chemicals, etc. **Investigators** who had discovered **such** items have **often** been led to believe that the whole incident **was a** human hoax or prank **of** some kind. **It** is also quire common to find ordinary tire tracks in inaccessible fields where **landings** have been reported." Keel warns **as** that **we should** not permit ourselves to be **misled by** these "negative factors". Keel **points** out that even in these cases **a** thorough investigation **should be** made. "We have discovered that a multiple group of these negative factors often leads to positive proof that a UFO event DID OCCUR."

Other odd factors inherent in UFO contacts is that "ancient **Greek** *is* often employed by the UFO occupants. Greek names and **phrases** *are* frequently **used** for their non-existent **planets.** Many of die entities adopt Greek- **nouns** *as* their personal names. The **witnesses very** rarely realize **this** or understand it. Prepare yourself by obtaining and studying **a book** on Greek mythology."

Keel also **suggests** that we should also study "our **own** techniques *of* **psychological** warfare **which** are often employed by the UFOs". Diversionary landings or seemingly important incidents frequently are *staged* a few miles from an area where a truly significant UFO activity **Is** taking place, The diversion wins all of our attention and publicity and the important activity *goes* unnoticed.

Like Scott, Mr. Keel informs us that we should discard all preconceptions: "You must learn to accept **only** the correlative evidence and ignore the assorted spec-

ulations which have dominated UFO-logy. % are interested only in hard facts. All of these facts indicate that we are dealing with an environmental phenomenon, but that we have been misled into believing the extraterrestrial thesis."

Milton Scott of **Philadelphia** claims that the UFOs are playing a game with earthlings. (Photo credit: Gray Barker)

Thus unlike Milton Scott, John Keel is convinced that the flying saucers, although very real, ARE NOT from other planets. "So long as we accepted the ET concept, the phenomenon and its source was safe and free from interference. Deliberate hoaxes were executed to sustain skepticism and **convince** government agencies that the phenomenon was non-real. The UFO buffery was convinced of the ET thesis, which was unacceptable to both the general public and the scientific community, and by loudly advocating it, they succeeded in heaping ridicule upon the subject. Thus the UFO source was able to operate unhindered for twenty long years."

HALLUCINATORY EFFECTS

UFO believers usually rebel at any suggestion that the UFO phenomenon may be hallucinatory or psychological. However, Keel points out: "In the past three years many psychological factors have been discovered and various groups of psychologists and psychiatrists are now actively engaged in UFO research. Unfortunately very few UFOlogists are trained or equipped to understand or even to investigate the underlying psychological factors. You should read at **least** one good **book** on *psychiatry* and/or **psychology.** "

As far as the contact stories are concerned, Keel tells us that "at least some of these cases in the past three years have proven to be hallucinations because it seems that the effects were produced in the witnesses' minds by an exterior influence. These effects are similar to hypnosis. While the witnesses' bodies undergo one sequence or experience, false memories of another sequence of experiences are planted in their minds-

"Frequently the true (but forgotten) experience surfaces from the witnesses subconscious later on in the form of a dream or nightmare. We cannot outline the whole process here, but it must be considered as a very important factor in many cases."

IMPORTANT FACTORS IN UFO SIGHTINGS

Some of the important factors to look for in UFO sightings according to Mr. Keel include:

"EMOTIONAL REACTIONS - In low-level sightings, auto pursuits, etc. the emotional and physiological responses of the witnesses are extremely important. Get them to explain in detail how they felt immediately before, during and after the sighting. Did they suffer fear, nausea, dizziness? Did they have unusual dreams afterward? In some cases these reactions are more important than the sighting itself.

"SOUNDS - The sounds accompanying the objects can be of great importance. Many of these sounds have proven to be 'mental' in nature. That is they were not audible movements of air, but were electrical responses in the brains of the observers. Beeping sounds frequently indicate that the witness was subjected to an unconscious experience. Such witnesses may find that they are unable to explain lapses of time or geographical transfers during such sightings. Such witnesses should be examined by a qualified psychiatrist whenever possible.

"EYE BURN - Witnesses who suffer from burned or inflamed eyes after viewing a UFO should be examined immediately by a professional doctor and a full medical report should be obtained. In those cases involving 'eye burn' weeks or months previous to the investigation, the investigator should get the witness to draw up a full statement explaining in full the reactions suffered. Medical documentation is most important.

"DREAMS - Many witnesses suffer unusual nightmares weeks before their UFO sighting. Others have strange nightmares for weeks afterward. These dreams are important, and you should obtain full descriptions of them. Some witnesses begin to have prophetic dreams after their UFO experience."

In landing cases when definite markings are found on the ground they should be photographed and measurements carefully made. For the past twenty years hundreds of landings have been neglected even though the markings are always similar to size and formation. If we had collected and documented photos of all these landings we would now have an impressive body of correlative evidence."

In further investigating important sightings, landings and contact experiences, under no circumstances should any witness be hypnotized by anyone other than a qualified psychiatrist. Amateur hypnotists have ruined several important cases in recent years.

MEN IN BLACK

During this same period of three years which John Keel speaks of there has been a growing number of cases which involve the MIB or men in black. These arrange individuals have been known to warn UFO witnesses not to reveal what they have seen long before' the case is ever made public. Keel comments on the activities of these MIB by pointing out that many different investigators in 'flap' areas have now had confirmatory experiences with the MIB and only a small percentage of these cases have been published. There are several different types of MIB. One group appears to be more psychic or hallucinatory than real. They appear and disappear suddenly in bedrooms and the witnesses often experience paralysis or a sudden rise in temperature during their presence. We now have dozens of such cases in our files.

Another type now common throughout the U.S. is represented by men who travel in pairs. The same description is always given. One man is tall, blond (usually has a crewcut), fair-complected and seems to be a Scandinavian. His companion is shorter, with angular features and a dark olive complexion. The blond usually does most of the talking while the other remains in the background. There seems to be several identical pairs of these individuals operating simultaneously in several states.

Other types of MIB include men with oriental features, dark complexions, slight stature and a heavy, undefinable accent. These men sometimes pose as salesmen or

Here is the first photo of the so-called MIS (Men in Black) ever published to our knowledge. It was taken by Timothy Grew. Beckley and James W. Moseley during an investigation of strange MIB type visitors who watched the home of researcher John J. Robinson in Jersey City, New Jersey. (Photo credit: Saucer News, Box 2228, Clarksburg, W. Va.)

MORE ON MOTHMAN

Several **issues ago we** devoted much of **this** column to our personal on-the-spot investigation of **Mothman.** A wing-typed UFOnaut who has been **seen** by dozens of persons in and near Point Pleasant, West Virginia.

Recently we received a letter from Michael A. Campbell of New York suggesting the reason why Mothman **has been seen** in this area. He concluded, after two years of research, that an intricate pattern showed **that the** only possible reason for **these** creatures (five or more) to be seen in this section of West Virginia "is that **they** must have been **sent to** study the **technological** installation at Green Bank". He also sent **us** a map plotting the sightings and pointed **out** that he reached his conclusions **after he** found that the two circles (see illustration) *intersect* at Green Bank.

He also offered his opinion that the Flatwoods creature and Mothman are one and the same - their methods of **attack** being similar (hit **and run).** Also when comparing the two pictures, in Mr. Campbell's opinion: "you will note that the Flatwood being **has a** large 'hood'

which **could** be **wings** folded".

STRANGE NEW LINK IN EARTH THEORY FOUND

The question of whether or not **at least** some UFOs are Earth made, that **is** either made by known Earthly **groups** (i.e. **Russia,** Germany, United **Stares)** or some secret group, **has** caused much controversy over the years. Some people have suggested that they were **the devices** constructed centuries ago by **a** race of beings who once **populated** Earth **and** as theory has it migrated to **other** planets- (perhaps paying **us visits** now). One such **person** was Richard S. Shaver who many years before the Kenneth Arnold sighting **told** of seeing such **devices** while in huge underground **caves** built by **these** ancestory of ours thousands of years ago.

Even more recently a strange manuscript **was** received **by noted UFO** publisher Gray Barker from a writer who offered impressive proof that he **was** a noted science author. He **told** Barker that **he had** written a strange **manuscript, but** because of its **contents,** could not have it published under his real name.

The result of further correspon-

dence produced **a** most **unusual book** entitled DOCUMENT **96** which **claims** to hold at least the **partial key** to the UFO mystery. The author offers several **new** theories **on** how Earth made UFOs are piloted and constructed and even tells **about** the mysterious **disappearance** of a Mr. Rex Ball whom the author claims discovered **an** underground **saucer base** some **35** years **ago** in the state of Illinois.

New words **such as** Zamn and Gazamn, related to power principles and Cosmocybernetics **and Cos**mocyberloid **Beings,** new mind stretching concepts are used and explained.

Most probably **researchers who** have **long** ago **made up** their mind that all UFOs are **interplanetary** will by-pass this volume **as** containing nothing more than speculation or **perhaps** even **claim** that it **is** made up. On the other hand serious investigators **whose** minds are **still open may** find here **a glimpse** of **what is** really happening. **In** fact Gray Barker suggests that this **volume** may *be* written on two levels **and** that one should read between the **lines.** Those interested may **want to** purchase copies now before the supply *is* gone (only **a** limited printing **has** been made). Mr. Barker **is** 'allowing **us** to offer **this** volume **to** readers of **this** magazine *at* only **$4.93.**

Also **our own** volume **which** pinpoints Earth **as a possible** location for many UFOs **(only** this time inside the Earth) - THE SHAVER MYSTERY AND THE INNER EARTH – is now into its **second** printing. Those **who have** enjoyed the works of both Richard Shaver and Dr. Raymond Bernard will in particular find this **book** to be **of unusual** interest. Enhanced **by** well done illustrations, readers will also read of the Jersey Devil, Mothman, Monsters, ESP, Mind Travel, *etc.* Some reviewers have called it **the** most **startling** and different **book** written **on the** subject of **UFOs** and the offbeat. This *too* **is available** *at* only *$4.95,*

Orders **for these books**, as well **as** news clippings, personal reports, **photographs** and comments (both pro and con) should be sent directly to this columnist,

PLOTTED **COURSE** OF **FLATWOODS** AND **MOTH MAN**

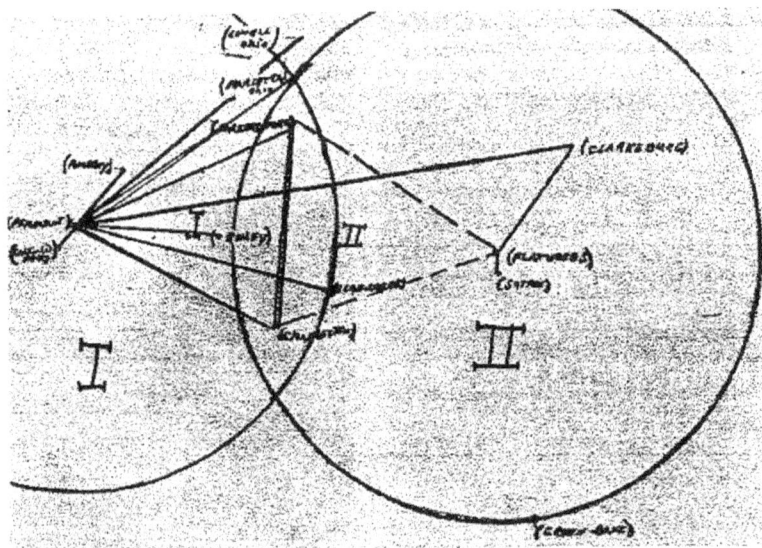

Though **the** map *is* inaccurate, I can assume you get *an* idea of the *situation.* The **circles** intersect at Marietta, Ohio, and *an* area in between two small towns. In Triangle I, Circle I, a pattern is formed showing possibly that Moth Man was a " Home Body". But then, in Triangle I, Circle 1, it **is** *most* apparently a continuation of the previous pattern. The distance between *cities* in (I) is 38 mi., 40 mi.; the red line *at* Clarksburg indicates a distance of 38 mi. to Flatwoods. At *first*, I thought that Moth Man had a range of 80 miles top distance; but remember 38 mi. is the key. It is exactly 38 miles from Clarksburg to Flatwoods! (Michael A. Campbell)

ON THE TRAIL OF THE FLYING SAUCERS

TIMOTHY GREEN BECKLEY
Director
Interplanetary News Service

Issue No. 66
October 1969

Usually conventions held by scientific organizations turn out to be long drawn out affairs consisting of various authorities in their chosen fields reading papers, on their latest speculations and "findings".

Not so the Congress of Scientific Ufologists! This year's annual meeting was held under the direction of Charleston, West Virginia's own Ralph Jarrett, director of a local group called UFO Investigators. This year's affair was attended by representatives from some 32 international UFO organizations boosting a total combined membership of somewhere around *50,000* buffs.

Talk at *the* closed sessions seemed to center mainly around such important aspects of the saucer enigma as recent men in black *cases;* the outcome of the Condon report; the possibility that at least some UFOs represent a manifestation of psychic phenomena; and documented evidence offered by this columnist which indicates that the UFOnauts (saucer pilots) may not be overly happy with *our* recent interest in the moon and colonization *of* same.

As with the five previous congresses, several delegates reported odd occurrences took on several forms. Several delegates reported that during their stay at the hotel Darnel Boone, they received sinister phone calls from a mysterious entity who

represented himself as being Dr. Heinrich.

Apparently Heinrich warned those who received these calls about releasing certain, information on the concept of free energy.

Heinrich gave the impression that he was an agent for the highly secret group of international financiers who are worried that the general application of free energy (well known to saucer fans who have followed the work of Otis T. Carr, Howard Menger and others) would cause destruction of our economic system and would result in their losing millions of dollars.

One Ohio delegate who did a pre-recorded radio show with famed Charleston MC, Hugh McPherson, later called up she program manager of the station and requested that his interview not be aired. Apparently he had been called and warned by Heinrich not to go through with the broadcast.

At first Heinrich was attributed to the work of either *a* hoaxer or practical joker. However directly after receiving a phone call one. researcher immediately called back the hotel switchboard operator to see if the call had originated from inside or outside the hotel. Shockingly the operator claimed that no such call had gone through her board—a certain impossibility. So *if* a hoaxer was at

work he *was* most definitely a clever one.

Somehow no one could come to any positive conclusions regarding these mysterious calls and the voice behind Heinrich, for his accent could just not be placed. Bur several delegates commented that the pattern was identical to many MIB cases of recent vintage.

Also several other delegates reported various forms of mysterious difficulties with their hotel room phones and still others claim they got *the* eerie impression they were being watched on various occasions.

One of the *most* important findings discussed behind closed doors at the congress was the discovery of a weird fossil near Louisville, Kentucky by Melvin R. Gray.

At first the fossil looks like nothing more than a meteor, but according to Mr. B. Ratliff this fossil may actually be a space *ship that* crashed to Earth, killing *its* crew, eons *ago.*

Ratliff told those present that after six months of close study by his group, the Tri-State Unidentified Flying Object Committee, they were convinced that this fossil contained the impressions of a total of seven three-inch tall humanoid creatures. Three of the creatures actually look, according to Ratliff, as if they were killed in their space suits. Two of the "aliens" are in a sitting position and one even looks as if he is holding on to something, or perhaps looking out: a window of the ship.

Realizing that imagination and tricks of the mind can often be played on those who seek to find bits of pre-cultures in rocks, this columnist spent quite sometime alone studying this fossil. Although we cannot come to any positive conclusions at this time, we are quite impressed with what we *saw.* Although the ' creatures" themselves could be almost anything, we were shocked by the details shown in one "UFOnaut's" arm and hand. In fact so clear *was* the impression that we could actually make out the knuckles in his fingers.

Also, for the first time, an award was presented *in* honor of the late Capt. Robert Loftin, author of *Identified Flying* Saucers, to the person who had done *the* most for the Congress during the past year. This

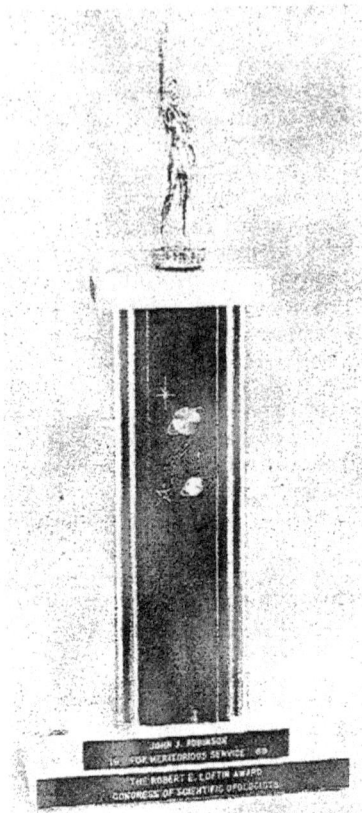

Capt. Robert Loftin award presented in Charleston to John J. Robinson for his meritorious service to the Congress of Scientific UFOlogists.

year's **award** was given to **John J.** Robinson. well **known UFO** investigator *and* **assistant** editor of two important UFO publications—Saucer news **and** Searchlight.

Saucer personalities (from left to right) Rick Hilberg, Ed Biebel, and Ralph Jarrett discuss saucer mystery over local Charleston TV show before start of the Convention.

Press converage for this **year's** Congress of Scientific UFOlogists **was** at *an* all time high. For days before the convention the local **papers** primed **numbers of** *news* stories listing the upcoming events. This **press** coverage resulted in **a** large crowd **in** attendance at the open session held at the Charleston Civic Center.

Speakers on die program included such long-time researchers **as** Gray Barker and **James** W. Moseley through whose efforts the widely **read** *Saucer News* has *been* published *since* 1954.

Other speakers included Rick Hilberg and Ed Biebel of Cleveland. Ohio and Rev. Richard Basile who offered several interesting possibilities regarding the origin for flying **saucers.** The four-hour show **was** rounded out with a lengthy illustrated lecture by this columnist. We showed **numerous** close-ups of UFOs and their pilots. some never before **released** to she public, and **discussed at** length recent predictions which **have** been given by several contactees warning **us** *that* strange dangers *can* be expected with our astronauts landing on the **surface** of *the* moon.

A VISITOR FROM SATURN

Another **new** silent contactee was present **at** the *Congress.* She **was** Barbara Hudson, an attractive middle-aged woman who **has** lived **mow of** her *life* in New **York** *City.*

Her story was presented for the first time by Gary, Indiana radio personality, Warren Freiberg, **over** radio station WWCA **via** phone huck-up. Covering both **Gary** and Chicago, **the show was** "one **of the** best in recent months". in fact Warren **informs us** that **after the show** dozens of listeners **called die station** commencing upon **the program.**

Barbara Hudson's *story* **is of** unusual interest and seems **to tie** in with even more recent **saucer** occurrences:

"At *the* time of the *weird* event I **am about to** describe, **I was** living with me parents in Manhattan *at* **276** West 115th Street· it **was** sometime after 1:00 P.M. during the month **of** February 1960 **when** the doorbell rang. I **was** sitting on *the* side **of** the **bed** changing she diaper **of** my five-month-old daughter. Debrah. Walking the few **steps** from my

Barbara Hudson discusses her saucer contacts by phone with Gary's Warren Freiberg.

bedroom to **the** entrance **to** the apartment, I opened **the** door **a** few inches TO *see* who **was** outside, since I **had** not been **expecting** anyone **to** call at this particular hour.

"Standing **in** the **hallway was a** man **about six** feet in **height,** quite slender, and *as* I recall **now,** dressed *in a* navy blue *suit.* dark tie and. a white **shirt.** Even in the darkness of *the* half-lit hall. he seemed to be **quite** fair skinned. had **dark wavy hair** and deeply **set eyes.**

"After staring at him *for* **several** seconds in silence, he remarked that he **was** the exterminator and **had** been *sent* by the management of our apartment to spray *the* **kitchen and** bathroom.

"So I opened the door to let him in, only suddenly to have the *idea* dawn on me *that* he **was** much too well **dressed** for this sore of job. Also ail the exterminators I had ever **seen bad** worn uniforms with their company's name **on** die front **or back.** But then he did **have several** *tools* of his **trade, including** an insect sprayer and *a* rather peculiar **black briefcase.**

"He went directly **to** the kitchen and **started to** spray around *the* pipes near the sink—seeming **to** know what he **was** doing. However I **was** still **quite** uneasy and began **wondering** who he really was **and** what he really had **in** mind. At the **same** moment that I **was** thinking this. *as* if he had **read** my mind, **he** turned and smiled **and** came over **to** where I **was sitting** with my young daughter. **He looked** directly into my **eyes** and said for me 'not to be **afraid'** of him that he 'would do me no harm'. He then crossed the room and went over **to** the night table, near the bedroom door. and reached for the **bonk** that was

48

lying under it.

'The **book was a** copy of *Flying Saucers Have Landed* by George Adamski and Desmond **Leslie**. The 'exterminator' **picked up** the book. fondled it in both hands, **and** asked: 'Do you believe m this?' I said: 'I do.' and **asked** him why he had **asked** me.

"He never answered my question, but simply put down the **book on** top of the night **stand** and with *a* son of half **smile** on *his* face **said**: 'What planet do you think these flying **saucers** come from?' I said **perhaps** Mars **and** Venus. having just completed **the book** by Adamski and Leslie in which Adamski tells **about** his supposed contacts with people from **these** two planets. **and** elsewhere n our solar system. To this **he asked what** i thought the **pilots** of these **ships** might look like. I replied that I thought they looked n o different **than you** or I and that maybe *he* or **even** I could *come* from another world in **space.**

"*At* this **he** grinned **and** leaned forward **kissing** me **on** the cheek. He than started toward the door. Almost in a *trance* I went **ahead** of him and opened it. Once outside **he** turned and **said**: 'I'll be seeing you again.' With that, he starred down the stairs, stopping only when **he had** reached the bottom. He then turned around and once **again** questioned me. This time the smile oil **his face had** faded **away**, and **looking at me in** *a* more **serious** mood he said: 'Whet **planer do** you think I'm from?' Without thinking I **said**, probably Mars; then I laughed. To this he remarked: **'Would you** believe Saturn?'

"I closed the door and suddenly a cold **shiver ran** over my entire body *as* I **recalled his** departing remark. I rushed to she. **window in** an effort *to* **see in** what directions he had gone, or **hi what** sort of **vehicle** he had **arrived.** But strangely enough I never **saw** him leave the building. It *was* almost as if he **had** dematerialized."

Despite the statement to Barbara that she would **see** him again, a second meeting with this individual **has not** transpired. However, the above **account** is neither die first nor the **last** encounter **with what** Barbara **Hudson** has good reason to believe are people visiting from other planets.

She claims to *have* seen their ships on many occasions. one time within yards in an out-of-the-way area of Pennsylvania where one had landed **and was** actually raking on men and equipment.

In fact. her story in many way, is similar to those of Adamski, Menger, Fry and **several** others. **However.** she admittedly does not **have** any physical evidence of these experiences, and for this reason is nor looking for publicity at the moment- She has cold us that when the right rime comes far her to "tell **all**" the story will be released through this writer *in* the form of quite a story.

And although we have heard many other experiences related by **Barbara** Hudson. some which *are* very amazing **and** if *true* of tremendous importance. we **have** promised *to* **keep** silent on these **incidents** for the time being. All we can *say* for *certain* is that here is **a** young lady whose knowledge of UFOs is considerable, not from a researcher's point of *view*, but from someone who **actually knows** what is going on.

SPACE PEOPLE WARN ASTRONAUTS NOT TO LAND ON MOON

For untold **centuries** man has looked **up into** the sky and wondered about our nearest; neighbor *in* space—the moon. is it inhabited? What causes the many mysterious changes on its surface? As of this **writing** mankind **is on** the threshold of finding **out.** (As of **this** printing, **he has** landed **and saw** nothing mysterious. – Rap.)

At the same time. warnings have been released by several contactees telling us that *the* **space people are** going to "quarantine" Earth until **we** learn **to** control our use of nuclear **weapons.**

it **is** a known fact that several astronomers **have** reported mysterious lights **and** movements on the moon's **surface**. This **has** lead to good reasoned speculation that alien beings who survey us in flying **saucers are** using the moon **as** a base. According **to** several sources they wilt undoubtedly endeavor **to** hinder **us** if we attempt to colonize **she** lunar surface.

These same contactees tell us that if we **land on** the moon there will be repercussions on Earth—earthquakes. explosions. tires and power failures. (Sic! – **Rap.**) They are primarily concerned *in* preventing **us** from using the moon for military purposes.

Already **these** warnings seem *to* be

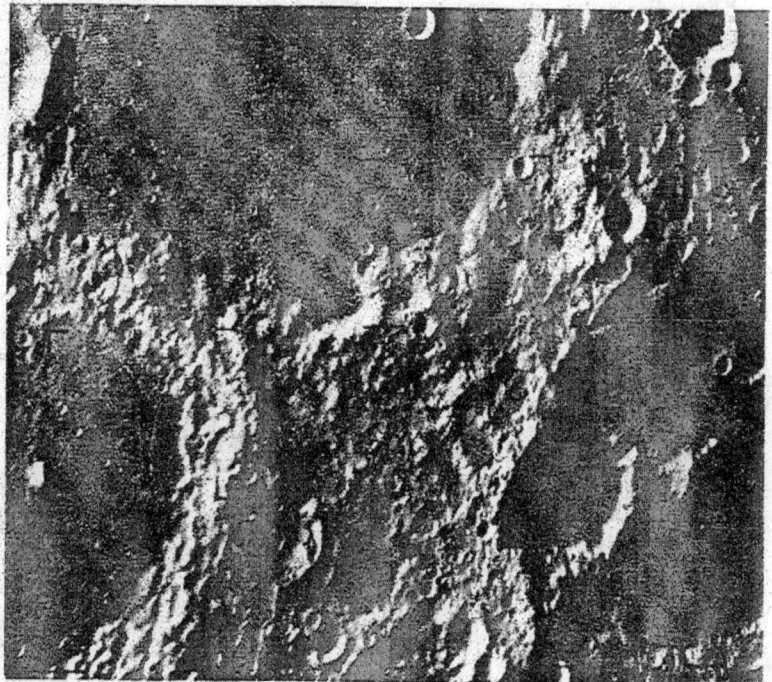

Section of the Lunar surface where Rob Short's space contacts claim craters hide saucer bases. (Photo courtesy NASA)

49

coming true. In a short span of three weeks. there have been several totally unexplained power failures in New Mexico. Texas. New Jersey and New York. In one recent incident in California. two satellites were prevented from being launched when mysteriously enough the power failed at the base at which the launch was to take place for no apparent reason.

In **Joshua** Tree. California contactee Bob Short. 01 the Solar **Space** Foundation (Box 622) released the following information which he claims was received through a special planetary communique he' **has** with she **space** people.

"N.A.S.A. AND SPACE–LUNAR LANDING PROGRAM. We also tell you, that there will **be** changes in the program for the LUNAR EXPLORATION. by the organization known on your **planet** as the National Aeronautics and Space **Administration.** This SHALL BE A CHANGE OF SCHEDULING. and *a* CHANGE OF DEGREES OF AREA FOR LANDING upon the surface of your satellite, which we call Luna, which you call the moon. (We also call it **Lana.**—Rap.)

" We will also tell you, that **there are** photographs **which** have been **taken** which **the public, perhaps. may** never *see.* that **show** installations or. the **southwest quadrant of** the area, which you call **the backside of Luna**, **and** there **are** silos or openings into the interior of **Luna** which **are** found **in the** southeast and central to northwest portions of the lunar surface which faces your Earth planet. We *have* learned *to* make use **of** the volcanic **activity on** your lunar surface for purposes of energy. **and for** purposes **of** heat exchange for certain devices **which** then derive energy. This your Earth scientists also **are aware of** and **that** this **is** the **reason** for TIMED CYCLES OF THERMAL ACTIVITY in *those* volcanic **regions. however,** this will possibly never become public knowledge."

Quite interestingly enough we have received word from a good **source inside NASA** that strange **unexplained signals** have lately been discovered coming from several of our Mariner probes going **to** Mars.

These signals are **taking** the form of messages **and** information which was

never programed to be sen!: **back** by the Mariner. in one extremely interesting incident. the power on one of the Mariner probes was completely shut off for some unknown reason for a good three hours. *in* fact it looked like the satellite had gone completely dead, and **NASA** officials had just about **given** the probe **up** for lost

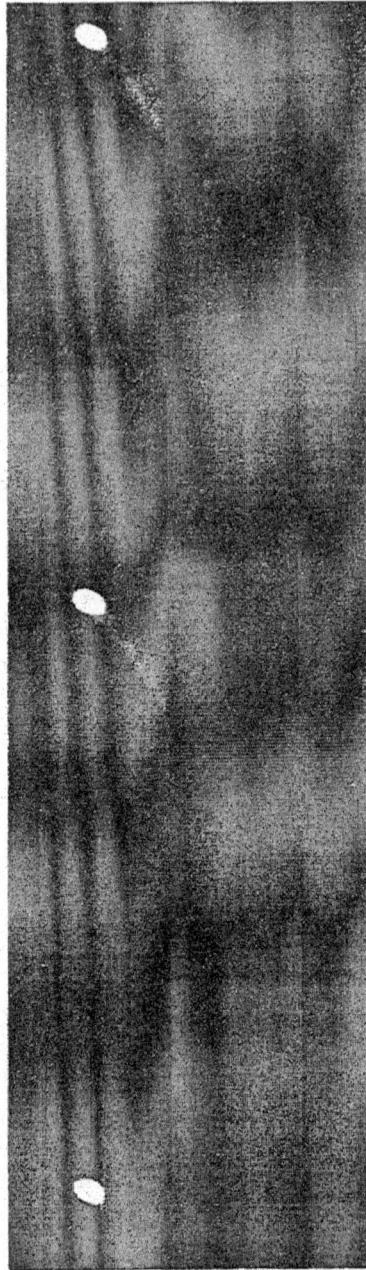

Three stills taken from **motion picture** from NASA files showing UFO seen in space by James McDivitt over Hawaii. This UFO is still un-identified.

when it starred sending back puzzling messages and codes which, according to **our** source. were most unusual.

As readers probably already **know,** just about every astronaut to date has reportedly seen **some** sort of UFO **while in** orbit. The most famous being the object which **was** actually photographed by James McDivitt *on* June 3.1965.

While in orbit. McDivitt **actually tracked** three "unknowns". One was a cylindrical shaped object over Hawaii. The second "had **big arms sticking** out **of** it". And **the** third **was** like "a bright **star** moving **fast".**

Going **back** sometime **before** this, **even** Gordon Cooper commented: "I **also** had the **idea** there might be **some** interesting forms *of* life *out* in space *for* us to discover **and. get** acquainted **with.** I don't believe in fairy tales. but **as far as** I'm concerned there **have** been far too **many** unexplained **examples** of unidentified objects **sighted** around **this** Earth for **us to** role out **the** possibility **char** *soma* form of life **exists** out **beyond** our own world. I **certainly** don't pretend **that** the examples **we know** about **necessarily prove** anything. **But the fact** that **many experienced** pilots have reported **strange sights** which **cannot** easily be explained. did heighten my curiosity **about space."**

According to secret government sources, **one** of *the* recent Apollo **astronauts was** overheard commenting **in a** Florida **restaurant about** the **reality of** UFOs and **the fact that** his **spaceship** had been **followed** closely by **alien craft** during *its* second orbit **of the** moon's surface. In fact, for a **brief** period of time no word was received from the space **capsule** because of a mysterious force which seemed *to* be **preventing the ship's** signals from reaching NASA ground control officials.

What does **all** this **mean?** According to several "silent" contactees. **we are** coming through **a** period in time where **we** *are* being tested by *these* alien beings. They *have* bees **keeping a** watchful *eye* **on** us for centuries, but now **that we are** going out **into** space, **they** are more concerned **than ever** about our attitudes and reasons for exploring the moon's surface.

And although they are friendly by nature. their first concern *is* toward the peaceful used of outer space and the well being of hundreds of other planets upon which life exists near enough to Earth to be effected with our possible war-like advances in the next 100 years.

To this end they are going to cause many terrible disasters which should be taken as a warning chat they mean business.

These warnings will include drastic increases in earthquakes, tidal waves, power failures—anything that will put a dog into the spokes of our space program.

From what sources, you may ask, are these warnings and predictions coming? The source is at least a dozen silent contactees who for the most part have been receiving this information through telepathic or audio-visual means. Some of these contactees, such as Ted Owens, have recently begun to receive publicity. However, for the most part, those involved in this work have given instructions that at no times are their names to be used in connection with this material.

In fact some of these silent contactees are well known researchers in the UFO field who have never publicly discussed their contacts for obvious reasons.

For many years one of these researchers was the late Wilbert B. Smith of Ontario, Canada, who for quite awhile in the early 1950's was head of the official Canadian government sponsored Project Magnet. Despite his high position in the government and his seemingly objective attitude toward the UFO enigma, Smith was also in constant mental communications with space visitors.

Although much of this information is still confidential, only recently has it been leaking out through the kind efforts of an organization known as the Ottawa New Sciences Club which Wilbert Smith founded and directed for some time.

Their files are a massive documentation- which indicate that these often dismissed means of communicating with space beings may indeed have a great amount of truth to them,

In fact, over the years Smith, and

the organization he represented, had built up sort of an underground network of contactees who much to his surprise, were all receiving identical information.

Much of this information is of a technical nature and thus would be of little interest to readers. However a great deal of information was also gathered and compiled dealing with the subjects of philosophy, economics, living standards on other planets, religion, general scientific information, and most important of all the use of atomic power.

Smith's biggest claim to fame, however, was his conviction that he had in his position an actual chunk of a UFO which had apparently exploded somewhere over Canada. The documented evidence Smith offered and the amount of research work done on this discovery is truly a credit to him.

Other of Smith's ideas and concepts can be directly linked with his own personal contacts and information being sent him constantly by these other "silent" contactees. One of his most unusual, but important, discoveries was of what he called the binding forces which he believed were measurable waves of magnetic forces which existed ail over Earth. It was through these forces that he attempted to track UFOs, since they were known to fly where these "forces" were strongest.

Smith was a great man; few people realize this even today. He became a legend in his own time despite the fact that not many researchers outside of Ottawa ever became familiar with his work. He never looked for publicity, and on the occasions it was given to him, he was always very careful to state his case as scientifically as possible.

Here was a man who was totally convinced about life in outer space, about alien brings and the effects he saw them having upon our world in the years ahead as we too planned to step outside of our own world for the first time.

Although some of this material has been. released in drips and drabs over the past few years by the Ottawa New Sciences Club (publishers of Topside] this columnist. with their kind permission, has combined all of

Wilbert B. Smith's works, his research and findings, together with additional investigations by Ills group into a new book entitled The *Boys' From Topside* (Smith's favorite slogan for the pilots of the saucers).

This volume, which should be ready for release by the time *this* column appears, also has an introduction by noted Saucer Contactee Dr. George Hunt Williamson; whose research into the cultural aspects of UFOs throughout history is also well known- Williamson and Smith apparently shared many similar feelings, and one can only wonder if their contacts were of an identical nature and source.

In addition, since Smith was for many year's Canada's foremost investigator, we have added a lengthy section to this book entitled Canadian *Saucer Scrap* Book which goes into great detail about many of the lesser known sightings, contacts, silencing cases and even photos taken over this country.

All in all, this is a volume which both scientific UFOlogists, since Smith was a scientist of great repute, and those who are interested in the subjective and contact aspects, will want to own. We have spent many months putting this volume together and our printer (none other than Ray Palmer's Amherst Press) had informed us that it will be a beautiful book with four-color cover, many photos and illustrations. And although the cost of each copy is considerably higher than most of the books we have either published or distributed in the past, we are placing the price at a most reasonable

Since our publisher, Gray Barker, has promised an international advertising campaign, in all probability the first edition will quickly be sold out. Therefore we suggest that all *those* readers who are interested in receiving a copy send in immediately. Our address is still the same:

We are also in need of news stories, ideas, opinions, speculation, sightings, and photographs for this column. These should also be sent to the above address. Until next issue happy saucering, folks!

★★★★★★★★★★★★

UFO REPORT

The most widely read – and quoted – UFO magazine in the world!

When you're **first** in **breaking** the latest news of UFO sightings, **landings,** and contacts..,

When you're **first** in reports from around the world and in depth investigations...

When you're **first** in breaking through to **new** frontiers of **knowledge** and new theories...

...these **are the** ingredients that make for leadership – and that's why **UFO Report** is the world's foremost **UFO** magazine!

On Friday evening, Nov. 14, 1969, **observatories** all over Europe **sighted two bright** flashing unknowns near the path of Apollo 12, which **was** on its way to **putting** America's second **team** of astronauts on the moon. **Seen** through huge telescopes, one object **appeared** to be following the **space** craft and one seemed to **be** moving in front of it. Both objects **were** blinking on and off rapidly. On Saturday, Nov. 15th, our **three astronauts,** Pete Conrad, Dick Gordon and Allan Bean, **reported** to Mission Control in Houston, that they had indeed **spotted** two **bogeys** 132,000 **mites** out. Why doesn't **NASA** tell us **the** whole story behind

May 1970

APOLLO 12's MYSTERIOUS ENCOUNTER WITH FLYING SAUCERS

By Timothy Green Beckley and Harold Salkin

APOLLO 12 MISSION CUMMENTARY, 11/15/69, 2:18 p.m. CST
Space Craft: We have had an object which is in the same place all the time and appears to be tumbling. We have had it with us ever since yesterday and it just seems to be tagging along with us . . . It's usually out our center hatch window when our ROLL angle is about 35 . . . maybe that will give you a clue and somebody can figure out . . . what we are really looking at.

You may not have heard this on **your** TV or radio—it wasn't carried in any newspapers—but the Apollo 12 astronauts, Pete Conrad, Dick Gordon and Allan Bean, reported **a** strange encounter with two bogeys 132,000 miles out, on **the** way to putting America's second team of astronauts on the moon.

Out of the thousands of UFO reports originating from reliable witnesses, a good percentage of the flying saucers have been **detected** surprisingly near or directly over key military installations, including Cape

NASA in Washington called headquarters in Houston for explanation of these two objects. Answer—"Clouds!"

According to Dr. Garry Henderson, a top space research scientist with General Dynamics, all our astronauts have seen these objects (UFOs], but have been ordered not to discuss their sightings with anyone!

Kennedy. The evidence now shows that the UFOs are entering a new phase in their world-wide surveillance—close maneuvers near our own reconnaisance flights into space. In fact, according to Dr. Garry Henderson, a top space research scientist with General Dynamics, *all* our astronauts have seen these objects, but have been **told** not to discuss their sightings with *anyone!*

Even before Apollo 12 left Earth's atmosphere, strange disturbing events were already taking place. Less than 30 seconds after *a* perfect lift-off, the space craft was reportedly hit by a bolt of lightning. Pete Conrad told Mission Control, "I don't know what happened here. We had everything in the world drop out!"

Since the nearest lightning was reported **by** the Weather Bureau to be 20 miles away, **we** are reasonably *safe* in saying that this was merely the first of many strange events on this epoch-making journey. Before they touched down in the Pacific 10

days later the astronauts **had** been:

• Tailed **by** two brilliantly flashing objects;

• Mystified **by** unexplained sounds on their radio;

• Startled **by** unaccountable seismic disturbances on the lunar surface:

• Sending back pictures of a mysterious blue halo encircling one of our spacemen;

• Unable to identify the "ghost light*' of Burma, which loomed into sight as they re-entered Earth's atmosphere.

By early Friday evening, Nov. 14th, ground control must have realized something was up. Observatories all over Europe sighted two bright flashing unknowns near the path *of* the space *craft.* Seen through huge *tele-*scopes, one object appeared to be following the ship and one seemed to be moving in front of it. Both objects were blinking on and off rapidly, and could not be immediately identified.

(Continued on page 88)

Photograph taken by astronaut McDivitt shows the object he observed during the 20th orbit of Apollo 12

SAGA ☐

Continued

So when, shortly after nine p.m., the three astronauts reported that at least one object was tumbling along after them, a NASA official said, "They weren't concerned but intrigued."

Three possible explanations were offered by Houston technicians as to what might be behind the sighting; the S-IVB booster, an sla protective panel, "or it could be the backup crew flying train on you!"

Pete Conrad then reported that two objects were now in view, and that one of the UFOs was not nearly as bright as the other. He proceeded to ask for the exact location of any known space debris in the area of the ship.

Mission Control informed the three men aboard Apollo 12 that the S-IVB booster should be 180 degrees away. Ta this Cmad replied that his bogeys were approximately 20 degrees apart, and therefore could not possibly be the S-IVB booster* which was then beyond their viewing range.

The following is taken directly from the Apollo 12 Mission commentary received at approximately 10:25 p.m. CST:

Space Cmft: O.K. I wonder what that could be then?

CAPCOM (Houston): O.K. We'll go back to our drawing board!

Space Craft: The object is very bright and it is obviously something that is tumbling. It is tumbling one and one-half revs per second or at least it is flashing at us about that. Dick is going to tell you what star it is nearing. He is messing with his chart right now.

CAPCOM: Roger. We are standing by.

CAPCOM: 12, Houston

Space Craft: Go ahead.

CAPCOM: As best we can tell, looking at things down hew—on those sla panels, we assume that they weren't imparted any great amoung of DELTA V—like anything more than one or so feet per second when they separated. Your sla panels would probably be only about 300 miles away from you right now.

At this point Cmad breaks mto the conversation and says that me of the objects, "whatever it might be," has just broken ranks and is leaving them at a rapid pace. The exact commentary was as follows:

Space Craft: That could be true, but, gee whiz, when we (just) turned around, I saw one of those sla panels leaving the area at a high rate of speed and it looked to me like it was leaving us at a pretty good clip, like it got a lot more than a foot per second or so.

CAPCOM: Well, since we don't really have any idea how they left or what their trajectory could be, it's kind of tough really to say just what the heck that could be

Dick Gordon cuts in:

Space Craft: O.K. We'll assume it's friendly anyway, O.K.?

CAPCOM: Roger. If it makes any noise, it's probably just the mind in the rigging!

Kim Senstad, public information officer at the Apollo command post, was questimed about the explanations offered for the mystery. While reading the space-

- ☐ SAGA

men's dialogue over long distance phone, he commented that when they first sighted the unknown, "they were rather surprised." Asked why they would be surprised if this was the normal trajectory cl the S-IVB booster or the protective shield, he gave an unusually candid comment: "Well . . . (brief pause) . . . I can't answer that question, frankly."

After further prodding, he exclaimed, "Oh Christ, this transcript is really unbelievable!"

Apollo Control's final comment on the sighting *was* that they had "no definite agreement as to what the crew might have sighted."

So, with ground-elapsed time *at* only 36 hours, 40 minutes into the flight, the Apollo team had been jolted from what had been scheduled as a "matter-of-fact" flight. Far from being routine, *this* was to be one of the most bizarre—as well as scientifically revealing—expeditions to date.

Several times, as the craft sped toward the lunar surface, scientists monitoring the "chatter" of the command module were stunned to hear unexplainable sounds that were not emanating either from the ground or from the capsule itself. At one point, it was even suggested that the astronauts "must be talking to somebody strange now."

According to investigator John Keel, weird noises have been heard on many occasions during previous space shots. Whistles, beeps, sounds of "fire engines" and even unintelligible language have been among those recorded.

In the midst of Cmad and Bean's limbering-up exercises on the surface of the mom, they told ground control that they were receiving weird background noises. At 6:45 a.m. on Wednesday the Apollo 12 log reads:

Bean: Do you hear a lot of background noises, Fete?

Conrad: Kind of static and things?

Bean: I keep hearing a whistle.

Conrad: That's what I hear. O.K.

Ten minutes later, Dick Gordon in the mother ship orbiting the moon reported to Houston the following:

Gordon: Hey, Houston, do you hear this constant beep in the backgroond?

CAPCOM: That's affirmative. We've heard it now for about the past 45 minutes.

Gordon: That's right, so have we. What is it?

Ground control then said it was unable to isolate the cause.

Keel says, in the UFO newsletter, *Searchlight*, "By far the most baffling and interesting case (of noises heard) occurred during Astronaut Gordon Cooper's fourth pass over Hawaii in Faith 7 on May 15, 1963. At that point, Cooper's voice *transmission was* interrupted by "unintelligible foreign language transmission on channels resewed for space flights." NASA recorded this transmission, but ha5 never been able to translate it, or identify it's source.

According to Navy Capt. Walter Schirra, Jr., on his Apollo 7 mission, strange music filled the cabin. It seemed to be bars of the song, *Where Angels Fear to Tread.* No explanation was ever given,

but it was shown that the song was neither emanating from the ground or the capsule.

The Apollo 11 flight had its own share of unnerving "sound effects." On July 22nd, noised like those of a fire engine surged through the airways from outer space. Mission Control asked, "You sure you don't have anybody else in there with you?" There was complete silence!

Next cam the sound of what seemed to be a high-pitched giggle recorded at high speed. This was followed by a further combination of noises, including the wail of a siren and the hum of a power saw.

Next day, at 10:30 p.m., there were more noises that resembled a train whistle and the chugging of a steam locomotive. NASA was unable to locate the source of the disturbance but jokingly told Buzz Aldrin "not to exercise so strenuously." This commentary was followed by further interruptions in the conversation by what seemed to he a rubber toy of some type that when squeezed gives off a whistle.

Who is using our "reserved" air waves to beam irrational noises, sounds and music to our astronauts? The mystery is unsolved.

Flying saucer buffs have long theorized that the UFOnauts operate on the moon from hidden bases with sliding camouflaged roofs that open onto large craters. This would explain why m astronauts have not seen any "direct" signs of life on the lunar landscape. We cannot discount the fact that for the past 100 years or more, mysterious lights and configurations have been seen over many of the larger craters on the moon. For instance, on July 29, 1953, the late John J. O'Neil, space science editor of the N.Y. *Herald Tribune*, was observing the moon through his powerful telescope when he suddenly realized that he was focussed on an "anomaly," something his rational mind told him could not be there. It seemed to be a bridge at least 12 miles long, stretching in a perfectly straight line across a crater in Mare Crisium. It couldn't have been a mirage or any other illusion since he saw its shadow and the sunlight streaming in beneath it.

Astronomer James W. Greenacre, of the Lowell Observatory in Flagstaff, Ariz., told several of his colleagues that on October 29, 1963 he observed a dull red glow in the Crater Aristarchus. Over a period of time, Prof. Greenacre described seeing many similar sights. including a formation of some 20 brilliant lights which seemed to have linked themselves in a pattern like that of a "theater marquee."

Just as it looked as if the return trip to earth would be without event, the space-travelling trio of Apollo 12 had a climactic ending to their 10-day mission.

As they passed over India, at 11:47 a.m. on November 24th, the spokesman for Apollo 12 reported in a startled voice that they were all watching a bright red object flashing brilliantly against the earth. Their verbatim transmission follows:

Space Craft: Also, right in the center of the Earth, now we have some real bright tight shining, staying on that Dick is looking at it with the binoculars. it's real bright.

CAPCOM: Roger. Understand. Does it appear to be coming from your nadir

(Continued

point, which should be just off the eastern coast of India now? (Nadir refers to the point in a line directly underneath the space ship.)

Space Craft: Yes. Looks like it's coming just about out of the center of what we're looking at. I would say down from Burma and east of India.

CAPCOM: Roger. That's just about your nadir.

Space Craft: I can't imagine what this is.

CAPCOM: We can't either. We're checking the possibilities.

The conversation continued with the astronauts describing the luminous appearance of the unidentified object.

Space Craft: It's a steady light, and it appears in size to be as big as any of the thunderstorms flashing.

Space Craft: It's as big as Venus at least.

CAPCOM: Roger. Understand.

Space Craft: It's hard to tell if it is exactly in the center of the Earth or not, it's pretty close to being right in the center. Maybe just a little bit to our right—whatever that means. Just a little bit to the side that the Sun did not go behind the Earth on.

CAPCOM: Roger. Understand.

At 11:57 a.m., 10 minutes later, ground control asked if the bright light was still visible. The astronauts replied that the UFO had disappeared as they continued toward splash-down.

If this wasn't enough, when the pictures were developed showing the Apollo 12 space men walking about on the surface of the moon, a strange silvery-blue halo seemed to have attached itself to Astronaut Pete Conrad. The "aura" was unexplainable! Experts in the photographic and developing field stated that no known flaw or oddity in the film itself could have caused this enigmatic effect.

Dr. Garry Henderson, in a question-and-answer period following a lecture at the planetarium in Calgary, Canada, told feature writer John Hopkins of the Calgary Herald that American astronauts flying in space have not only viewed UFOs, but have photographed them on several occasions. According to Dr. Henderson+ one of the nation's top space re-search scientists with General Dynamics in Texas, NASA has instructed the astronauts never to breathe a word of their UFO encounters. The space scientist then went on to say to a stunned audience, that he had talked to one astronaut, who told him that NASA has many actual photos of these craft, taken at close range by hand and movie cameras.

Dr. Henderson said the reason for the government's silence on these mysterious probes, is that NASA is worried that Congress may not appropriate additional funds for our space shots. "The whole thing is still under a great deal of ridicule," he said.

His comments to the press are confirmed by a recent disclosure of an official of the Central Intelligence Agency (CIA). One of our Government sources in Washington, on the staff of the U.S. Information Agency (USIA), has leaked to us the information that the CIA has the evidence that UFOs are real objects under intelligent guidance.

At about the same time, Dr. Jams E. McDonald, senior physicist in the Institute of Atmospheric Physics, University of Arizona, told members of the news media that he had seen a "Top Secret" CIA order which called for the debunking of all UFO sightings. The order was signed by CIA Agent P.G. Strong. Asked how he had obtained the report, McDonald said he was shown the confidential document while on a visit to Wright-Patterson Air Force Base, Dayton, Ohio.

"The report was declassified on the spot, and I was permitted to read it and make notes. When I returned three months later, I asked to make Xerox copies of the report. The request bounced up to the base commander, and he passed it on to the CIA, which then classified the report again," McDonald said.

The CIA's stated reason for debunking saucer reports was that with less official recognition of UFOs there would be a corresponding drop k~public interest Cl there would be fewer reported sightings. The CIA said in this guarded, confidential report that they considered such research groups as the Tucson-based Aerial Phenomena Research Organization (APRO) as subversive fronts.

During another Mercury flight, Gordon Cooper radioed back that a red object with a green tail had been sighted from his capsule window as he passed on his final orbit over Australia.

The sighting took place on May 16th, and at the time Cooper said the UFO was of a "good size" and "it was higher than I was. It wasn't even in the vicinity of the horizon . . ." indicating that the bogey was not a star or other object, either natural or man-made. Sometime later Cooper made the following statement: "I also had the idea there might be some interesting forms of life out in space for us to discover and get acquainted with. I don't believe in fairy tales, but as far as I'm concerned there have been far too many unexplained examples of unidentified objects sighted around this earth to rule out the possibility that some form of life exists out beyond our world. I certainly don't pretend that the examples we know about necessarily prove anything. But the fact that many experienced pilots have reported strange sights which cannot easily be explained, did heighten my curiosity about space" (Quote from the book We Seven).

According to Maj. Donald E. Keyhoe, former head of the Washington based National Investigation Committee on Aerial Phenomena (NICAP), the first flight in our Gemini series was followed by four unknowns into orbit. Keyhoe claims he got his information from several scientists who were on duty at Capt Kennedy and were tracking the flight of the GT-1 on radar. Suddenly, four objects joined the course of the Gemini and proceeded to follow it out into space. They continued right along with it for a complete orbit and then streaked off.

On June 3, 1965, Maj. James McDivitt and our first space walker, Maj. Edward White, were blasted into orbit.

During their trip, which was to last 97 hours, the astronauts described viewing from their window a total of three unidentified objects that cascaded in the heavens bath above and below them. They also found their flight hampered by several unexplained blackouts on the ground!

Maj. McDivitt said the first bogey was a cylindrical object, sighted over Hawaii. Aiming his hand-held movie camera in the direction of the mysterious sphere, he was able to take five frames of film that show the UFO as it made a close fly-by. It shows that the object was an egg-shad craft with a long tail of light and a fanlike glow.

At 6:55 p.m., on the 21st orbit, Mission Control gave the following report:

This is Gemini Control. We are ROW 30 hours and nine minutes into the mission. Spacecraft Gemini 4 has just completed a pass over the state on its 20th orbit. In voice communication with Gus Grissom, spacecraft communicator. Command Pilot Jim McDivitt reported he had sighted another object in space. He described it only as an object that appeared to have big arms sticking out. He said he took some motion pictures of this object, but was having some difficulty because of the sun

A few seconds later Gus Grissom asked whether McDivitt was still looking "at that thing out there." His reply was, "No, I've lost it. It had big arms sticking out of

(Continued

it . . . I only had it for just a minute. I got a couple of pictures of it with the movie camera and one with the Hasselblad. But I was in free drift and before I could get the control back, I drifted into the sun and lost it."

Minutes passed before Mission Control said it was checking with the Space Detection and Tracking System to locate the object McDivitt reported he had seen.

A later investigation showed that the nearest object in space would have been slightly more than 1,200 miles away from the craft.

Forty minutes after Mission Control released its report, it told newsmen it was having extreme problems communicating with the spacemen because of an unexplained power failure that had occurred on board the ship, *The Coastal Sentry Quebec.* The difficulty was quickly corrected, although no explanation for the blackout was ever offered.

The history of blackouts in connection with saucer incidents is lengthy and well established. Strangely enough, during the 31st orbit of GT-4 over Australia, another power failure was reported. This time it was from the tracking station at Tannarive. It took nearly four hours for technicians to find the trouble and get back on the air. Again no explanation was forthcoming. Perhaps these failures were only coincidences—but if they were then they are only a pair of several such "coincidences" which have repeated themselves flight after flight, and support the documented evidence which tells us that most, if not all, our astronauts have been followed in space by craft of a completely unknown purpose and origin.

This is a verbatim transcript of the communication between Gemini 4 and Cape Kennedy, regarding the sighting:

CC: Roger, could you give us an estimate as to how far that satellite was from you yesterday?

Space Craft: I couldn't really tell; it looked like quite a large object. It looked like I was approaching it rather rapidly. I'd say 10 miles or so.

CC: Ten miles?

Space Craft: That would only be a guess. It was close enough that I could see . . .

CC: See what?

Space Craft: (Garbled transmission)

CC: You're coming off pretty badly there. I couldn't read that.

Space Craft: O.K.

CC: That came through good.

Space Craft: All right, I said I got close enough to . . .

CC: Close enough to it to what? The nearest we can tell, there wasn't anything that close to you. Pegasus was about 1,200 miles away.

Space Craft: No, not quite that close. That far away.

CC: Pretty good eyeball, all right.

Space Craft: I took a picture, I just hope it comes out.

CC: So do we.

This ended the voice relay between the space craft and the ground. The next morning McDivitt told Mission Control that he would guess that the distance of the UFO from his capsule was "between 10 to 20 miles."

The final sighting by McDivitt and

☐ SAGA

White occurred during the 38th orbit. Officials said McDivitt described the object, seen passing low over China, as resembling "a bright star moving fast." According to a Houston release, he did not attempt to take pictures of it.

Seconds after the lift-off of Gemini 5, which sent astronauts Cooper and Conrad into an eight-day orbit, three unidentified objects were observed by James R. Peek of Orlando, Fla., in the vicinity of Cape Kennedy.

Peek told the *Orlando Sentinel* that he was returning home after the launching, and suddenly saw an object "travelling at very high speed" in the vicinity of the launch area. "It looked like a silver or brilliant green phosphorescent light just east of the contrail left by the rocket. It made a sort of S-turn in and around the contrail, became elliptical in shape as it turned, then changed into a clearly defined disc."

Luckily Peek had his 35mm camera with him and took a photo of the UFO as it vanished in a southerly direction. When the picture was developed, he discovered that the camera had actually recorded the presence of not one but three objects.

Even the *Condon Report*, which must UFOlogists believe to be a government whitewash, admits there is no credible explanation for the sighting of a large UFO and smaller "particles" seen in the vicinity of Gemini 7.

A close reading of the transcript reveals that Mike Lovell and Frank Borman were paced by a mysterious object while passing over Cape Kennedy on their second orbit. Paul Haney, spokesman for the two, said the report was "one of the biggest puzzlers" and "certainly was unusual and unexpected."

The exact conversation between Houston and the capsule centered around the sighting:

Space Craft: Gemini 7 here. Houston how do you read?

CAPCOM: Loud and clear. 7 go ahead.

Space Craft: Bogey at 10 o'clock high.

CAPCOM: This is Houston. Say again 7.

Space Craft: Said we have a bogey at 10 o'clock high.

CAPCOM: Roger. Gemini 7, is that the booster or is that an actual sighting?

Space Craft: We have several, looks like debris up here. Actual sighting.

CAPCOM: You have any more information? Estimate distance or size?

Space Craft: We also have the booster in sight.

CAPCOM: Understand you also have the booster in sight, Roger.

space Craft: Yeah, we have a very, very many—like, like hundreds of little particles banked on the left about three to seven miles.

CAPCOM: Understand you have many small particles going by on your left. At what distance?

Space Craft: Oh about—it looks like a path of the vehicle at 90 degrees.

CAPCOM: Roger, understand that they are about three to four miles away.

Space Craft: They are past now they are in polar orbit.

CAPCOM: Roger, understand they were about three or four miles away.

Space Cmft: That's what it appeared like. That's roger.

CAPCOM: Were these particles in addition to the booster and the bogey at 10 o'clock high?

Space Craft: Roger—(Lovell) I have the booster on my side, it's a brilliant body in the sun, against a black background with trillions of particles on it.

CAPCOM: Roger. What direction is it from you?

Space Craft: It's about at my two o'clock position.

CAPCOM: Does that mean that it's ahead of you?

Space Craft: It's ahead of us at two o'clock slowly tumbling.

The *Condon Report* states: "The general reconstruction of the sighting . . . is that in addition to the booster travelling in an orbit similar to that of the spacecraft there was another bright object (bogey) together with many illuminated particles. It might be conjectured that the bogey and particles were fragments from the launching of Gemini 7, but this is impossible if they were travelling in a polar orbit as they appeared to the astronauts to be doing."

Borman and Lovell also returned to earth with several unusual photos of objects that we fail to find mentioned in the transcript. One is a beautiful color shot that shows the earth below and, quite brightly silhouetted against the blue sky, two brightly glowing objects with a contrail of some type. We are led to believe that neither of the UFOs were seen by either of the astronauts from their position inside the ship. But the UFOs in this color photograph are identical to the one seen and captured on film by James Lucci in Brighton Township, Pa., on August 8, 1965. Another puzzle for NASA to ponder!

Among the puzzling aspects of the Gemini 10 flight, which lifted off on July 18, 1966, was that astronauts Gordon Cooper and John Young were keeping very much to themselves. Paul Haney, the voice of Mission Control, told news reporters that, "This has to be one of the most untalkative flights to date. We can only recall hearing from (the astronauts) on two or three occasions."

Silence was broken at 6:14 p.m., however, when the crew of the ship reported two unexpected objects following in their flight path:

Space Craft: This is 10, Houston. We have two bright objects up here in our orbital path. I don't think they are stars—they look like we are going right along with them.

CAPCOM: Roger. 10, Houston.

Space Craft: 10, go.

CAPCOM: Where are the objects from you?

Space Craft: Roger.

CAPCOM: If you can get us a bearing, maybe we can track them down.

Space Craft: They just disappeared. I guess they were—guess they were satellites of some kind.

The reason for the extended periods of silence on the part of Young and Cooper has never been explained. We can only conclude that NASA has a policy of keeping our astronauts from discussing their sightings!

Gemini 10 had a second rendezvous at 4:20 the following morning:

Space Craft: . . . to the east we have an

(Continued

extremely bright object. I believe it's too bright to be a planet. It's north of Orion about six or eight degrees. Right now it's approximately eight degrees. Is it the Gemini 8 Agena? Over.

CAPCOM: *Roger. We copy. Stand by.*

Space Craft: *Pictures that it makes (sic) just about an equilateral triangle with the belt stars in Orion and with Pleidas. It's a . . .*

CAPCOM: *Do you notice anything moving relative to the stars?*

Space Craft: *Possible. I haven't noticed any movement so far and unfortunately the stars are disappearing now and I can only see this object and one or two other first magnitude. . . sun starting to come up.*

CAPCOM: *Roger. Copy that.*

Although no *positive* identification was *ever* made, both Houston and the astronauts were inclined to rule out the possibility of it being the Gemini 8 Agena rock-t *because* of its position.

At a press conference on August 1st, >th spacemen seemed hesitant to talk about the subject of UFO's, and skipped over questions on the topic very rapidly. *They* did admit, however, that no solution to *what they had* observed was as yet forthcoming. *It has not been to this* date!

Shortly after the Gemini 10 flight, a "silent contactee" with whom we are in constant touch told us that NASA was very much interested in UFOs, and that officials at Cape Kennedy had a great deal of inform ation about "outer-space" craft.

This contactee's story involved an initial meeting with a dome-shaped object and their quite-human occupants along a highway in West Virginia. He had a number of similar rendezvous in the following weeks, and his story was corroborated by more than a dozen eyewitnesses, including a respected Baptist minister, a medical doctor, as well as business and professional people

Two weeks after the first *contact*, an official of the town of Cocoa Beach, Fla. adjoining *Cape Kennedy*, showed up in the West Virginia city and spent several days visiting with the contactee. Making a noticeable effort to appear nonchalant about the case, the Florida official whom we shall call "George Cater," nevertheless discussed *every* aspect of the contact. He then invited the contactee and his wife to "take a well-needed vacation" in Florida. In fact, he would be host to the couple at Cocoa Beach. The invitation was *accepted.*

During *Christmas* week, the couple drove to Florida and spent the holidays in the Cape Kennedy area. Their host took them on numerous tours of the base, pointing out the latest advancements in space technology. While making the rounds, they were introduced *to several* dozen *NASA* officials and staff personnel. One man who spoke with them at length about UFOs was introduced as "Charles Smith." but *the* contactee later told us. "I recognized him from photos as being James Webb," the chief of the entire U.S. space program.

The contactee related his story many times during the five days at Cape Kennedy. He was quizzed and -re-quizzed, but he never "lost his cool," according to his wife. Despite *the* bizarre-sounding facts of

☐ SAGA'

the *case. his* listeners showed no *signs of* surprise. Several NASA technicians even threw in details of the *construction* of the unearthly machines, which agreed with what the contactee has been firsthand. He reasoned that the men at Cape Kennedy must have been given information by *someone* on which *to* base their comments.

On the third *day of the visit, the* contactee was allowed to see a huge wall chart of some distant star system. One of *the stars* was *pointed out to* him by a scientist. "That," he said, "is where your friends are coming from!"

After the travellers returned home, they learned that George Cater was not only an official of Cocoa Beach, but had a top security clearance in the space program. This would explain his *making* a special trip *to West Virginia to check* out the UFO episode for NASA.

When the contactee told us about his visit to the *Cape,* we called George Cater to check out his story. *What* followed was a classic in the annals of evasive dialogue. For 11 minutes we attempted to dig out the facts. From the very beginning, Cater appeared suspicious of our intentions. He avoided each question by stating that he had "no comment." Only after repeated prodding did he even admit *that* the contactee had *been* in his office. This could only lead us to believe that he was covering up. and the contactee was telling the truth.

For months following this visit there were three radar trucks stationed in a triangular pattern several miles from the contactee's home. Their antennas were aligned in the direction of *his* farmhouse. The contactee told us *that* when *the* saucers first started landing on his farm, military jet planes came zooming overhead. On one occasion, the spacecraft *was* hovering a few hundred feet *in the* air, when two jets flew in from different directions. *almost* colliding in mid-air. After that, the pilots of the saucers descended very rapidly when landing on the West Virginian's property. A number of reliable witnesses told us that NASA had not even gone to the trouble of hiding the identity of the trucks. The large letters "NASA" were still *present* on the sides of the vehicles.

Indeed, NASA scientists should be *ac*quainted with UFOs by this time, because their *own* installations have *frequently* been visited *by* these elusive aerial *espion*age agents. For years, Cape Kennedy has been the scene of many unexplained saucer flaps. On Saturday, December 5, 1965. at 11:05 p.m., just a week after the launch of Mariner 4, mysterious multi-colored lights were sighted high in *the sky* above *the* rocket complex. An Air Force spokesman related how a flood of calls had come in, inquiring about reports of these

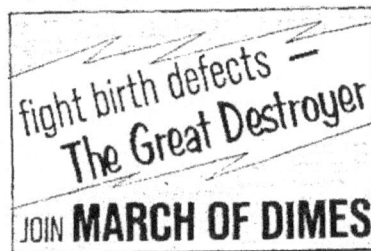

phosphorescent orbs. Officials at the well-known space center were reportedly concerned over these events. Security personnel at the Cape reported a craft of similar design had been seen seven years earlier.

More than 50 frantic calls poured *into* the Miami International Airport, and at the same time residents in the vicinity of Patrick Air Force Base reportedly were viewing *a* green and red sphere' with *a slight* smoke *trail.*

One of the witnesses, E. P. Brown, observed a cigar-shaped streak heading over him home. "It was *as* green as could be," Brown said, *"My* wife told me, 'You tell anybody and they'll think you're crazy.'"

The mysterious lights reappeared on December 8th. Sightings were reported by several individuals. who told the Air Force that the spheres were in the same position *as* those seen two days before.

Not only have U.S. military bases been harrassed by these alien *eyes* in the sky, but identical reports have come from other parts of the free world and from behind the Iron Curtain, In 1961 UFOs almost precipitated an international crisis, when a factory near Moscow that built the guidance *systems* for the Russian space program exploded. During the investigation that followed, workers told how they had seen "myriads of intensely luminous small globes." After *the* explosion a *large* UFO was seen hovering over the factory. It disappeared when jets approached. But the *greatest* mystery of all was the fact *that* no personnel *on the* grounds were injured, for it seems the alarm siren had sounded some minutes before the explosion and all the workers had time to take shelter. At the inquiry it was found that no one had touched the alarm.

In May of the same year two Russian cosmonauts—a male and a female—lost their lives in outer space. They were launched together in one capsule from Baikonur, near the Aral Sea. Tracking stations in non-Communist nations intercepted and recorded their conversation. Their last message radioed back informed the ground that they were losing control of the capsule:

'While we are studying the program . . . the situation becomes critical for us . . . Something went wrong. . . We are changing our course . . . I am talking to the director, do you understand? . . . If we do not get out, the world will not learn about it anyway. . . You will know what to do. . . What? What? Here! Here there is something! There is something!. . ."

These were the last words heard. Contact was lost at eight p.m. Moscow time. In replaying the taped conversation, one can feel the excitement and shock of the two cosmonauts in their tight quarters.

Was the brave Russian team the victim of *a* close approach by one of these bogeys? Have our astronauts been directed as to what *steps* to take *should they get too* near an "unknown" in *space?*

Indeed, as mankind *poises on the* threshold of planetary travel, are celestial *beings* from far-off worlds in the limitless void of outer *space* attempting to communicate or *spy* on our cosmic voyagers? An avalanche of evidence now shows that we may well be in the midst of a grand interplanetary espionage *game!*

★ THE END

According to many authorities, there have
been more sightings of unexplained
phenomena above this town than anywhere
else in North America!

CALVERT, TEXAS: FLYING SAUCER WAY STATION

By Timothy Green Beckley

Evidence continues to mount that alien beings have established bases in selective regions around the globe.

Data now being meticulously sifted and evaluated by researchers strongly suggests that the crews of these so-called flying saucers are currently in the process of carrying out a program that will ultimately affect all mankind—a program that may prove to be of monumental proportions.

For more than 25 years, the U.S. southwest has been a focal point for repeated UFO activity. Little more than a decade ago, the Air Force, in a highly classified "Confidential" document, reported that Texas ranked third in continual visitations by unidentified flying objects.

With a population slightly more than 2,000, Calvert is essentially like many other peaceful ranching communities nestled deep in this country's cattle-raising belt. What makes Calvert so unique is that in this area—divided by the Brazos River and hidden away in central Texas's Robertson County—UFOs have virtually become nightly callers. Witnesses have included a bank president, a retired Navy officer, as well as law enforcement officials.

In addition to the many multiple witness sightings constantly being reported around Calvert, there has also been a parallel flurry of related ground-level phenomena, including:

• The interference of normal radio reception;

• Unexplained tracks on the ground;

• Mysterious deaths and disappearances of livestock;

• Credible reports of landings and contacts with UFO occupants; and

• Peculiar noises coming from an unknown source deep underground.

Not in the least surprising, to those who have carefully charted previous UFO behavioral patterns, is that this area of Texas is also heavily dotted with military security systems designed to defend this country in case of enemy attack. Within a radius of 100 miles of Calvert are numerous underground missile silos, mobile radar units, Air Force and Army bases, as well as many top secret military installations. In fact, only individuals with special clearance from the Pentagon are privileged to know the precise nature of these installations which are vital to the protection of our nation.

According to one of Calvert's most solid citizens, there have probably been more sightings of unexplained phenomena above this tiny town than anywhere else in North America, Gracia Unger, editor of the Calvert Tribune, maintains that reports of UFOs date back for many years in the area, but became much more frequent during the past 18 months, reaching near-epidemic proportions during November and December 1973.

From her cramped editorial office, the 31-year-old, dark-haired journalist freely talked about her involvement with UFOs, noting however that not everyone agrees with her open-minded attitude on the subject. "I know something weird is going on around these parts! Unfortunately, I have found it exceedingly difficult to get any substantial cooperation on this UFO problem from some eyewitnesses and the government. Though I've personally investigated more than 200 valid sightings—and had a good number of my own—there is a lot more happening which folks aren't willing to talk about to anyone! Those who have encountered these things are thought of as being crazy. It more or less comes down to this: people who have seen UFOs believe in them, and people who have

Among many seemingly related side effects of Calvert's "unwelcome tourists," are the ability of UFOs to cause major power blackouts, dim street lights, interrupt telephone service, and stall automobiles . . . not to mention talk over ham radio sets . . .

★ UFO REPORT

not been exposed to *the phenomenon* directly, laugh at those who have."

Gracia Unger—who, in addition to her newspaper chores recently made an unsuccessful bid for the office of mayor—contends that these mysterious discs are nothing new, either to herself or the town.

'Old-timers recall sightings from as far back as the late 1890s. Many of *the* events that have transpired over the ensuing years have gone far beyond mere aerial appearances. From time to time, some remarkable—no, *incredible*—ground level mysteries have occurred which tie in directly with UFOs, and have convinced me that Calvert is being used 'as a way station by *these* beings."

To *dale*, Gracia *says* she has seen a variety of strange craft, "at least 50 of them." Her *first* and "best" *sighting dates* back to 1956.

"*...As the UFO bobbed overhead, we became aware of aircraft and helicopter activity to the north. At one point, one of our military planes circled directly above the UFOs but kept a respectable—and safe— distance. Checking with officials at Gray Air Force Base, it was admitted that there had been a routine reconnaissance flight in progress that night. However, they emphatically denied any knowledge of flying saucers...*"

"I often think about what happened, and can vividly recall the details of my experience because it shook me so. At the time, I had just turned 12, and on the evening in question was driving along with my dad—an executive tor Southern Pacific Railroad—along State Highway 6, a few miles east of town. It was way after midnight—around three a.m., I believe—and we were returning home after visiting some friends of the family.

'With absolutely no advance warning, from out of the blackness of space, came these two glowing objects, which proceeded to follow us down a rather deserted stretch of road. We were really frightened, and didn't know what to expect. Finally, curiosity getting the best of us, my dad stopped the car, we

got out, and watched as the *two* objects merged into one, growing larger by degrees, much like a balloon being blown up. Eventually, it moved off, hovering about 30 feet in the air over a nearby pasture. Without making a sound, this object began shining a large and extremely powerful searchlight on a herd of resting cattle. Next it moved in our direction, coming to within 25 feet of us, throwing its eerie spotlight upon us in the process. Our instincts told us to leave immediately and we returned to the car. The UFO—we didn't know what it was then, of course—followed all the way into Calvert, and then zipped off to a high position in the sky, turning pinkish-red as it soared upward. My father cautioned me not to tell anyone about the incident, because, he said no one would believe us. Dad died the next year and so I decided to keep my mouth shut, as he said I should."

Sightings *have been* made on a continuing basis over the years. But, *according* to all reliable information, Calvert did not receive its largest percentage of "phantoms of the air" until November 1973.

I suppose I was among the first to bring the matter to the attention of folks around here," television repairman Virgil Chappell said, A ham radio enthusiast for many years, Chappell insists he initially became aware of his "new neighbors" when a citizens band radio he operates as a hobby began picking up odd receptions and acting very strangely.

"Almost every night during the early part of November, heavy interference plagued amateur broadcasters in the area. preventing us from communicating with one another as we regularly do. Instead of hearing the normal messages from fellow hams, all I could pick up was a series of clicks," Chappell said, "closely akin to Morse code. Being somewhat of an expert in codes, however, I can vouch for the fact that it was decisively different from anything I had heard before. Why, even the tonal pitch of the *'noise'* was odd, varying greatly from high to low. It was definitely—as far as I'm concerned—an intelligent type of signal. I don't profess to know where it came from, and I don't know who was behind it. All I can positively state is that *it* was eerie to listen to!"

The realization that something was definitely wrong came when the stocky. middle-aged Texan ventured out into his yard on November 15th, and peered into the sky. What he saw puzzled and amazed him. "The air all around was aglow with a multitude of twinkling lights. It was like a Christmas tree— *that's* about the best way I can describe the scene. All around and above me

were these blinking spheres. I ran inside the house, yelled to my wife to follow me back outside, and simultaneously grabbed a pair of binoculars, which I thought would give me a better view of what I was certain were not airplanes, stars, or those satellites that come over every so often."

Taking a closer took through his field glasses. Chappell admitted he only managed to make out the vivid colors of the "lights," and could not focus the binoculars *enough* to determine *any* solid, physical form that might have existed behind the glowing orbs. "They were vaguely round, sort of egg-shaped. *But* those colors *were...* well. . .I'll never forget them! They were the *most* beautiful hues of purple, red, yellow, and blue. Right out of a rainbow, I'd have to say."

As for the maneuverability of the UFOs, Chappell says they hovered in one spot for 30 minutes, and then moved on to hover in *another* portion of the sky. *At times they* moved gracefully, as if acting out an aerial ballet.

Asked to estimate their size, Chappell said this was exceedingly difficult for him to do with any degree of accuracy. "For the most part, they remained pretty high. However, several times they fluttered earthward, coming down. as it were, over a grove of trees 500 feet from *where* we stood."

During the course of their night-long vigil, Mr. and Mrs. Chapped were joined by a dozen nearby residents who had been alerted to the strange goings-on by telephone. Among those who were able to verify the activities was banker Billy R. Hall.

As former president of the Calvert Bank and present chairman of the Robinson State Bank, Billy Hall is not one to embellish facts. Active in both the financial and civic affairs of Calvert, *the* astute businessman was deeply affected by what he observed. "I am *not* one to believe in flying saucers and aliens from outer space," Hall said at the beginning of our conversation, "I'd heard about such matters, of course, but always assumed there was a logical explanation for what people had seen. You can imagine my shock when I picked up a pair of binoculars and focused them on what was definitely not a star, a balloon, or any conventional aircraft."

With the aid of powerful field glasses, Hall insists he saw a disc-shaped vehicle with a bubble-like structure on top. "The craft itself was a gunmetal gray." the banter continued. "I watched it as it hovered in one spot for 45 minutes or so, before going into the house to catch the 10 o'clock news. On television, a commentator mentioned other sightings, but said official word had come to

Steve Abraham (above) says this UFO followed him down a lonely back road.
Gracia Unger (below), editor of the *Calvert Tribune*.

the station that everyone was seeing flares being shot into the atmosphere from Fort Hood."

Billy Hall, however, does not accept this explanation. "I know what I saw," he argues, "There was something 'unknown' in the sky that night and I'd like very much to find out what it was'."

The telephone switchboard at the *Calvert Tribune* was jammed a good part of the next day with calls from confused and startled residents seeking an explanation for the phenomenon. Of course, no one had any. And over the next 60 days, sightings were reported almost daily.

On November 19th, two women who live in the nearby town of Rosebud were pursued by a flaming UFO when they neared Calvert. "It happened so quickly, we didn't know how to react," Faye Seeley and Faye Hileman agreed. "First it was a mere speck, like a star, off to the left side of our auto and then—whoosh!—it was on the right side of us," Mrs. Seeley said. "It came down to about 30 feet above the ground, and sat there as if daring us to come closer. 1 wasn't about to take a chance that this thing did not have our best interests at heart," the terrified housewife told the *Dallas Times Herald*. Turning their car around in an attempt

to escape did not change the situation. "It simply rose straight into the air a short distance and began to follow us again," Mrs. Hileman added. "It came after us quickly for a while, as if trying to catch up. But when we saw the lights of a car up ahead it slowed down. Then, as we caught up with the other automobile, the light from the object dimmed entirely, shooting up into the sky out of sight."

Over the years, thousands of UFOs have been seen near bodies of water, and reports from Calvert are no different. The sightings around this Texas community seem to support the contention among ufologists that flying saucers are capable of hiding underwater, where their activities cannot be seen by humans.

A sizeable portion of observations in the area have taken place near a small steel bridge which crosses the Brazos River a scant six miles east of town. A year and a half ago, several persons fishing near this bridge saw a brilliant ball of white light appear above the water, zoom over the span, and disappear without a sound. "No one seemed to take these reports seriously," Gracia said, "but from what has transpired at this spot since, we can only conclude that the early observations were accurate and honest."

Poised as she talked, but with a trace of tension in her voice, Gracia Unger recounted the strange events of the past 18 months, beginning with an

---

"...We watched spellbound as two strange-looking objects hovered over the Brazos River. They could not have been military aircraft because as we watched them one of our planes came into view. Compared to it, these UFOs were three times larger. Why doesn't someone tell us what is going on!..."

---

account of what she, herself, saw close to the Brazos River bridge on Nov. 21, 1973. Three other witnesses were present at the time, near the 200-foot-long span, located in an area of cotton fields and grazing land.

"For several nights we had been receiving reports of eerie colored lights hanging over the Brazos River at a low altitude. Since all prior sightings had been made just off Farm Road 979, we decided to watch the sky *from* this vantage point. Around seven o'clock on the evening in question, we caught

sight of two pulsating orbs, which passed across the sky very slowly and then landed on the Brazos River channel."

Gracia described them as "big—over 125 feet in length" and shaped "rather like a brick with the ends worn off." Also visible to the naked eye was a dimly lighted dome on top and a wildly blinking series of red, white, and blue lights. According to her account, after the UFOs hovered for 25 to 30 seconds on the surface of the water, they simultaneously "settled into the river, extinguished all their lights, and vanished toward the murky bottom."

Stunned, Gracia, who was with her husband Jack Unger, watched the spectacle along with Tommy Blann and his wife Linda, both of Merlin, Tex. Later, over a period of several hours, I interviewed Tommy Blann, who told me that the UFOs were first noticed when they were about 1,000 feet in the air.

To prove their experience was real, Blann offered a convincing photograph of one of the craft, taken, he says. as the UFO passed noiselessly over some telephone lines at about 25 miles per hour. He described the ship as being "extremely large" and joined together in the center by what appeared to be "four ball-type structures."

A freelance reporter for several newspapers, Blann says at the time he took the photo, he was using a 50mm lens with an exposure of about two seconds. "I positively believe this picture will substantiate our account!" he said firmly.

Calmly relating the details of his sighting, Tommy Blann also revealed an interesting highlight of the encounter. "As the *UFOs* bobbed around overhead, we came aware of aircraft and helicopter activity to the north. At one point, one of our military planes circled directly above the UFOs, but kept a respectable—and safe—distance. Checking *with* officials at Gray Air Force Base—the closest military installation from where they could have originated—it was admitted that there had been a routine reconnaissance mission in progress that night. However, the officer I spoke with emphatically denied any knowledge of 'flying saucers.' To my way of thinking, there is no way on Earth," Blann exclaimed, raising his voice, "that their pilots could have missed seeing the UFOs unless they were totally blind!"

For the next seven days, according to Gracia, who has kept a detailed diary of all the events that have transpired in the vicinity of Calvert, UFOs darted and flitted around in the sky, sometimes vanishing from sight at terrific speeds. "The wild dogs, coyotes, and wolves are the first to pick up the presence of a UFO," she revealed while thumbing

(Continued

UFO REPORT ★

CALVERT, TEXAS

through stacks of typed reports. "They begin to bark furiously, *then* howl, and just before the UFO appears, they *run* wildly through the pastures and woods. and sometimes even dash confusedly out onto the highway. Our own dog becomes very alert, and begins to tilt her head upward as if searching for something, but she makes no sound." The editor's contention is that even though UFOs may not make any sound audible to the human ear, they may be operating at a pitch that *is* painful to an animal.

One of the witnesses who saw UFOs hovering over the Brazos River on subsequent nights, was the manager of a focal drive-in grocery store, Duncan Mack. After repeated sightings, the middle-aged businessman confided that his initial observations were anything but casual. "For more than a week, I would step out in the driveway that circles our store, and see *these* peculiar lights maneuvering back and forth above the bridge. They were much larger than any *star* or planet, and came in an assortment of colors. For the most part, we couldn't make *out* any specific form behind these lights, because of their distance from our viewing spot."

With Duncan Mack on one occasion were Ruth Mears and her 16-year-old daughter, Nancy. "We watched. spellbound, as *two* strange-looking objects hovered over the Brazos River. They couldn't have been military craft

because, as we watched them, one of *our* planes came into clear view. Compared to it, these UFOs were three times larger. Why doesn't somebody tell us what's going on?" Mrs. Mears asked repeatedly.

According to another resident, Lillian Juarez, a tavern owner, pulsating lights have landed again and again behind her home on Farm Road 1644, only a short distance from the Brazos bridge. "They scared my family at first," the 40-year-old Mexican woman told Gracia Unger, "but we've almost gotten

> "...During the 'crisis' period of November-December *1973*, a woman who refused to give her name 'for obvious reasons' called the *Tribune* to tell of a frightening face-to-face confrontation with a hairy creature on *the* Brazos bridge.."

used to having them around." The highlight of the many close approaches to the Juarez property came when a white and blue sphere landed in a field behind their farmhouse. Because they were terrified by the strange light *that* touched down so close, for more than an hour the family refused to leave the farmhouse to check out their uninvited visitor until the craft disappeared

While landings and actual confrontations with "space men" near Calvert have been rare, they have occurred.

During the "crisis" period of

November-December 1973, a woman who refused to give her name "for obvious reasons" called the Tribune to tell of a frightening face-to-face confrontation with a hairy creature on the Brazos bridge. The anonymous woman stated that the path of tier car had been blocked by a huge, stiffly walking, seven-foot-tall "monster" moving in the midst of a heavy fog. The incident occurred at six a.m. while the woman was driving into town for groceries.

Finally, on Dec. 11, 1973, one of the silvery UFOs landed in a pasture near the home of Mr. and Mrs. Cleo Smitherman, leaving behind actual physical evidence of its visit.

Nita Smitherman and her grandson, Brent, were returning home along Old Hearne Road, about a half mile south of Calvert. This area is somewhat hidden in a valley near to, but secluded from, neighbors.

As Mrs. Smitherman drove along the twisting back road, she paid little attention to her five-year-old grandson, who kept insisting that his Granny look at the "space men and spaceship out in the pasture."

Pestered beyond the point of patience, Nita Smitherman took her eyes *off* the road long enough to see a strange object hovering over *their* calf pen, *just* as young Brent had claimed.

'Sure enough," the perturbed housewife told Gracia Unger, "when I finally did look where my grandson was pointing, there was this UFO hovering right over *our* pasture and blinking very bright red lights."

Mrs. Smitherman also said that a tower-like structure was visible on its

Virgil Chapell (below) picked up *a* strange code *from* aliens on his citizens band radio.

63

upper portion, with an intensely vivid red light on *top.* At each end of the craft—which seemed oval—there were long antennae that glowed deep red, with a pulsating effect."The light on the west end was huge," she told the *Tribune's* editor, "and it was more of a maroon color."

Driving into her yard, Mrs. Smitherman stared as the UFO floated from side to side no more than 50 yards away. "There it was, glowing like coals in a fireplace," she recalled. "I yelled to my husband and he came running out of the front door in time to see the UFO taking off with a zipping sound to the east. It disappeared behind a row of trees, coming down in an empty field, where it rested for some time before finally streaking off."

The site of the landing was inspected the following day by a team of researchers composed of Gracia Unger and Tommy and Linda Blann. "While we could not verify little Brent's tale of ufonauts, we did find, upon close examination, that the UFO had left a sizable impression in the soft soil. From our careful analysis of this physical evidence," Gracia explained, "we were able to draw at least one conclusion. Whatever landed was quite large—at least 30 feet in length!"

Exactly one week later, on December 19th, a truckload of farm workers were terrified on the Eugene Gibson, Jr. farm—not far from the scene of the previous incident—when a UFO followed them at treetop level, stopping when they stopped, backing up when they backed up, and moving ahead when they did. That same night, a photo was taken of a UFO in *the* air over *the* highway near Chilton, Tex. The 15-second time exposure shows the object floating through the sky in a very irregular pattern. The tracings of its flight resemble the jagged pattern of lightning.

Among the many seemingly related side effects of Calvert's "unwelcomed tourists," are the ability of UFOs to cause major power blackouts, dim street lights, interrupt telephone service, and stall automobiles.

"Residents between Calvert and Bremond (10 miles northwest of Calvert) have reported that their street arc lights go off at night for short periods of time, and then turn back on again," Gracia Unger reported. "It seems that all lights in a certain area go off at the same time. This is a very peculiar phenomenon, since the arcs are regulated by sensory devices, which turn them off at the earliest hint of sunlight. Thus, only some exceptionally brilliant object passing low overhead could trigger this built-in and supposedly foolproof device."

In one of the strangest incidents yet

reported, Leroy Butler, telephone line repairman for Gulf States Utilities, claims he mended a broken power line near Franklin, Tex., that "could only have been done by the force of a large object landing on it from above." Cross arms and posts were snapped off 15 feet above the ground, and wires twisted in half. Butler stressed that *the* wires were definitely "broken by weight resting on them and were *not torn down."* He later got a calf from the main office of Gulf States Utilities, when he listed the cause of interruption of service as a "UFO landing on the lines."

Another peculiar effect was noted in early December by a salesman for a dry cleaning company in Temple, Tex. "The phone rang early one morning," Gracia said, "and on the other end was a nearly incoherent fellow who told me a UFO *had* followed him as he made his rounds out of Waco. The man, who pleaded that his name not be disclosed, stated that the flaming blue object threw a bright floodlight on his truck, and

> "...The UFO looked *to* be 20 feet wide and about 12 feet in height. I was driving along at about *50* miles per hour when we spotted this thing as we came around a bend in the road. Immediately I slowed down to get a better look'..."

stayed with him as he drove in the early hours of the morning through several deserted communities.

"When the UFO finally streaked off, his car motor stalled while he was driving along at 65 miles per hour, and his power steering locked. Needing the services of a repair shop, the vehicle was immediately towed to the nearest gas station, where it was discovered that the truck's alternator had mysteriously burned out. In addition—and here is another anomaly—the salesman's watch had stopped running and a jeweler later told him the battery inside the timepiece had become fused." No plausible explanation, as could be expected, was forthcoming for these incredible puzzles-within-a-puzzle!

Earlier, less than 50 miles away, lights were shut off and giant generators brought to a grinding halt when a small circular disc less than five feet in diameter streaked past a police officer and security guard at Monticelto's newly constructed power plant. "I heard about it from a friend who is a disc jockey at a local radio station," Tommy Blann told me. "Apparently the power facility was knocked out for a number of hours." According to Blann,

this is not the first time these miniature UFOs, often referred to as monitoring discs, have been observed. Blann states, "We had a report back in October 1973 from a welder who was employed at a foundry in McGregor, Tex. He was working outside, when this 'little ball' came up to him, apparently watching what he was doing. Suddenly it flared up, blinding him momentarily, and then sped off into *the* night. *Later he came down* with chills, and was unable to warm up for quite some times."

On *top* of all these enigmas, feed and gram *store* owner Steve Abraham (among those who reported the dimming of arc lights) said that for three consecutive weeks in late November and early December heavy-duty fences around his ranch were broken down night after night by an unknown prowler. Unexplained was the fact that there were never any tracks of any kind—animal, human, or motor vehicle—near the barbed wire fences. Upon closer examination, it almost looked as if the fencing had *been* broken—or *melted*—by something or someone, with superhuman strength. "No normal person could cut through these wires without utilizing bulky equipment. No one was ever seen approaching or leaving the area—we had it patrolled at all hours—nor was there any apparent reason for anyone to go through all the trouble of doing this."

Later, Abraham told of seeing a ghostly figure while on the way to his rural home one evening. "I kept quiet about what happened for a long time, because I was afraid of being embarrassed," he sheepishly admitted. "But finally, I just had to tell someone about it."

The following is a verbatim transcript of an interview conducted with Steve Abraham several months after the major wave of sightings around Calvert:

'We were on our way to Marlin, Tex., to bring back my wife, who was visiting her mother in the hospital. I was driving my daughter's car, which seemed to be the only vehicle on the road. It was a clear night, well lighted by the moon. As we neared Fish Creek bridge, located midway between Marlin and Bremond—15 miles from Calvert proper—I noticed an 'image' out of the corner of my eye. Squinting a bit, I could see it resembled a bell, with a reddish-orange glow emanating from its bottom. The object was poised above a large tree, situated *next* to an abandoned farmhouse on Highway 6. After a few seconds the glow dimmed and then seemed to blink *off* completely. Then, just as abruptly as the glow died, it came back on again, this time brighter than before

It proceeded to stay with us another few minutes before going out a second time. Suddenly, in its place appeared a spotlight complete with the same reddish-orange glow at its base. My daughter and I both saw this phenomenon simultaneously, for each of us muttered, 'Good Lord. what is that!' The UFO came down at a rapid speed toward the highway and over our car, moving in a side-to-side fashion. 1 thought it was going to slam into us. but as it got closer, it turned upward and went over the top of the trees lining the creek. In a few seconds, it seemed to have disappeared behind the trees.

"When first seen. my daughter and I thought that someone was firing flares across the highway, because of the orange glow and the speed of the light, However, we soon remembered that this area was totally uninhabited.

The UFO looked to be 20 feet wide and about 12 feet in height. I was driving along at 50 miles per hour when we spotted this thing as we came around a bend in the road. Immediately, I slowed down to get a better took. When we originally caught sight of the UFO, it was hovering over a clump of trees 700 feet from our auto."

At 53, Steve Abraham is emphatic about what he saw. "During WW II, I spent more than three years in the Air Force. in addition, I have worked out in the fields around here on many a night, and have witnessed nothing even remotely similar to this before. The UFO had the brightness of a lightning boll, and could move and change direction faster than our most advanced military jets."

Gracia Unger managed to compile an impressive fog of eyewitness accounts before they decreased late in December. Many of the observers were obviously reluctant to have their identities made public, though several offered to sign notarized affidavits attesting to the reality of what they had seen.

An abridged summary of only the major sightings of this flap period follows. In the cases where eyewitnesses requested anonymity, we have reframed from revealing their true identity, giving only their initials:

• Felix R. Luna. an 18-year-old student, watched a triangular pattern of lights over the Brazos River bridge in November. Luna, who works part-time at a nearby manufacturing plant, says he is able to "sense" when UFOs are in the area, A peculiar feeling apparently sweeps over his body on these occasions. His entire family, who live on the edge of town, watched a bright white light rising and falling in the sky over their home until it disappeared at dawn.

• Mr. and Mrs. D.L. were followed by an egg-shaped UFO which "stayed with them," then cast a powerful beam of light on them as they drove into Calvert, through the Brazos bottomlands.

• Martha and Buddy Smitherman, manager of a dress shop and the town constable, respectively, have seen "flying saucers" from the front porch of their home which is located at the edge of town, Mrs. Smitherman says she has seen mysterious "ground flashes" emanating from the area of reported landings near the Brazos River,

• Irene Whitlow, a dental technician, and Thelma Conitz, school librarian, watched a "bar of white light" appear in the west just before sunset. The UFO stayed in the sky until about 90 minutes after dark. It did not move and didn't resemble any fixed star or planet.

• Uldene Casey, a former medical technician, saw a similar craft several days before Christmas. The UFO resembled a tubular-shaped fluorescent light bulb.

• Y. S., foreman of a 2,000 acre ranch near the Brazos River. had a brilliant pulsating ball follow above the

---

"... Law enforcement officials may be counted among the hundreds of stunned witnesses of UFOs. Police departments in several communities have found it necessary to set up files to hold the many authenticated sightings ..."

---

cab of his truck for more than 30 minutes, as he was returning late one night to Calvert. It kept "an extremely bright floodlight" on him most of the time.

• Alfred Conitz and his wife, Helen, witnessed a "flat pie pan" that moved erratically at low level as if it were about to land. It never did. The couple watched the UFO for well over a half hour, and were close enough to definitely determine it was not a plane. balloon, or similar object.

• G C and M.L., two deer hunters, were camping at Steele Creek, near Bremond, Tex., early on the morning of December 7th. One of the men was in a deer stand about 50 yards from his friend. At daybreak, "something" threw an intensely bright light down on him. He looked toward his friend's deer blind, thinking he had shone a flashlight on him, only to hear his buddy cry out for help. Peering toward the sky, he saw a tremendous UFO hovering directly above him. The man fired his deer rifle repeatedly at the UFO, and could hear the bullets strike metal each time. One hunter became so nervous that he almost panicked, but mercifully the glistening object lifted

straight up and disappeared in a matter of seconds.

Skeptics will find it hard to accept these reports of weird visitations. Yet, beside these sightings, there remain other aspects of the Calvert UFO enigma which even the most open-minded believer will probably find difficult to accept.

Early one morning, after a heavy rainfall, Alfred Conitz found himself confronted with a mystery which tie has been, even up until today, hard pressed to explain in "Earthly" terms. "I own a sizable piece of land on the fringes of Calvert," he explained. "About four o'clock, I went to the pasture to check on the livestock to see how they had weathered the rather violent storm that had just passed. Arriving at the main gate to my property. i couldn't help but notice that I was not the first to come along our rather secluded back road so early in the morning. For fresh in the mud were the tracks of what appeared to be a small automobile. Thinking that something was wrong, 1 decided to follow the tracks to see where they led, My suspicions were correct, for they vanished right up ahead of me. This 'car' had not turned around, nor did it back up. The tracks simply came to an abrupt halt in the soft soil."

Totally perplexed, Gracia Unger had to shrug her shoulders when asked tor a rational explanation for the mysterious tracks. "I have to admit, it didn't look like the car could possibly have left the area. The tracks ended on the road, and did not begin again anywhere else. At first I didn't believe the matter warranted serious attention, but then I remembered the Conitz property is on the same road where a ball of light followed a car full of people. The tracks were the only ones on the road, and were conspicuous, since they sank right down into the muddy earth."

Though Mrs. Unger could offer no logical reason for their presence, Alfred Conitz theorized that a small vehicle such as a Volkswagen might have driven down the lonely road and been picked up by a waiting UFO. "No missing persons have been reported in the area," Gracia reminded me when I brought up Conitz's speculative theory. "But of course, I'm not about to rule anything out," she added.

Checking out other sources, however, I soon was amazed to learn that although confirmed human disappearances are seemingly rare, an outbreak of puzzling animal slayings and kidnappings has recently occurred in four states—including Texas. "On the Kings Ranch down toward Houston," Tommy Blann told me, "they have been missing a lot of animals. Thoroughbred horses and top quality cattle mainly. UFOs have been seen there almost every

UFO REPORT ★

night. I am told the ranchers do a lot of artificial insemination on the animals there, but what the possible connection **may** be I wouldn't venture to guess, **Kings** Ranch is approximately 75 miles south of **Calvert**, in a sparsely populated area.

UFO activity in and around Calvert eased up at the end of 1973, but the "invaders" returned in full force right after the New Year.

On **Feb. 4, 1974**, a fireball was seen crossing the skies by a half-dozen persons, and even ran Charles Juarez, Sr., a laborer at a **steel mill**, *off* **the road** as he **was** driving with a car full of co-workers. **"I find** it hard to talk about what happened," **he** said, "and sometimes I even have vivid **dreams** about what I encountered. **I'd** like to forget about that **damn** thing, but I can't! This **huge** ball of fire threw sparks down at us, and passed over the deserted **road** so close **that** we thought it was going to collide with us head-on."

Among other witnesses was Harry Wilson, a 65-year-old retired Navy officer, who admitted that he did not get a good look at the **object**. "It flew by so **rapidly I** couldn't focus my eyes on it in time to see it clearly. It was positively one of the most jolting moments of my life, though. It passed overhead, traveling thousands of miles an hour."

Claude Cannon, an electrician, looked on as a **huge** glowing ball sped from west to east. "It was deep orange **and** threw off sparks in all directions, like a Roman **candle**" This is how he describes what occurred: "I was headed north on Farm Road 979, about 8:15 **or** 8:30 at **night**. All of a **sudden,** the heavens were lit up like it was noon! Then this bolide streaked across the sky. First it was only a brilliant ball of fire, with a trail behind it. This trail was almost invisible, until the object **flared** up, sending flames spewing in its wake. It was headed toward the east. I suppose it took no more than 30 **seconds,** or a minute at most, to cross from horizon to horizon. If I counted correctly, it made a **total** of four **bursts."**

Law enforcement officials may also be counted among the hundreds of stunned witnesses. Police departments in several communities have found it necessary to set up files to hold the many authenticated **sightings**. However, despite observations made by their own **men,** authorities admit they are powerless to do anything about the situation.

A **deputy** sheriff, who asked that his name not **be published**—"I don't want to lose my job"—says he **watched** a UFO for more than 45 minutes in **broad** daylight as it moved slowly over the town of Benchley, **Tex.**, 20 miles **south** of Calvert. "We get sightings almost every night," the deputy said, "but what **can** we do? Our hands are **literally tied!**

*

U F O REPORT

After all, the government keeps saying that flying **saucers** don't even **exist. We're not** in the business of chasing **ghosts.** What would we do if we caught an alien being anyway?"

Sightings died down during the hot **summer** months of 1974, but they did not disappear completely. At 8:30 on the evening of June 27th, Mrs. Alice Tribble of Calvert **saw** a blue-glowing UFO in her backyard. **"I had just let my** little dog out, when I saw something hovering over our old **oak** tree. It was weird! **I kept** saying, **'What can** that **be?'** It was bluish-white and had a band of red lights around it- The object stood silently amidst a clear, star-filled sky. It was **very** large—at feast 50 **feet** across. After hovering in one spot for 15 minutes it shot right up—going like a million miles a second, vanishing into space as if **someone** had shut **of** the light!" According to Gracia Unger, reports continue to *cross* her desk, **even**

> . . **Indeed, if** UFOs are using this **particular area as a base** or **way station**—as now seems obvious—where are they hiding? Tommy **Blann** says **he personally knows** of caverns which exist **beneath** farmlands on *the* **edge of town . . .**"

now, **on the average of several times per** month.

That reputable individuals have seen strange objects above **Calvert** cannot **be** denied. The existing evidence is now overwhelming. But why have the ufonauts chosen this sector of the southwest as a **base?**

This question—a major part of the cosmic jigsaw puzzle yet to **be put** together — is **one** on which Tommy Blann is outspoken. "Calvert ties right in the middle of one of **the** greatest concentrations of military installations to be found anywhere in this country. To give you an idea of what I mean, there's Gray Air Force **Base** in Killeen, about 60 miles northwest of Calvert. Around the perimeter of this base, the government has set up mobile radar units, positioned on the back of flatbed trucks, These units can be moved about the **badlands** from one **spot** to another at a moment's notice, supposedly for the express purpose of tracking **enemy** missiles coming in from the Gulf of Mexico.

"Nicknamed *the* 'Red **Eye** Radar Units,' I have **been** told by a reliable **source** that they have picked up speeding unidentified objects on a number of occasions. Several months ago, a *UFO* **was supposedly monitored on these radar** screens for more than 10

minutes. Apparently it reached the point where jet interceptors **almost had** to be scrambled to check out and identify the approaching 'bogie.' From what **I'm** led to believe, the object shot off into space **moments** before **a red alert** *was* to be **sounded."**

An independent investigator for many **years,** Blann briefed **me** on the fact that central Texas, where Calvert is located, has been a hotbed of UFO activity for years, "In the Air Force's Project *Blue Book Special* Report *No.* 74, published graphs show that this **precise** portion of the Lone Star State has always been among the high concentration points for **saucer** sightings." According to this **knowledgeable** expert, **this** section of the U.S. is also **known** for its tight security, which cloaks in a veil of tight secrecy the various scientific and military research projects being **developed** there.

"In this area of **Texas, there** are at least three strategically **placed** underground missile silos," Blann told me. "No one really seems to have any idea of what **goes on in these** particular silos, but we have been told these installations are extremely important to the well-being of our country. Other than that, we are **kept in the dark!"**

An active member of several scientifically oriented organizations, including the American Meteorological Society, Tommy **Blann asserts that he** has developed "inside informants," closely affiliated with various government programs.

I have **been** informed by knowledgeable **people** that several of these military installations are **closely** tied in with our aerospace program. In McGregor, Tex., for example, **there is even** a large **civilian corporation** called Rocket-Dyne, which is instrumental in producing parts for both our **guided** missiles and spaceships." Word has filtered out to Blann that **Rocket-Dyne** is working on a program to perfect a **new** type of economical and lightweight rocket fuel *which* is said to far surpass anything the Soviet Union currently **has.**

Ostensibly, Fort Hood, located within 15 miles of Calvert, is an Army base. However, high-ranking Air Force personnel are **also** stationed there, who are engaged in secret defense work. Many of those **who have** seen UFOs report that they have either originated at—or headed in the direction of—Fort Hood, On several occasions, base officials have stated that UFO reports were misinterpretations of such conventional objects as flares and balloons sent aloft as part of **some** routine nighttime test. Near-paralyzed witnesses have, in most instances, refused to accept these **explanations.**

Moreover, at the world's largest airport, Dallas-Fort Worth, a task force has been formed to **investigate** UFOs which have constantly shown up on regular flight **paths** leading into the **area.** Located almost on a straight line and just 80 miles due north of Calvert, this modern facility has been the scene of as many as a dozen sightings **on** any given **evening.** The **UFOs** have reportedly hovered over and landed in clearings just west of the 17,000-acre field In one case, **three** families saw **an object** at close range hovering about 50 feet above their heads.

After thoroughly checking out the sightings, Fred Ford, operations **officer** at **the airport, admitted** *that* a great many questions remained unanswered. "As a matter **of safety** *for* the hundreds of airplanes using our facilities, we have instructed our operations crews and public **safety officers** to immediately **report** anything they cannot identify."

The mere thought that flying **saucers might** be appearing en masse less than 100 miles **from** Calvert is **enough** to send chills up any concerned investigator's **spine.** Yet the **facts** cannot be denied!

From examination of past flying saucer flap periods, we have come to team that UFOs are frequently seen around **or** near key space and military installations. No doubt they **are** keeping a dose **surveillance** on the development of our technology, just as we **maintain** a watchful **eye** on any **important** advancement made by foreign adversaries.

Indeed, if UFOs are using this particular area as a base or way station— as now seems to be obvious—where are they hiding? Tommy Blann says he personally **knows of** caverns which exist beneath farmland on the outskirts of town. "There is a complex **network** of caves and tunnels which connect somewhere underground. A check of geographical survey maps will show that Calvert is built directly on top of a fault line which zigzags for miles in all **directions."**

Disclosing for the *first* time an incredible facet of his findings, Blann told me that ranchers and farmers in the area have reported hearing peculiar noises coming from deep beneath their feet. "Individuals living five or six miles outside Calvert have **told me** how they have repeatedly been driven out of their homes into the cool evening air by the sound of generators. It appears to **them** as if a steady droning noise is originating from all directions but is **loudest** when ears are placed to the ground. This bit of information has led me to conclude that UFOs operating around here have established **bases** for themselves far beneath the Earth's crust."

Going a step further, Tommy Blann claims ufonauts are probably obtaining the **necessary** energy to power their ships and **bases by** making use of existing underground bodies of water. "This portion of the state is crisscrossect with hot mineral streams that flow silently deep inside the Earth. **Placed** under extreme pressure, these streams

could **make** one hell of a hydrodynamic generator, supplying **any space** visitors **with** all the energy they need and *without* **having to** construct *anything* at *all* **above ground which would** give *their presence* away."

While Tommy Blann and Gracia Unger, may differ on individual aspects of the UFO puzzle, they both remain firm in their belief that an event of tremendous importance is likely to happen at any time.

Blann **says:** "**Most people** could not **handle** the situation, if what **I think** is about to happen **does.** Before long, **some** type of upheaval in the Earth's physical structure **is, I** definitely believe, going to take **place.** When it happens there will be an immediate change in our way of thinking. These UFOs **seen** around Calvert—and elsewhere for that matter—seem to be establishing contact, if only by means of a brief sighting, with a few chosen individuals who are helping to pave the way toward a **better** understanding of the **universe** we live in."

Whatever the outcome—whatever the eventual, long-range goaf of **the** ufonauts may be—**many** UFO investigators are watching the heavens above this area in Texas. The general consensus, based upon an in-depth examination of existing reports and accumulated **data,** is that an event of tremendous universal importance will occur here in the not-too-distant future. On this point, almost all the eye witnesses to Calvert's **UFO mystery** agree! ★

'Mr. UFO' wings in from far-out New York

Timothy **Green** Beckley, UFO author, **to address** New **Space** Age Convention

By TODD FLETCHER

A man known as "Mr. U F O to those who are convinced of extraterrestrial space travelers is in the area to meet with local believers.

New York's Timothy Green Beckley, who says his main interest with the UFOs is cataloging sightings, is staying with Tacoma's Wayne Aho, the area's leading UFO watcher, while attending the New Space Age Convention in Seattle.

Beckley reports his findings in his New York-based publication, UFO *Review*. the worlds only publication devoted entirely to UFOs. Published four tittles a year. the Review *was* started by Beckley more than four years ago, shortly after the movie *Close* Encounters of *the Third Kind* was released.

"I felt following the movie, the time was right tor such a publication," said the president of Global Communications.

The paper now has more than 40,000 readers in 37 countries including the Soviet Union and several small African nations.

❝ (UFOs) mean acceptance of truth in human thinking. **❞**
— UFO **authority** Timothy Beckley

Roughly 800 to 1,000 persons read the paper in the Tacoma-Seattle area, he said.

The paper offers such stories as "UFOs in Fast Food Business? 'Saucer King' vs. Burger King" which recounts an incident of a family eating at a restaurant that only they seemed to know about. The paper also carries ads for such items as the "amazing Telecrystal" which will allow the wearer to communicate with other dimensions

Beckley began publishing a UFO newsletter when he was 14, and the 35-year-old New Jersey native has written six books on UFOs including *Space Brothers*

and *He People* of the *Planet Clarion.*

He claims he made his **first** sighting in New Jersey when he was 10, when he says he saw two discs (lying in circles over the cloud layer.

"The next day I read In the paper that government officials dismissed the sighting *as* being weather balloons," said Beckley, "but I could tell the objects were solid, not weather balloons, and that they were driven by intelligent life."

Beckley's claims a second sighting in 1981 in England.

He says that excuses and co-

verups such as he experienced with his first sighting are what Is keeping the world back from finding out if UFOs really exist.

"We have the intelligence and capability to identify them," said Beckley, "but it means acceptance of truth in human thinking."

Beckley says that people attending the conference in Seattle today and tomorrow will come away with a better understanding of the universe and of themselves. Beckley will deliver two lectures entitled, "Will the host of heaven save us from a nuclear holocaust?" and "Top-secret military-industrial coverup of UFOs."

Other topics to be discussed at the convention, which will take place at the Seattle Center's Nisqually Room, include spiritual transformation and holistic health.

The New Space Age Convention is dedicated to all veterans and commemorates the June 24, 1947, sighting of flying saucers at Mount Rainier

The convention runs today and tomorrow from 11 a.m. to 7 p.m. Cost is $10 a day for adults; $7.50 for seniors and students.

THE NEW YORK COLUMN

Vol. No. 454   25 cents   Mar. 19-25, 1971

OCCULT SYMPOSIUM

A forum and discussion on:

WITCHCRAFT
WHITE MAGIC
TALISMANS

THE TAROT CARDS
PSYCHIC PHENOMENA

Some of the conclave at Wendell Willkie Hall for the Spring Occult Symposium.

Which Witch to Watch?

By R.E. MONTEMOJADO

We found seats on the side of the auditorium, between a fat woman with sequined eyeglasses and a young fellow doing an unbathed Bela Lugosi routine in a doorway to our left, complete with cape, beads and his best attempt at looking sinister. We, and about 200 others, were at Wendell Willkie Memorial Hall for the Spring Occult Symposium, a gathering of self-proclaimed experts on witchcraft, magic, talismans, satanism, tarot cards and psychic phenomena for which the audience was charged a fairly non-mystic $2.50 each.

Apparently satanism is good business these days, for the cash was rolling in in a steady stream and a side table by the doorway was doing a brisk trade in books on the supernatural. At the front of the smoky room was a black-draped table with candles and sticks of sandalwood incense burning at either end; to the left of the dais stood a portable blackboard bearing a sequence of mystic symbols. Behind the dais sat three witches, one of whom was droning on unremittingly about her ability to chase ghosts from her West Village apartment and to predict every airplane crash in the last few years. Seems she hears mystic voices talking to her.

The gathering was sponsored by the New York School of Occult Arts and Sciences and by E.S.P. Magazine and had been advertised in several newspapers. A telephone call earlier in the day had put me in touch with Timothy Green Beckley, director of the School and publisher-editor of the magazine, who cordially invited me to attend. Beckley, a young man in his late twenties

or early thirties, wore a white flowing blue shirt and hair over his shoulders. On the cover page of a lecture agency brochure touting his services, he appears closely cropped, well shaved and wearing a business suit and tie. The brochure describes him as a "noted author, lecturer, syndicated columnist" and "a leading student and researcher of . . . flying saucers, prophecy, hypnotism, sea monsters (sea monsters!), and psychic phenomena." His syndicated writings appear in such household journals as "Probe," "Saucer News" and "Beyond." Not satisfied

continued on page 3

Draped in black is Witch Anna, High Priestess of the "New York coven of witches."

Which Witch to Watch?

MONTEMOJADO — cont. from p. 1

with the transitory erudition of the weekly press, he has authored such memorable works as "Inside the Saucers," "Alien Invaders" and a treatise on c r a f t and voodoo. Not at all a *SIZE* of mundane or limited talents. He also kept a *sharp* eye

h e till throughout the evening. Banding **me** a brochure proclaiming "why E.S.P. Magazine is a runaway best-seller," Beckley noted that its first issue, due to come out shortly, is expected to have a newsstand run of about 100,000 copies. A one-dollar sample copy offers to explain whether flying saucers are from outer space or a "secret psychic force" from earth.

The panel included Gertrude Cooper, witch, amulet and talisman expert, astrologer and alleged incarnation of one Aleister Crowley, and Witch Hazel, a young girl draped in black, doing her best to be exotic. She is, by the way, High Priestess of what is straightfacedly described as a "New York coven of witches."

Also on the evening's panel was a tarot card reader, supposedl an expert one *at* that. @ believe his name may be Paul Karasik), in a black academic gown lined with white satin, under which he wore an irridescent purple *silk* outfit **and** bare feet. **His explanation of** tarot card reading became *so* esoteric and confusing that at one point of the three witches at the dais leaned across to whisper "What the hell are you talking about?"

The crowd was predominantly young, into the twenties and mid-thirties, some wearing suits, others dressed casually, a few in hippie outfits and, not unexpectedly, some creatures from the back lot of the Twilight Zone. A few had come for the entertainment value of the evening (and were, consequently, bored and disappointed by the straight-forward lack of excitement), but most were either true believers or undecided. A choreographer in the audience

told me that this **was** the second such meeting she had attended in the last two years and that, while she had some doubts about it all, she felt that she at least might meet some interesting people and might, perhaps, find some answers. Tim Beckley's view is that the audience consists mostly of believers, because "most non-believers have already made up their minds that it's all nonsense" and don't bother to come.

Also in the audience were a sprinkling of dedicated satanists, obvious by the depth of their attention and the trappings of their devotion hanging about them on chafes and thongs. A release prepared for the meeting claims that there are at least 5,000 practicing witches (male and female) in New York and perhaps twice that number in Los Angeles, with active covens in St. Louis, New Orleans, De-

troit, Seattle and *dozens* of other cities. These people are a little frightening in the intensity of their belief and in their devotion to a private morality (or amorality, as the case may be).

Some people follow their mystic beliefs as a form of interventionist religion, providing them the opportunity to combat the feeling of helplessness with which they face the trials of daily life. The supernatural is also attractive as a denial of involvement, for it offers simplistic explanations to those ill-equipped to cope with the complexities of a troubled age.

Waiting in the lobby of the building later in the evening, I had a closer look at the departing audience and spent some time talking to them. On the whole, they were articulate, outgoing people with a healthy and

questioning **attitude, who recognized, as do I, that there are a** lot of **unexplained phenomena** about **as and a lot of** recorded events for **which conventional science has no ready explanations. The personnel** associated with **the evening's program, I must** admit, were pleasant, openly **invited inquiry, and did their best to** provide an objective opportunity *to* **question** *their* wares.

Just before we departed into a *sudden* downpour, I recognized **Witch Hazel,** *heading* out to *the* **street.** 1 introduced myself, teamed that she's originally from a small town in Kansas, and *asked* her whether she believes in the casting of evil spells. "Most assuredly," she responded. & we shook hands *in the* drafty hallway, *she* promised *to do her* very best on CoB Edison, the Internal Revenue Service and Mayor Lindsay's proposed **tax** increase.

Noted tarot card reader Paul Karasik lectures to the audience of would-be witches and warlocks.

INVASION OF THE SPACE GIANTS

Authorities around the world have been flooded with reports of giant aliens whose mysterious actions have left them completely baffled

By Timothy Green Beckley

T was a humid evening in **late August 1963. The** moon was full, and *the* stars twinkled brilliantly. Near the town of Sagrada Famíla, Brazil, the Eustagulo family lived in a *modest* home in a rural area. They never heard of flying saucers.

On this particular evening the two Eustagulo boys, Fernando, 11, and Ronaldo, 9, **were** told to go to the well in the garden **and clean the** family **coffee** filter. The two went **down** the little stone stairway that led to the well with their friend Marcos. The night was so clear and luminous, **they** didn't immediately recognize the sphere that was floating in front of them as they stood in front of the well cranking the **pulley** to bring up a **bucketful** of water.

When they *first saw* **the object, it was** above the trees, practically touching the branches. The boys could make out people **sitting** one behind the other in four or five rows inside the **craft.** Then suddenly a door popped open, making a humming noise. Two luminous parallel bands speared the **ground** near a flower bed **and a slender** being, about 10-feet-tall, glided on the two **bands** of light to the ground, **landing near** the foot of the **stone** stairway.

The being rode down the beams, with his arms outstretched, in a **slow sliding** movement- Once he reached the ground he walked about 20 feet, with his back stiff, legs open. and **arms** stretched out, balancing himself. **He moved,** swinging his **body** from left to right continuously until he reached a rock in the yard **and** proceeded to sit down. All three boys agreed that the **being wore a transparent helmet over his head, and had only one visible** eye of **dark color in the** middle of his forehead. It was actually a **giant-sued saucerian Cyclops! The ufonaut was** wearing high boots, which had long, thick triangular spikes protuding from each other. The spikes made **strange impressions**

in the soft earth. which could be **seen** for days following the sighting,

The **trousers** he being **wore,** seemed to be fastened to the boots in a ring fashion. The moment the being hit the **ground, his suit seemed to inflate as if** it filled with air. His **garment** was very shiny and similar to leather. Fernando said *that the* being had a copper colored **box** on **his back, and a square** pack which covered part of his chest. He said this **pack** gave off flashes of light. and he though! it was either a camera **or** flashlight. In the craft's open **doorway** the boys could plainly see the other occupants sitting behind **control** panels **turning knobs** and flicking switches.

Frozen in their tracks, the boys Said the being reached for one of **them** *as* if he meant to sweep him up in his giant hands **and** carry him to the waiting *ship*. Fearing the worst, Fernando *picked* up **a brick** and was about to heave it at the spaceman, who **was** seated **on** the rock, when the being stood up and stared at the youth. Fernando was unable to move, or threw *the* brick. It was as if **the** being had gained control over his body and his movements.

As if **surprised** by the **boy's** hostile action, **the** "spaceman" **took a few** steps **back,** his mouth opening in a vertical fashion, **showing** a row of white teeth with **two** larger ones at the corners of the mouth—**one directed downward, the** other up. The being proceeded to enter the ship, gliding up the shafts of light still beaming down. This time, however, the Cyclops floated skyward with his hands pressed against his body and not outstretched as before.

Looking through the door of the open ship, the boys saw **that** all the crew members were about the same size **and stature** and wore the **same** transparent helmet. The youngsters also **felt** that one **of** the being on board was a female. since it had long hair

pulled tightly in a bun. while all the others appeared to be bald.

As in many cases already reported, the boys felt that the **occupant** *was* not really attempting to **hurt** them. They could not explain how they got this impression, but their fear had **disappeared.** The boys were also quite certain that he **would** return again. When **asked** how they knew **this,** they answered that it was just a feeling, as *if* **someone** was talking to them. A local Brazilian UFO researcher explained this as a telepathic **suggestion** and claimed that others in **the** vicinity had also reported strange objects in the **skies** that evening.

Another of the many cases of giant **ufonauts** was reported in the *Australian Flying Saucer Review.* It was raining heavily at dawn on Oct. 18, 1963. Eugenia Douglas was driving **with** a truckload of coal, between Monte **Maix** and **Isla** Verde, in Argentina, when a brilliant **headlight, apparently** from an approachingcar, blinded him. As another "auto" approached, Douglas realized that the vehicle had only one headlight. He slowed **down** to avoid a collision, and as he did the light became so bright he could **not** look at it any longer. He stepped **on the** brakes and put his head on the steering wheel. The truck was **now on the edge** of the **road.** Douglas **go!** out **of** the truck **and** through **the veil of rain** saw a circular metallic **craft about 35** *feet high* **in front** *of him.*

Douglas **told** an investigator from the Review **that,** "Suddenly another light *of* lesser intensity appeared in **the** vehicle, It came **from an** open door. Several **tall** figures **passed** through the opening. They were human-like but extremely tall." He estimated their height at approximately **13** feet **and** they were dressed in **tight** fitting metallic suits.

According to the died report. the occupants wore strange headgear with **protru-**

sions that looked like small *antennae*. Douglas **said** there was nothing repulsive about the big **men.** yet he was terribly frightened.

The moment his presence was discovered by the aliens, a ray of red fight flashed, burning *his* skin. Eugenic Douglas was in such a state of fright that he could think of nothing but grabbing his revolver **and firing three** shots at the tall being. Then he started to run on the road toward the **town** of Monte Maix.

But the "burning light" from the ship followed him wherever he went. When he reached the village, Douglas noticed that **as** the red beam touched electric lights in the street, they turned violet and then green. A strong smell of gas immediately spread all around the area.

As he came **la** the nearest home he began to shout for help. This was the house of a Mr. Ribas, who **had** died *the* night before. Unexpectedly, the candles around the cas-

ket and all the electric lights in the house turned green. A strange smell instantly filled the room.

Hearing the **shouts** outside *and seeing* the *weird happenings* Inside, *the* Ribas family rushed out of their house to find Douglas with an **overcoat** over **his head and a gun** in his hand. Neighbors appeared on the scene to stare at **the green** street lights. In the meantime the ufonauts had disappeared into the night.

Douglas was taken to the **police station** where **he showed** burns on his face and hands, and again related his weird experience. The **police officer** then **remembered** that **he** had received a number of calls about the electric lights changing **color** throughout **the** town, which was attributed to irregularities at the local power plant. Douglas was examined by a Dr. Dabolas, who stated that the burns had been caused by radiations similar to those from an overexposure

to ultraviolet rays.

The following day **the** villagers went to the site where Douglas met the strange machine with **S**t**e** giants, and found large footprints (19½ inches long), partially washed away by **the** rain. Burnt out cables were also found in the truck.

There had **been many** observations of flying saucer "giants" in **South** America, but sightings of these beings *seem* to abound in Argentina. *Saucer* News **(September 1965)** contains a brief report concerning an incredible incident which occurred in **the** town of Torren. During February of that year. a UFO landed in full view of a group of extremely excited and frightened farmers. Two **strange** beings, towering over seven feet tall, **emerged** from the **craft** and walked toward the villagers. As in the Douglas case they had an apparatus on their **foreheads** which gave **off** small rays **of many** *colored* light. **The beings then** went into **one** of the **nearby** houses and attempted to kidnap the farmer who lived there. They were unsuccessful, due to the combined efforts of his friends who came to his rescue.

On the **same evening** *the craft* landed *again, and* this *time the* fanners opened fire on the giants. To their horror and dismay the bullets had no effect. Despite the ability to withstand the fussilade, the spacemen were easily discouraged from their *kidnap* mission. Interestingly, one of the farmers who fought the spacemen hand-to-hand later **came** down with a *strange* **skin** disease.

Brazil has also had its share of visits by these giants. In August 1958, three **men** on the outskirts of **Mindui** reportedly observed a pair of eight-foot-tall beings dressed **in** brilliant red clothing. They watched the spacemen **walk** up a hill to **their** UFO. and **take off.**

On Feb. 14, 1965, on a beach near **G**u**a**rani. Brazil, five local residents observed the landing of an **unusually** large object. Three of those present went back to **a nearby** motel to get additional witnesses. While they were gone. **the** two remaining UFO witnes-**ses cautiously approached** the ship from behind sand dunes until they managed to maneuver within 60 feet of the craft. From this position they noticed that **three beings** had **alighted** from the **ship. The ufonauts** were thin. tall **creatures** about eight **feet** tall, wearing a dark, one piece suit **which** fit very tightly around their bodies.

Before anyone else could arrive at **the** site. the *craft* took off. However those who did return **could** see traces of footprints **and** unusual circles where the object had rested.

Several hours later on the same evening, **Nilo D**omingues, while **resting** on a beach in Atlantida, Brazil, saw a **UFO** land **and immediately** turn on what appeared to be a bright spotlight that moved about on the sand. A porthole **could** be seen **on the** craft and from a door on its underside *came* 'another strong light. Suddenly the object **look oft** rapidly and disappeared. Half an hour later, **D**omingues returned to the beach with his son and found strange markings in the sand, which looked like the ship and its crew had returned **during** *his* brief **absence.**

From Vilovi, Spain, comes a sighting of an enormous hairy monster seen on Feb. **27,** 1968. The "animal" reportedly left huge footprints in the ground **and** walked the countryside at night scaring animals. Several horses were reportedly **attacked** by *the*

★ UFO **REPORT**

{Continued

SPACE GIANTS

beast. There have been frequent reports of UFOs in the area.

A Rumanian migrant in Australia reportedly saw three giant creatures in purple and yellow clothing about 200 miles north of Brisbane. This sighting was carried in The News of Jan. 17, 1969: "Mr. George Vas, a repairman, his wife, Malanka, and daughters Olga, 14, and Maria, 13. all say they watched the spacemen collecting sugar cane and other plant specimens for 10 minutes. Mr. Vas said he and his family were asleep in their caravan at the edge of the road. About 4:30 a.m. they were awakened by the barking of their dog. Ica He heard a load buzzing noise like a big swarm of wasps, and said he saw an object land; it was between 25 and 30 yards in diameter and looked like a Mexican sombrero. It gave off a brilliant violet color. Mr. Vas said he and his family watched as three spacemen—about three times larger than humans—descended from the ship. They had blocky arms and legs and shapeless bodies. They gave off a purple-yellowish glow. After gathering specimens for about 10 minutes. the spacemen returned to their ship. The craft than went straight up. traveling very quickly. As it look off, the hair on (everyone's) body stood up as if affected by a form of magnetism. Mr Vas said this was his third sighting of 'spacemen.' He saw one as a child in Rumania in 1918. and another near Belgrade in 1946."

Although the appearance of these giant ufonauts have been less frequent in North America, information has been obtained of at least 25 reports centering around sightings of these creatures. Mary Lou Guenther. a Canadian researcher, reports that on Sept. 19. 1963. about 8 p.m., a UFO hovered over a field across from a school yard in Saskatoon. Canada. As the UFO passed over the vacant lot. it dropped a large container of some type. After the UFO took off. the young witnesses, including 11-year-old Brian Whitehead, started walking in the direction of the "box." When they were within 15 feet of the object. someone or something stood up. The being was about 10 feet tall, and suddenly started moving toward the children. moaning and holding his hands out as he came at them.

Brian described the alien as being dressed in clothes which "were like a cloak worn by a monk." The "suit" was white like a huge crayon. When questioned whether he saw pants legs, Brian seemed puzzled and said. "I don't know: sometimes I could see right through him."

After the children had calmed down, the police were summoned, and they arrived

about 45 minutes after the incident took place. The investigation centered afound the field for several days, and details of it were sketchy. The boys were questioned separately and asked to draw sketches, which apparently matched. According to Mrs. Guenther. The following evening some boys while in the playground saw the same UFO return and again hover above the tot. They thought they saw an extremely large man lying on the ground because they saw 'arms and legs move.' The object then disappeared, and they saw nothing else."

During a widespread wave of saucer sightings in Mexico in 1965 there were several cases involving giants In September, a group of saucer occupants estimated to be 10 feet in height, with brilliant red eyes and no mouths or noses, were seen by three women who claim they popped out in front of them during a stroll through a suburb of Mexico City. The beings

> ". . . After watching a flaming fireball land in the immediate area, seven witnesses climbed a hill in Flatwoods, W. Va. When they reached the top of the hill they were surprised to see a dull orange globe resting on the ground. From the glow surrounding the object emerged a 15-foot-tall being . . ."

were dressed in shiny gray suits and boots "just like out of the comic strips." After seeing the beings, the women said they ran away in panic and when they eventually decided to return to the site the ufonauts had departed.

Not to be outdone, the U.S. has had it share of this type of creature.

On the evening of Sept. 14, 1952, seven witnesses, including a National Guardsman, climbed a hill in Flatwoods, W. Va., after watching a flaming fireball land in the immediate area. When they reached the top of the hill. they were startled to see a dull orange glob resting on the ground. From the glow surrounding the object emerged a 15-foot-tall being which towered over the witnesses. Its face, everyone agreed, was round and blood red. No one noticed a nose or mouth, only eyes, or eye-like openings. which projected "greenish-orange" beams of light. Around the red "face" and reaching upward to a mint was a dark hood-like

shape, which could have been a helmet.

Watching the "monster" gliding over the ground in their direction, the witnesses took off, running back down the hill and clearing a four-fool gate without opening it.

Later, questioned by researcher Gray Barker, the witnesses stated that an awful odor, like rotten eggs, covered the entire area. This stench was so horrible that they were sick to their stomachs for hours afterward.

Returning to the area with Gene Lemon, the Guardsman, Barker found the site covered with mysterious "ski marks." The impressions were about 10 feet apart in the tail grass and led from the tree. where the "monster" was last seen standing, to the location of the alleged "fireball"

Oddly enough, at the exact time of these seven witnesses' experience, residents from surrounding states were calling local police departments. TV and radio stations, and military installations to report peculiar aerial observations which were generally interpreted as meteorites.

The Air Force sent an investigator to Flatwoods a few weeks later and convinced at least m e witness that what they had seen was a top secret government rocket, propelled by an ammonia-like fuel. No answer has been offered to explain the appearance of the 15-foot-tall monster. Thus it must be listed as another appearance made by giant saucerians!

A young Van Nuys, Calif., electrician, Ted Kittredge. came forward in June 1956, with his account of meeting three seven-foot-tall 'visitors' who appeared quite friendly, had long flowing hair. and spoke English, "as if they had memorized thousands of conversations and were repeating the words on tape."

Kittredge said his stepbrother, with whom he shared his home. slept through the entire episode. Kittredge himself was awakened by the barking of his dogs and upon stepping outside to investigate saw a huge golden colored ball in his yard.

"Three men approached me without hesitation and told me not to be frightened," he said. "I was realty scared. In fact the whole thing seemed like a dream. Only I know it wasn't. Several other people in the Valley had seen the same thing, even talked with the men. I just hope I never see it again, that's all."

Kittredge also appears to have had a brush with a mysterious group who try to silence saucer witnesses. After appearing on a TV show in Van Nuys he got a phone call in the middle of the night, warning him that it would be wise not to talk about his contact. "I was Sold to stop worrying and stop talking," Kittredge said. "I could hear

· UFO REPORT

VARIETY

FILMS   VIDEO   TV FILMS   RADIO   MUSIC   STAGE

WEDNESDAY, DECEMBER 23, 1970

Literati

Flying Saucers Anyone?
D.C. and N.Y publicist Harold D. Salkin working with Timothy Green Beckley, editor-publisher of ESP (the occult field) on an article for Saga which quotes show biz celebrities who claim to have seen or believe in UFO. Among these who have been reported as claiming or believing in Unidentified Flying. Objects (flying saucers, in parlance) are mentioned Arthur Godfrey, Jackie Gleason, Sammy

Davis Jr., Gloria Swanson, Richie Havens. Stuart Whitman (a news story not verified. purportedly quoted him as having seen an object during the 1965 blackout), Cassius Clay (reportedly while training in New York's Central Park for his last fight). Corinne Calvet, Betsy Palmer, Buddy Hackett, Buddy Rich, et al.

Salkin and Beckley cover themselves by mentioning them as being either fans of or claimed viewers of UFOs.

machines clicking in the background and (he voice said 'We know all about what's going on. You just keep your mouth shut and forget about it.' "This type of phone call has been received by many people after a dose sighting or contact.

While going for a late walk on the sand near Rite Park, N.Y., in September 1961. Stan Suban, of Brooklyn, claims that he saw a creature at feast seven feet in *height* near a burning fire. The young Columbia University student maintains that his sighting occurred around 2:30 a.m.: "A sphere of white light hung suspended around the fire. Near the water I could see five or six persons whom I took to be skin divers. I could see the black 'wet' suits with the white strings drawn at their arms. They were all about 6½ feet tall and well built. I was about 50 yards from the fire and was attempting to get a closer look at what was going on. Then *a figure*, much larger than the rest, approached from the direction of the water. It came up to the fire and bent over it and remained in that position for some time Then he walked around the fire several times, stopped and took off what appeared to be sweat pants. What then terrified me was the appearance of this figure. He was white as snow, seven to 7½ feet tall. and had *no* distinguishable facial features

I couldn't believe my eyes but stared at him in fascination and terror. At this *time* I hid *behind* a concrete block which was about seven feet high." The "alien' even towered above this structure. "After looking at the creature for several minutes I knew he was not of this world. He walked with an animated gait I was impressed with the massive power it seemed to have within itself. I do not believe the 'person'was human."

Minutes later, the creature disappeared as it moved out of the firelight toward the ocean. Because of the constant shifting of the sand no impressions were found to confirm *Stan* Suban's tale, but he is very definite about what he saw.

One of the strangest encounters involving giant-sized saucer occupants occurred *to* six teenagers in Daniels Park just south of Denver, Colo., on the *evening* of Apr. 8, 1966.

The group of teenagers consisted of Alan Scrivner. Donald Otis. Michael Simington, all 17 years old. and Patricia Retherford, Kaye Hurley, both 16, and Mary Zolar, 18. At about 5:30 p.m. they drove to Daniels Park, which is a short ride from the heart of Denver. They parked their car and waited, joking as they went, a distance of some 350 feet to an old dugout shelter where they proceeded to build a fire and have a picnic.

About 9:30, Scrivner told reporter William Logna of the *Rocky Mountain* News, "We were all inside the shelter and thought we heard a sound like someone walking on top of the roof." Scrivner and Donald Otis took a flashlight and went out to have a look. "We couldn't see anything. It seemed real quiet outside, and then we noticed this *buzzing* sound. There was something out there rustling around and it would stop when Don and I would stop. Up near my *car* we looked *out* into a nearby field and saw something that looked like another car with big round tail lights. The lights moved around and then were gone. We went back to the shelter. where the others (were waiting), and they told us they had seen a big figure or

something pass in the light outside. They said it was a tot taller than me. and I'm six feet one inch " Scrivner *estimated* that the being was seven feet tall.

"We decided to *leave* and *as we walked to* the car, Don yelled *about* a light. There was a white light that shot out real bright across from us. and two blue lights, dimmer. and a brighter one below us "

Four of the teenagers stood on the hood of the car to get a better view. They saw four objects that looked like "footballs with domes on them, sort of squashed spheres. This strange sound was all around us It didn't come from one direction. It was pulsating."

Scrivner told reporter Logan that three of the objects were off to *(he* right. "Two that hovered and one that went up and down— and the fourth came around from the left. The last one changed its color to red after it got close to us."

Red rays seemed to be comma out of the bottom of the *object* "on and off" as if the object was trying to blast off unsuccessfully. Scrivner continued: "We decided to drive out of there. My *car* wouldn't work right. It's a 1954 Ford, but *has* a new engine and works *fine*. but the engine kept (conking out) like the ignition was going on and off. There was nettling *but* static on the radio."

After Scrivner finally managed to get the car started, he reported that the *others* all saw *a* huge light on the road behind them. "It was 30 feet behind us and came up right behind our car and then it went out. The strange thing is I *couldn't*. . . see the light in the rear view mirror."

Police Chief John C. MacLvor said the

teenagers seemed quite sincere and "two of the girls were really frightened." The chief commented, "I'm inclined to think they really saw something."

Emil Slaboda, Wire News Editor of *The Trentonian*. has been one of the few dedicated newsmen who has tried to get the facts about flying saucers across to the public. His investigations of *several* sightings which have taken place in New Jersey have turned out to be valuable contributions to UFO research.

In his *Across the Board* column of *Feb. 5*, 1967, Slaboda wrote: "The following two stories are true to the best of my knowledge- They happened in the Trenton area and both cases were reported to the police. The principals, however. wanted to remain anonymous and for *good reason* . . . monster and flying saucer stories often bring ridicule to the tellers! Although only a select group of people know it. a monster, presumably from a saucer, visited Washington Crossing Park, N.J.. and scared the daylights out of four nocturnal visitors to the park some five weeks ago,"

Slaboda reported that two men and two women were driving through the park when they noticed an unusual shadow pass over their car. "Although there was no sound of engines, the four passed off the shadow as that of an airplane heading for nearby Mercer Airport. They stopped the car moments later and two of the group left the car for a short walk." Suddenly, there was an alarming roar, "as if some animal were nearby." Hurrying back to their *parked* auto. the couple saw an eight-foot-tall creature gliding toward them over a grassy knoll- "It

definitely did not walk like an animal *or* anything human." one of the witnesses explained.

Slaboda interviewed a brother of one of the witnesses who told the newsman. "I don't know what they saw out there, but I do know that whatever *it was*, it certainly scared the heck out of them."

The second encounter reported by Emil Slaboda occurred oft Friday. Mar 3, 1967. not far from the same Washington Crossing Park. "*Two* 19-year-old girls were driving down Bear Tavern Road, in Ewing Township. They were in the vicinity of the Mountain View Golf Course when the UFO put in its appearance " The girls told the Ewing Police that the craft was about 20 feet long, cigar shaped and was lit up along its entire length. When the object dipped down in front of their *car*, the girl driving slammed on the brakes and began to scream-

It has been suggested by the late Ivan Sanderson, John Keel. and many others that many UFO occupants are actually "androids"—manufactured creations. This would mean we are dealing with non-thinking, nonfeeling beings and are faced with the task of trying to understand machines which are merely "programmed."

The space giants, from eyewitness reports, could be the machines created by ufonauts to land on Earth and perform various mysterious tasks. Imagine what the Russian "Moon-rover" would look like in the eyes of a lunar creature.

What is astounding about the space giant phenomenon is that these "creatures" have been sighted throughout the world. But perhaps the most important *aspect* of this mystery is this: witnesses have always *seen* different shaped *beings in* different locations and one type of *giant Has* never been sighted in another area. Have the masters of the giants or the giants themselves carved up the Earth into spheres *of* influence *to* accomplish—who knows what? Research indicates that giants have walked the Earth in the past. Were they from space? If so, why have they returned?   ★ THE END

Space Sports Adventure Animals Girls Guns Astrology Action

73

DOUBLE-LENGTH BONUS
MIND MANIPULATION: THE NEW UFO TERROR TACTIC

There has been a frightening increase of cases where aliens have begun controlling the minds **of** human beings!

Here is an investigative look **at** this new threat to the human race!

by
Timothy Green Beckley

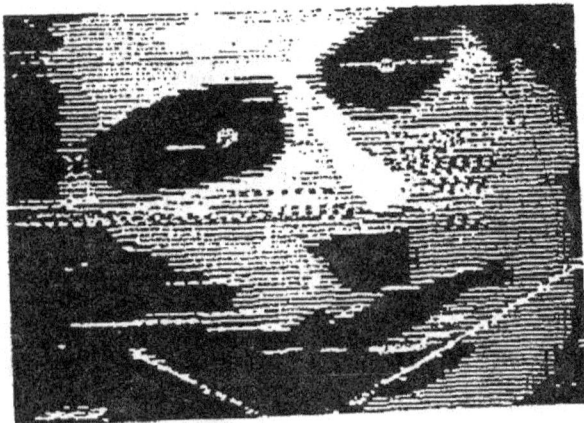

There are mounting indications *that* **UFOs** have a long-term plan *of* operation in store for Earth and its inhabitants. Data, meticulously collected in a worldwide research effort, would seem to support that stunning theory.

UFO literature *is* filled with hundreds of cases in which unsuspecting observers have *been* subjected to continuous harassments following an encounter with a flying saucer. Many times *the* witness finds his home plagued by a host of inexplicable phenomena. In other cases, eerie, mechanical-sounding voices, purported to be "messages" from an alien source, begin emanating from their radios, TV *sets,* or telephones. In addition, mysterious strangers dressed in dark 'clothing, commonly referred to as the Men in Black, or MiB, visit the often confused eyewitness and warn *him* not to speak about his sighting to anyone.

Many observers, however. endure far more harrowing experiences than these. As terrifying as these incidents may seem, *they* are no comparison *to* the instances which appear to be actual cases of *UFO possession.*

Often, while interviewing a UFO eyewitness or contactee, I find myself face-to-face with an individual who is convinced he is slowly—but surely—losing *touch* with reality. Having come that close *to* the unknown, the individual *feels* his very existence is being threatened by an *alien force* bent on gaining total control of his body and soul!

Some witnesses persist in believing that they are being "haunted" day and night by an invisible specter whose main objective is *to* capture their *free* will and make them the "property" of someone—*or something*—else.

Cases of UFO *possession* are *actually* quite common! Yet *very* little is known about it because of the scarcity of research into the subject. Investigators have remained extremely cautious about digging too deeply into this particular *area.* Their hesitancy, however, may be justified.

An exhaustive study of my own *shows* that accounts *of* UFO possession are almost always identical. Frightfully *so!* The following patterns have emerged, again and again:

• After a close encounter with a UFO the eyewitness goes through *a* period of anxiety, during which he is unable to consciously remember certain aspects of the incident.

• Within months—sometimes weeks or even days—the personality of the observer actually changes. Eventually. it may alter to the point where he finds it impossible *to* get *along* with workers, close friends, or even family. Personal tragedy seems to strike many of those who have had ground level encounters with UFOs. Much could be written about individuals whose entire personal world crumbles around them following such an experience.

• In some cases, the eyewitness discovers he has developed certain 'gifts" or abilities. Though they may appear to be beneficial at first, too frequently this is not the case. Among these unusual abilities are extraordinary powers of ESP, precognition, or psychokinesis. in addition, a heightened intelligence level or an unusual increase in physical strength may be noticed. Such peculiarities willi often manifest themselves shortly before a person is about to be possessed. Shortly after this, he may begin slipping into a "trance," during which time it appears as if an alien intelligence has "taken over" his body and is using his brain.

It was during my in depth investigation of an extensive UFO wave in the U.S. Southwest (see *Calvert, Texas: Flying Saucer Way* Station. Spring 1975, UFO REPORT) that I met Paul Clark, a tall, slimly-bull! man in his mid 20s. (Because of the seriousness and the possible repercussions this article may cause, we have decided to change the names of those individuals involved.)

His story is one of the most believable accounts of alien possession that I have ever heard. And I'm convinced it is *not* a hoax.

During the course of three, rather lengthy, conversations with Paul I felt I learned much about him. Like so many other American boys, he spent his teen-age years playing baseball. listening to music, and chasing girls. Paul never paid close attention to his schoolwork, with the result that his grades were "just average." Nevertheless, he was well liked by his fellow classmates, and also managed to get along amicably with his elders.

Now, at 25, this same "average young man" feels destitute, as if he doesn't have a friend in the world. Nearly a total recluse, he shuns any activity which might expose him to public scrutiny. He is divorced from his bride of four years, and has quit or been fired from numerous jobs.

Of course, these radical changes in his life did not occur overnight, but, rather were a painfully slow period of moral and physical deterioration.

Paul was more than willing to tell me the details of his ordeal. As we talked, it became apparent that he was anxious to get the matter off his chest. The problem had obviously been weighing him down for too many years.

"For the longest time, I thought I was going insane," Paul said. "Often my best friends would accuse me of behaving irrationally and t wouldn't have a clue about what they were referring to. My mind, on those occasions, was an absolute blank. I found myself going to doctors and psychiatrists, but even they couldn't offer me an explanation that could account for these amnesia attacks."

Whatever the cause of his trouble, it was obvious that it was rooted in an eerie confrontation with a visitor from outer space! The event took place on a Friday night in August 1967. At the time. Paul lived with his parents on a rather secluded ranch near Waco, Tex., which was surrounded by trees, dense thickets, and bramble. Here is his personal account of what happened on that fateful summer evening:

'The weather had been unbearably hot all day, with temperatures soaring into the 90s. I got permission from my folks to spend the night outdoors, camped in back of our ranch house with a couple of friends.

"We set up a makeshift shelter, turned on a portable radio, and proceeded to shoot the breeze. The sky was as clear as I'd ever seen it, with stars twinkling against a background of absolute blackness.

'Around 10 p.m., the air began to gradually get cooler. In the distance we could hear an occasional rumble of thunder, and once in a while the sky would light up with a flash of lightning. ft was a great sight."

Unfortunately, the beauty of the night was short-lived. It was shattered less than two hours later.

"Shortly after midnight, we lowered the flame of our kerosene lantern and retired," Paul Clark continued, a slight *trace* of tension building in his voice, "Immediately, I turned over and closed my eyes. Before long, however, a peculiar high-pitched whine woke me up. The nearest I can come to describing this would be to say it sounded like a million bees buzzing.

Sitting up, Paul peered into the darkness and saw nothing. Within a few moments, however, he managed to pinpoint the source of the noise. It was coming from the woods near the ranch. With his curiosity now aroused, Paul decided to investigate.

I didn't want to wake my friends, so I tiptoed over to the area, hoping to catch a glimpse of whatever was causing the noise. I recall wandering aimlessly farther and farther away from our back-yard camp, as if I was being pulled by an invisible rope. All around me, the whine continued to grow in intensity, until finally it encircled me on all sides."

At this point, Paul sighted his first UFO.

"Up ahead of me, between the trees and bushes, was a glowing light the size of a basketball. As t approached to within 25 feet of *it*, I could see the light was actually a pulsating sphere."

In an attempt to block out the loud irritating noise that now was growing in intensity. Paul put his hands over his ears. This had little effect, however. "My head began to swim, and my eyes started to water Next thing I knew, I was on my hands and knees—somehow I must have fallen without realizing it—crawling on the ground, trying to get back to the safety of my friends."

He was unsuccessful!

Upon "coming to," Paul found himself in his parents' living room. His head was pounding from "the worst headache I've ever experienced." Standing around him were his mother and father and his two fronds.

Paul says he found it difficult to understand what they were trying to tell him. "It was as if they *were* talking to *a* complete stranger," he said. I had, for all intents and purposes, lost my identity. I had no idea who i was or where I was." While he tried to calm his nerves and gather his thoughts. Paul's friends filled him in on what had happened.

"They said they had suddenly been awakened by a brilliant flash off in the woods. They noticed that 1 wasn't in my sleeping bag nor did they see me nearby, and they became worried. Considering all the possibilities, they felt I might have wandered off in my sleep and fallen into one of the many ravines in the area," Paul said

Using a flashlight to guide them through the underbrush, Paul's friends began calling out his name. Their worry grew into fear, because he did not respond to their cries.

Five minutes later their search ended when they found Paul stretched out on the ground face down. "Lifting me to my feet, they explained how I seemed to be in another world, dazed and looking right through them. My eyes, they claimed, were rolled back in their sockets and my skin had turned as white as a sheet. in addition, they said my flesh felt ice-cold, like that of a corpse."

On the way back to the house they noticed something else. Paul's head had swollen like a balloon. His forehead appeared enlarged and extended several inches beyond normal. "It was

(Continued

UFO MIND MANIPULATION
(Continued)

'puffed up' as if I'd been stung by a mass of bees."

This condition rapidly disappeared and Paul's head returned to normal by the time the three boys reached the safety of his parents' quiet ranch house.

For weeks afterward, Paul Clark felt worn out, "as if I'd been drained of all my energy." He found it extremely difficult to concentrate long enough to do even the most mundane chores All he could do was mope about the house, and he spent a good portion of the time sleeping.

As the months went by, Paul regained his strength. However, even as he returned to normal, physically, he couldn't help but wonder about what had really happened on that late summer night.

"My friends came up with a rather logical explanation. They concluded that I'd been walking in my sleep—I'd never done that before, to my knowledge—and that a thunderstorm had come up in the middle of the night and I had barely missed being struck by lightning They figured a bolt had struck near where I stood, and after traveling over the surface of the ground had reached me. Along the way, the lightning must have lost a great deal of force. Otherwise, they theorized, I would surely have been instantly killed."

Though their explanation seemed reasonable, Paul couldn't shake the persistent feeling that a lot more was involved. "I recalled the bright light dancing about, and the strange buzzing that literally ran through my skull." He knew there had to be another answer—even if it was an unpleasant one.

After several years had passed, Paul became engaged to and later married his high school sweetheart, Irene.

"After we got married, I took a fob as a ranch hand near Calvert, Tex. And though the week was tiring, it paid pretty well. Each week, I was able to put some money in the bank, figuring some day I would have enough saved to buy a small place of our own, and perhaps even start a small cattle business."

Since that night in back of his parents' house, Paul suffered both mentally and physically. Dizzy spells, headaches, and fainting became common. "I'd be seated at the kitchen table, and all of a sudden my wife would be applying cold compresses to my forehead. I'd pass right out reading the newspaper or eating,"

Gradually his condition deteriorated. During this difficult period which followed his UFO experience, Paul became keenly fascinated with science and began reading books on physics and engineering, subjects which he had never before Showed even a mild mterest in. "It was as if I were furthering my education," he insisted. "I didn't know why I found these topics so fascinating. My mind seemed to be developing—expanding—at a rapid clip."

Coinciding with this heightened curiosity and intelligence, Paul found himself growing extremely moody. As the months passed, and after discussing his suspicions with his wife, that ufonauts were trying to control him, it became more difficult for Paul to be around other people—including his wife, parents, and co-workers, "I had a hard time keeping my thoughts together." He started showing up late for work, and then not showing up at all.

Finally, he quit, not wanting to wait until he was fired. A string of lesser paying jobs followed, but they all ended the same way.

Then things went from bad to worse!

"My mind was incapable of thinking straight. It was always a million miles away, toying with some advanced mathematical formula or scientific equation. The funny part of all this was that I still didn't know the reason why I was so hung up on these things. After all, I wasn't a scientist or an engineer, just a simple country boy." During this period, personal tragedy struck the darks. Their year-old son, suddenly died. Doctors diagnosed the infant had succumbed to a cerebral hemorrhage.

In early 1973, Paul's wife left him and filed for divorce. One of the reasons she gave was that she felt the boy's death was somehow related to Paul's condition. She felt that the UFO issue had broken up their previously happy marriage. This same pattern is often repeated as UFO witnesses have found their formerly normal lives turned into nightmares.

Paul didn't even bother to contest the divorce action. "Even though I loved Irene dearly, she didn't matter that much to me any more. It was as though I had a special mission on Earth. It was 'beyond me' to lead an ordinary existence!"

Irene's decision to leave came after Paul's second encounter with mysterious unidentified objects. Not knowing what to expect—or what her husband was capable of doing—she decided to leave.

"Again, I must tell you what happened as seen through another person's eyes. My mind is almost a total blank when it comes to the events of that night."

Paul and his wife were driving home from Belmont, Tex., where they had spent the evening with relatives. "It was around 1:30 am, and I was speeding along the darkened back roads to avoid traffic, when suddenly a large, yellowish ball of fire appeared on the road ahead, immediately, I slammed on the breaks because otherwise I would have collided head-on with the object." The UFO slowly lifted from the road top position a few feet above the pavement, and began drifting toward the side of the road. About 30 seconds passed before it stopped and hovered next to a grove of trees.

It was then that a frightened Paul Clark insists he was directed, as if by magic, to leave his car and walk toward the UFO that now remained stationary. Just as in his first UFO experience, the nighttime air was now filled with an eerie loud whine, similar to a shrill scream.

'My wife pleaded with me not to leave the car, but I was no longer in control of my movements. It was as if my body was being made to react, pulling me in the direction 'they' wanted?"

Walking toward the light, Paul says he heard a voice inside his head. This "inner voice" demanded that he walk straight ahead and not look back.

Meanwhile, inside the parked car,
(Continued

(Continued from page 56)

Irene Clark was almost hysterical. **"She** considered going for help, but was afraid **the police** might **think** she was daffy," Paul said. "So, in desperation, and because there wasn't anything else to do, she decided to 'sit tight', hoping I would return soon."

When he did, havoc followed.

"Somehow I **wound up back** in my car. Opoening the car, my wife says I looked like a 'monster'—that's exactly the way she put it! **My** face was more alien' in appearance than human. My features had changed grotesquely, eyes bulging out of their **sockets."** She compared his face to the creation of a master makeup artist on **the set** of a *science* fiction movie.

Shaking nervously, **Mrs.** Clark tried to get Paul to climb into the back seat where he could **he** down and remain calm white she **drove** to *the* **nearest** hospital. Irene **thought** a wild beast, or perhaps a poisonous snake, had attacked **her** husband, instead of complying with her wishes, Paul **pushed** her aside with a "violent shove" that **sent** her sprawling against the opposite **door.**

Paul slid into the driver's seat and grabbed the steering wheel in a rage. "Supposedly I was talking incoherently, as if in a trance." When he gripped the wheel, it bent **out of** *shape like it* **was** made of **putty.**

Within a minute of this remarkable feat—one that would require extraordinary strength—Pauf stumped against the dashboard, with his eyes shut and his **forehead dripping perspiration.**

To Paul. it was all a dream, "I don't remember a damn thing after leaving the car and hearing the hypnotic sounding voice and seeing the lighted object If it wasn't for the steering wheel being twisted, I'd say my wife probably made up the whole crazy story." Since his second meeting with a UFO **Paul** feels more strongly than ever he is being influenced by alien beings. Since his last encounter with ufonauts, Paul Clark's life has stabilized somewhat. He has learned to cope with **the** "force" trying **to** control him. At this time, this "average student" is **on** the threshold of obtaining a **degree** in electrical engineering!

While Paul's narrative is intriguing in itself, Clark is **by** no means the only person to have **been selected** to receive such "special" treatment at **the hands** of ufonauts. Even high-ranking government officials have received "communications" and been "manipulated."

Somewhere in a locked file cabinet, hidden in some **obscure** office in the Pentagon, is a two-inch-thick file that contains perhaps the best-documented UFO possession **case of** the decade. The episode actually involves an Air Force officer, the Office of Naval Intelligence, and the CIA.

Until just a few months ago, this manila fodder was closely guarded—stamped "Top Secret." It's **contents** were finally leaked to an enterprising scriptwriter, **Robert Emenegger,** on assignment from Sandier Institutional Films, producers of a syndicated **documentary on UFOs.** The source of this "leak" was, surprisingly enough. Lt. Col. Robert **Friend,** U S.A.F., **former** head of **Project** Blue Book and well-known UFO debunker for the government.

New retired, Friend **seems** to have done an "about-face" on the question of UFOs. Not only does he think they exist, but **he also seems** to give serious **consideration** to the even **more puzzling** UFO contactee cases.

A most revealing interview **with** Friend appears in the book, *UFOs, Past,* Present and Future. In this interview, the former Blue Book spokesman describes a case which contains all the typical elements of a **"UFO possession."**

While head of the Air Force's UFO project, Friend says he was informed as a "matter of courtesy" that a well respected Rear Admiral was especially interested in a woman living in Maine who **claimed** to be receiving highly advanced and technologically correct information from extraterrestrial **beings** These entities were said to contact her while she sat in a trance-like state. The admiral, with the approval of the Air Force, sent **two** of his **most** responsible and **trusted** men to investigate.

Relaxing **in** a chair **before** them, the **woman** expressed her willingness to answer any questions they **might** have. At **this** point, she no longer seemed to have control of her physical self. Her body was **ostensibly** "taken over" by members of an intergalactic organization referred to as the "Universal Assedation of Planets."

A few minutes into this unprecedented "conversation," one of the officers present, a Navy commander, was told that further answers would be directed through *him.* The officer was instructed to hold a pen lying on a nearby table. The "spacemen" then took control of his hand and proceeded to respond to questions through a *process* known in parapsychological circles as "automatic writing."

Colonel Friend **notes** that news of **this** highly provocative **experiment** reached Washington almost before the men returned. Top officials at the Central Intelligence Agency also heard **about the episode and demanded to** know more. It was Friend's duty to find out what he could.

(Continued'

There were giants in the Earth in those days. Men of Steel. Super Heroes Possessing Great Powers. It is an era bygone but not forgotten! Left to Right: "Sir" Timothy Green Beckley (knighted by the Earl of Clancarty). The Honorable Dr. Frank E Stranges. The Elegant Mr John A Keel, and **the "Big Daddy" of pop UFO culture, the late Gray Barker. (From the Tim Beckley Library)**

★ UFO REPORT

77

(Continued from page 58)

"It was in 1959," he told researcher scriptwriter Emenegger, "when I was invited to attend a meeting in the security section of a government building in Washington. I was briefed on an experiment that had been conducted with this same Naval commander before a group of CIA members and military personnel. It was described how, after going into a trance, the commander contacted a supposed extraterrestrial being. Several questions were put to him, and answers came back such as: 'Do you favor any government group or race?' Both were 'No.' 'Can we see a spaceship?' The commander, still in a trance, told the group to go to the window and they'd have proof. The group went to the window, where they supposedly observed a UFO. I was told that when a call was made for a radar confirmation, the tower reported that that particular Quadrant of the sky was blanked out on radar at that time."

Friend says that after being briefed on all the details he asked if the officer could attempt a contact for him personally. While he watched, the commander went into a deep trance.

"Questions were put to him, and he printed the answers in rather large letters, using rapid but jerky motions very unlike fits natural handwriting. During the course of the questioning, we were told the names of some of the so-called extraterrestrials. One was 'Crill,' another 'Alomar,' and another 'Affa,' purportedly from the planet Uranus."

The former head of Blue Book admits that he was puzzled. "All those involved were found to be highly credible and responsible professional government men." After turning in his report, Friend was told by a superior to forget the entire affair. He was informed that the CIA was making their own study, and therefore the Air Force had been instructed to "lay off."

What was his reaction to this command? As might be expected, it was a military one. "Well, when a general tells a colonel to forget it—you forget it!" Friend later discovered that every witness present in that government office on the day the Naval officer went into a trance was relocated or transferred to other duty. "To this day," concludes the ex-Air Force officer, "it's an unresolved incident to me. I just don't know what to make of it . . . It seems totally unique in all my experience with investigations of UFOs."

Had he cooperated to any degree with civilians, Colonel Friend probably wouldn't have been so awed with this case. For many years private organizations have patiently gathered and investigated similar cases. Indeed, whole

sects have been founded, based on similar "trance" messages.

There are hundreds of so-called "mental contactees" who claim to receive information and data of a highly advanced scientific and philosophical nature. in fad, during the 1950s and 60s, this method of communicating with UFO occupants (better known as 'channeling") became so popular that entities calling themselves "Asthar," 'Agar," and "Monka" were heard from daily, somewhere in the world. As far back as the 1920s, the "I AM" religious movement gathered a tremendous number of supporters. Their entire doctrine was derived from messages purportedly delivered through their leader from a "higher" source. And even earlier, around the turn of the century, Madame Blavatsky founded the Theosophical Society. Her "guide" was a long-deceased Tibetan master. Today, Madame Blavatsky might find that her white-robed monk was a silvery-garbed "Venusian - The "source" appears to be the same; only the "messengers" have changed!

There is no doubt that this phenomenon is widespread and it is by no means limited to the U.S. Cases of mind-altering UFO possession seem to be occurring on a global scale and at an alarming rate. There have been reports of entire towns being placed under a strange "spell," with the simultaneous appearance of flying saucers in the area.

A large-scale attempt to invade and seize the minds of human beings occurred on Apr. 29, 1967, when a coastal village on the outskirts of Rio de Janeiro became the target of a strange aerial visitor.

For approximately one hour on that day, the hundreds of citizens of Barra de Tijuca. Brazil, were literally forced into establishing contact with an unearthly intelligence, which quickly subdued every single person in town.

The series of disturbing events began at noon. when an emergency telephone call reached Or. Jeronemo Rodrigues Morales, chief physician at Barra de Tijuca's general hospital.

An excited voice explained how a man in his late 60s had fatten unconscious on the beach near town. The caller seemed alarmed because he felt certain the man had suffered a heart attack.

Apologizing to his waiting patients, Dr. Morales immediately drove to the scene. Upon arriving he found the man brushing sand from his clothes. He was standing and quietly talking to a crowd of people who had gathered to offer help. "I was merely walking about the sand dunes," the man explained. "I had been watching the birds high above the water, when suddenly I blacked out."

An on-the-spot examination, conducted in the hospital's old ambulance, ruled out the possibility of a heart attack and Dr. Morales decided that the man had suffered a mild case of sunstroke.

Knowing he was needed back at the hospital, the physician headed back to his waiting patients. Within minutes, however, the ambulance's shortwave radio blurted out the disturbing news that a fisherman had been discovered in shallow water beneath a nearby bridge, and was said to be trembling from shock.

Dr. Morales quickly drove to the area and arrived just in time to see the "stricken" fisherman casually drying himself off, and inquiring what all the excitement was about.

When the doctor explained that he had blacked out, the man seemed insulted. "I'm not sick," he argued, "I feel perfectly well." He assured Dr. Morales that he had been tossing his nets into these waters every day for 20 years without any difficulty, and would do so for 20 more.

Within a short while. Dr. Morales received word of six other "stricken" individuals. All followed the identical pattern: people keeling over, then reviving themselves without aid, and, after a flurry of excitement vehemently insisting that "it was absolutely nothing."

The next episode, which occurred a little after one p.m., involved a young woman who had been innocently strolling along the beach with her three-year-old child at her side. Suddenly they both "passed out." Because of the child's age, Dr. Morales insisted the youngster be taken to the hospital for an extensive examination. The worried mother readily agreed.

While carrying the young boy into the emergency ward, Dr. Morales happened to glance skyward. High above, glistening in the sun, was a tremendous elongated object—a UFO. He watched as the shiny craft wobbled back and forth. It went through an entire series of gyrations. Several times it dropped lower in the sky, offering a better look at its metallic surface. Then, just as rapidly, it would dart back to its former position high in the clear blue sky.

During lunch, several other physicians and nurses on the hospital staff excitedly commented on their own sightings of a "cigar-shaped" craft which they had noticed suspended over the town that day since noon.

Coincidental? Most unlikely. Three days later, the same craft appeared again. Once more, a number of people dropped unconscious to the ground. During these two days, many other individuals were treated at the hospital for headaches and dizziness, no rational cause being found for their illness. From the evidence we have uncovered, the cause seems apparent.

Individuals in the grips of UFO possession often behave irrationally and have even been known to commit criminal acts.

Former NASA Mars mapping expert, Dr. Jacques Vallee, in his third book, *Passport to Magonia*, writes of a chilling account of UFO possession that occurred behind the Iron Curtain. "In the Soviet Union," Vallee reports, "not very long ago. an eminent scientist in the field of plasma research died under suspicious circumstances — he was murdered by a mentally disturbed woman who pushed him into the path of a train which was speeding into a Moscow subway station. The accused claimed that a 'voice' from space had instructed her *to* kill *this* particular man, and she felt unable to resist the order."

Furthermore. the French-born scientist says he has heard from "trustworthy sources" that Russian criminologists are disturbed about the recent increase in cases of this nature. "Quite often," Vallee maintains. "mentally unstable people are known to run wildly across a street. protesting they are being pursued by *Martians*, but the present wave of mental troubles is an aspect of the UFO problem that deserves special attention … " We have long known that UFOs show no political preferences or respect for national boundaries. Aggressive acts have been committed worldwide by individuals who insist that they are in contact with extraterrestrials. Once contact has been established, they *are* doomed to do what is asked; whether they approve *or* not!

Here in the U.S., Brad Steiger, a respected former English professor turned author and parapsychologist, has been diligently gathering volumes of pertinent date. in the last few years, he has managed *to* amass an impressive collection of material dealing with the many peculiar side effects experienced by flying saucer eyewitnesses He has gathered statistics on all sorts of "UFO oddities." including: episodes involving instantaneous teleportation of observers; cases of enhanced psychic abilities; and information pertaining to the bane of all UFO researchers—the Men in Black. These areas all contain elements of the UFO possession syndrome.

A short time ago, Brad told me he had talked to a young serviceman who complained of hearing "beeps" inside his head. The loud and annoying noise began immediately after a UFO flew directly over him. Steiger was *further* convinced of the man's credibility because, "as another researcher and I sat with the young man in a motel room

hundreds *of* miles away from my home, I heard him describe every room in my house and correctly identify objects within each room."

Another victim of UFO possession, a veteran of WW II, told Steiger how he was walking up a street in Italy one night shortly after the Allied occupation, when he heard a buzzing noise above *him*. The next thing he knew, *he was in northern France.* Not only had he traveled by some unknown means, but four months *had elapsed of which he had no recall.* As if to compensate for the loss of time, however, the soldier found he had suddenly developed clairvoyant abilities, which he did not posseas before the incident occurred. "Today, tie lives in a large midwestern city," Steiger said. "more disturbed than *dated* by his 'gift' from unknown donors."

In the July 1975, issue of Probe the Unknown magazine. Steiger talked about the morbid experience of a young married couple, Sam and Mary, who, in their spare time, had been attempting to track down and verify sightings of humanoid creatures made in their home state. They made it a regular policy to notify Brad of their individual findings.

One evening, after returning home from an interview with the witnesses of a humanoid sighting, Mary began feeling strange. A terrific headache sent her off to bed early. Once asleep, she was visited in her dreams by "grotesque entities," who told tier that they wanted her, and that she must leave her husband. They threatened violence if she did not obey. in subsequent "dreams," the confused woman saw "grim, dark-complexioned men beat Sam *to* death." Here, again, UFO researchers have noted many similar instances, where space entities have shown they are able to manipulate the dreams of earthlings. Their "hold," once obtained, is enormous.

Mary's experience didn't end there, however, and the torment continued, becoming more oppressive with each day. Shortly afterwards, her telephone became—as Steiger so aptly phrased it—"an instrument of fear." Mary was awakened late one night, in the middle of one of *her* bizarre nightmares, by the ringing of the phone. Answering, she heard a cold. calculating voice ask in a mechanical, 'Wow are you ready to *come* over to our side?"

According to Steiger, Mary was later visited by a man who appeared at her front door, flashing impressive-looking telephone company credentials He was anxious to know about her "problems." Sam later *checked* the man's papers and found his "impressive cre-

dentials" to be fakes. The man didn't work for the phone company—in any capacity.

Immediately following the stranger's appearance, Mary began falling into deep. coma-like trances. These trances were usually prefaced "by a headache, a pain in the back of her neck, then a lapse of consciousness," and she seemed powerless to prevent their occurrence.

Needing assistance, the young couple contacted Steiger. He suggested they minimize the situation in their minds. "The important thing is not to play their game," the author warned. "In many ways, their effect [that of the MIB] is like an echo. Cry out in fear, and they'll give *you* good reason to fear them." They took Steiger's advice and were greatly relieved to find that the phenomena came to an abrupt halt.

Sam and Mary were left in peace— but other individuals have not been set free so easily.

Take the case of Hans Lauritzen. A trained engineer, *Hans* is not the type of person to be easily frightened or duped. Writing from his home in Copenhagen, Denmark, this reliable UFO witness filled me in on the details of his Dec. 7. 1967, encounter with two disc-shaped craft. "At the time, I was on a walking *tour* with tour friends in a wooded area not far from Hareskoven. Because *of* a severe case of hepatitis, I found it difficult to keep up the brisk pace of my associates. I had to stop several times, because I was so tired. At that time my liver was extremely distended."

As the group passed a clearing, Lauritzen asked his friends if he might rest a few minutes. They, of *course*, said it was O.K. "Suddenly, we all saw two great yellow globes about 50 yards from where we were standing. For some reason, at this point I asked if I could walk into the woods for 10 minutes. My friends agreed. I had no intention of walking toward the UFOs. as we could riot see them any more. I seemed to be walking in a trance—like one who is being guided, I just walked. Then, I felt the presence of something above, but could not see anything."

At this point, Hans began to feel a throbbing pressure in his head, which seemed to bring on a telepathic conversation with whomever was "guiding" him. They told me that I should give—and not *receive*. And that I should not be alone. And they said, 'You are only standing here by the help of your friends.' Then, whoever was doing the talking seemed surprised and said, 'This is the first time.' I don't know exactly what he was referring to, except that he probably meant that it was the

TRENTONIAN
Trenton, NJ
circa 1968(?)

Across the Board

Claims UFOs Have Bases on Earth

By Emil Slaboda
Wire News Editor

There's a full page cartoon in the latest issue of "The New Yorker" magazine that depicts a flying saucer shooting off *pin-wheels* and Roman candles—the whole bit. It shows a visibly excited housewife running *into* the kitchen from the bade yard, evidently to make a telephone call to the *Air* Force *and* report the space *visitor.* .

Cairo, *cool* and collected, her husband says to her: "Why bother? They'll *only* tell you it's marsh gas

It broke me up along with several other staffers. But the sad *tad is* that it has probably occurred many, many times.

What with all the adverse publicity and ridicule that occompanies many sightings, it's understandable that many of our citizens prefer to keep their sightings a secret. Caught . off guard, these "pillars of society" sometimes reveal their unique experiences many months, and sometimes years, after.

* * *

Luckily, there are sincere, honest individuals who, with a passion, want to unravel the mystery. *So they spend a* lot of time (and money) seeking out the sightings, the witnesses and related evidence hoping the pieces of the puzzle will resolve themselves into *a* whole.

Such a person is Timothy Green Beckley, director of the "Interplanetary News Service," with its headquarters to New Brunswick.

Beckley, along with a highly expert group of associates, has come up with a possible answer to the origin of the UFOs

'If we admit the *possibility* that these objects are real and probably from outside the range of this *planet*," Beckley writes, 'then you must also admit that they have bases somewhere within easy reach of their target, the earth."

Where are the bases? Beckley's theory is two-fold. First he takes aim on our nearest neighbor, the moon. "For many centuries mysterious lights and objects have been reported in the vicinity of the moon. On July 29, 1953, the late John O'Neil saw a strange phenomenon on the moon. He described it as a bridge at least 12 miles in length stretching in a perfectly straight line across a crater situated in Mars Crisium. Other astronomers reported the same thing- Other manifestations on the moon include strange lights of red, green and orange colors, dust clouds and shadows of unknown origin also have been observed."

Beckley adds that if space visitors were to pick bases on planet earth, "It is only logical that they would go out of their way to avoid highly populated areas. It *is* my belief," he continues, "backed up by many startling, but factual incidents, that the UFOs have bases both in the Antarctic region of our planet and in undersea hangars."

pointing out that for many years UFO reports have been on the rise in the Antarctic' area, Beckley added, "Just recently a report from two Argentine bases confirmed by British and Chilean scientists of the appearance July 3, 1965, of an unusual celestial body. The object was photographed and said to be shaped like a double, convex lens."

The UFO made no noise and moved rapidly eastward. He adds *that* an earlier report from another British base said the craft caused geomagnetic instruments to go wild-

* * *

Beckley explains that earthbound saucers could hide very easily in undersea hangars. "Throughout history," he added, "ship crews have told of *seeing* strange pinwheels of light and disk-shaped objects drifting along the bottom of the water. We have a number of reports which would seem to indicate that these mysterious underwater UFOs have crashed into our sea-going vessels,"

In *any* event, if Beckley's theories have aroused your interest, you'll have a chance to hear him expound his views on the flying-saucer enigma over Station WTTM on May 12. He just *may* be site to change your thinking on the matter.

trance state much of *the time,* "I just had *to* follow whoever was pulling me strings. Afterwards, I became extremely frightened as to what might be going on. I began to imagine all sorts of weird things!"

As it was, this "feeling" began to spread throughout fits entire nervous system. After severs! months, pain would frequently shoot through his arms. chest, back, and neck "I had never experienced such strong pains before in all my life," Hans declared. Gradually, however, the effects of the pain began to subside.

Then Lauritzen found that he was frequently becoming overwhelmed by the most pleasurable states of mind. "it was so wonderful," he stated, *"that* it cannot be described," On other occa-

sions, the contactee said he felt a strong fear and anxiety, so much *so* that he *was* afraid to *leave* his apartment. "I *went* through periods of extreme sorrow, depression, and desperation. I have never *experienced such* severe mental suffering in all *my* life."

*

At was at this point that he began to realize he no longer had any free will to Slink and believe as he wished. "I would converse with people, voicing opinions on a wide range of topics. *Later.* I discovered that whatever I had heard, I had to believe and act accordingly. Of course this created great confusion. Strange thoughts *started* to come into *focus.* I knew they did not originate inside me because they were often of a very negative and destructive character. It was not possible for *me* to *stop* these thoughts or overpower *them.* although I tried. . . believe me, I tried!"

Hans said that he Had never before thought it possible that *such* a chaotic State of affairs could possibly exist in one person's mind!

Eight years have since passed and Hans finds himself once again leading a normal existence. When asked for his comments on the entire episode, he replied, "It has been the most wonderful and pleasurable experience of *my* entire life. On the other hand, it has also been the *most* painful. horrible, thing

that has ever happened to me. Before. I had a bad liver. *Now.* I am strong and healthy *again,* I am most thankful to the UFOs for having cured my otherwise chronic hepatitis, without which I would never have been able to resume my work and *other* normal activities."

Obviously both *positive* and negative factors have been experienced fay those who have come within *close* range of these strange craft.

Realizing that something most peculiar is manifesting itself, we are still left with a gnawing question: Is an invasion force poised at our atmospheric doorstep? And *if* so, is their proposed takeover being done for our *own* welfare, or for some as yet unknown, and perhaps *sinister,* reason?

---

first time they had met anyone quite bke myself. They told me that I had a very strong power, and that it would soon become even stronger." Hans asked the invisible voice "to make it so this power could not be misused-"

With this final request, the conversation ended. For some time afterwards, Harm continued to walk *in* a trance. Eventually, he found himself at the place where he had first seen the yellow globes. "There was an open area which I decided to cross. I don't remember walking across it. All at a sudden, I heard my friends calling for me. I looked at my watch and saw that more than an hour had elapsed." Returning to his friends. Hans was told that they had been searching for him during this period. "They thought that I had gotten lost."

r a n g e things then started to happen. Hans found himself *running* to their parked automobile. Only an hour

before, he had barely been able to walk because of his liver condition. "I realized that I had been cured of my otherwise chronic hepatitis. On my next visit to the clinic, the doctors told me that my liver had returned to its normal size. Blood tests showed *that* it was functioning as any healthy liver should!" The medical experts could not offer any explanation for the change in Hans Lauritzen's physical condition. "I didn't dare tell them about my contact," he admitted.

The oddest part of his story remains to be told. Soon after the experience. the Danish engineer found his entire life and personality beginning to change. "I felt something spreading inside my body. Something was actually moving up along my spine from my lower back to the neck and to the back of my head. This movement was accompanied by a pleasurable feeling. It made me stand up and make strange movements and turns." He explained that he was in a

Logically, we would like to believe that the metallic ships described eons ago by the pharaohs as "celestial sun discs." are manned by a super-race of benevolent "space brothers," who harbor genuine concern *for* our world. But, then again, is this really the case? Are we actually being aided in our moment of need by "interplanetary wise men," or is *some* devious scheme unfolding as we ponder (his very question? Could it be that an interplanetary battle is being waged by rival starmen to gain control of Homo Sapiens? Maybe, as some outspoken researchers have stated, a "war of the worlds" is being waged, not here on the physical plane, but in some other dimension.

'Veteran investigators of the paranormal will undoubtedly recognize that attemps to gain mastery over the human race are nothing new. As intriguing *as* cases of UFO possession may be, a direct comparison can easily be found in the lore of the occult. Indeed, spirit and demonic possession has been written about for centuries. it is almost a commonplace phenomenon in theological and psychic circles. Only *recently*, because of the immense popularity of the motion picture The *Exorcist*, has the subject *come* to the attention of the general public. Many moviegoers found this picture uncomfortably realistic.

Like the hideous *demons* of old, it would seem that at feast some UFOnauts have developed the ability to control certain individuls they have selected to do their bidding. Many times, I *have* sympathetically tooted on—much like the young priest *in The Exorcist*—as a UFO observer undergoes *a* dramatic charge in character and personality. It is uncanny—and difficult to rationally explain.

There is, however, another school of thought regarding *this* phenomena.

Individualssuch as Paul Clark, whose story we detailed earlier, insist that any direct manipulation of humans by space people is being done for our benefit.

"I've *been* led *to* believe," says Paul, "that there is a grand event slated to occur in the not too distant future. I have no idea when this event will transpire, or what it will consist of, but I *do* know that it will be earthshaking, and will affect almost everyone."

Another good example of what seems to be a "positive" case of UFO possession, involves none other than Uri Geller, the extraordinary psychic. Reportedly, he is able to accomplish a variety of astonishing feats, including the bending of metal by means of psychokinesis; interfering with, and rendering inoperable, various electrical and mechanical devices: and beaming in on the telepathic thoughts of others. Geller has recently been linked with extraterrestrials. He openly acknow-[edges that his powers originate from a source "outside" himself.

Dr. Andrija Puharich, the man responsible for bringing *Uri to* this country several years ago, admits that his gifted protege is an agent for inhabitants of a

zone. All the remarkable things that go on around Uri are, he says, directed by *these* "solar beings."

Though it has a definite Space Age twist, Uri's biography contains aft the ingredients found in a suspenseful occult or gothic novel. During the occasions *he* slips into a hypnotic trance, Uri's features are said to change. In addition, a strange voice—definitely not his own—is heard from the psychic's mouth. Regaining consciousness. Uri has; no recollection of what has transpired. And although Puharich has attempted to record these "foreign" tongues for posterity, he has constantly run into problems. When the tape is replayed, it is frequently blank. Other times, the cassette itself will vanish. *right out of the recorder?*

Both Uri Geller and Paul Clark are adamant that there is a specific reason why they have been "railed" to represent this unearthly power- They agree that some monumental even! is stated

to happen within a short *time*, and it's essential we be fully prepared for it.

Geller and Clark also agree that the ufonauts are using them *for* the good of Mankind. We are told that they have a definitive plan, and have simply decided *to* utilize human *agents to get the* job done faster,

Whatever the answers might tie, an exhaustive study of the UFO puzzle shows "higher powers" are at play. They are attempting *to* systematically guide or influence our destiny. A sufficient number of strange occurrences have been reported. which prove beyond a reasonable doubt, *that at* least *some of* these "other-world travelers" are *out* to control the course *of* our civilization—*if not by physical force then by the direct manipulation of human* minds! ★

Tucson, Sunday. September 4, 1983

Daily Star

35 gather in Safford to share tales of unearthly 'encounters'

By Don Dale
The Arizona Daily Star

SAFFORD — Cosmic communication or simple whirlwind, whatever it was, the spinning swirl of water on tiny Dankworth Lake yesterday lasted for several minutes, creating a whirlpool of whitecaps and shaking the spellbound UFO conventioneers.

"That's a real UFO." said one, who advised using infrared photography to capture its image.

"It could come right up out of there," another said of the alleged unidentified flying object.

"I have one (spaceship) that's been assigned to me," said a woman who claimed she has been in communication with a vehicle from Jupiter.

Thirty-five people from all over the country who say they have been contacted by aliens shared their tales yesterday.

The whirlpool capped the first day of the second annual convention organized by UFO Contact Center International.

"The true contactees get to the point where they have to talk to someone, want to get it off their chests," said Dan Edwards. He and his wife. Aileen, both of whom claim contact with aliens, organized the convention (or that reason.

The two are directors of UFO Contact Center International, based in Mesa. One of "hundreds" of UFO-related groups worldwide, it specializes in gathering information on alleged personal contacts with alien crafts or beings, Edwards said.

(Scientists who have extensively investigated) reports of visits to Earth by extraterrestrial beings and vehicles say no evidence exists that any such visits have ever occurred.)

The convention, which continues today and tomorrow at this state-owned lake on Arizona 666 south of Safford, features speakers such as Tim Courtney of Phoenix and Tim Beckley of New York City. But file crux of the meeting is the average "contactee" with an experience to share.

Take Helene, of the Safford area, for example. She does not want her name made public, because UFO contactees can be harassed as heretics or kooks.

In 1976, when Helene was living in British Columbia, she was dying of pancreatic cancer, she said. But a couple of months before the date doctors predicted she would die, a voice called her out of bed, out of her house and into a clearing several miles away, she claimed. There she saw a brilliant light and a spacecraft, she slid.

"From the center of this large craft came a cylinder of light, us! in this cylinder these two beings came down," Helene aid. "They were small humanoids," wearing "tight-fitting. metallic-looking suits."

They floated her up to the ship, where another being used a number of strange instruments to cure her can-

cer, she said. The reason, they told her, was that they might need her help in the future, she said.

She showed a small, circular scar on her stomach that she said was left by one of the instruments.

Healthy now, Helene has become active in the contact group and claims to be able to translate unearthly symbols that were placed in her mind as a child. They tell how to survive what she said is the coming destruction of the Earth and include map coordinates of "safe areas."

Much of Arizona, incidentally, is a "safe area," she said.

Or take Monique Shahrivar of San Clemente, Calif., who said she has "experienced telepathy" and seen what she believed were alien beings.

Or take Courtney, one of the speakers, an ordinary-seeming builder and house-designer from Phoenix who said his life has changed "utterly" after what he believes was a close encounter with extraterrestrial beings on the Beeline Highway south of Payson.

Or take Beckley, called "Mr. UFO" by the contactees because of his expertise and many books on the subject. Now the editor of UFO Review, Beckley said his interest was piqued at the age of 10 when he sighted two chandelier-like images that he thinks were spacecraft

"This is something that is happening all over the world," Beckley said. He has information on "up to 2,000 contacts," and the stories "keep repeating themselves over and over again."

Beckley said two probable reasons for these contacts are the aliens' concern that humans may destroy themselves, and the creating of a "spiritual awareness" among the contactees.

"Maybe the god Moses talked to is part of the same thing these people are communicating with," Beckley said.

Edwards said his "research" indicates there are many people who have had contact with aliens but have no knowledge of the experience. They need help bringing their knowledge to a conscious level, he said.

Some of the symptoms of contacts, he said, are pains in the shoulder, back or knee; crying for no reason; surges in so-called ESP ability; buzzing or ringing in the ear; close brushes with death; and an affinity with eagles.

"We've noticed that a lot of the contactees are of Jewish or Indian heritage," Edwards said.

As for those who seem to actually believe they have had contact with extraterrestrials, tears may well up in their eyes as they relate their alleged experiences.

Edwards said his group is needed to give those people an outlet.

"We're contacts helping contacts," Edwards said, inviting people to write to him at P.O. Box 873, Mesa 85201.

THE TOWN HAUNTED BY

FLYING SAUCERS

By **Arthur** Shuttlewood as fold to Timothy Green Beckley

On almost any clear night you can gaze up at the sky above Warminster, England, and become part of a mystery which has made this otherwise tranquil locate one of the strangest places on Earth.

As this is being written, on the average of two UFO reports are brought to my attention every week. As a result, over the last nine years, I have seen myself slowly change from that of a skeptical chief reporter and feature editor of the Warminster Journal—a highly respected newspaper—to an individual whose consciousness has expanded to encompass previously unimaginable areas.

During my on-the-spot studies I have come across ample evidence to prove that this community has been (and still is) playing host to an unprecedented armada of unexplainable aerial and ground level phenomena which include:

* Disturbing sounds that fill the air with a thunderous roar:
* Unexplained deaths of small animals and birds:
* Strange solid-looking craft that dematerialize in plain view of confused witnesses:
* Objects disappearing that belong to UFO observers; and
* Accounts of actual meetings with UFO-nauts.

The first inkling of anything "uncanny" about Warminster came at six a.m. on Christmas morning. 1964. At that time a middle-aged woman was forcibly tossed about and then thrown' violently to the ground by an invisible shock wave which originated a short distance above her.

Weird crackling noises paralyzed Mrs. Marjorie Bye while she was on her way to services at Christ Church. Mrs. Bye told me later that as she walked along the cobblestone streets. a high-pitched hum began to fill the air. It sounded to her as if a jet plane was about to take off from an unseen runway several feet from where she stood riveted to the ground. As the noise grew progressively louder, a powerful force pulled her legs out from under

her and toppled the crying woman to the pavement.

Shock waves of an unknown magnitude continued to pound at her head. neck, and shoulders that numbed her completely. Helpless, she was pinned down to the ground by fingers of sound that left her weak and jelly-legged, so that even when "it" passed she had great difficulty reaching the church

AS the precise moment at the strange attack upon Mrs. Bye. the stage was being set for Warminster's postmaster to undergo a similar horrifying experience.

Working late the previous night, Roger Rump did not expect such an early call oo Christmas morning. This credible—and frightened—participant in the early stages of the Warminster UFO story told me he was jerked out of a sound sleep by 2

pounding on the roof of his home which is only a short distance from Christ Church.

"There was this terrific clatter," Mr. Rump tole! me, "as though the tiles on the roof were being rattled about and plucked off by some superhuman arm. This was followed by a scrambling sound. as if they were being hurriedly replaced." Roger Rump said that he then sat "boil upright" in bed and listened carefully, noting that on top of all this noise, he could hear a loud humming draw.

He added that it seemed as though all the tiles were being roughly manhandled and jostled together before being thrust into their respective niches again. Upon inspection, none of She tiles were chipped or damaged anti the roofing was intact.

A terrified Mildred Head, wife of an ex-policeman and once a seamstress at

Since *1964, the* peaceful **town** of **Warminster, England,** has literally been overwhelmed by **visits** from unidentified flying objects. **Does** some **strange vortex** *exist here* which **acts as a cosmic** beacon, beckoning **UFOs** earthward?

Warminster Hospital sat **quiet** and **shaker,** *as* she told **me** *how* **she** was *awakened* at her **home** *at* 1:25 a.m. on Christmas morning. "Our **ceiling came alive** *with* **strange sounds** that **lashed** the **roof,"** she said. "It was **as** if prickly **holly bushes** were **being** pulled **across** *it.* or like **a ca?** sharpening its claws. *it* ended with a noise I **can** only describe **as** giant **hailstones** pelting **down** with all their might."

Most of these aerial **"attacks"—there** were about **20—took place** *in* the southern **sector** of town, and were apparently **responsible** for *the* death of small *creatures* and birds who were **collapsing** without any apparent reason.

During this period, reports came in—**sometimes** as many as **three or four a day—of** dead mice found *in* the gardens of **"affected"** *homes.* Their bodies were **covered** with **burn** marks, *and* many holes perforated their skins.

During the **first few months of** 1965, **household pets** were *adversely* **affected by** the **weird rooftop sounds.** Dogs **crawled** into **kennels, under** tables *or* kitchen **sinks, barking** *and* **whimpering,** when **homes** were **attacked by** the **unknown noises.** *Cats* arched their backs. *fur* bristling, **as** they **twisted and turned** *in* rapid *circles* at the height of the *bizarre* **aerial** battering. Many **pets** *in* **these affected houses** were **sick** and **cringed** *in corners.* **One** *woman* from **Westbury Road** openly **cried** when **she** recalled her **pet's** ordeal. In an **upstairs-** room her faithful cat "Budgie" lay stiff-legged *in death* after a

roof **bombardment. The shock had paralyzed** it!

A *flock* **of** pigeons were killed **in** flight after tangling with the **"Thing" (as** our **intruder** came to be **known).** They came **into** fatal contact with **deadly sound beams** in the **woods** near Crockerton, *in* **February** 1965. Stiff-winged, they **plummeted** *to* the **ground** into a clearing on Longleat Estate belonging to the Marquis of Bath. **Two** *witnesses* **judged** that rigor **mortis** had *set* in instantaneously.

David Holton, a surgical chiropodist and naturalist, **told** me of another **surprising development** after having **examined two stricken pheasants shortly** after their **death fall.** The **two** birds were **found** *or,* his **estate** by *a* man noted for his **hunting** ability. The **shooting season** was over and his **wife** was surprised **to see** him walk **up** the **front steps** of their **large** house, carrying a **brace** of **lifeless** game birds. He was **unarmed** and she knew he had not shot them. **His** wife, a **local councilor, told** me he had **stumbled** upon the **dead** birds in **a** *thicket* **on** their spacious estate. **She wondered if they** had **been bludgeoned** to a **mangled** mass of **rigid** limbs and **fluttering** *feathers* by **jet aircraft crashing** the **sound barrier.** David **Holton told** me he **thought** the **birds were** killed by **sound waves of** an intensity **Earth creatures were** not **accustomed** *to.*

Following the initial **"attack"** of Warminster's "aerial **turbulence," my** office **phone was** kept busy by *dazed* residents **who** were **observing** all **types** of craft in the sky. "Flying trains" and "railway coaches" with glowing windows *were* said to be hurtling about in space.

In late May and early June of 1965, I *was* still laughing at such reports and *re*jecting them as too ridiculous and farfetched *for* publication in *the Warminster Journal.*

My skepticism had its first big challenge when similar sightings *started* cropping up in the neighboring counties of Weston, Siper Mare, and Cheltenham.

As far as I am concerned, the initial breakthrough came with the testimony of Kathleen Penton of Warminster on June 19th. She told about her sighting while seated in front of my desk. "It was *a* fantastic spectacle—so much so that *my* husband and daughter thought I was *go*ing crazy when I told them about *it* Safer. I was opening an upstairs 'window, as *it was* a stuffy night, when I saw this shining craft going along sideways in tire sky from right to left. It glided quite slowly in front *of* a fine *of* trees. Porthole-type windows ran along the whole length of the ship, which—to my eyes—was enormous. Its windows were lit up. the color of yellow flames in a coal fire.

"It *was* much like a railroad car," she added, "only with rounded ends. And it did not travel lengthwise, but was gently gliding sideways." Mrs. Penton's sighting, which lasted about five minutes, was confirmed by six local residents who *tele*phoned the newspaper within a matter of a few hours. And all their observations tallied. I was admittedly puzzled and determined to find out what was behind this phenomenon.

News of the events at Warminster soon spread- Magazines and daily newspapers all over Britain began featuring stories on what was happening in our community. Unfortunately, in many *instances* they gave the erroneous impression that our *Citizens* were cowering in panic, trying to shield their eyes and ears from this unknown terror.

TV and radio coverage soon reached an all-time *high* and in August 1965, even the staunchly conservative British Broadcasting Company sent *a* camera crew *to* record the testimony of anyone who would step forward and relate their experiences.

Rachel Atwill, *the* attractive wife of a *pi*tot, did exactly this. In front of *a* BBC commentator *Mrs. Atill* told how she had both heard harsh grating sounds and saw *what was* causing *it.* Her traumatic experience took place at approximately 3:45 a.m. on Tuesday, August 10th, when she was awakened *by a* "terrible noise" that caused *the* bed and floor to quake. "I went to the bedroom window and looked out," she said, "and between *the two* bungalows opposite us, about 200 yards above the range of hills beyond, I saw a bright object like a massive *star.* I have never believed in flying saucer stories, but I cannot describe this as being anything else. What I witnessed was definitely domed on top and was huge in size, an unwinking light of great brilliance!"

Rachel Atwill said that she *was* not overly frightened by this "thing" but was terribly shaken by the awful noise that came from it.

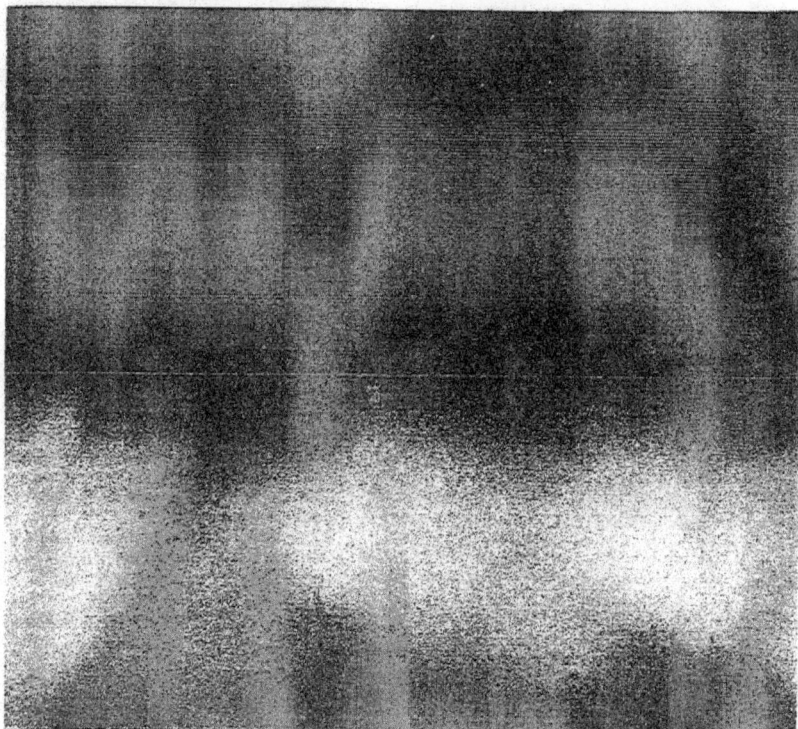

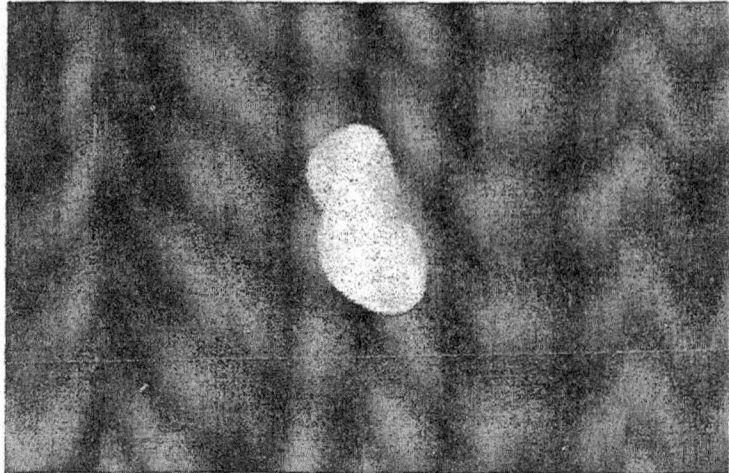

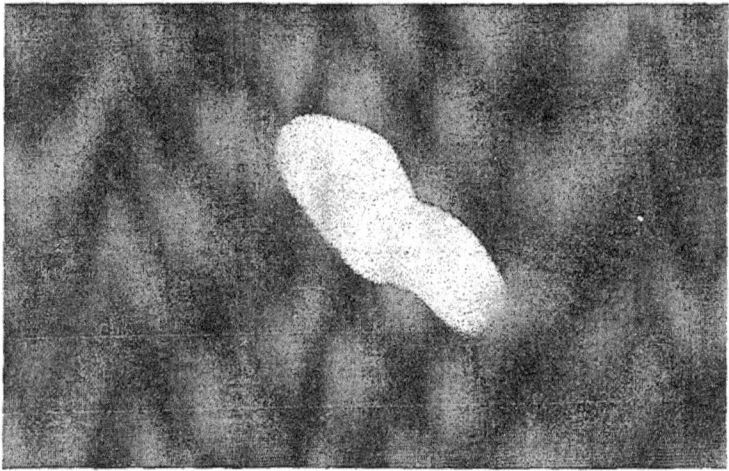

After a while the horrible humming di-minished, and finally the noise stopped altogether."The entire episode lasted for *25 minutes."* she said. "The noise was most upsetting . . . I felt as if there was *a* tight band of steel around my forehead *. . . a pounding and* hammering *at* my eardrums. I drank some *brandy after-wards;* I was dreadfully cold and could not stop trembling. Then I filled two hot water bottles and went to bed. The *strange* thing was," Rachel Atwill concluded. "that not one of my neighbors on this private estate saw or heard anything unusual,"

After word leaked out about what was happening in Warminster, we found our-selves plagued by people from around the world, who came to see what was W-ing place for themselves. The curious set up camp for as long as a week at a time, or until they were satisfied *that what they* had read was not some concocted *tale* created by an over imaginative journalist.

On many occasions I was among the skywatching groups when something definitely not of earthly origin was spotted moving across the horizon. Because of the obvious importance of the situation at Warminster, we often invited government and military officials to check out the situation for themselves. In most cases we were politely, but firmly, informed that a natural solution could *be* found *for* what we had seen. *But* despite this negative at-titude, the Defense Minister would never deny specific *cases!*

Given patience, no sincere investigator ever leaves Warminster without visual confirmation of otherworldly contacts. Around Warminster, extending in a com-plete circle are a number of key observa-tion sites from where UFOs can be readily watched performing their aerial acrobat-ics. The names *given* these select vantage points—Heaven's Gate. Lord's *Hill,* Ja-cob's Ladder, Starr Hill, and *Cradle Hill*—would seem to imply that previous cultures that settled nearby and gave these sites *their* names, were familiar with this locale's extraordinary contribution to extraterrestrial (or interdimensional) rela-tions.

Actually Warminster **is steeped** *in enigmas—both* **modern and** ancient. *The* strategically placed rural and peaceful community of ·14,000 is surrounded by prehistoric relics, stone monoliths, and ritualistic circles.

Stonehenge, a gigantic complex of rocks built by an unknown society, is lo-cated to the east of our town. Standing like a lone sentry on the Salisbury Plain, this *strange* structure was, according to one theory, built as an astronomical ob-servatory centuries ago. Several hundred years later, the Druids, *an* almost extinct religious sect, used the stone pillars of this *ancient* monolithic structure for equi-noctial religious gatherings and claimed it as their own work of art. Scholars, how-ever, tell us that Stonehenge's true origin dates back thousands of years!

Avebury, to the north, has a similar his-tory and like Stonehenge consists of a series of stones which supposedly had a mathematical purpose?

With so many mystical anomalies in the area, it should not come as a surprise that Warminster has become the modern foc-

al *point* for *visits from* flying saucers.

It *is* almost as if some strange *vortex* exists here which acts *as a* cosmic bea-con, beckoning UFOs earthward end wel-coming them *to* this serene terrestrial lo-cale.

Personally, I have had more than 800 *authentic* UFO sightings and have even had the opportunity to come in close con-tact with the occupants of these phantas-magorical objects.

The UFOs sighted over Warminster take on various shapes and come in a multitude of colors. They have been seen as: glowing spheres; luminous teardrops; ovoid jewels that range from bloodred rubies to winking diamonds of flashing Sight; from lustrous gray daytime pearls to fiery green emeralds that decorate the nighttime heavens.

Seen through a three-inch telescope at night, a hovering spacecraft is a glorious firefly of radiating colors, pulsating from the center to its outward edges in a con-tinuous stream of flickering and living energy patterns, with white. amber, green. red, and blue predominating.

The most common daylight variety is a gunmetal gray that sparkles with silvery majesty when sunrays strike it through passing fleecy clouds. Basic shapes *are* round, bell-like, and torpedo. Sizes vary, we find, as do conventional aircraft de-signed for different tasks and responsi-bilities on our own planet.

Longer and larger airships, which are not so common. are described by wit-nesses as aerial submarines—silver white "tighter-than-air" craft, *or* illuminated round-ended *railway* coaches in flight, complete with portholes along the *sides. The* majority of these phenomena *are most often* seen in the distance, and they're silent, as the smaller types in-variably are. unless they swoop close to the ground. Then a distinctive buzzing or droning sound is audible, which is similar to millions of swarming bees.

Especially active in the sky over Cradle *Hill.* is what I term "a thinking light" or "brain beacon."

These are simply tiny circular bright lights that change direction rapidly, sometimes at bewildering speeds. They are usually amber *or* white and sur-rounded by a *glowing* aura or halo along their *edges.* We *have* seen specimens of this type at night come toward us—and in

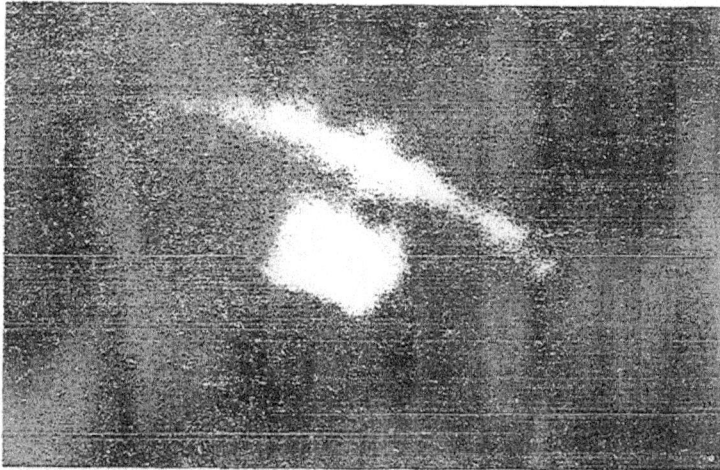

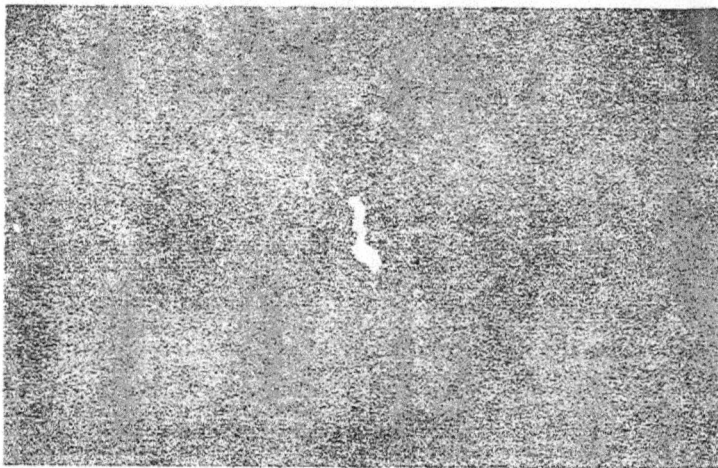

fact *go* right past us—at a distance of only four to six feet. They frequently emit a high, piercing, whistle-like noise, which *causes* ears *to* throb in pain.

We are confident that these *are* remote controlled mechanical and electrical robots. sent out from larger *craft* on close survey operations. These unmanned surveyors are *no* doubt a tremendous help *to* travelers farther aloft. who are anxious to learn all they can about us.

Except on Aug. 1, 1971 when we saw three silvery discs suddenly appear near ground level, daytime *UFOs* usually burst into view above the horizon. The sun glitaring over their metallic surfaces, they often make right-angled turns before suddenly stopping and hovering. Occasionally they make a fluttering descent much as an autumn leaf falls in a breeze

At night, *fast* moving UFOs can be seen coming in over the horizon, stopping at a point *over* nearly treetops, where they slow down and then erupt into brilliant red balls of light. Then they gradually change *to* an oval or ellipsoid shape *and* switch from red to gold or amber color,

In addition to the various types of flying saucers seen here. this area *has* been the

focal point of dozens of UFO-related incidents which defy logical understanding and explanation These events, we believe the evidence shows. are highly *indicative* of a continuing surveillance by beings who originate from some totally alien world.

For example, numerous UFO watchers at Cradle Hill and Starr Hill can confirm that articles have vanished from cars and vans, even when their doors have been locked—then miraculously turned up again. safe and sound, when drivers and passengers arrived home after a night of skywatching

George Woods. a Merseyside area resident, turned UFO enthusiast, has braved inclement weather several times to gaze at the Warminster phenomena After his first visit. Woods discovered that his tape recorder had *been* skillfully tampered with by someone or "something' unknown

A repair shop owner verified that Woods's machine had been *expertly* taken apart, with components laid out in *reverse* order on top of the mechanism. A silly prank? This is hardly possible, as no

Confirmed

one in the house had access to the equipment.

Another visitor bought a record while staying in Warminster for a few days. The disc was a new one, only recently released, and was in the locked car of one of the men skywatching at Starr Hill.

The driver, after locking the car, joined us at a gateway in front of an abandoned farm. Glancing back, he saw a shadowy form silhouetted against a car window. He counted the people at the gats and realized that the dark figure wasn't a member of our party. Then he ran back to his car and unlocked it. No one was inside. yet in the few seconds it took Neil Beverly to count the skywatchers, "someone" had been in the car. What was more amazing was that the new record was badly warped, wax-soft, and had obvious thumb impressions at the edges.

Also, a camera in the glove compartment had been dismantled, with its film "mischievously" turned around. Another container of film, this one developed, had been replaced backwards.

We have helped others search, in vain, for "lost" items such as glasses, knitting needles and wool, packs of cigarettes, small food baskets, coffee flasks, cameras, and so on. All were invariably "Found" later, often after arriving home.

These mystifying experiences late? increased my feeling that much more than purely physics! spaceships were at work. Not only did solid objects belonging to skywatchers seem to vanish, but UFOs themselves on occasion have been known to drift in and out of sight—and always in front of witnesses.

On a Sunday afternoon not too long ago I was with 30 trustworthy individuals when we all spotted an object about the size of a full moon. The UFO. elliptical in shape and having a semi-spherical dome. hung in a cloudless clear blue sky. Gray in color, the object was struck by a bright shaft of sunlight, transforming it into a brilliant, living jewel of dazzling magnificence.

We watched the hovering object for

about a minute. during which several observers (including an ex-Royal Air Force bomber crewman) ran to get movie cameras. Before they could return, the UFO, which we estimated was hovering at an altitude of about 700 yards, began to lift like a failing leaf and without warning "{Sashed out."

We refused to believe that anything so obviously solid could disappear before our eyes. So we spread out and formed a large circle in a field bordering the roadside. Between us, with every member gazing at a different point on the horizon. we hoped to pick up the glittering object when it reappeared. Obviously it had sped from the peaceful scene at such blazing speed that it had deceived our eyes.

> "... There is ample evidence ... that Warminster is a 'window' area to another plane of existence—or perhaps there are unique 'properties' here that serve as some sort of landing beacon to some far off intelligent life ..."

We waited in vain for about three minutes, when: "My God—look!" shrieked one of the women. We looked again, and there. in precisely the same patch of clear blue sky where it had abruptly vanished, the craft was reassembling itself. Little by little, over a span of roughly three robs; &-, the UFO turned into a solid form again. We stood with our mouths open in total amazement, watching what assuredly had to be a once-in-a-lifetime experience.

Gradually. in muted undertones of half-gray and white, tile filaments started to interlace in mid air as the entire object began to re-form. The strands ceased to interweave as the "filing-in" operation finished, and there again in all its metallic

might was the UFO.

Sometime later, in April 1973, in a field in Gwent, Monmouthshire, Wales, two little girls and an engineer were astounded when the luminous and glowing object standing before them literally disappeared as they approached it.

Saucer lore abounds with dozens, if no: hundreds, of such "vanishing acts" made by these elusive craft. Perhaps this ability to weave in and out of Earth's physical dimension is a good answer to why we were so often frustrate;; in attempts to photograph UFOs. We often took pictures of what we knew to be typical UFO shapes, only to wince at the ridiculous results when our negatives were developed. We frequently ended up with prints emblazoned with rows of triangles and pyramids: weird animal heads; bodies and legs; wriggling shakes and serpents; or series of stairways and towering stone columns.

There is ample evidence to support my theory that Warminster is a "window" area to another plane of existence—or perhaps there are unique "properties" here that serve as some sort of landing beacon to some far off intelligent life. I can state for a fact that much of what has happened does not indicate the existence of ordinary astronauts from another galaxy. The pattern of events is far too complex and disturbing to simply conclude this.

And take my word for it —it's much safer to watch the skies around Warminster in the company of others. Many nights we have heard frightening sounds which could not be identified as belonging to man or beast.

At 2:30 one March morning in 1966, I stood at the edge of a cluster of trees near Cradle Hill, eyes raised towards 6 starless sky. the mist swirling in gray spirals around me. The first sound came from a barn nearby. it was a heavy footstep. I walked toward the building and no one was in or around it. Yet the sound was repeated several times. as though someone of giant size were walking, or clumping, in front of me, I hurried to catch up to it, but the "thing" changed its direction and I heard a shrill cackle that chilled my spine. For a few frightful seconds I was rooted to the spot; then fear of the unknown overcame me and I fled down the trail, twisting my ankle in my rush to escape.

Bob Strong, another veteran skywatcher who has photographed UFOs many times, had a similar experience. While a glowing-bodied "thing" swished down over Cradle Hill, he heard heavy footsteps thumping behind him, but when he turned around he realized no mortal was near.

It is reassuring to learn that the footsteps of these "ghostly walkers" have been heard by more than 27 people in the notorious area around Cradle Hill. On one occasion a research party hurriedly jumped out of the way and separated into two groups when an invisible prowler charged between them. Several other individuals, including myself, have been victims of coat-tugging "invisibles" at both Cradle and Starr Hills. In January 1974, Pauline Trubridge, who was standing near the barn where my initial encounter had taken place, screamed to her husband for help when the hem of her dress was violently tugged. Six of us scoured the area for more than an hour, finding no sign of the intruder.

One of our realty close confrontations with alien intelligence came on the evening of Aug. 27, 1969 while 13 people were in our skywatching party at Cradle Hill. Among those on the hill, besides myself, wars an ex-naval commander's wife, Mrs. Kathleen Bent; her friend Mrs. Eileen Keck; Ian Cowan and his wife Kathryn; Mrs. Gwen Smith; Christopher Trubridge; his student friend Robert Coates; Julian Butler; and John Dunscome.

At precisely 10:10 p.m. our attention was attracted to what can best be described as a "burning bush" about 600 yards southwest of our vantage point on Cradle Hill.

At first we thought it was rubbish being burned by a farmer, but we all commented how strange it was that this "circular" flame should suddenly erupt, without warning, as no smouldering or smoke was notice*) prior to this by our ever watchful group.

Chris Trubridge and Robert Coates immediately started to run to the site while the rest of us followed more warily.

The burning effect "died" on the ground and was replaced by a large orange ellipsoid that hung motionless about 100 feet above the ground. It was glowing and immobile for almost three minutes.

While several members of our party discussed the rather sudden change, the object started to move southeasterly across Cop Heap in the direction of Starr Hill.

It was enormous! The UFO moved slowly, almost sedately, throwing off a bright and fitful halo around the craft's main body.

Shortly thereafter we saw a second, similar-shaped object much higher in the sky that was keeping pace with the bright orange UFO closer to the ground.

Our attention, however, was soon to be abruptly interrupted from the visual treat before us. We heard) cries coming from the field, and running wildly toward us came Chris and Robert. They were trembling and their faces were ashen.

They drank not coffee to recover from their experience. Then They blurted out an amazing story of a face-to-face encounter with a strange "being."

Standing before a crackling fire, they told us that they had run ahead to get a better look at the "burning bush." Upon reaching "Kidnapper's Hole" (so-called because in 1911 several horses vanished one night, presumedly toppling down a deep well) they saw the flame die out—and in its place stood a tall figure dressed in a shiny tight-fitting suit that reflected the beam of their searchlight.

A gold-colored "sash" was around its neck and shoulder that wound about the waist. No words were exchanged between anyone.

Bob is slightly over six feet tall. He estimated the figure to be a good foot taller than himself. Chris continued this. They also said that the "being" had long dark hair falling to shoulder length, bright eyes, and a rather "feminine" set of features. The "visitor" did not move, but the two men, overwhelmed by fear, would not approach closer than 30 yards.

As their searchlight swept over the huge form they decided not to dally any more, and ran back to the hilltop to report in staccato phrases what had happened.

While the two men were being questioned closely by the rest of the Observers I wandered across the field. I had a flashlight in my sweating palm and with it beamed a friendly message (in Morse code) out into the darkness to relieve any apprehension on the part of our unexpected "guest." And while I sensed an unseen tingle in the air, my visual perception did not pick up any "spaceman" wandering about.

A slightly different alien form made itself known to a group of us standing on Starr Hill in the winter of 1972.

When Diana Granville-Mathews and I arrived before 8:30 p.m., we were immediately aware of a "supercharged" atmosphere, which I can best describe as similar to the feeling one gets shortly before a thunderstorm when the air, is full of electricity. We heard thumping noises from clumps of bushes to our left as we walked near a barn. We imagined the noises were being made by a wild animal, such as a badger or fox, but soon realized that our own movements made no noises!

We owe shortly joined by John and Angela Bennett and Neil and Sally Pike. Neil is a bank employee, his wife the daughter of a former chief detective in the Wiltshire Constabulary. John is a former police officer. Another clumping sound caused us all to look at the hedgerow to our left That's when we saw the three giant figures standing in a triangle at the edge of a field a good distance away. They were all of eight feet tall, had donned heads, no apparent necks, wide shoulders tapering to slim waists, and long arms that dangled at their sides Their outlines were clearly discernible, even though it was dark.

All six of us felt terribly cold and apprehensive, as we sensed that those ghostly forms were not to be taken as friends.

Yet, in seconds, the entire atmosphere changed. A beautiful fragrance wafted toward us that was accompanied by blasts of warm air that took the chill from our

bodies and minds. We started to walk down a dirt track and the tall figures, transparent and oddly impressive, glided parallel to us, at a distance of not more than 10 yards, but keeping to the hedgerows. When we stopped at the tower end of what is known as Mortar Clump, the figures again took up their triangular positions in front of us near some bustles and scrubland.

We found ourselves, quite unselfconsciously, talking to these ghostly giants, conveying love and trust to them; but they, in turn, didn't utter a sound. Yet, at this point, we sensed no suspicions or hostility from the trio, just a measured, calm, detached appraisal of us, and a warmth of emotion silently transmitted.

Neil waited over to one of the figures and bowed his head toward it while still talking. When he returned he told us that he had in fact passed right through the eerie form! The figures remained for 25 minutes before the roaring exhaust of cars approaching the area cut the night air and led to the abrupt disappearance of our friends.

All these stories—no matter how bizarre they sound—are easily verifiable. All observers, whose names are on file, will attest to what has been reported here. Over a nine year period I have faithfully recorded in over 35 notebooks each event I have personally witnessed or had been told about. Admittedly many of the incidents which have occurred around Warminster are incredible to our way of thinking, but we must keep in mind that they represent a truly alien pattern of behavior.

As for the reasoning behind this mass "invasion" of Warminster, I feel strongly that Salisbury Plain is a "window" to another dimension through which a superior race of beings can pass easily to our realm. From the ancient structures which still remain intact, it is possible to assume that this location has—for the longest period of time—been of immense importance to whoever pilots flying sauce"

It may be that such monuments as Stonehenge were constructed to act as homing devices to travelers far away from their bases. Or perhaps they were built as a gesture of greeting to these voyagers whose presence was a welcome sign in ancient times, and whose return in our era may offer dope and courage to those on our planet who must face and cope with an uncertain future.

Some of the UFOs we have encountered may have a true basis in reality—that is actual hardware we can see and touch—while others are believed to be of a "higher" source. Only time and further dose encounters can determine this.

In any case, there is no longer any doubt in my mind that these transient passersby from space and time have much in store for us, and Warminster seems to be a key spot from which they plan to carry out their operation!

★ THE END

SCIENTISTS CHANGING ATTITUDE TOWARD FLYING SAUCERS

Spring 974

By Timothy **Green** Beckley

Despite an effective blackout concerning UFO news in the mass media, the list of impressive sightings continues to grow

As a result of this wave of new reports streaming in from around the world, nighly regarded scientists, professors, and businessmen are beginning to openly admit their increased concern and growing interest in the UFO phenomena

An Apollo 17 Moon walker, a pioneer of private aviation, and a top research *scientist* are among those impatient for the truth concerning the "mysterious hovenng discs" we have come to call flying saucers

What are they? Where do they come from? How did they get here? Is there an intelligence controlling them? If so. what *do* the beings look like? And most important of all—what do they want?

Questions such as these have plagued serious researchers for decades And today, they're just as troubling to the impressive list of backers calling for an all-out no-nonsense investigation of the flying saucer *enigma*.

The ranks of UFO believers now harbors such converts as

- Dr. Thornton **Page**. astronomer·
  * John Northrop, aviation pioneer,
- Or **Leo Sprinkle**. Associate Professor of Psychology, University of Wyoming.
- James Hurtak, professor, California Institute of Arts,

- **Eugene A. Cernan**, astronaut, **and** Commander of the Apollo 17 Moon flight;
- Or. Garry **Henderson, senior re**search scientist. **General Dynamics** Corporation;
- Dr. *James* Harder, Assistant *Professor* of Civil Engineering, University of California;
- Prof. Hermann Oberth. "Father of Astronautics": and
- Dr. Berthold Eric Schwarz, psychiatrist.

Sightings of intelligently controlled strange objects tor centuries have stirred popular emotion and at times have caused crises *and* panics. However, it has not been until modern times that men of science have given the *subject serious* consideration.

During a meeting of fellow scientists in Boston. Dr. Thornton Page, a highly acclaimed Wesleyan University astronomer. voiced his belief that there is a worldwide mystery involving UFOs and that this puzzle should be investigated and solved at once.

Dr. Page based his statement *on* a number of "conclusive" cases obtained firsthand. One report Dr. Page strongly emphasized was supported by eyewitness testimony **from** *two* police officers as well as dozens of additional observers.

On *a* mountaintop, high above the quiet city of Deadwood. S.D., *two* spellbound police officers sat in their darkened patrol

90

car watching a huge white sphere hanging motionless in the pitch-black sky.

The evening of September 22nd had started out typically for *the* pair of lawmen until a little before 2:30 a.m., when one of them happened to glance up and noticed a globe-shaped object gliding noiselessly in from *the* northeast.

To get a better view of the object the two men abandoned their regular patrol of U.S. Highway 14 and proceeded to a more advantageous viewing point high above the city.

Getting out of their car the lawmen turned their spotlight in the *direction of* the suspended object. The instant the light beam hit the UFO, ?he object turned into a black silhouette in the moonlit sky.

After approximately 20 minutes the officers noticed a smaller white object, moving from the northwest toward the larger UFO. Suddenly, another object streaked *in* from the southeast and hovered near the larger ship. After a while the larger craft moved to the right, then down, then to the left, and tip again, as if drawing *a* square in *the* air. During this process, the larger ship sen; out occasions! blue shafts of light toward the ground that lasted from three to five seconds.

Again *the two* officers aimed their spotlight on the object only to have the "mother ship" blink out once more.

Amid this excitement the radio in their patrol car crackled with news: others in nearby communities had reported seeing this same formation.

Finally, 30 minutes after their initial appearance, the smaller objects shot off in the directions they had come. Yet, the original ship remained in its same *position* for at least 25 minutes snore. Then, it moved off *toward* the southeast, picking up more speed with every second.

Dazed and confused, the officers began the drive down the mountain road They hurried to Deadwood's police headquarters, where a complete report was filed.

Before their sighting, they admitted they had been hard-nosed skeptics about flying saucers arid had disregarded sightings which had been pouring into their station for several weeks. They now realized what they had seen and what others had observed and it could no longer be dismissed.

Although the above account sounds as if it might have *Seen taken from* a dramatic film script, this incident was true *according to* Dr. Thornton Page. He, and other men of similar backgrounds are suggesting that the secrecy lid be at last taken off and the public be told *the* truth about UFOs,

One of the most positive statements to be **fade** about UFOs in recent years comes from **a pioneer of aviation in America.**

In a lecture before students and faculty at Cal Tech University, John Northrop emphasized his belief that *flying saucers* are the work of a race of beings 10,000 years technologically more advanced than our own.

Northrop, now 91, was the co-founder of tile huge Lockheed Aircraft Corporation and president of Northrop Aviation.

He is generally considered *as we* of *a* handful of men responsible for the success of early commercial aviation in this country.

"I am of the opinion that the people who are responsible for piloting the UFOs seers in our skies are physicists from some other world keeping *a watchful eye* or our development over the centuries.'. he said.

Furthermore, Northrop said that he *feels* that these ships were "being flown by scientists from some other realm much more advanced and scientifically sophisticated *than* our own."

Although the aviation expert admitted he had never seen a UFO himself, he is convinced that they are "very real." According to Northrop, one of his close friends and chief pilots observed *something* which defies all explanation.

"Test pilot Max Stanley was en route from *Texas* to California flying one of our planes when he sighted a strange translucent object at around 80,000 *feet.* it defied all known principles of aeronautics. and ever flew 'sideways' during the *time* it was within Max's viewing range.

"I don't know what Stanley saw but there are hundreds of similar reports coming from equally reliable sources: pilots, radar technicians, astronomers, military personnel, and police officers."

Northrop, whose career in aeronautical engineering spans nearly 60 years, said, "I am convinced that there was a phenomenon in the sky, at that time. which did not show characteristics which could be explained by physical *laws* as we know them."

Regarding the Condon report which received so much publicity several years ago. Northrop feels this could be one of the *biggest* blunders *of* our present era. "I think the serious scientific community of the 21st Century will end up laughing at Cordon's whitewash. I have indications that it was one of the most deliberate cover ups ever perpetrated on the American public."

Northrop told the audience of 1,200 students and faculty that UFOs were nothing new, and 'reports obviously 90 back as far as 25,000 years."

Perhaps the biggest surprise of all came when he told those present, that he was berth puzzled and concerned over the worldwide increase of "close level" sighting in which otherwise "trustworthy" citizens were claiming to have actually come within a short distance of these objects, and in some cases even spoken to their humanoid occupants.

Indeed. Northrop's public comments (and similar pro-UFO statements from other men of prominence) appear to have been made at a very crucial time. For at this moment all reports indicate that we are in the *midst of a* new wave of sightings. *And* this *time, the results could* be catastrophic. It is a flap that *as yet has* not attracted the full attention of the press, but does seem to have brought about an unexpected change in the attitude of the establishment.

Reports filtering into the UFO Research Committee of Seattle, *Wash., since early*

Saucer Fans Are Here Dishing Out Their Data

NEW YORK POST, THURSDAY, JUNE 22, 1967

From California, Hawaii, England and television-land the believers are drifting into New York this weekend to tell about flying saucers.

They are convinced unidentified flying objects are usually spacecraft from other planets manned by a higher form of intelligence than earth people.

Their big show, billed as the 1967 Congress of Scientific Ufologists, commemorates the 20th anniversary of the first recorded "flying saucer" sighting June 24, 1947, by Kenneth Arnold near Mt. Rainier, Washington.

The objects he saw, "looked like saucers skipping over the water," and since then the faithful have enlarged on his theme.

The three-day convention at the Hotel Commodore tomorrow through Sunday will feature speeches by other saucer-sighters, by persons convinced they have traveled to other planets, by those who say they've talked with men (?) from outer space.

"We're trying to inform the public," explained Timothy Green Beckley, 22-year-old managing editor of Saucer News, quarterly publication sponsoring the convention.

Earthlings May Attend

"But we expect people will enjoy themselves too," he added.

For just $2 the public can hear the speakers and make the grand tour of exhibits, including:

—"A life-sized model of a humanoid from Outer Space.

—"Weird flying saucer paintings.

—"An electronic flying saucer detector.

INSTRUCTION—ADV.

COLLEGE

—"A prototype of an actual saucer now being constructed."

—"Exclusive motion pictures of flying saucers from other world."

The list of believers who'll attend include:

¶Gray Barker, author of "They Knew Too Much About Flying Saucers."

¶Art Ford, the radio and television personality who believes six Navy planes which disappeared mysteriously off the Florida coast in 1945 were kidnapped by creatures from outer space.

¶Howard Menger, who says he made a trip to Venus and wrote a book about it, "From Outer Space to You."

¶James Randi, a magician and escape artist.

¶Stewart Robb, a psychic researcher who's writing a book, "Reports from Beyond."

¶Frank Stranges, who's made a 90-minute film about UFO's he'll show at the convention.

And a special attraction will be Roy Thinnes, star of the TV series, "The Invaders."

Some of our people do have

pretty far-out things to say," Beckley admitted. "We don't endorse all of them, but we do present them and let people decide for themselves.

"Flying saucers have been seen over a period of 200 years. They've been detected by radar and seen by police officers, mayors and governors."

The responsibility of such witnesses, Beckley maintained, confirms that "we are dealing here with some kind of craft."

Some believers have seen objects land and leave scorched places on the ground. Others

tell of two-to-four-foot beings cavorting outside the ship.

"The flying saucer phenomenon is a world-wide enigma," Beckley said. "It covers the entire globe and the United Nations is interested."

The reason the public doesn't know or hear more about flying saucers, Beckley explained, is because the security force for space visitors have warned the believers against talking.

Gray Barker's speech tomorrow night will center about the mysterious visitors who warn believers about disclosing what they know.

What do homeowners

lik a

NEW YORK'S FIRST FLYING SAUCER CONVENTION

Attendance - 8,000

World-wide publicity again for Timothy Green Beckley

N.Y. POST

CHANGING ATTITUDE

(Continued '

1973. break down into four very specific types: multiple witnesses; physical evidence; low-level sightings (or close encounters); and contacts. A good portion of these sightings *have* come from reliable persons who have *seen* things in the sky and on the ground which, supposedly. should not exist—but *do*!

Rod Dyke, UFORC's director, admits that his organization is now sifting through hundreds of clippings coming in from all over the U.S. trial will. eventually be placed in one of these tour categories.

The following have been taken from this large stack of reports to illustrate these basic types of sightings:

Multiple Witnesses—Dozens of *eye*-witnesses watched *as* an unidentified object, which one woman described as being "the strangest thing I ever saw." hovered above *Santa* Ana, Calif., on Jan. 2, 1973.

From separate parts of the city reports flowed into police headquarters of "the mysterious lighted object." All reports

★ UFO REPORT

said that the UFO was of gigantic proportions, measuring more than *50* feel in *diameter*, with a round hat-like dome *on* its upper half.

The UFO *was* said to *have a* circular ring *of* multicolored *lights* around a central rim, and had two antennae protruding from a brightly lit door *in* the center of the craft.

One of *the* observers totd a member of a local UFO organization *that* she could hear a noise like that of an "electric generator" as the unidentified craft disappeared, traveling at an accelerating speed.

Startling multiple witness sightings have been flowing in from all over the U.S. with Dighton, Kans. undoubtedly holding the honors for the most UFO witnesses in one community—more than 1,000!

"Although we may *be a* small town, we're big enough to be of some interest to whoever is inside those ships." claimed Police Chief M. R. Shelton acknowledging that Dighton had been the center of a great deal of UFO activity.

"During the past few months, beginning in early 1973, almost everyone here, *some* 1,050 residents, have told some

kind *of story* related to *UFOs, "* he reported. Why, I even chased one myself in the patrol car at speeds up to 100 miles per hour." The object, Chief Shelton admits, easily outran him.

Physical Evidence—The constant vigil by *ufologists* determined to uncover physical evidence directly linked to saucer *activity*, may have been successful *in* recent months. Documented cases of scorched earth, dismembered trees, and "a *strange* foreign substance" have been among the forms of *evidence* left behind as a reminder that UFOs are actual hardware of an unknown origin.

Driving along Weatherby Road in Fort Elizabeth, N. J., on Dec. 11, 1972, Mr. and Mrs. Charles Willis were the first to report seeing *an* unidentified object *as* it descended toward Earth. "We were driving along at about 9 p.m.," the couple reported, "when we *noticed* this glowing object flying above the road ahead of our car. Within seconds the sphere came down to treetop level and proceeded to hover there for a brief period before crossing over to the other side of the road and crashing, *cr* landing, in the woods."

The frightened couple raced to a nearby phone and placed a call to the State

Police at Morris Barracks. Responding to this and similar reports. Trooper Leonard Anderson arrived at the site, which is located about a half mile east of Port Cumberland Road, and what he found baffled him and has remained a controversy ever since.

"When 1 got to the scene of the reported crash," Anderson said, "I was surprised to see that something had literally carved out an area two feet in diameter back in the woods where this object had supposedly come to rest. This portion of ground was bare of all vegetation and pine needles, and in; the center was a round hole two inches wide and four inches deep. It was a real wild area and I don't see how anything could have gotten in there *except from above*."

Bill Gowan of Ellenboro. N. C., also saw evidence of a UFO landing on Jan. 5, 1973. when a strange object landed briefly in his backyard and then took off again, *almost* immediately, leaving behind 'some weird greenish looking stuff' which remained mixed with the freshly fallen snow.

Gowan was on the phone with radio newscaster Pat Nanney giving a report on student activities at his high school, when all of a sudden the radio in the next room began emitting weird crackling noises, "I glanced out the kitchen window and there was this object moving slowly a few feet above the snow-covered ground," he said. "After wobbling for a few minutes it tilted on its side and started, coming straight down. Moments later it landed.

"I would say that the object was only about a fool high and maybe half that size n diameter. It was more squarish than round and a roaring flame shot out of the end of it

"I hung up on Pat and ran outside to get a closer look. As I did, whatever it was went straight up for about 50 feet and then there was an exploding noise, like a rifle being fire#. After that it took off like a whiz and disappeared over the trees."

Examining the area, Gowan was excited to find that there were severs! small black particles left in a circle around a three-inch hole in the ice and snow. In addition, the hole was almost completely filled with a foul-smelling green substance.

A sample of the material was collected and placed in a seeded container and Gowan said he was willing to give it up for analysis but so far there have been no qualified takers.

Saucer researchers have files full of documented cases in which power failures have been attributed to close approaches made by UFOs. Thus, Stan Gordon, director of the Westmoreland County UFO Study Group, believes there is strong evidence that UFOs may have been responsible for a malfunction in the radar system at Greater Pittsburgh Airport on Jan. 25, 1973. Gordon believes that this type of report, when checked out completely otters an unquestionable form of "physical evidence."

Although airport personnel blamed the malfunction, (which delayed the landing of more than 20 jet liners for a period extending from 1 p.m. to 2 p.m., and from 3:30 p.m. until 1 a.m.), on a "hardware failure in an antenna," *Stan's* group believes otherwise.

According to Gordon his phone was kept busy throughout the day and night by calls from residents living in the vicinity of the airport. In a lengthy news item featured in The *News Dispatch* of Jeannette, Pa., the following day, Gordon said that there were many UFO sightings over the entire area. He cited reports including "a formation of five or six bright, round objects" that were said to hover over homes near *the* airport for more than 10 minutes before separating into two different formations.

Verifying Gordon's statements were police from North Huntingdon Township who added that they had received two calls about a UFO seen about 9 p.m. One of the callers told police seven youths had spotted a UFO in the sky over the Northwin Senior High School. There were additional sightings of a huge cigar-shaped. wingless object near Derry, Pa.

Low-Level Sightings and Close Encounters — There are those who say that Gerald Summrey lives in fear of being abdueled by a flying saucer. He has apparently read the many accounts told of Betty and Barney Hill, a New Hampshire couple that recalled (under hypnotic regression) of being kidnapped and taken aboard a strange ship from another planet.

Reporters from the Charlotte, N. C., News, agree that Gerald has a St to be concerned about. Beginning In early January 1973. the 47-year-oid professional truck driver from Harrisburg, Pa., began noticing a low hovering light in the shy that followed him as he drove along the open road. Several times, over a period of two weeks, the light would seem to get closer only to reverse itself when Gerald slowed (town, hoping to get a better look at it.

His fellow truckers were initially skeptical of their friend's constant chatter about his new found friend but many of them became less skeptical when a news photographer, Tommy Franklin, and reporter Edith Low followed the trucker in their own car on one of Summey's long hauls. Several miles out. they too spotted the object as it suddenly appeared some distance off to the side of the highway. On several occasions *they* watched the object with binoculars and even managed to get a photo showing a blurred blotch of tight against a dark background,

"We all fetr a sense of awe at the sight. This was definitely not a plane, weather balloon, or a stationary object (i.e., planet or star). Of this we are certain," said the pair from the newspaper.

Numerous sightings of the low-level variety have been reported in the Harris* burg. Pa.. area over the past two years. On one occasion a formation of more than 15 UFOs were observed by the townspeople.

Hundreds. perhaps thousands of tow-level sightings have been made within the last few months. Georgia, Mississippi, and Florida were among the areas being closely watched by UFOs for an unknown purpose during the summer months of 1973.

Farther north, New York City had its share of saucer sightings during this

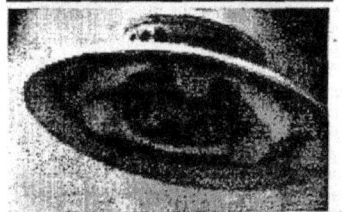

same peak period. Unfortunately, very few of the sightings made in the metropolitan are? *ever* appeared in print. Yet my own telephone lines are frequently kept busy by people who have seen strange objects in the sky. *Such is* the case with a young lady by the name of Pat (she has requested her full name be kept **confidential**) who telephoned on the morning of June 1, 1973 to tell me of an incident that had happened only the night before, during an unusually heavy thunderstorm.

"Eleven of us were seated around my friend's **apartment** in Brooklyn looking out the window, commenting on *the* electrical *storm.* At about nine p.m., we began to notice what 1 can best describe as weird lights **floating** outside. To get a bet*ter* view. we left the apartment and went up to the roof since we **realized** right away that *what* we were seeing was not any form of lightning. We looked up and there in the cloud covered sky were two bright lights shining from behind some dark clouds spaced a good distance apart. The lights were flashing on and off—as if responding to each other."

Pat claims that this spectacle continued until about 10:30. The young and attrac*tive* witness, who is employed by a leading advertising firm in Manhattan, thought it quite strange that about seven or eight airplanes had also passed during the "disturbance," and she guessed that they might've been dispatched to observe the phenomenon.

Because of the unusual aspects of this sighting I called a local newspaper to see if anyone had phoned in an account.

The city editor of the *Brooklyn Home Reporter,* told me that although she had received no reports of anything **unusual** that particular evening. an obviously frightened man had **called** about a week earlier and claimed that he had **seen** a brightly glowing sphere land in the water near the Verrazano Bridge.

Contacts—Although there have been many **reports** of contacts made by UFO .occupants in recent months, few ever **get publicized** because of the notoriety involved.

A contact backed up by additional eyewitness testimony of UFOs in the nearby vicinity lends weight to a claim made by a Cherokee County, S.C., youth whose identity is being withheld "to protect him from cranks."

According to a front **page** story in the Jan. 26. 1973, edition of the *Gaffney* Ledger. a 24-year-old resident was driving south along Highway 18 approximately 15 miles south of Gaffney when his at*tention* was attracted to a cluster of flashing red lights on the road in front of him.

His initial thought was that the lights belonged to a police patrol car that had **caught** up with a speeding motorist. It wasn't until he got much closer that he received his initial shock. There, in his automobile's headlight beams was a domed. saucer-shaped **object resting** on three tripod legs in the middle of the road. In front of the ship were a dozen "humanlike" men who seemed to be trying to "fix something" on the underside of the ship.

The editors of the Ledger say the youth told them that the men around *the* ship were all wearing outfits resembling white **coveralls** to which were affixed various

★ **UFO** REPORT

buckles and belts. The men were of average height, had Caucasian-like faces and had the same style jet black hair. On their hands were what appeared to be white gloves.

The UFOnauts did not seem to care about the young man's presence nor the fact that he was watching their activities.

Even **more** incredible, the youth told editor Rodger Painter that he couldn't believe his own eyes, for the "men" appeared to waft in and out of view. His actual words were that they "sort of wiggled like worms. in and out of my field of vision."

Another bizarre **episode** occurred **in** the area during the same week when a woman reported that her car had been followed by a similar **object** along a road not too far from the alleged landing spot.

Other reports were made to the newspaper by three additional witnesses who said they saw a group of mysterious lights moving **in the same area.** one of them on the very night the landing took place!

Although a surprising number of scien*tists* are beginning to take such UFO reports at face value, only a handful have begun considering the likelihood of actual contact. Among those who have been

---

. . . The scientific establishment is just getting around to examining the UFO enigma. A courageous few have been anxiously seeking answers to this puzzle for some time.. ."

---

keeping a keen eye on **activities** in this category is Dr. Leo Sprinkle an Associate Professor of **Psychology** at the University of Wyoming.

Dr. Sprinkle maintains that if anything is to be definitely proved regarding the existence of UFOs it will come **when** we contact their **occupants.** Professor Sprinkle has **stated** on numerous occasions that he is convinced that many rational and sober individuals have had some sort of contact with UFOnauts. However. Sprinkle is not convinced that these episodes **are** of a strictly physical nature. "I have been attempting to assimilate just how much the paranormal plays in such encounters. There is enough evidence, however, to **suggest** *that* a lot of what is transpiring may have psychic overtones."

Whatever his conclusions. Professor Sprinkle **admits** two "very real" sightings of his own. "Before my initial experience I was a scoffer, but my first sighting turned me into a reserved skeptic. After my second observation I had to admit to myself that I had become an 'unwilling' believer."

Sprinkle has frankly stated many times before various academic gatherings that it is his personal belief that "the physical. biological, psycho-social, and the spiritual implications of the UFO phenomena

are real and quite **staggering.**"

A similar attitude has been expressed by James Hurtak, professor at the California Institute of the Arts. in Valencia. In an address delivered to an audience of lay**men** and scientists (including former astronaut Edgar Mitchell) at a conference on Acupuncture and Kirlian Photography sponsored in February 1973 by the prestigious Foundation for Parasensory Investigation in New York. Hurtak said that he believed "man is not the only intelligent creature in the cosmos." The dynamic professor offered evidence he gathered personally. that supported his theory that our planet has been visited for thousands of years by beings from other galaxies. Among this evidence were scripts written in ancient Tibet which have only recently been translated by researchers. They **suggest,** a la Chariots of *the Gods?* that extraterrestrial beings may have intermingled with Earth races in the past and played an intricate part in the development of various cultures.

Since the early days of our Manned Space Program I have kept abreast of all comments made by our astronauts. or by anyone closely associated with our space program, concerning **strange** flying objects- Sightings of UFOs made by our planetary travelers have been kept under pretty tight security. Yet a number at our space voyagers have made comments—quite positive ones— concerning unknown objects seen in space. A good deal of evidence which suggests our space probes have been closely watched and followed was presented by this writer in an issue of *Sage (see* May '70 issue) and author Joseph Goodavage in the March and April 1974 issues of SAGA.

The most recent **public statement** of this type came from astronaut Eugene A. Cernan, commander of the Apollo 17 mission to the Moon. Returning from the lunar surface he had a chance to ponder the things he **both** saw and "felt,"

"When you get out there, and you look at the infinity of time and the infinity of space, which is something none of us can really understand, but exists—and I know it because I saw it—you begin to notice how small our Earth actually is in comparison to the vastness of the universe,

"Statistically, there has to be an infinite number of other Earths and an *infinite* number of other civilizations.

"I think it's exciting, scientifically and philosophically and *any* other way, for people, young and old. to think that in the future we may be able to get to go **farther** out there, or there may be other civilizations we can make contact with."

On UFOs specifically, Cernan had this to say: "I'm one of **those guys** who has never **seen** a UFO but I've been asked, and I've publicly thought they were something being constructed and flown by some other civilization."

The retired astronaut also thinks that our present civilization is not the only highly technological one that has existed on our planet. "Maybe infinity goes backward as well as it does forward. Maybe the Moon can tell us something about the existence of some ancient civilization, not necessarily on Earth, not necessarily on the Moon. but possibly within our own universe. and give us an insight into what

(Continued on page 88)

(Continued.

it is really all about Understanding something that is relatively untouched, that is two, three. even four billion years old, is part of the teaming process to what is behind us, and what may be in front of us,"

Another astronaut. Ronald Evans, says UFOs may be real. He told a news conference at Arionza State University on Feb. 6, 1973. that there is "a distinct possibility" that UFOs exist. Evans pointed out, however, that he did not see anything of this nature around Earth of the Moon, "unless you mean all kinds of particles that are flying around through space."

The astronaut added that when his craft went behind the Moon and he left the radios on, even though messages from the Earth would be cut off. he heard "a strange sound like a 'whooo.' " In several previous flights scientists monitoring the "chatter" of our spacemen have been stunned to hear unexplainable sounds that were not coming from either the ground or from the capsule itself.

On the Apollo 12 flight astronaut Allan Bean told Houston that he kept hearing a sound like "a whistle" in the background.

On the much earlier Faith 7 mission (May 1963) Gordon Cooper claims he heard "unintelligible language transmitted over restricted NASA radio frequencies.' Later, during the Apollo 11 Moon mission, unnerving "sound effects" came across the air waves. The point of origin for all these "sounds" and "voices" is still unknown.

Dr. Garry Henderson, a senior research scientist of General Dyanmics Corporation in Texas. says not only that he is a believer in the reality of "spaceships" but that just about all of our astronauts have seen and even photographed these craft! This startling disclosure was made at the Planetarium in Calgary, Canada, where Dr. Henderson was invited to speak.

According to this research scientist, NASA has fifes bulging with photographs and testimony gathered from our spacemen, This material is not being released because the space agency is afraid that their funds for future space exploration wilt be stashed even more by the government. "People are still terrified to talk about these things; it's still a laughing matter to many. especially in Congress and the government. No one wants to be responsible for sticking his neck out."

Why does such an attitude exist among the government, military, and scientific establishment? Dr. James Harder. Assistant Professor of Civil Engineering, University of California, offers this theory: "There has been a strong feeling aroused about UFOs, particularly the extraterrestrial hypothesis. This is entirely understandable in view of Man's historic record of considering himself the central figure in the natural scene; the extraterrestrial theory tends inevitably to undermine the collective ego of the human race. These feelings have no place in the scientific assessment of facts, but 1 confees that they have at times affected me."

Dr. Harder believes that over the last 26 years a vast amount of evidence has been accumulated concerning the existence of these objects. "Most of this is little known to the genera) public, or to most scientists." he said, "but on the basis of the data and ordinary rules of evidence, as

would be applied to civil or criminal courts, the physical reality of UFOs has been proved beyond a reasonable doubt. With some effort, we can accept this on an intellectual level but find difficulty in accepting it on an emotional one, in such a way that the facts give a feeling of reality. in this respect, we might recall the attitude many of us have toward our own deaths; we accept the facts intellectually but find it difficult to accept them emotionally."

As we can see, the scientific establishment is just getting around to examining the UFO enigma. A courageous few, such as Dr. J. Allen Hynek, have anxiously been seeking answers to this puzzle for some time.

Another exception to science's rigid attitude, by a man who has always been far-reaching in his thoughts, is Professor Hermann Oberth, the acknowledged "Fathe? of Astronautics."

Oberth is one of the most renowned space scientists in the world. He has been striving since early in this century to realize the dream of Jules Verne—Man venturing forth into outer space.

During WW II, Professor Oberth was director of Germany's rocket program, the first successful application of liquid fuel propulsion for guided missiles. Under his leadership such men as Werner von Braun gained their experience.

As long as 10 years ago. Oberth was poking a pointed finger at his colleagues warning them that a great danger existed in ignoring the steady flow of UFO reports.

Oberth is extremely outspoken when it comes to this subject, especially the contactee aspects of the mystery. After meeting two so-called contactees who attended a UFO congress in Germany, Oberth remarked: "I thought before this conference that these contactees were deceptive, hysterical, or schizophrenic individuals but 1 have to say they made an impression on me. I am willing to bet one to 100 that these individuals are completely normal and saw and experienced something."

Asked why the UFOnauts haven't tried communicating with us more directly and

openly, Oberth commented. "Perhaps they consider us uncivilized—like monkeys in the jungle. Our own atmosphere may be poisonous for the people who pilot these crafts. Perhaps there are bacteria in our atmosphere that might endanger their lives. Consequently they do not step out of their spaceships without being fully prepared."

Hermann Oberth is open-minded enough to admit that contacts may have indeed taken place and he is all for stepping up the investigation of the UFO puzzle on a worldwide basis. "We are only in the embryological stages of research in this field." he contends. We have to wait with this UFO question until a more serious study has been made. We need some physical evidence in our hands."

Studying the subject from a slightly different view is Dr. Berthold Eric Schwarz, assistant attending psychiatrist at Montclair Community Hospital in New Jersey. Aside from monitoring UFO activities in the area. Dr. Schwarz has devoted a great deal of time to parapsychology and has written several technical papers on his research in this field, Like Professor Oberth, Berthold Schwarz is enormously interested in (lie "contactee enigma" and has often stated his theory that many of these individuals did, in fact. have actual experiences beyond the normal world. After interviewing witnesses in four separate close encounter cases he concluded that there was no psychopathological reason for these particular individuals to have these experiences.

Recently. while accompanying a woman in her mid-40s who insisted that she has been under almost constant surveillance by UFOs that used an area not far from her home in Massachusetts as a landing base. Dr. Schwarz himself witnessed a strange phenomenon in the form of two glowing globes whose colors constantly changed. The luminous spheres appeared to glide noiselessly in front of him for several minutes. Then both objects merged into one solid form. separated again, and finally took off,

Dr. Schwarz's battery operated tape recorder refused to function even though a fresh set of batteries had been placed in the machine earlier that day. However. the two motion picture cameras he carried continued to work throughout a good part of the dramatic experience and Dr. Schwarz captured the episode on film.

Dr. Schwarz admits that he is bewildered not only over his own close encounter. but many similar cases he has personally looked into.

"Psychiatric studies of all witnesses so tar have showed them to be of normal intelligence and there are no signs of psychodynamic motivation for conscious or unconscious fabrication. Thus, it seems entirely reasonable that these incidents are factual and objectively accurate. If there is any question it is most likely in the interpretation of these accounts." Dr. Schwarz said.

And so it seems the mounting evidence is impossible to ignore. Undoubtedly the government possesses bulging files crammed with fantastic cases the scientific community knows nothing about. As

> "...They suggest that extraterrestrial beings may have intermingled with Earth races in the past and played an intricate part in the development of various cultures.. ."

Timothy Beckley and Maureen Connelly examine movie film of UFOs.

Richard S. Heyza / Seattle Times

(Continued from page 88)

John Northrop said recently, "I am not about to believe that the Air Force has given up collecting reports, nor is the government about to release its classified files to any scientific body for evaluation."

As it stands now, the UFO mystery is a long way from being solved, but with such

respected men working on a thorough study we may cut the time down to a matter of a few years, perhaps even months before something concrete and conclusive is discovered.

And although the list of men quoted in this article is impressive there are many more scientists and other qualified men

working on private research projects just waiting for the "proper time" to release their findings.

Whatever the end results may be, let's hope as does the "Father of American aviation" that UFOs are "of tremendous value to all mankind on Earth."

★ THE END

UFO 'believer' on lecture tour brings his stories to Tacoma

by Don Duncan
Times staff reporter

Timothy Beckley, veteran East Coast UFO writer, calls Hangar 18 at Wright-Patterson Air Force Base in Dayton, Ohio, "our cosmic Watergate."

Beckley contends that inside the fenced and guarded hangar are *pieces* of an alien spacecraft that crash-landed on earth some years ago, along with deep-frozen bodies of nine small, bluish-skinned visitors from outer space who died in the craft.

"It is our government's best-kept *secret*," says Beckley, who is in "the Puget Sound area for a series of lectures and talk-show appearances. He is being accompanied by Maureen Connelly of Tacoma, who says she has had several personal experiences with UFOs.

Beckley, the 35-year-old editor of UFO Review, the nation's only newspaper devoted exclusively to sightings of unidentified flying objects, bases his belief on interviews he and his staff investigator, Lee Spiegel, have had with people who once worked inside the hangar.

Beckley says that among those who think there is a real likelihood the stories are true is Gordon Cooper, the astronaut, "and if you can't trust Gordon Cooper, who can you trust?"

The author contends that our government has been engaged in a high level cover-up of UFOs for years, aim he offers as evidence numerous documents obtained under the Freedom of Information Act, along with stories by military personnel that their films of UFOs have been impounded by the government "and never seen again."

Timothy Beckley is a good-natured, moon-faced man who has written half a dozen books about UFOs. He said he published his first mimeographed newsletters on the subject when he was 14 years old.

Despite *seeing* his, first "strange *lights* in the *sky*" over New Jersey when he was 10, and having made several subsequent "sighting" in this country and England, Beckley candidly admits he never personally has seen a

Beckley further concedes there is a "lunatic fringe" that has *attached* itself to *the* subject of' UFOs.

But, *having* said that, he offers photographs, movie film and hundreds of eye-witness accounts to back his belief that millions of earthlings have seen spacecraft in the skies, that hundreds have seen them close up on the ground, and that a handful have seen alien visitors walking around outside spacecraft or "been inside actual spaceships."

Beckley said he thinks there are several types of alien visitors — the small bluish-skinned workers, who are not over 4 feet tall, and the larger "brains-behind-the-, spacecraft" who resemble Caucasians, wear business suits and dresses and live and work among us.

The author is full of stranger-than-fiction stories:

— In 1975, two Iranian Air Force jets were sent out to intercept a brightly lighted object in the skies near Tehran. According to a U.S. Defense Department report, the object was tracked by radar and seen by the crew of a commercial airliner.

As the jet pilots neared the object, their radios went dead, their weapons system jammed and they lost all power until the large object, with flashing lights, sped away "faster than any aircraft they had ever seen."

— A female University of Michigan student told a professor she was driving along a deserted road when she saw a saucerlike object, with tripod landing gear. She stopped and saw three well-dressed men find women, walk down a ladder and drive off in a car. She filed a report with the local sheriff, who laughed.

Several weeks later, in a super market, she saw "two of the three men, and the woman," at a checkout counter. She tried to follow them, "and they simply vanished."

Beckley can spin such stories by the hour.

"UFOs are not a subject you can exhaust easily" said Beckley.

large cigar-shaped spacecraft pass overhead when he was in New Mexico in 1945.

"We figure there are two or three reported sightings every 24 hours and probably a lot more than that that don't get reported."

Beckley —"

Hardly out of high school, Tim was the editor, Jerome Clark, Assistant Editor- Gray Barker, Brinsley Le Poer Trench and George Fawcett was on the Advisory Board, and Barry Hoffman did the cover art. What a job to type stencils.

INTERPLANETARY NEWS SERVICE

96

Publisher presents his space case

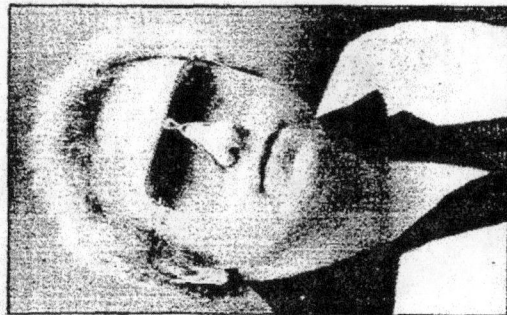

Lawrence Maddry

**TIMOTHY BECKLEY, . . .
. . . publisher of UFO Review**

Timothy Beckley is the Johnny Appleseed of flying saucer reports.

If there is a light in the sky over a trailer park in Kansas that has hayseeds scratching their heads on Saturday night, Beckley will be there come Monday morning. He will write about it and spread the word,

He is the editor and publisher of UFO **Review,** the only publication in America that deals exclusively with sightings of unidentified flying objects. In planting the UFO reports in his tabloid, he is entirely indiscriminate,

If a woman in San Diego says her gall bladder was improved by the advice of little men in a flying saucer, Beckley will print it beside an advertisement that states: "Reach Out To Other Dimensions When You Wear Your Amazing Telecrystal!" (Only $15, the telecrystal comes complete with a chain and a beautifully channeled message from "Crystal

Love," who dwells in another solar system, we are told.)

Beckley arrived in Norfolk this week for a round of television appearances and radio talk shows, and a chat in the newspaper office. A moon-faced man wearing rose-tinted sunglasses and purple tennis sneakers, he considers himself the country's expert on UFOs, space creatures, flying saucers and unexplained things that blink, bump or thump in the night,

"There have been thousands of sightings of UFOs all over the country," he said. "It is simply too much to be a coincidence."

about 3 or 4 feet tall. They are not very communicative. They fly down in their spaceships to collect soil and water samples. There have been 5,000 reports of this type."

The second type of UFOnaut is a much more intelligent creature, a mastermind, which he says probably lives on Earth and might be encountered at the laundromat or the ballpark without anyone's knowing it,

My favorite is type three.

"Type three includes strange saucertians, weird beings who have been seen over the years," he said. "These include the Mothmen and Big Foot people,"

"Mothman?"

"Oh yes," he said. "Mothman was this being about 8 feet tall. He had glowing red eyes and a wingspan of about 11 or 12 feet. Mothman was seen in the 1960s in West Virginia. There were several dozen witnesses, I talked with some of them.

"The first persons to observe Mothman was a couple in their teens who had been drinking beer in an abandoned area where the government stored TNT. The Mothman with

glowing red eyes chased their car for quite a distance. Others reported seeing the same creature."

Mothman, he said, has rarely been seen outside West Virginia, which must be good news to the Orkin people.

Beckley said the strange saucertians were often seen in remote areas at the same time UFOs appeared. The Big Foot creatures have been seen in 37 states, Beckley said.

"A Big Foot was seen in the state of Washington 10 years ago," he said. "Now it seems to be moving into Ohio and New Jersey. I was in Athens, Ohio, a few years ago tracking a report of a UFOnaut leaving strange indentions in the ground, I canvassed a neighborhood looking for verifications.

"I found that two or three reported seeing a giant, hairy monster about 8 feet tall with a horrendous smell associated with it."

"A what kind of smell?"

"A horrendous smell," he replied. "One woman reported that the Big Foot raced across a field behind her house. She said the creature moved faster than an Olympic runner and left giant footprints in the soft soil

beneath her window. No one knows why it was running so fast or why."

"Maybe it was trying to flee its own odor?"

Beckley didn't think that funny, though he confirmed that there had been many sightings of UFOs near my hometown of Lumberton, N.C., about 10 years ago. Several farmers reported mysterious lights in the sky, some claiming that the glowing objects resembled giant versions of the headlamps on John Deere tractors.

When a Federal Aviation Administration official for the region issued a statement saying that the sightings were probably the lights on Piedmont planes, a hue and cry of protest arose from the local farmers. One explained in a letter to the local newspaper that he knew he wasn't looking at a Piedmont plane because the lights tie saw seemed to be moving about with some sense of purpose and direction.

Beckley didn't think that was funny either. Gathering his garment bag, he strode directly to the elevator and departed to spread his message of UFOs and weird space creatures to whoever would read or listen.

"I was talking with Larry Bryant of Alexandria before coming down here," he sa "He used to live in Norfolk. Larry is a member of Concerned Citizens *Against* Sauc Secrecy, an organization that wants 3,000 government documents released to the publi under the Freedom of Information Act,"

Beckley contends that the documents, in the possession of the *CIA*, the FBI and the S Department, would prove the existence not only of flying saucers but of space creatures.

"Of particular interest is the governmer report of a crash of a flying saucer in 1950 which contained the charred remains of spat creatures," he confided,

Beckley has never seen a space creatur but is certain they exist and fly overhead fr time to time.

"There are three basic types of UFOnauts," he said. "First are the little me

The Virginian-Pilot, Friday, August 5, 1983

57

SAUCERS OVER OUR CITIES

Recently, scores of UFOs have been seen cavorting over our largest population centers, from New York to San Francisco. Are they planning a repeat of the massive blackout of 1965—when they were spotted near power plants?

UFO

UFOs are being reported in ever increasing numbers from all over the U. S. Statistics show that there are more than a dozen sightings every 24 hours. . . . And while small-town newspapers are prone to headline even the "milder" episodes on their front pages, the big metropolitan dailies avoid like the plague reporting the antics of these shimmering "phantoms of the sky."

To an investigator who has access to the steady stream of information, it is obvious that the UFOs have recently begun a new phase in their operations here on Earth. in the last few months, flying saucers have been seen hovering and darting about over our largest towns and cities; in effect, zeroing in on our population centers. New York, Chicago, Cincinnati, and Philadelphia are only a few of the "target' zones. Apparently they are now daring the authorities and the dwindling corps of skeptics to contest the validity of their existence. The ever-mounting number of landing and contact cases makes it increasingly difficult to do so.

Located a mere five miles from Wall Street in lower Manhattan, the borough of Staten Island is a pear-shaped island, roughly 13 miles long by seven miles wide, and has recently become the focal point for repeated UFO activity.

The night of Feb. 14, 1975, was cold and blustery as Daniel Kish walked his German shepherd along Barclay Avenue, in the rural Annadale section of the island. The wind whistled through the long naked branches of the trees, creating an eerie, unsettling sound.

Kish walked the same route with his dog nearly every night.

"Rip, my German shepherd, was walking by my side, when suddenly, his ears went up and he started sniffing the air. Then he turned around, tugging on his leash, trying like mad to break loose and get the hell out of there. It was like he'd seen a ghost!"

The German shepherd continued to lunge against his collar "He gave such a terrific jerk at one point that the sturdy metal chain attached to his collar snapped. He was really scared!" With this, Rip raced for home. "He hid under the bed, and we couldn't get him out for the longest time. Finally, we managed to coax him out. but he wasn't the same. He was whimpering, and we could tell that his heart was beating unusually fast, Rip didn't calm down and return to normal all that night, nor most of the next day."

Daniel Kish admits he didn't know what to make of the dog's peculiar behavior.

It wasn't until several weeks later, in fact. that he learned that a UFO had been seen at precisely the same time he was out walking his dog—and within a few hundred yards of where they were strolling.

"It really scared me." Mike Kileen admitted, referring to his eerie confrontation with an unidentified flying object, Mike and a friend, Chuck Damore, were bundled up in their warmest clothing as they walked along desolate Barclay Avenue in the dim light of dusk, returning from the home of a classmate. They had decided to take the long way back to their respective houses, in order to

Above: Dulles International Airport in Virginia has been me target of a virtual UFO siege. Below: On June 17, 1975, Capt. Joseph Walters observed two UFOs on radar at Homestead Air Force Base- After Captain Walters reported his sighting to the Miami News, he was later found to be unavailable for comment.

stop off at a local pond to see if it was frozen over. The 15-year-old Tottenville High School students hoped it would be, so that they could go ice-skating the following afternoon.

As they ventured cautiously onto the ice to test its strength Mike chanced to glance upward. Hanging stationary above the trees 300 feet away, was a strange object which he could not immediately identify.

"It was definitely the oddest thing I've ever seen,"the young witness said as we tailed in his parents' kitchen, his bewildered mother standing nearby "I'm positive it couldn't have been a helicopter or an airplane. First of all, it didn't budge an inch for the longest time, and also there was no sound of engines or propellers to be heard."

The two youngsters watched intently, as the UFO hovered over a densely-wooded area, dipping occasionally below treetop level.

Together, they noted as many details as they could under the circumstances. "The UFO stood out like a red-hot poker, glowing a brilliant shade of orange in the night sky," Mike noted. Its shape closely resembled that of a football. Asked to calculate the size of the

craft, the witness estimated the UFO to be "somewhere around 25 feet in diameter."

After several minutes, the object changed form. "I had to blink twice to make certain I wasn't imagining it," Mite said. "its new shape was that of a sphere."

Moments after this transformation, the UFO flew off to the northwest.

Questioned about the episode, Chuck Damore agreed that the entire affair gave him a rather nervous feeling. "My knees were shaking from the combination of the cold and seeing this thing—

this flying saucer—that by all rights shouldn't have been hovering there. It was so close that you got the impression that if you wanted to, you could reach out and touch it.

"We watched it for close to 10 minutes," Chuck added. "I know that a lot of folks will think we're making up the whole story—but that's not so. My only regret is that no one else was present to vouch for its appearance.

As it turned out, the boys did not need additional witnesses. The evidence they sought was available in abundance.

Chuck insists that the UFO had a very specific outline. "It wasn't a reflection or a bird that we saw. It was definitely a *machine* of some sort!"

Like his buddy. Chuck Damore **was puzzled by** the UFO's ability to alter its **shape.** "One second it looked like a goose egg, and the next moment— *presto!*—it actually shrank in size and turned into a ball "

After calming down, the pair headed for the warmth of their parents' homes. Initially, they **had decided** to **keep their** unusual experience a closely-guarded secret. Only after returning to the **same** area the next day, and making a startling discovery in the process, did they decide to report **what** they had **seen.**

This is what Mike Kileen reports they **found: "We went back** early the follow-

An unexplained glowing light, sometimes spinning, at other times "seeming to have flares burning from its sides," was seen over Philadelphia on Oct. 8, 1975.

ing morning, and decided to take a walk through the woods to the point where the UFO seemed to have been hovering. As we **reached** the vicinity, we halted in our tracks. Immediately, we saw that the tops of **several** trees **had** been sheared off **as** high as 10 feet above the ground. Bark on a lot of the other trees had been burned— scorched—as if by a **tremendous** blast **of heat.** The soil itself was charred. Everything—all the shrubs and thickets—in a radius of approximately 50 **feet** appeared to **be** flattened out, as if by a giant object."

Feeling it **was their** civic duty to report their sighting, the high school students contacted the Annadale Police Department, **and** the *Staten **Island** Advance,*

a daily newspaper. Both the press and local law enforcement officials were impressed with the evidence.

When word of the incident reached me, I noted *that* there **was** a better-than-average chance I could document **an** apparent landing of a *UFO,* so I contacted the two boys directly.

Together, we drove to the **scene,** which I **found exactly as described. After driving** down a winding, unpaved dirt road, we arrived at the spot. Five-inch-thick branches, the size of a baseball bat, had been **snapped** in two, **high in** *the* **trees.**

If this was a **hoax, it was** *an* **extremely** elaborate one.

And **for** what reason?

In addition, the soil and dead leaves showed every indication of having been seared by intense heat or radiation. *Also,* of major importance—a circular patch of ground covering a radius of **40 feet had been pressed down** into the frozen ground, Smaller tree **trunks were found** to **be broken** off close to the

earth. **The area** *bore* a remarkable **resemblance** to **the so-called** "'saucer nests" **discovered in Canada** and Australia following recent UFO activity in these two countries. In each instance, **the earth** *was* **found** "pressed down,"

always in a clockwise direction, as if something extremely heavy had settled on the **ground.** Photos taken from the the air give the impression that a giant *prehistoric* bird had *made a nest for* itself. The same **pattern** was visible in Staten Island!

Indeed, this case had all the signs of being genuine.

A check with the local residents turned **up** no further clues that might shed some light on the case **or** offer **a possible solution. No** one reported seeing or hearing anything in *the* least **bit** suspicious—that is except for Daniel Kish and his dog, Rip.

It was only by accident, in fact, that Kish's **story came to my** attention. "After *a* **friend told me what** had supposedly happened. **I** retraced my activities and found that the sighting made **by** those **young fellows took** place near **where** I was **walking** my dog, **and** at precisely the **same** hour. Can **you** beat that? Frankly, I can't explain why I didn't see anything **odd,** but perhaps (the **object)** was **just** too low, and the trees **blocked my view.** There's no question in **my** mind that old Rip sensed something peculiar."

And while he had never **seen the "unknown"** that night, **Daniel** Kish admitted, after a little prodding, that he had **seen** unusual "things" in the sky prior to this occasion. **"One** evening, late in 1974, I was returning from a nearby shopping center with **my** wife, Margaret. We were driving **along, when** suddenly **we** saw this tremendous 'cigar' floating across the road. The object had a clearly visible row of lighted windows. It was down real close, so that we had no trouble making out the details."

San Francisco and vicinity have been repeatedly visited by strange objects in the sky. Three glowing UFOs were sighted near the city on the evening of Nov. 2, 1975. Below: San Antonio was the site of a bizarre encounter when Alois Olenick was temporarily blinded after observing a red dome-shaped craft that hovered within 30 feet of him.

During the course of a lengthy conversation, Mrs. Kish insisted that she has been seeing UFOs over Staten Island for nearly 15 years—more or less on a regular basis! "In the early 1960's my youngest son shouted for me to come out of the house one night and take a look through his telescope." What she saw jolted her. "There was this pulsating object, bobbing up and down." Margaret says the UFO had a bubble-like dome on top.

Mrs. Kish says that she has seen a steadily increasing number of objects in recent months. "If you ask me, I think they are probably from outer space!"

The more checking I did, the more I began to realize something truly weird was happening on this small island located only a few miles from Times Square. There were the usual sightings, plus a host of other, totally bizarre, aspects to contend with.

Other witnesses came forward after hearing me discuss the subject on local radio and TV talk shows. Their observations added to my bulging flies.

Several sightings, it should be noted, have been made surprisingly near the Verrazano Narrows Bridge, which connects Staten Island with neighboring Brooklyn. One person placed a call to the Brooklyn Home Reporter, a small weekly community newspaper, after watching a strange object descend into the lower harbor. In a frightened voice, the witness described seeing a brilliant ball of fire zoom down low over the bridge, and moments later land on the water, where it sank rapidly from sight.

Another observer, Claudia Montelione, of Brooklyn, stared "dumbfounded" as a UFO passed above the huge span in January 1975. "I had stopped for a traffic light," she said, "when I happened to peer out of a side window." There, swaying back and forth over an apartment building near the bridge, was this reddish glowing ship with a circular band of rotating, multi-colored tights around its edges." Moments later, the UFO sped out over the harbor, passing breathtakingly close to the steel towers of the bridge. "Other people must have seen it as well," Claudia said. "There were three other people in the car with me, and they were all impressed."

On a clear, cloudless night, it is possible to see for miles out over the span of water that separates Staten Island from Manhattan and Brooklyn. Depending on the prevailing weather conditions, it can be a picturesque sight. Over the years, this area's quaint back roads have built up a reputation for being a favorite "lovers' lane," frequented by youngsters living in the nearby suburbs. From time to time, a nervous teenager has approached me in the strictest of confidence, to report a sighting that's never been publicized. Usually, the story they tell is one I've heard many times before. One warm evening during August 1974, for example, a young couple was parked enjoying the view, when suddenly an entire fleet of disc-shaped objects, flashing colored lights appeared In the twilight- They counted five UFOs in the armada. The sighting, to quote them precisely, "made our hair curl!"

As has happened so Often before when dealing with UFO flaps, the Staten island wave left us a fair share of bizarre and totally puzzling events to contend with. There were reports of a strange hairy "monster" and mysterious "government agents,"

A number of the participants in the flap claim that a blue van, with the words, "U.S. Air Force" stenciled on its side, cruised the neighborhood for days after the "saucer-nest" was uncovered on Barclay Avenue. One observer said that the occupants of this vehicle did not wear regulation uniforms, but instead dressed in white coveralls with thick-soled boots. And although these men kept a close watch on the comings and goings of witnesses, at no time did they try and talk with any of those involved. When a suspicious resident finally decided to confront the driver of the van, the vehicle disappeared. There were no signs of tire tracks on the shoulder of the road where it had been parked, despite the fact that it was raining lightly, making the sides of the road even muddier than usual. "They should have left some tracks," the man said. A check with the Air Force showed that they had never ordered an investigation in mat area.

Who were these men? So-called military imposters have often appeared

One of two teenagers who witnessed the landing of a UFO on New York's Staten Island points to the broken trunks of small trees which were found at the site.

at the sight of a UFO landing, particularly in cases where physical evidence has been left behind. Several years ago, the Pentagon issued a memorandum warning local Air Force commands to be on guard against such imposters.

In previous issues of UFO Report. other authors have speculated on the link between flying saucers and the creature known as Bigfoot. Dozens of fully documented episodes are on file in which UFO sightings are accompanied by reports of "beasties," as they are sometimes called, being seen. Frequently, these tall, hairy humanoids,

Mike Cooper and Jim James watched a rapidly moving UFO fly toward the heart of Tucson, Ariz., in September 1975.

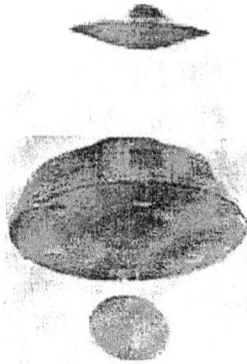

CITIES

(Continued)

which closely resemble **apes** but with superior **intelligence**, will appear **just** prior to or shortly after a UFO flap. Such was the case with a Staten Island episode.

Hysterical callers telephoned the *Staten Island Advance* on Dec. 7, 1974, to tell of a "large, hair-covered mammal' that **walked on two feet and screamed** at the top of its lungs. Police made a two-hour search of an area around S t Andrew's Episcopal Church and an adjacent **golf course. As more reports came in,** a helicopter was ordered into the air to *search* **for the creature** from treetop level. **A posse combed** the vicinity on foot. but **could** find **nothing. The** hairy visitor had **vanished** without **a trace just** like the "military imposters"

were to **do later on!**

Actually, the UFO flap **in** and around New York City has been slowly but steadily increasing in tempo. It is apparent that the ufonauts have had their eye on the highly populated East Coast for some time. In fact. **sightings of low-flying discs are** considered **a com-**mon sight throughout towns across the **river in New** Jersey.

Although **no part of the Garden State has** gone untouched in **recent months,** northern **New** Jersey **seems** to have been particularly "hard hit." Directly opposite **the** northern tip of Manhattan are the **communities of Fort Lee,** En-glewood Cliffs, Fair Lawn. and Pater-**son.** Many of the residents of these towns commute to **New** York daily by bus or **car** over the George Washington Bridge. For all intents and purposes, the **people who** live in these towns **are New**

Yorkers, peering out of their high-rise apartments at night **and looking at** the lights of the largest city **in** the country. **With** no effort at all, from their **vantage** point across the Hudson, they **can** see such sights as the **Empire** State **Build-**ing, the World Trade Center and dus-ters of other skyscrapers scattered about Manhattan.

While taping a show for Tele-prompter-TV (an independent cable **television** station **in New** York) on location at a famous **resort motel** in New Jersey. I was approached after **the** program by a dignified highly-respected physician, in his free time he is vice-president of a large foundation which provides *college* scholarships to **minorities.** He had **been** listening to my conversation with Lourdes Ramann, the attractive female host of the show. The topic of **discussion had** been *flying* **saucers.**

"Of course, I've never told anyone beside my wife about this. Because of **the** nature of my profession **and my** connection with a foundation—which is entitled to federal grants—you can ap-preciate **my** reluctance to have *my name* associated with anything like UFOs." After I promised **that his identity** would remain confidential, the doctor began relating his story. It was a truly unusual *one!*

"I was driving on one of the back roads on the outskirts of Paterson, N.J., returning **home** from a party. It was rather late—about three a.m., on a cold December morning in 1974. I **had** turned the radio up quite loud **in** order to **keep** myself awake. Since I had never **had** any previous trouble with the radio, you can imagine my surprise when the music was interrupted by a blast of static. No matter where I turned the dial, the interference continued."

The doctor says that intermingled with the static **was a beeping sound. "Over** *the* **roar of** the crackle **and** noise, I could distinctly hear a peculiar *beep.* It seemed to **be intelligent—as** if some-one were trying to send a **message in** code." As he rounded a bend in *the* road, he saw something **in** the sky that made him slam on the brakes. "Here I am like only person out at this ungodly hour, and I have to see 'it.' " The "it" was a large cigar-shaped craft of size-able dimensions.

The doctor claimed the UFO hung **suspended** in **the sky** "as if dangling from an invisible wire." As in many cases of **this type,** the **object** made absolutely no sound. The **body** of the craft was surrounded by an **orange** glow that totally mesmerized **the** doctor, "so much so **that** I couldn't take my eyes off it." Almost hypnotized by the spectacle, **the doctor** polled over **to** the side of the road and **parked.**

The spellbound witness was even more dumbfounded when a number of smaller, diamond-shaped craft-each one "about 30 feet in diameter"—shot out of a concealed "trap door" in the base of the elongated cylinder. Without a sound, this strange "vessel" **then** sped across the sky to take up a stationary position about a quarter of a mile to the **west.** Within a **matter** of minutes, **three** of the mini-UFOs ren-dezvoused **nearby.** Together, the trio formed a **triangular** pattern in the heavens **before** taking **off at** a rapid clip toward the island of Manhattan. And, immediately after this, the **doctor** tes-tified, three more objects **emerged** from the bottom of the "parent" craft, and disappeared in an identical manner.

As if this wasn't enough for **the** doctor, an additional aerial ballet began taking place in another portion of the **sky.** "To **the** east, I caught sight of a formation of three sparkling jewels. By that time I was **ready** to **accept** any-thing..." As the physician watched, these **pulsating** globes entered the "mother ship" one by one, seemingly replacing those that had left earlier. This procedure was followed a few minutes later when **yet** another fleet *entered* the **craft.** "It appeared as if this big, cigar-shaped *craft* was acting as some sort of *'aircraft* carrier,' *sending* out a fresh, steady stream of flying saucers and taking **aboard** those that **were** returning. Who's to say **what their super-secret** mission might **have** been?"

Regardless of the late hour, **the** doctor found it extremely difficult to fall asleep that night. "If my wife had been **awake** when I came in that morning, sometime after 4:30, she would have found me shaking like *a* leaf. I tossed and turned until dawn—I don't believe I got more than an hour's rest altogether. The bags showed under my eyes the next day. **Luckily,** it **was a weekend,** so I didn't have **patients** to **treat."**

Although the highly respected physi-cian didn't report his sighting to "a living soul," he **has never forgotten the inci-dent.** "It's not **the type** of thing you can easily forget." he said in earnest. "What I want to know **is,** where were **they** going, and what did they have **inten-tions of** doing?

While we **may** not have the specific answers the doctor seeks, **we do know** that UFOs have caused repeated havoc in the suburbs of New York City. The spring and summer months of 1975 brought a rash of sightings, and mys-terious objects were frequently reported in the **area.**

On **the** evening of **July 5th, excited** residents of Fort Lee, Paterson, and Fair Lawn. N.J., called **the** Hackensack *Record* to tell of a "**round flying object, strung** with dazzling white lights and topped with a tong red light." Pilot James Quodomine, an employee at the Caldwell Wright Airport, insists that he flew within feet of the strange craft and watched it swoop down *toward* the ground, turn around and fly off. Another perplexed witness, Tom Cahill, told police that a UFO **hovered over his car on Route** 46. "it was huge, oval-shaped with bluish lights. I watched it for a white, and then it shot off into the sky in less than a **second." And as puzzled as** *these* observers might have been, they were certainly not atone. Police in several New Jersey counties noted a disruption of their patrol car radios on **several** occasions that night. Each time, UFOs *were* **seen** *in the* **vicinity**

While it may be hard to accept that such close encounters **are** going on within sight of Manhattan's skyscrapers, the facts remain unchallengable.

Because of this constant activity. it shouldn't come as a terrific shock if tomorrow, or the next day, a flying *saucer should* cruise *down Fifth Avenue* at high **noon.** with hundreds of thousands of people watching the spectacle.

In case anyone thinks that we are too farfetchedin our daydreams, such incidents have already occurred—at **least** on a small scale.

In August 1975, movie producer Lloyd Kauffman (whose **credits include such** films as *The* **Divine** Obsession **and** *Silent Night, Bloody* Night}, was standing outside the famous Plaza Hotel on 59th Street and Fifth Avenue, in New York City, trying to hail a taxi. Across the street from where he stood is Central Park. As he stepped out of the **hotel** onto the street, he happened to glance across the thoroughfare in time to see a dazzling display. "I know I can't prove it," the young, bearded producer told **me,** "but it had to be from 'out of this world.' I mean this object literally made no sound. **On** top of that it moved so gracefully, that it reminded **me** of a glidingswan.

Kauffman says that the **UFO came complete with** a "band of white light" which circled its base. The movie producer estimated the object's size as that of a "jumbo jet." He expressed surprise that there was nothing about the sighting in any of the newspapers the next day. "I'm almost positive other **people** saw it—I **mean, it was so big,** how could they miss it?" Apparently they did!

When heavyweight boxing champ Muhammad Ali and a contingent of aides and reporters observed not one but two UFOs "like light bulbs" over Central Park **in** 1971, **New** York's daily newspapers ignored the story, although it was carried on the **wire** services. Ironically, **a** United **Press** international newsman was among the dozen witnesses. **However,** the UFO sighting by Ali did make the front pages of **papers** across the country.

Luckily. **UFO** news fares much **better in other parts of the** country. Up until a year ago, it **was rare** to hear of a flying saucer being sighted over **any** highly populated community. For the most part reports **were** confinedto rural areas and other sparsely populated locales, **such** as swamps, deserts, or mountainous regions.

But **times have** changed!

Here is a brief rundown of only a few of the many documented reports that *have* **come** to our attention in 1974 and 1975 from **sizable** cities and communities across **North** America.

• *Cincinnati,* Ohio (**Pop.** 452,000): In the pre-dawn hours, police spotted a UFO **80** degrees above the horizon. For more than two hours on Oct. 27, 1975, the disc bobbed "up and down," always remaining in the same sector of **m e sky.** Finally, the UFO moved *off* **in** a southeasterly direction. leaving **more** than a dozen police officials bewildered. Sgt. Lester **Muse** confirmed that several of his **men** had seen "a white light with little red lights **on each end."** He could not explain the phenomenon.

• *Chicago, Ill.* (Pop, **3,369,000) UFOs were seen** on at least two separate occasions in 1975 above the Windy City.

On August 7th, more than a dozen residents of the north side watched a strange object "make horseshoe movements, then hover and **move** vertically." Some *witnesses* described **the** illuminated **sphere** in terms **of** "red, white, green, and blue lights." Others insisted it "had a whitish **glow** inside and an orange glow aroundits **middle." Among** the stunned observers were police officials from three counties.

Just **two** months later, residents of Chicago were aroused during the wee **hours** of **the morning** by a "blinding **strobe** light" **that** was said to change **shape.** "It was like watching a Roman candle explode," is the **way Mrs. Cynthia** Zusel described *the* aerial spectacle. The Chicago **housewife** told friends **that** she originally **sighted** the UFO **when s h e** raised **the shade** in her bedroom around three a.m. to *see what* was **"causing the sun to** come up so early." There "dancing" in the night sky, was a globe of dazzling brightness. "It **looked** like a **star.** It was changing shape as it was glimmering. I nearly fainted!" the **witness** said, her voice showing tension. Many of the Oct. 8th **sightings** clustered around O'Hare Airport, where many witnesses saw "bright red" UFOs "playing tag" with **each** other.

• *Atlantic* City, *N.J.* (**Pop.** 47,000): Veteran policeman **Frank** Ingargiola, and Sonny Schwartz. a columnist for the Atlantic City Free Press, encountered a UFO which **paced** the officer's patrol car and **appeared to** be on the verge of "gobblingus up." **The** incident, which attracted **widespread attention,** took place on Jan. 20,1976 at 5:15 a.m. According to **the** witnesses, the **object** came to **within** 100 feet of their **car.** at an **altitude** of no more than 30 feet. Hovering in the vicinity for close to an hour, the UFO at one point closed in **on** Ingargiola and Schwartz. It was only after the two **men** turned on **the** patrol car's brilliant spotlight and **beamed** it in the direction of the object, that the craft retreated and **disappeared** out to sea. Additional sightings from the Atlantic City area were **reported** for **a** week following this hair-raising incident.

• *Las Vegas, Nev.* (Pop. 126.000): For more than a *week* in mid-January 1976, observers in **widely scattered parts of** *the* Las Vegas Valley reported sighting UFOs. **Descriptions of the objects** varied from "a **cigar-shaped ship,** flying at **extremely** high altitudes" to a "shiny **disc** that **appeared** over the **North** Las Vegas civic center, veering sharply west **and** flying **out** of viewing **range** over Mount Charleston, at speeds faster than any jet ever seen." **During the** *midst* **of** *the* flap, a musician by **me** name of Johnny Sands claims he was abducted **and taken aboard an object** that took the form **of** "the **Goodyear** blimp, only longer, with flashing lights on its bullet-shaped ends, and a darker doughnut-like **ring around** the fuselage." Inside the craft he claims he **was** examined by several creatures **with** "squinted eyes, and gills under their ears."

• California. No thorough roundup of UFO **sightings** in metropolitan areas **would be complete** without a summary of the recent flurry of events **in** **California. Long a** hotbed of flying saucer activity, the Golden State has had its share of **recent occurrences.** In the past few months **the** populated areas surrounding Los **Angeles** and San Francisco have been particularly hard hit.

In Compton (pop. 78,000), **a** suburb of L.A., **two** college freshmen, **Chico** McCall and Alvin Logan, say they got a better-man-average look at a pair of UFOs which joined **together** in midair. The two honor students claim that the **objects were disc-shaped,** with **a** central **band of blinkinglights.** While a check with the **local** sheriff's office failed to turn up **any other** reports **on the** night of **Feb.** 5, 1976, a spokesman for the department noted that "two **weeks ago,** a woman did call to say she had **seen** men from outer **space.** We finally dispatched a **deputy** to calm her down!" No additionalinformationwas forthcoming, **and** the **sheriffs** office refused to divulge the **identity of the** shaken women.

Not to be outdone, **San Francisco and** vicinity have been visited by UFOs

Astronauts' experiences prove there's a heaver

HEAVEN IS not at the other end of the universe — it's right over our heads, say spiritual researchers.

Each planet has its own spiritual zones populated by evolved beings, say Rev. Diane Tessman and Timothy Green Beckley in the book Your Passport to Heaven (Inner Light Publications, 1985).

"Each planet in this solar system, as well as throughout the vast cosmos, is made up of various spiritual planes, the lower ones purely physical in nature and the people residing there materialistic in overall content," they explain.

"This is the type of plane we currently reside on. As we leave the physical by way of the soul, we discover that the planes directly above us are much like the planet Earth.

"As we journey higher we come closer to God's kingdom, which is spiritual and not physical essence."

Tessman and Beckley *feel* that *the* higher realms are located about 5,000 miles up,

Blips

"High altitude radar has often picked up blips of unknown origin coming from just such an altitude," they explain.

"Such blips have often registered as being upwards of *five* miles across, *as* if they were some sort of 'sky island' *floating* in the upward regions of our atmosphere

Yet *as* massive as these blips are, *nothing* can *be* seen through a telescope, indicating that we're dealing with unseen realms or kingdoms."

Bizarre

The authors *also* note that the astronauts' bizarre experiences while *in the* limbo of space also indicate to them that heaven is nearby

"Our astronauts heard strange voices coming through their earphone speaking in languages they are not familiar with," they explain.

"On *the* Apollo 12 mission, one of our lunar walkers also actually heard the

... say two spiritual researchers

chords of *the* song Wher Angels Fear To Trea while he was bouncin *about* in the free-fail grav ity of space.

"NASA also picked u the emission *but the* could not trace its origin: 'Sines they were con municating on *a* speck channel with the astr nauts, they felt convince that the song was not bein broadcast by anyone her on Earth

'To our minds," the au thors conclude, "this seem to be a way of telling u that *the* angels of the Lor are *always* dose at hand

— JOHN TURNE

TIMOTHY BECKLEY, co-author of Your Passport to Heaven, holds a copy of his UFO Review.

on several recent occasions. In Vacaville, for example, three glowing oval *objects* were seen on *the* evening of Nov. 2, 1975, hovering in the sky above this peaceful tree-lined community. Robert Perry told police that he was riding along on his motorcycle, when he saw a large light through the *trees* near a water treatment plant Perry claims the UFO rose from the ground and hovered over the *trees* for several minutes. Shortly thereafter, two similar craft rose from the ground and joined *the* first one. Other communities near San Francisco that *have* recently reported UFOs include Modesto, where on Feb. 14, 1976, *more* than *a* dozen residents watched as a UFO cavorted over the downtown section of the city. Local authorities tried to deride *the* sightings *as* nothing more than (he reflection of a searchlight on low-hanging clouds, but the populace did not buy the official explanation. Only a *few* days earlier, Mrs. Vicki Richter, a reserve deputy *for* the Yolo County Sheriff's Department, in Woodland, watched *in* awe as a brightly lit UFO hung motionless in midair, and was later joined by a second object. Together the *two* craft remained *in* the vicinity for a half-hour, finally flitting off to the north. Similar sightings have

been made in this *same* area near San Francisco on previous occasions.

● *Texas:* Perhaps tire most thrilling *encounter* involving a UFO took place on Oct. *23*, 1974, as *two* pilots were preparing to land at San Antonio International Airport. The "bright red ball" was first spotted at 3,500 feet *off* the wing tip of an Eastern jumbo *jet* piloted by Capt. Jerry Noyes. The object, kept pace with the airliner for several *minutes*, and then *shot* up 2,000 feet in an incredible burst of speed. A Braniff *pilot*, flying above Captain Noyes' plane, watched the proceedings with fascination, fearing *that*, at *any* moment, the UFO might come after him.

Perhaps related to the appearance of UFOs, was a weird creature said *to* be "half-bird, half-man" which *came* complete with "bulging pink eyes," and was seen roaming around the state. Police were busy answering calls from excited residents of Brownsville. On Jan- 3, *1976*, a man living on the outskirts of town testified that he was awakened by the sound *of* something *scratching* against *the* side of his house-trailer. Alverico Guaradd and his family were so frightened that they got *into* their car and began driving away. The headlights of the vehicle fell upon a five-foot-tall being with "a *large* beak and a bat-like face with white feathers."

Because of the urgency of the accounts, a research group has been formed *to* check into reports originating in the Lone Star State. Dedicated to scientific investigation on a local level, the *Texas UFO Study Group* is being fun by Tommy Roy Blann who, along with newspaper editor Gracia Unger, detailed many of the recent Texas sightings, landings, and contacts in the Spring 1975 issue of *UFO Report*

Lawrence, Kans. (Pop. 45,000; fifth largest city in state): Traffic came to a complete standstill on Oct. 27, 1975, when two "wed lighted" UFOs were seen above this bustling city. Richard Ross, a meteorologist from *the* University of Kansas, gave the *press* this account: "About *50* or *60* cars with observers pulled off the road . . . The objects *were* first blue, *then* alternately changed to yellow, red, and orange. A lot of people saw them and nobody seems to know what they were. There was no sound. They just hung there for a while and then disappeared. I have to call them *UFOs* because that's what they were!"

● *Lawton, Okla.* (Pop. 74,000); third largest city in state and the site of a large Army installation): At first the object was thought to have been a Skyhook balloon launched from Holloman Air Force Base. However, a spokesman there discounted this explanation, stating that "all their balloons were accounted for." Taking up a position directly above the County Courthouse, the UFO caused massive telephone problems when police and military switchboards were jammed with calls. The unexplained "visitor" was picked up on radar and seen simultaneously from the ground and air. The UFO stayed in the vicinity of Lawton for 24 hours before vanishing The UFO moved silently above the town, often in *the* direction opposite to the wind, proving that it could not have been some sort of lighter-than-air device

● *Philadelphia. Pa.* (Pop. 1,950,000): An unexplained glowing light. sometimes "spinning" and at other times *'seeming* to have flares burning from its side," was observed by scores of people as it flew across *the* smoke-filled skyline on Oct. 8, 1975. All told, 50 calls were received by the police and at Philadelphia's international Airport for the period covering four a.m. to six a.m.

Officer Michael Baldassaro and Sgt. Michael Romano added their names to the rosier of puzzled onlookers. "It was pretty bright with 'flares appearing from either side," Romano said. "It seemed to spin—rotate—and would go up and down and crosswise and in a circular motion." A spokesman for the Federal Aviation Administration (FAA) discounted the likelihood that it might have been the landing lights of an aircraft approaching the airport.

• Portland, Oregon (Pop. 398,000): Observers saw a "large, burning ember" falling out of the sky about 9:15 p.m., Sept. 10, 1975. The Portland Journal confirmed that the object was "enormous, with a greenish tinge and a tail." According to reports, it lingered over the city for some time before "going down in a southwesterly direction and disappearing with a flash." One woman saw it crash near Portland's Aurora Airport, but no debris could be found. Another observer added that "it was bright as a street lamp."

• Pensacola, Fla. (Pop. 59,000): Ed Gillotte, assistant chief of the FAA's radar flight-control tower at Sherman Field, says he saw a UFO. "flying in a zigzag pattern high above the city's Yacht Club." He described it as a "blowtorch" rather than a pinpoint of light.

• Pontiac, Mich. (Pop. 85,000): Members of the Harrington School basketball team saw a solid object 20 feet in diameter, flying in the direction of the Pontiac Metropolitan Stadium around 11 p.m. on June 23, 1975. "It was silvery and circular" or "looked like a flying saucer," were common descriptions. One eyewitness said the UFO had a band of light which revolved constantly. Another observed a series of windows.

• Greensboro, N.C. (Pop. 144,000; second largest city in state): A UFO landed in a wooded area behind the Manor apartment complex. The object was seen for 10 minutes beginning at 12:30 a.m. on June 16, 1975. The observers included a businessman, his wife, and a friend. High grass and weeds were found flattened in a circular pattern at the landing site. The witnesses, who asked not to be identified by name, told APRO field investigator Dr. Arlan Andrews that the object "came straight down out of a cloud, hovered for more than five minutes, moved up and down, and then finally landed. It remained on the ground until its lights went out."

• Tucson, Arizona (Pop. 263,000): Two teenage boys—Mike Cooper and Jim Jones—said they were sitting on a wall along Pinal Drive at 8:30 p.m. on Sept. 3,1975, when a UFO sped by, heading for the heart of Tucson. The youths claimed that the rapidly moving craft was flying "high up." Suddenly, it turned

around and went back toward Phoenix. APRO, with headquarters in the city. said they were attempting to verify other reports, including the sighting of a 'luminous cigar" seen by two women traveling on Highway I-10.

• Miami, Fla. (Pop. 325,000): Capt. Joseph Waiters did a complete about-face after reporting that he had picked up two unidentified blips on radar at Homestead Air Force Base. The incident happened on June 17, 1975, at nine p.m. Captain Walters first called the Miami News, explaining, "We spotted these two objects traveling at 240 knots. They were on the screen for about 15 seconds." Later, two people telephoned the newspaper to tell of their own sightings. "There were these two cylindrical streaks moving across the sky," Joyce Farkwell stated. When a call was placed to Homestead to get additional information the News was told, "We never see UFOs here." Captain Walters was not available for comment. After hours of trying to track him down, the commanding officer called the newspaper back and explained that the objects on the radar screen were caused by "St. Elmo's fire." He concluded: "I'm sorry if I have given you the impression this is a whitewash." The National Weather Service emphatically rejected the explanation. "St. Elmo's fire is a coronal discharge of static electricity from the edge of thunderstorms," said Dick West of the Weather Bureau. "It is basically stationary and could not be picked up on radar." Though the Air Force claims they ceased investigating UFOs in 1969, it is obvious that information is screened from the press and public.

• San Antonio, Texas (Pop. 654,000): third largest city in the state): Alois Olenick told the sheriff's office that he went through a period of temporary blindness after watching a "cherry red" dome-shaped craft which hovered within 30 feet of the ground near him. Olenick said the UFO first caught his attention when he heard a "terrific wind" approaching from the east. The witness was able to see "two bald-headed men seated behind a control panel through a glass-enclosed cockpit atop the craft. Olenick said a bright light which surrounded the UFO left him partially blinded for three days. He said the blindness was similar to that caused by watching an arc-welding process without protective glasses.

• Charleston, W. Va. (Pop. 71,000): Elmer Salisbury, his daughter Kim, and her friend Julie Carey were playing basketball in Cameron High School playground on May 12, 1975. Salisbury said they could feel the static electricity thrown off by a green-blue globe which hovered above their automobile as they pulled away from the schoolyard. As the strange form hovered nearby, the car's electrical system went dead.

• Savannah, Ga. (Pop. 118,000): On Jan. 3, 1975, several area residents

reported a UFO which hovered over the town's busy traffic circle. making a sound like a "swarm of buzzing bees." Descriptions of the object were identical. The UFO was said to be composed of a bright gray metal, round at the bottom and with a structure on top "like a pyramid with the point cut off."

• Spokane, Wash. (Pop. 170,000): Mr. and Mrs. Jack Campbell observed what they maintain was a UFO: the date of their sighting was Nov. 26, 1974. "It was about five p.m. when we saw the object climb from the northwest, streak

CONTINUED

CONTINUED from page...
across the sky and disappear over the horizon in the southeast," stated Mrs. Campbell. "The bright body had a red tall or streak in its wake. It was faster than anything I've ever seen. I am sure it wasn't a shooting star or meteor because it raced all the way from horizon to horizon."

• Concord, N.H. (Pop. 30,000—state capital): Police were among those who watched in amazement as four brightly lit spheres, one beaming down a powerful searchlight, stood in the sky like a "sore thumb" over the capital. Patrolman James McGonigle, Jr., was among the many observers. He said the UFO "parked itself' quite high in the sky and proceeded to shoot vertical shades of light into space. A steady white beam

was topped by a flashing green light and a brilliant red light below. Officer McGonigle made his observation between 3:30 and 4:30 a.m. on Aug. 12, 1974. Northfield Police Chief Kris Meinhold reported a similar sighting. "They were something I'd never seen before," he maintained. With him were two other patrolmen. Photos of the UFOs were taken but showed nothing.

It is fascinating to note that no section of the country has been left out of the continuing UFO wave. Reports are evenly divided among the north, south, east, and west. Taking all the data into consideration, it would seem as if the occupants of these craft are no longer interested in playing peek-a-boo with

the human race. If they wanted to, the ufonauts could remain in hiding—far removed from public scrutiny. No longer satisfied with showing up only in secluded areas, they now appear bent on proving their existence. Day by day, the number of scoffers and cynics dwindle. The intelligences behind the UFOs are obviously out to show the people that they are indeed real, and not figments of overworked imaginations.

Whatever their plans may entail, obviously the ufonauts have all of us in mind. Their calculated and constantly increasing appearances over our largest cities are bound to bear fruit before too long. All the evidence adds up to one striking conclusion:

Flying saucers are anxious to make themselves known!

★

Over the centuries, scientists and philosophers *have gazed* at the seemingly endless sea of twinkling stars, and pondered the question: Is Earth the only haven of life in the universe? Are we unique—a product of *evolution* purely by chance?

At *this* very moment, huge dish-shaped scanning *devices* probe the heavens in a relentless attempt to pick up radio signals beamed from beyond our *own* solar system. We are led to believe that the long-&-wailed contact with *some* as-yet-undiscovered planet-neighbor could come any day.

Perhaps, though, our money is being unnecessarily wasted *on* such projects. Just *maybe* we are squandering our time and money in vain. For, there is a constantly expanding *file* of convincing evidence which indicates that communication with aliens has already been established—and not by radio wave, but *face-to-face!*

Staggering?

Incredible?

An unlikely theory?

According to available data, there has been—in recent years—a global increase in the number of low-level sightings *of* flying saucers; instances in which mysterious craft have maneuvered within a few yards of startled observers, *or* touched down upon the Earth. Included in this growing volume of reports are a surprising number of episodes involving *actual confrontations* between aliens and humans.

Overlooked in *this* surge of UFO activity and reported contactees, one lone individual may hold the missing clues we need to unravel the complex UFO enigma.

Carl Higdon, 41, of Rawlins, Wyo., remains bewildered by what happened to him on a cold autumn afternoon last Year. Little did he suspect, before starting out on what was supposed to be an ordinary hunting trip, that by the end of the day he would serve as an unofficial *emissary* to *a* group of "foreigners," who were anything but ordinary in appearance or behavior.

To this day, many *of* the events of October 25, 1974, remain nothing more than a hazy dream to Higdon. His memory was "blanked out" and it was only under hypnosis that he began to remember the circumstances of his strange experience. Careful analysis of this particular episode could well provide us with *the* answers to questions we have long been asking:

● Why UFOs visit *earth;*

● How they manage to travel *at* such incredible speeds; and

● How the realm from which they Originate relates to our *own* state of existence.

Higdon's experience is equal in importance to the famed case *of Betty* and Barney Hill (the *New* Hampshire couple who claimed—under hypnosis—that they had been *kidnapped* and given a physical examination by a group of UFO occupants). For Carl Higdon not only professes to have conversed with these entities, but he also claims he was taken *for* a ride *in* their spacecraft to an uncharted planet millions of miles away.

As incredible as it may sound, a surprising number *of* scientific investigators am convinced his voyage offers substantial proof for the extraterrestrial theory which has been *so* popular for years among UFOlogists. They point to the following evidence:

● Placed in *a* deep hypnotic *trance* on two separate occasions, Carl Higdon's story *held* up;

● The *impossible* movement, over a considerable distance, of a truck belonging to the witness;

● The subsequent *testimony* of additional witnesses who claim they saw strange objects in the sky on the day in question; and

● Scarred lung tissue which showed up on X-rays prior to the occurrence, subsequently vanished without a *trace.*

Employed for the last 20 years by the AM Wells Service Co. (Riverton, Wyo.) as an oil-field driller, Carl Higdon is accustomed to working in *the* outdoors, Never before has he had *anything* happen to him which could *be* construed as an unworldly experience.

"I'd like to think *it* was just *a* nightmare, except I *know* it was real," Higdon said. *"I've* tried to shake my mind dear of all thoughts pertaining to what took place, but frankly that's totally out *of* the question at this point"

His *story* begins innocently enough.

Like many Americans. Carl recently began to feel a pinch *on* his wallet He watched the price of feeding his wife and *four* children increase each week, and decided to try his hand at hurting to fill the meat freezer. Being an experienced *sportsman,* he quickly began bagging wild *game.* It was during the peak of elk hunting season that his extraordinary experience took place.

"I was all set to leave for work (Higdon is a foreman) when *one of my* key men phoned to tell me that he was sick. Realizing that nothing could be accomplished *with* him at home, I decided to take the *day* off." Driving toward McCarthy Canyon in Carbon County, in one *of* his company's pickup trucks. Higdon came across two *motorists* having trouble with their van. 'I pulled in front of 'em and helped 'em. During our chat, they told me the hunting *was* much better *farther* back in a remote section of the Medicine Bow National Forest." Higdon changed his plans immediately and headed in the new direction, to a locate some 40 miles south of Rawlins.

"Around four o'clock, I parked my two-wheel-drive on a knoll and putted out *my thermos* to pour *a* cup *of* coffee.

An old friend, *Gary* Eaton, walked over to where I had stopped and together we surveyed the area- *After a* few minutes, Gary told me he was going on higher up *into the* forest Jokingly he suggested he might scare down *some elk* for me." Higdon then *decided* to investigate an *area* beyond a nearby hill.

"I walked maybe five *minutes* until I came to a *rise* in the ground. Down below in a *clearing* were five elk, huddled closely together. From my vantage point, several hundred yards away, I could *see* that one *of* them was a really outstanding animal. I lined *him* up in my telescopic sight and fired *my* gun, a magnum rifle." The magnum is no lightweight weapon and pulling the trigger usually results in a sharp jolt to the hunter. "It can give your shoulder a mean *whack* if you're not careful," Higdon said.

What happened next transported him into an unknown dimension, and Carl still finds it difficult to understand.

"I couldn't believe *my senses!* Instead of a powerful blast, the 7mm bullet left the gun's barrel *noiselessly*

Kidnapped By Aliens!
The true Story Of Carl Higdon's Incredible Contact

Little did Carl Higdon suspect, before *starting* out
on an ordinary hunting trip *in* the Wyoming
wilderness, that by the end of the day
he would be abducted by UFOnauts!

By Timothy Green Beckley

ARTIST'S conception of the 'man' Higdon encountered.

and in slow motion. *It* floated like a butterfly, finally falling to *the* ground about 50 feet from where I stood. I was awe-struck—I froze. All *around* me there *was* a painful silence. Not a chirping bird or the rustling of leaves on nearby trees could be heard. The only sensation I could detect *was* a tingling feeling which crawled up my spine. This was similar to the feeling you *often get* before a fierce thunderstorm, when the air is full of static electricity."

Suddenly, *the* deadly *quiet* was broken by the snapping of a twig. "Turning *to* my left, I saw a 'man' standing *there*. At first I thought he was just another hunter, so I lowered my gun. Then he moved out of the shadows, into the light, and immediately I realized something was terribly wrong."

There, confronting Higdon was a humanoid creators.

"My heart skipped *a* beat and my knees were shaking so badly I could hardly stand. I thought. 'Well, I should have *stayed in* McCarthy Canyon like I'd originally planned!' "

Higdon maintains the being was rather peculiar, but not altogether nonhuman. "He was definitely man-like. *In* height, I'd estimate he *stood* well *over* six *feet,* and weighed around *180* pounds. This *was* definitely no ghost! *Good* Lord. he *was* flesh and blood. Amen."

Higdon also said that the being was *dressed* in a tight fitting, one-piece outfit, "similar *to* a wet-suit scuba divers wear." Around his waist, the creature wore a thick metal belt. In *the* middle of this was a six-pointed star. and directly underneath the star on the belt was an unidentifiable emblem. Crisscrossing its chest were a couple of belts that looked to be *a* harness.

"It was definitely a male!" and its *most* unusual feature was *the odd* appearance of his head and face. "Personally, *I* took getting used to, in order for me to look *at* him without getting a *queasy feeling* in *the* pit of my stomach." *According* to Higdon, the UFOnaut's face ran directly into his neck. "No chin was visible. His *face* just seemed *to* blend right *into* his *throat.* He had no jaw bone."

Recalling as much detail as possible, Higdon said that the being's skin was yellow, "very similar *to an* Oriental's."

'The visitor had no detectable ears. His eyes were small, and lacked eye brows." When *the* being opened his slit *of a* mouth, Higdon saw two sets of extremely large *teeth—three* on *top* and three below. The most outstanding feature however was definitely the creature's head. "The dome of his skull was covered with the coarsest hair imaginable It looked as if he had straw growing out of his head!" Golden in color, each strand poked up a couple of inches from his scalp. Sticking out of his forehead were two antenna-like rods.

"Without any prior communication this creature said, 'How you doin'?' I was trying to stay calm, so I responded with a weak, 'Pretty good'" At this point the alien then asked Higdon if he was hungry. Not waiting for a reply, the creature floated a small packet at him. He waved a pointed object where his right hand should have been, and it levitated over to me.

"I opened the packet and found four pills inside. He told me, in English, to take one of them. That it would last four days. Now, normally I don't like taking pills, not even an aspirin, but something happened. It's as if I had no control over my actions. So I just swallowed one of 'em, and put the other three into my jacket pocket."

Directly behind the alien, Higdon noticed the sun's rays reflecting on something in the glade. "There, not far from us, was a transparent, cube-shaped object resting on the ground. To me it looked like a huge Christmas package. You know—flat on all sides, like a box. I couldn't see any landing gear or entrance."

As to its size, Higdon was emphatic. "It was much smaller than any of our commercial or military planes. In fact, you're going to think I'm crazy, but this thing couldn't have been more than five feet high, seven feet long, and four-and-a-half feet wide. Tiny is the only word I can think of to accurately describe it's size!"

Realizing that Higdon had seen his ship, the being asked, "Do you want to come along?" Higdon, realizing he had no choice, only shrugged his shoulders.

"Before I was able to move a muscle, I found myself inside this contraption. It was instantaneous. How I was able to fit inside, remains a riddle. They must have shrunk me, that's the only explanation that seems plausible. My memory fails me, here. I recall my head starting to reel—my hands sweating. Somehow the pill this fellow gave me must have deadened at least some of my senses, otherwise I'm positive I would have been crying and perhaps even fainted. I may be strong, but I'm only human!"

Through a transparent partition, Higdon saw the elk he'd been hunting earlier. All five were on board in a separate compartment "I'm kind of fuzzy as to how they managed to contain such wild beasts. They were motionless. Paralyzed!"

Cart Higdon explained that he also was not able to move. "As we took off, I found myself strapped down to this seat with my hands held fast to the armrests of the chair. My legs were similarly bound."

Realizing that it was useless to struggle, Higdon reigned himself to his fate. Another being then appeared. "I have no idea where he came from—he was just there!" They covered his head with a football-like helmet. Wires stuck out in every direction. "I felt like the monster in an old Frankenstein movie." Unfortunately for Cart Higdon, this was no classic horror film, but reality.

Off in the distance, through the crystal-clear watts of the ship, Higdon said he saw a large sphere—"shaped similar to a basketball"—looming below. "We landed on what must have been their planet They told me it was 163,000 Tight miles' from earth." At no time did they say "light years," which is the terminology usually used for measuring the vast distances between two points in space. "Obviously to them the passage of time is different than it is to us. Again, I couldn't recall a great deal. until placed under hypnosis. Consciously, I don't even remember leaving the ship, though it came out later that I did."

From his seat aboard the "flying box car" Higdon was able to took at their

world Rising many stories above the ground was a towering platform, which reminded him of the "Space Needle" built especially for the Seattle World's Fair.

"All around this tower were revolving patterns of multi-colored lights, not unlike powerful spotlights. They were so intense that it was actually painful to keep my eyes open. These lights were so brilliant that I held my hands to my face as a protective shield. I vaguely remember shouting, 'Shut them off.. . they're burning me!' I just couldn't tolerate them." With this, one of the aliens commented, "Your sun burns us, too!"

After a short while they told Higdon they would take him back where they had originally found him, because he did not suit their purpose.

The next sequence of events Higdon can recall has him wandering down a dirt road, staggering from side to side, utterly confused. "I didn't know what had happened—who I was—or where I was, for that matter. The only thing I could think of was to get out of there as fast as possible and find someone who could help me."

In his hands was the rifle he had

been carrying earlier. "There I stood, shivering, eyes filled with tears and not knowing my own identity. I saw a truck parked off the road between some trees, and decided to crawl into it for shelter and to keep warm. I didn't realize the truck belonged to me."

Sprawled out in the van, Higdon heard a voice over a radio. "There was a two-way set under the dashboard, so I picked up the mike and held it close to my mouth. I managed to blurt out that I was sick and lost and desperately in need of assistance. When the voice on the other end asked me where I was, I told 'em I had seen a sign down the road which read, 'North Boundary National Forest'. This didn't seem to be of much help, however, as there was absolutely no indication as to what forest the sign was referring to."

By keeping in constant radio contact, a search party eventually located him. Even as they approached the area, they were bewildered over where they found Carl's pickup truck. It was stuck bumper-deep in mud, in the midst of a sink hole. A careful look at the situation told the rescuers it would have been

> "...Though I remain apprehensive over the events of last October, I firmly believe the American public is brave enough to accept the truth about such matters. Of course, I wish the entire episode hadn't happened, but since it did, I don't see any reason to keep it secret.."

impossible for Higdon to drive into such a hazardous locale.

"Using towing equipment, I was hauled out. They immediately took me to the nearest hospital, where I was placed under day-and-night observation. Not until the following evening did I begin to regain my memory and start to recall a few details of my ordeal.

"Though I remain apprehensive over the events of last October, I firmly believe the American public is brave enough to accept the truth about such matters. Of course I wish the whole episode hadn't occurred, but since it did, I don't see any reason to keep it secret. Some folks may think I've gone off my rocker, but anyone who knows me can tell you I'm not making up any of this."

Unlike the majority of reports involving direct, physical contact with UFO crew members, this case seems—after careful investigation—to be based upon much more than circumstantial evidence and hearsay. Known as a responsible community-minded individual with a genuine interest in the welfare of his family, Higdon is liked by both his neighbors and co-workers. Among those who believe his account are Margery Higdon, *his wife,* Don and Marilyn James, two other **residents of** Rawlins who observed a peculiar glow near where Carl was "lost" in the woods, Dr. *Leo* Sprinkle, a University of **Wyoming** psychologist and trained UFO investigator, and Dr. Walter W. Walker, an expert in the field of metallurgy.

Soft-spoken and not one to meddle in her husband's private affairs, Margery Higdon was nevertheless willing to shed as much light as she could on the episode.

"Having lived with my husband all these years, I'd know right away if he were lying. Never before have I seen *him* so shaken by anything. I'll *never* forget the expression on his face the night we found *him* way back in the Medicine *Bow* National Forest. He was trembling from head to toe and babbling to himself. Nothing he said made any *sense to me —now,* of course, it does!"

Margery Higdon says she realized

something was wrong when Carl's boss, Buddy Rosaker, telephoned to find out where her *husband had gone* off to. "He was upset because Carl had promised to return a borrowed company truck by late afternoon, and it was now seven p.m. I told Buddy that I hadn't *seen* Carl since I'd left for work that morning. I remember he told me he planned to *go* hunting, and the last time I saw him he was putting his gear together and cleaning his gun. I told Buddy I'd let him know *the* minute Carl stepped through the front door."

Fidgety and anxious to hear from her husband, *Margery* Higdon waited impatiently for any word of her missing spouse. Twenty minutes later, Buddy Rosaker telephoned again, telling her that Carl had radioed in from his truck. "Buddy told me not to worry, *but* in *the* next instant said I should get ready to go out, since Carl sounded delirious and that he didn't *seem to know who he was* or where the truck was parked. I felt that I couldn't handle the pressure alone, so I called on my friends Marilyn and Don James to come along with me. Finally, when we met the search team, we were told not to venture into the woods, but rather to wait on the outskirts, since most of the roads were unsuitable for travel.

As they sat shivering in the damp night air, all three saw. the forest suddenly come alive with an eerie phosphorescence. *"The* trees appeared to *be* ablaze. All around us the area was lit brightly as if the full moon had settled down somewhere amongst *the* trees. It was so light. I believe you could have spotted a dime on the road!"

Several minutes *later,* a strange aerial display erupted. "A light bobbed above a nearby grove of trees. At first

we thought it might be an airplane circling overhead, but it was much too low and traveling much too slowly. We didn't hear a sound coming from it. We also ruled out it being a helicopter. since we had asked for an aerial search and were told that none could be arranged before morning."

Minutes passed, and then a brilliant flash was seen coming from the forest. "I jumped for joy, figuring they had found my husband *and* were bringing him out. However, this *wasn't* the case, *since* the short-wave in our vehicle, tuned to the police broadcast band, advised us that they were still searching for Carl."

Around midnight, Marilyn James, who had been staring out the window, let out a *soft* cry and pointed to the sky in the direction of a hovering light. *It* moved! Wearily, her husband, Don, mumbled that we should try to get some sleep—that it *was* going to be a long vigil, and besides, the object *was* probably *just* a star. To this his wife answered. "Well, if it's only *a star,* why

is it moving and making loops?" We watched dumbfounded as it blinked alternately red, white, and green. Their sighting took place long before they learned of Carl's bizarre ordeal.

Reviewing the details of that terrible night in order to sort them out in her own mind, Margery Higdon went on to give a dramatic account of what happened.

"Checking my watch, I saw that it was just after 12 o'clock when they finally reached Carl. The rescue party consisted of Sheriff Ogburn, Deputy Sheriff Ed Tierney, Roy Flemming, Dave Martin, and Harold Schurtz. They radioed for us to wait for them at the boundary of the forest. While waiting, I kept remarking as to how light it was over the next hill, as if the sun were coming up long before dawn."

As soon as Carl was brought out Mrs. Higdon ran over to the truck he was sitting in and began to ask him what happened, how he had gotten lost. "When I first got to him," she later told an investigator, "he just looked at me like—well, like he was peering straight through me. The first thing I could think of to say to him that would help him get back to normal was. 'Oh honey, did you *get* any elk?' And the minute I said 'elk', he turned around and looked out the windshield with a horrified expression on his face. What really frightened me was when I tried to put a coat around his shoulders, he began to scream, 'Don't *touch* me! . . . Don't *touch me!*' It was like he *didn't recognize* me—or any of us, for that matter! I whispered to Don to take Carl's gun out of the truck. I truly didn't know what was wrong with him."

According to Margery Higdon, her

husband sat in the truck with his head on his lap. During a brief stop to *gas* up on the way to town, Carl jumped out of the van and ran over to the side of the road. "He was crying and holding out *his* hands over his eyes. The only thing he said was, 'Those lights, those lights, put those lights out. Help me, *God, help* me! Get those lights out!' We thought he was referring to the lights that had come on in the truck when the doors opened."

When they arrived at the Carbon County Memorial Hospital at two a.m., Carl was rushed into the emergency room for examination. Immediately he was subjected to an *extensive series* of *tests, including* X-rays, *blood samples,* and an electrocardiogram.

"Pacing up and down the corridors of the hospital, unable to relax," Mrs. Higdon recalled. "I couldn't help but wonder what had happened out there while Carl was hunting. At one point, the chief *intern* on duty came out of the emergency room, mumbling something to *the* effect that it was totally crazy. I believe his exact words were, 'This is

just like a science fiction movie.' I *didn't* know what to think"

Mrs. Higdon breathed a sign of relief when she was told all the tests had proved negative.

Taken *to* Carl's bedside, Margery was surprised to see a nurse administering *wet* compresses to his forehead and to his eyes. "All he kept doing was yelling about his 'pills,' his 'pills'. When we asked him *'What* pills?' he would just reply, 'The four-day pills.' Then he would *shout* something about 'the men in the black *suits,'* and the 'pick-up is—how *did* it *get* there?' The nurse asked. 'What *do* you mean? and Carl answered, 'Those men had a gun . . . They *just* pointed, and *it* disappeared.'"

After a particularly violent outburst, the doctor came into the room and shut off the overhead lights. "Getting closer to his bed. I saw that my husband's eyes were filled with tears. Besides his watering *eyes the* only other complaint he appeared to have was that his head hurt him badly. The nurse would try to stroke his forehead and he would cry. 'Oh! Oh, oh.'"

It was not until the following day, around five p.m., that *Carl* began to regain his senses. "Everything was a blur." he recalled. "My head felt like a balloon, and the room was swirling around me. The only things I can recall are the overhead lights and being pushed from one place to another. The best way I can describe what I felt is to say it seemed as if someone had hit me over the head with a baseball bat."

As more time passed, however, Carl was able to recall other bits of information. "I couldn't believe what my mind told me. Sure, I'd read about flying saucers—even seen a few high up, but never took the subject too seriously. Now, I don't know what to say. All I know is that I met a couple of realty 'funny looking' fellows out there, and my life hasn't been the same since. I'd like someone to tell me what's going on!"

Before being sent home from the hospital on Monday, October 26th, the doctors instructed Carl to take it easy and not exert himself. He stayed home for three weeks, leaving his house only for a stroll around the backyard. "He was even afraid to drive the family car," Margery remembered. "It was as if my husband wasn't certain he could do anything."

Luckily for Higdon, his story did not initially receive the wide attention it deserved. A brief account, containing only the barest of details, appeared in the Rawlins Daily Times on October 29th. A staff reporter, Sue Taylor, interviewed Higdon and came away sounding as if she were convinced something unexplained had occurred. Despite the lack of widespread publicity in the Higdon case, the story did attract the attention of a leading psychologist

Dr. R. Leo Sprinkle is a veteran in the UFO field. He has been an advisor to such organizations as the Aerial Phenomena Research Organization (APRO) of Tucson, Ariz., for many years. His meticulous work in the UFO field has convinced him that the flying saucer enigma should be seriously studied by his scientific colleagues.

An Associate Professor at the University of Wyoming in Laramie, he is not eager to seek publicity. Yet, regardless of the almost "supernatural" complexity of this incredible case, he has gone on record as being "intrigued" by the unusually high quality of available evidence.

Using hypnotic regression over a period of four grueling hours on November 2nd and 15th, Dr. Sprinkle was able to extract additional facts from Carl Higdon's subconscious memory.

In the presence of Mrs. Higdon, her four children, several relatives, and two associates, he filled in the periods in which Carl had "blacked out." With him during these sessions was Rick Keynon, a public school art teacher in Rawlins, and Robert Nantkes, a vocational rehabilitation counselor from Riverton, Wyo. Both men had alerted Dr. Sprinkle to the case, after it had been reported in the Daily Times.

Seated in a comfortable chair in the calm seclusion of his living room, Carl Higdon revealed many additional details which he had not been able to recall prior to the hypnotic sessions. The UFO contactee divulged the total scope of his strange meeting with the aliens and his subsequent "voyage" to another realm.

Drinking a cup of strong hot coffee to help calm his nerves, Higdon was told to take off his shoes and to make himself comfortable. Feet planted firmly on the floor, hands on his lap, he was instructed to concentrate his gaze on a swinging pendulum.

"Relax deeper! Relax deeper!" came the soothing voice of Dr. Sprinkle as he began inducing the hypnotic state.

"You will be able to go back to the time and get more information about this experience," the psychologist said softly. "You'll be able to understand and evaluate it, so that even if the feelings are bothersome to you, you'll be able to tolerate them . . . In your mind's eye, just see yourself going back . . . to the time you were driving the pick-up—going into that area. See yourself getting out of the truck with the rifle . . . going down the crest, looking at the elk."

Once hypnotized, Carl Higdon, began to relive his bizarre hunting experience. Comments made during the hypnotic session indicate that his experience included the following astounding events, none of which Carl could consciously remember;

● Emerging from the transparent cube on an unknown planet, and being escorted into a large building;

● Being placed before a "shield" for the purpose of getting a physical examination;

● Seeing other Earth people on this alien world;

● Being told that he would be returned to where they found him because he wasn't "what they needed!"; and

● Learning why they have been visiting Earth for centuries.

Flashing back to the precise moment the bullet left his rifle, Higdon repeated how it had come out of the barrel of the gun in slow motion.

"It sort of hit something in mid-air," he said, "falling to the ground 50 feet from where I stood, weapon in hand. I went over to where it landed, picked it up and put it in my canteen pouch."

Under hypnosis, his story remained unaltered. Only details which he had "forgotten" were added.

"...,At one point, the chief intern on duty come out of the emergency room, mumbling something to the effect that it was totally crazy. I believe his exact words were, 'This is just like a science fiction movie.' I didn't know what to think..."

Asked how he originally got inside the peculiar cube-shaped object. Carl stated matter-of-factly that the being,

who approached him from out of the woods, simply pointed the rod-like appendage where his right hand should have been, and "presto, we were there!"

Once buckled in a seat aboard the spacecraft, Higdon was able to see the forest around him. "You could see the trees and Earth below." The alien waved his mechanical "arm" at a control panel and they were launched into the blackness of space.

Recollecting more fully the interior of the cubicle in which he was held captive. Higdon described a row of "levers" surrounded by a series of letters. He also gave some fascinating details about the propulsion system used by the aliens. Here are parts of this conversation paraphrased from the original tape transcript:

Dr. Leo Sprinkle: O.K., new looking over to the levers. What was it that you were seeing? What did they look like?

Carl Higdon: The first one: automatic

CARL HIGDON . . . kidnaped by spacemen.

transmission . . . more like a sports car. *Second* one, the same: the third one, mostly the same, *but* it had letters on each end.

Sprinkle: How many letters did it seem to have?

Higdon: Eight

Sprinkle: What letters *were* they?

Higdon: E.P.H.D. *on the* top. D.H.P.E. on *the* bottom.

Sprinkle: Anything said about what that meant?

Higdon: No.

Sprinkle: What impression did you have? Did it suggest some kind of propulsion system . . . ?

Higdon: No. They traveled by magnetic force.,

Sprinkle: This is what they said to you?

Higdon: Yes. As fast as they want to travel.

Sprinkle: That second lever, you said, looked like an automatic transmission lever on a sports car. Could you see *how far* the level would move? Would it move several inches?

Higdon: Three or four inches down, four inches up. But it never moved white we were on the trip. It stayed in the center.

Sprinkle: Did you see any of the fevers move at all?

Higdon: The first one. *It* moved down- Don't remember it ever movin' again.

Later on, Higdon told the psychologist *that* these "levers" *were* approximately six inches long. *At the* top of each was a black knob, "like a shifting knob on a pick-up." *Next* to *one* of them was a six-pointed star identical to the one the alien wore on his belt. In front of him was *a* "mirror" which reflected the images of the five elk. No! being able to turn around, however, Higdon never directly saw the elk he had intended to kill. They seemed to *be in* a cage, "like a corral" with "cross pieces"—bars—preventing their moving around. It was as if he were gazing at some giant stuffed animals. The craft was empty except for a two-foot-high box in the center of the ship—whose function was never explained.

For a fleeting moment after lift-off, Higdon saw, through the transparent walls, the Earth drifting behind. "The next thing I saw was a 'ball'—like a basketball—where the earth had been before."

During their trip through the cosmos, the chief crew member—now joined by an "assistant"—identified himself by name.

Sprinkle: Did they call each other by name?

Higdon: Ausso One . . . I talked to him.

Sprinkle: Ausso One? Did he appear to be the expedition's leader?

Higdon: Yeah.

Carl Higdon also observed that at no point during the journey was he able to touch—or even get near—his kidnappes. 'They were careful about maintaining at least three or four foot *distance,*" he *said,* obviously perplexed about this. Another puzzle is that *he* never once saw them from other than *a* frontal view. "I was looking straight into their faces, never got a *side* view. If *you* wanted to communicate with them, you were looking right at them. You never looked at the side or the back; there was just a direct front view—that's all I ever got." Higdon seemed positive that the aliens were surrounded by a "force field" which protected them from earth's "foreign" elements.

Higdon: The "force fields" are around all of them. . . and me! You can move, *but* can't reach out *too* far . . . unless the "force field" expands. he (Ausso One) said. That's the way they travel without helmets—*or* any type of oxygen gear.

Sprinkle: So they can move on our planet without *the* use of a helmet, because they can regulate the size of the "force field"?

Higdon: They get oxygen *inside* the "force field."

Sprinkle: Did *he* say that they use oxygen at the *same* level—at the same rate—as on this planet?

Higdon: He didn't say anything about that.

Offering no explanation of their means of propulsion—"after all, I'm not really qualified to understand scientific terminology"—they did tell Higdon that their ship operated on the principal of "magnetic force." "*These* people can travel *as* fast as they want!" he said.

Perhaps their major scientific achievement—which puts their technology far beyond ours—is the means that they *use* to move from one location to another, instantaneously. Know as *teleportation,* this *feat* is accomplished by aiming their right "arm" in the direction they wish to travel. Ausso One used *the* term "gun" when referring to this apparatus. "He used his *right* arm . . . *to* point where he wants to go—and *he* goes. He moves freely . . . no, he said, we move freely, anywhere *we* want to go." Higdon believes he entered and left the ship by *this* process.

Asked for his opinion as to why he was given pills to swallow at the start of his ordeal, Carl believes they might have been a form of tranquilizer, "Maybe they hypnotized me, I don't know. I just relaxed."

Following a *flight* that seemed *to* him to be about *30* minutes, a sparkling *sphere* loomed on the horizon. "We landed where the lights were brightest," Carl said, "It must have been night, because the lights were in a confined area—casting outward maybe 100 yards in a circle," referring to what he says, was "artificial."

Dr. Sprinkle's tape recorder caught every hesitancy, every *change of* tone. There were moments when Higdon's voice was tinged with panic, anxiety, and utter disbelief.

The tapes of the hypnotic sessions were transcribed. More than 60 pages long, the transcript fills in numerous missing details about what took place on this alien base of operation. Their motives become a tot *clearer.*

The spacecraft came down *close* to a structure that resembled an airfield control tower. Higdon found himself being led into an elevator by Ausso One. He recalled entering without walking from the ship—as if he'd been "projected" there. From his perspective, the tower was shaped like a pine tree, "big at *the* bottom and small at the top." *Colored* lights ran up *and* down its sides, "like a string of bulbs on a Christmas tree." Also the lights were flashing *on* and *off,* similar to *those* on *a* landingstrip.

Escorted into "a cubicle-type office," Higdon was placed before a screen—or "shield as he calls it—which he says may have been used to examine him. Dr. Sprinkle, probing deeply into the sub-conscious recesses of his subject's mind, came up with the following:

Sprinkle: How *big* was the shield? Was it between him (Ausso One) and you?

Higdon: Yes. I couldn't *see* him when the shield *was* there. it was about . . . oh. I'm not sure- . . about four *feet* wide and about eight feet high. It blocked out all vision. You *can't see* anything except the shield.

Sprinkle: What did the shield look like?

Higdon: It looked like a wait coming toward me!

Sprinkle: Did it look like it was made *out* of metal? Could you tell any *texture?*

Higdon: Kind of glassy-like. You couldn't see through it Like slate, but it was real glossy.

Sprinkle: Could you tell how thick it was?

Higdon: No. I didn't get to *see* the side, it came from the front.

Sprinkle: Could you estimate how long the shield was in front of you?

Higdon: Oh, I guess about four of five minutes.

In order to stand in front of the shield, Higdon said he had to step up onto a W e platform. After his "examination" it vanished by "moving flush with the wall."

When asked to visualize *the* room, Higdon insists it was large—"maybe 24 by 30 feet"—but, with the exception of the screen, totally bare and all white.

Stepping down from the little platform, he was then ushered by Ausso One, through a long corridor. "We walked back down *a* hall The door opened and we stopped on a platform and went down and returned *to* the space cubicle.

From his confined quarters. Car! stared at *a* sight that *stocked* and puzzled him. He saw several individuals, nothing like Ausso One, standing near the tower. "They were talking amongst themselves, five of 'em. I don't know what it was, because, you know, they kept looking back and forth at each other, just like a group conversation." *These people were definitely Earthings,* Carl Higdon says.

Sprinkle: Were they adults? Were *they* young people?

Higdon: Three adults and two kids,

Sprinkle: What did they look like? Did *they* have dark hair? Light hair?

Higdon: One was gray-headed.

Sprinkle: How about the youngsters?

Higdon: One had blonde hair, one had brown.

Sprinkle: Did you get an idea of how young or old Hie kids were? Were they six *years* old or 12 years or . . . ?

Higdon: Brown *haired, about* 10 or

┌─────────────────────────────┐
│ " . . . Asked how he originally │
│ got inside the peculiar │
│ cube-shaped object, Carl │
│ stated matter-of-factly that │
│ the being, who approached │
│ him out of the woods, simply │
│ pointed the rod-like │
│ appendage where his right │
│ hand should have been, │
│ and 'presto, we │
│ were there!' ..." │
└─────────────────────────────┘

11. Blonde, 13 or 15.

Sprinkle: Could you get an idea of whether they were male or female?

Higdon: Female. Then there was a young boy . . . oh, 17 or 18, and *a* young girl, the same, about 17-18; brown and blonde haired.

Sprinkle: They were dressed in everyday clothes?

Higdon: Yes.

Sprinkle: Did *these* people seem *to* be surprised or puzzled or afraid?

Higdon: No.

This incredible *scene* would tend to support the contention of a number of contactees that claim aliens have been Kidnapping people for years.

Before leaving, Ausso One said he would return Higdon to a spot near where he had been taken. The alien told him that there was no further reason to detain him, because he did not serve that purpose. Ausso One's exact words were: "We'll take you back, since you're not any good for what we need!" He did not elaborate.

Cad Higdon *was* briefed on the main reason they travel such *a* vast distance. "They're comin' after food, Exploring. Hunting. Fishing. He was talking about fishing and hunting—and exploring our country- He *just* kept talking- Meat. Concentrated food's not *enough."* Looking foe birds, animals." Dr. Sprinkle managed to extract this account:

Sprinkle: They want animals for food?

Higdon: Food. Places to breed them on their planet.

Sprinkle: Did he say anything else about their planet?

Higdon: Fish . . . They don't have any place to keep 'em, so they have to keep coming back after them—out in *the* ocean.

Sprinkle: Did *he* say why they don't have any *place* to keep than . . . their lakes?

Higdon: Their *sea* won't take care of them. They *rite.* Not enough oxygen or something—they don't know for sure-

Sprinkle: But, they *can breed* other animals?

Higdon: Yes- Our animate can live there, just like *here.* But *the* fish, they've got a certain oxygen—or iodine—or something, he says, *that* they're trying to find out what it is.

Sprinkle: Did ha say anything else about the planet? Social, political, or economical?

Higdon: No. Just that he's a hunter or explorer. That's all *he* does.

At this point in the interview, Dr. Sprinkle noticed Carl beginning to grew very distressed, inquiring *as to the* reason for this *outbreak* of nervousness. Dr. Sprinkle and *the others* present were drawn right back into the vivid experience, as they watched Carl relive the pain caused by the bright lights around him on a far away world. His hands moved to his *face* as if he were trying to block out the rays of a powerful spotlight or beacon Ausso One explained that they lived under *a* different sun. "Our sun burns them (the beings) . . . that's the reason for the Mack su'ts, and standin' in the shade. Cloudy days not bad!"

With this, the creature pointed his "hand" at the control pane), causing one of the levers to move up. Unlike their original trip, there were no other aliens to be seen aboard the craft Nor were any elk present. They had apparently been taken off while Carl was undergoing his examination.

Wishing to retain *a* souvenir of his unexpected *voyage,* Higdon *hoped* that the alien would r at retrieve *his one* vital piece of proof that this experience *had* been genuine—the three remaining pills in his jacket pocket. Unfortunately—as in every previous *case* of this type—the proof was whisked away almost at the last second. "He just pointed and *they (the* pills) *floated* out of my *pocket."* Ausso

One had expressed a willingness to exchange mementos. "He wanted to keep my gun, but said this was not allowed."

The translucent cube hung *silently* in *the* air above Higdon's parked truck before the last act in this most amazing episode began to unfold. "When we got above the trees, Ausso One *aimed* his 'arm' *at my* pickup and it disappeared—*poof!*—vanished into thin air!"

Although he had no way of knowing it than, Higdon's borrowed company truck was instantaneously transported a distance (it five miles. It had *been* "lifted" from its parking spot on the grassy knoll in McCarthy Canyon, and "dropped" in an area where no vehicle could possibly maneuver. "Since I was in a state of mental stress, this fact did not have any impact on me until sometime later. I know that I could never have driven over that impossible terrain—even it I had been physically capable of driving, which I *most certainly was not!*"

Before Ausso One teleported him to the ground, Higdon's magnum rifle was returned. Resting next to the seal, on *the* floor of the cubicle, *the* gun suddenly levitated into his hands. Then suddenly, Higdon was back on the ground.

Sprinkle: Did *he say* anything to you when you were going?

Higdon: "We'll see you." A friendly good-bye.

Sprinkle: You don't remember how you got from the seat?

Higdon: From the seat *to the* ground . . . I don't know. I just went like *that.* (moving his hands) and I was *gone!*

Sprinkle: Did you feel yourself going down?

Higdon: No. Just like I said, you're sitting here and then you're over- there. Don't feel a thing.

Equating *the* sensation to jumping *out* of a high tree *but floating instead of* falling, Higdon was *glad* to have *his* feet planted firmly on Earth again. In his eagerness to return to civilization, Higdon slipped on a rock and tumbled head-over-heels for a distance of eight or nine feet Finding himself at the *bottom of* a shallow gully, he pulled himself up and began wandering aimlessly, with his eyes watering, *and* his head spinning.

Having extracted as much data as possible from his subject, Dr. Sprinkle *concluded* the session, easing Carl out from his deep slumber. Before being awakened, the thought was planted in *Carl's* mind *that* he *could* remember everything *that* transpired under hypnosis, and that he would no longer be tearful of his experience. accepting it, without discomfort, as an an event of great significance to his life.

Higdon opened his eyes and shook

peared at ease—memory *restored* to *a* large degree.

Of course many mysteries remain. Higdon, for one, freely admits that many riddles are still unsolved as of this writing. A prime example of one of the questions that still nags him, is how h e *was* able to fit into the tiny five by seven foot cubicle without any apparent difficulty. "Rationally, I *know* that in order for me, the aliens, and the elk *to get in* there, we must have been *shrunk*—there's no other way! I wouldn't venture how they accomplished this feat. Ausso One just pointed, and we were where he wanted us!"

Since the fantastic adventure took place, Higdon bas complained about sharp pams in the back of his head and neck. "I feel like I'd been pushed together like this," he said playing an imaginary accordion. "That's just the way my muscles feel—like they were compressed, and then yanked apart."

In the Winter 1974 issue of *UFO Report,* I mentioned the subject of spontaneous healing and miraculous remission, as it concerned those *who* had come within close range of a flying saucer. The case of Carl Higdon is a prime example of such an unexplainable recovery.

During 1958, Carl was hospitalized, because it was suspected he had contacted tuberculosis. X-rays showed traces of the disease. A series of examinations were conducted at regular six-month intervals, to make certain his condition did not worsen. In addition, doctors who treated him on these occasions confirmed that he also had numerous kidney stones.

Following his bizarre encounter X-rays showed no trace of the lung disease! Furthermore, it was determined that he has not produced any more kidney stones.

Evidence for the medical profession to ponder? Verification comes from attending physician Dr. R. C. Tongo, who treated Higdon at Carbon County Memorial Hospital. "He's now in A-1, super condition!" the doctor is reported to have said.

Among the vitally important puzzles remaining unsolved is why Ausso One remarked that they were returning Higdon to Earth because he wasn't "what They needed." Mulling this over, Higdon had a seemingly logical explanation. "Well, this may sound stupid, but nine years ago I had a vasectomy." This operation severs the duct through which sperm flows, making it impossible for him to impregnate a woman. "Maybe this is what they meant when they said, I wasn't any good! I kind of sense that they wanted young *people."*

Farfetched? Not if we *take into* consideration *the* reported instances of apparent crossbreeding between aliens and Earth people. Although there have been several *cases of* this type, the most popular *among* UFO writers is the well-known story of the Brazilian fanner who was seduced by a beautiful space maiden. Cart's thoughts on this matter are only conjecture, but they should be taken seriously. If the inhabitants of Ausso One's world are *taking* animals for breeding, why not humans?

The major *piece of* hard-core evidence is. of course the remains of the bullet which Higdon fired at the elk. it fell to the ground 50 feet from him, after striking an invisible "force field." Turned over for examination to Dr. Walter Walker, APRO's expert metallurgist, it apparently defies explanation. A 7mm bullet under ordinary conditions would travel at such tremendous velocity that its course would be impossible to chart- *The odds* against *locating* the spent bullet would be *millions-to-one.* Carl Higdon declares that after the buffe floated to the earth, he retrieved it and placed the *piece* of metal in his canteen pouch, where it was later found.

Higdon admits that when he first discovered the bullet in the bottom of his canteen, he had no idea what it was. "I'd *never* seen anything *like* it *before,* to compare *it to,"* he said. "Soon as I could, I took it to the Carbon *County* Sheriffs Department, where the officer in charge of ballistics analysis examined it through a microscope- He told me it was from a 7mm Magnum rifle, which is the caliber of my gun. Returning the chunk of metal, he noted that he had never seen a bullet in that shape *or* condition." The lawman further stated that he didn't think it was humanly possible to hammer the bullet into its current shape. Furthermore, he added that it didn't seem likely that me bullet had hit a solid object, such as *a* tree or a rock, and been compressed by such natural means. 'To him, it appeared as if the bullet had been turned inside out' by superhuman hands." Dr. Walker's findings coincided with those of the local authorities, for he too is convinced that there is no scientific explanation to *account for* the present shape of the bullet.

Dr. Sprinkle is emphatic in his belief that Higdon's encounter should be studied further. "My impression of Carl Higdon is that he *is a* man of *integrity* with average education, but *a* keen sense of curiosity about the world *around* him; he *is* an outdoorsman and seems to have developed good skills of estimating *size* and distance- Although the sighting of a single UFO witness often is hard to evaluate, the indirect evidence supports the tentative conclu-

cerely the events which he experienced."

Did his meeting with aliens actually take place?

Was Carl Higdon taken to another planet?

Did a physical examination occur while he was there?

Or was it all a nightmare? A hallucination?

Of course, there are other explanations which we may ponder, in addition to concluding that Carl Higdon's experience happened precisely as related. A number of seasoned UFO investigators—among them UFO Report columnist Charles Bowen—have recently theorized that the aliens may in actuality he projecting whole sequences of events onto the memory banks of contactees.

We can speculate that perhaps this is what happened to Carl Higdon. Maybe the "helmet" placed over his head in the early stages of his experience, served such a purpose. It might just be that Ausso One programmed the entire episode into his captive's brain. This could, indeed, account for many parts of the ordeal which would otherwise be difficult to explain rationally. Higdon admits, for example, that he was never allowed to touch the aliens, that he could only see them from a frontal view. Doesn't this almost sound as if he were being shown a motion picture? One that was being projected onto a screen inside his mind? We should not discount this possibility, no matter how extreme or bizarre it might seem at first glance.

To say, however, that the entire incident was, in reality, a "projection" or a programmed interplanetary drama, would not be in keeping with all the evidence. In addition to the remains of the "smashed" buffet, the location of Carl's vehicle, and the subsequent UFO sightings made by his wife and two friends, there have been other reports of strange aerial craft seen in the immediate vicinity of Rawlins in recent months.

Cars have been pursued in the dead of night. Peculiar, noiseless objects have been observed hovering and then darting about over power lines and treetops. Frightening, perhaps, 'is the unconfirmed accounts of a young girl who disappeared from a fair grounds recently. A mysterious light was seen bobbing around over the area on the day she vanished!

According to Margery Higdon, the authorities know more than they are willing to talk about. "They're in a sensitive spot, what with election time rolling around. The officials are worried about losing their jobs—they don't want people to know they believe in flying saucers?

A state of reasonable calm has returned to the Higdon household. Though Carl frequently thinks about

what happened on that eventful day last October, he is no longer upset by the recollection.

In fact, Carl reports that within the past few weeks, white returning home at night, he has been followed by a large green light. These subsequent close approaches made by UFOs indicate the extraterrestrials are still keeping a close watch on their earthly

communicant. Following an established pattern among contact cases, it is not too much to assume that further fateful meetings will take place.

Though his phone rings day and night, very few callers are of the crank variety. "People seem to accept it, now. I'm being truthful as I can tie. Tins all really happened! "

Rare Thrill for Tass: Joshing Over Its U.F.O. Report.

By ELEANOR BLAU

The report by the Soviet press agency Tass that lanky, three-eyed creatures took a stroll through a Soviet park last month has caused such reverberations in the United States that they have bounced back to Tass itself.

The agency reported Tuesday that major American television networks and newspapers, which it said typically avoid stories about unidentified flying objects, "played up the space adventure, frequently poking fun and suggesting that the beings from outer space might be a result of overzealous glasnost."

The Tass report, written by an American working for the agency, did not sound resentful It quoted Edwin Diamond, a New York Magazine media critic, who criticized what he called the story's shallowness, saying, "What did the Academy of Science think?" and "Where are the pictures?"

And it quoted Yervant Turzian of the Cornell University Astronomy Department, who said fellow academics regarded the story as a joke.

Drawing of Creature Is Broadcast

"Given the physical parameters of the universe, the possibility of life on other planets is high," be told Tass. "But the vast majority of these reports can be explained by such logical phenomena as unconventional aircraft in the sky or artificial satellites."

On the other hand, Tass found that "A Current Affair," the- syndicated news and entertainment show, was taking the report seriously enough to plan on sending a film crew to Voronezh. That is where Tass originally reported that three children had said they saw aliens emerge from a ball, wearing silvery overalls.

Last night, Soviet television viewers saw a picture of one of the creatures on the main nightly news program "Vremya," in the form of a scribbled drawing by one of the children. It showed a smiling stick figure inside a glowing two-legged sphere.

Vremya sounded- more skeptical than the original Tass report, but it offered without comment an interview with Vasya Surin, one of the purported witnesses.

'He Didn't Have a Head*

"We were scared," said Vasya, who appeared to be about 11. "It hovered over this tree. Then the door opened and a tail person of about three meters looked out. He didn't have a head, or shoulders either. He just had a kind of hump. There he had three eyes, two on each side and one in the middle."

Vasya said the alien had two holes instead of a nose, and could not turn its head, so it had to swivel its middle eye.

But "Vremya" cast some doubt on the reports of the sighting, noting, for instance, that there were no adult witnesses, even though a large apartment house overlooked the site.

Since the first U.F.O. sightings in the 1940's, spaceships have been described as sausages, cigars, balls, bananas, crescents, round straw hats, eggs, mushrooms, disks and, especially saucers. But, in the 1980's "Saucers are out; boomerangs are in," said Jim Speiser, a computer expert in Scottsdale, Ariz. He founded a national U.F.O. computer network in 1986 because he

thought there should be an exchange of information instead of disputes among people who reacted variously to U.F.O. stories, "from skeptics to wild-eyed gee-whiz believers."

In a telephone interview, Mr. Speiser said of the reported Soviet sighting: "I think Tass is exploring its new freedom and is not used to self-censorship. I don't disbelieve, but we have much better stories in this country."

Also surprised — but only because he thinks the media ignores U.F.O. reports — is Tim Beckley of Inner Light Publications. He edits U.F.O. Universe, a glossy magazine that prints 100,000 copies six times a year and distributes them internationally.

Mr. Beckley said that he is a journalist, not a scientist, and that he is almost as puzzled about U.F.O.'s now-as he was when he saw his First in 1967, as a 10-year-old in New Brunswick, N.J. "It's kind of a cosmic game these entities seem to be playing with us," he said.

THE NEW YORK TIMES

THURSDAY, OCTOBER 12, 1989

Photo by Chuck Pulin

Now and then. there's a fool such as I.

Halloween Holocaust

By Walli Elmlark

'Of course you should cover the Halloween shows; who better? cackle cackle"

This from my editor Michele Hush. Very funny Michele. Whooooooo better indeed? Actually. Michele has a point. She knows of my weird past. present, and if things continue along these lines, future. My skeleton in the closet (so to speak): I am a Witch. That is my religion, for Witchcraft (White Witchcraft) or Wicca as it is known (or should be) IS a religion. But. enough of that, this is a rock review. . . of sorts. My assignment was covering the two big Halloween shows in the city. Satan's celebration at Manhattan Center, boasting Ruby and the Rednecks. The Eight Balls, N.Y. Central, the Harlots of 42nd St.. The Magic Tramps and Satan himself (in the form of Israel Jones, the fire eater). Zacherle, local vampire

about the radiowaves, was guest ghoul, Witch Hazel was Monster of Ceremonies and yours truly, the Official White Witch of New York. was guest M.C. From there I was to travel uptown to THE bash at the Waldorf where Howard Stem was presenting The New York Dolls.

How does one describe the most fucked up affairs one has ever attended?

I arrived at Satan's Celebration about 8:30. All seemed well. Video cameramen greeted me and set up my spell-teaching bit, where the cameras would catch it all. Hazel. in flying black hair and Morticia type red gown, was her usual high-energy happy self. Zack was about to open the show looking divinely dead. The 8 Balls were all set to back him white he sang "The Monster Mash." The kids were loving everything. Zack introduced Witch Hazel and myself, and then had to rush off to his radio show. The 8 Balls were to play one or two

more songs, then make way for Ruby . . . and there was the beginning of the end.

Exactly who was at fault I was never able to ascertain. Ruby and her group never showed. I took over and covered for awhile after the 8 Balls' set. Hazel did a money spell and tossed silver dollars into the audience. but there . comes an end to how much schtick you can get away with. Backstage was utter pandemonium. . . people yelling,. "Who's next? Let the Tramps set up. they were to go on at 9:30 anyway." But the Tramps weren't there either. at least not enough of them. The kids were losing enthusiasm and getting restless. Amira, a belly dancer, was thrown to the wolves (werewolves of course) and kept the crowd occupied on the dance floor while 16 different hysterical bosses ran around backstage giving orders. . . all different. Finally, it was N.Y. Central that saved the evening. Calmly and

115

AMERICA'S ABOMINABLE SWAMPMAN

An entire family of these frightening creatures has been spotted deep in the Florida Everglades—and now scientists ore closing in on the strangest prey ever stalked on this continent

By Timothy Green Beckley

"The bushes parted violently and from out of the darkened swamp came a huge creature towering well over seven feet tall. Its body was covered from head to toe with white hair, and its face looked almost human. The 'beast' walked erect and had long, dangling arms which hung loosely and reached the knee. Its eyes, cat-like, curiously searched the Tents reflected by a roaring campfire just beyond . . .

"Our visitor stayed but a few seconds—just tong enough for a fleeting glimpse—then it was gone. What remained was a set of enormous tracks in the soft earth and a musty odor which made us gag for an hour after it was gone.. ."

This account vividly describes what was seen by an archaeological team in the swamps of the Everglades on the morning of Feb. 27, 1971. It was, however, only one of *eight* related sightings made by the scientific group as they went about their work of digging into *the* ruins of a prehistoric civilization.

Spearheading a drive to gather more information about the "thing" which has been nicknamed the "Skunk Man" (because of its highly offensive odor), is 42-year-old Miami adventurer Homer Osbon, who is known as "Buz" to his friends.

Osbon's credentials are impressive and include membership on the board of directors of the Miami Museum of Science as well as being past president of an organization known as The Peninsular Archaeological Society. He has single-handedly attempted to place Florida's "Abominable Swampman" on the map, and in so doing has caused more than a mild stirring of interest from the scientific world.

Osbon's team includes Dick Benson, professor at Miami Dade Community College, whose specialty is oceanographic sciences, and archaeologists Frank Hudson and James Spink. They

all claimed their work was constantly interrupted by an entire *family* of creatures who to this day remain under a heavy cloud of academic controversy.

Although the locale and terrain where similar creatures have been occasionally spotted may differ belief in the existence of such an ape-man, said to walk erect and possess a high degree of intelligence. has existed for years. Word of a humanoid-like animal first reached the public's attention in the early 1950s when Himalayan mountain climbers brought back stories of huge footprints they had discovered in the snow near impassable ice-covered mountain trails close to "The Top Of The World." The climbers promptly identified the tracks as belonging to a family of creatures they refer to as the "Yeti" or more familiar "Abominable Snowman." The remote mountain tribesmen stated that tor centuries their ancestors had known about the existence of a race of hairy monsters, giants who wanted absolutely no contact with human beings.

Although coming from highly credible sources, these "first hand" reports were never accepted by naturalists, zoologists, biologists, or "followers of evolution," who said such a half-man, half-primate species of "missing link" could not possibly exist. Thus the subject was consigned to obscurity for many years.

Actually, it turned out that reports of the "Yeti" *were* nothing new. For more than 150 years, stories were told of an enormous, hairy humanoid creature that was occasionally spotted wandering up and down the west coast of the U.*S.* and Canada.

The American Indians called him "Omah," "Sasquatch," or just plain "Bigfoot." And, although most of the reports centered around the wilds of California, Oregon, Washington, and British Columbia, "Bigfoot" has appa-

rently broadened his sphere of influence in recent years to cover a number of highly unlikely locales, far from these areas.

One of the current hotbeds of Yeti activity is the steaming Everglades, a mass of land and water so hostile and uncharted that its interior has never been fully explored.

Undoubtedly, any number of unidentified species of insect and plant life abound in these murky swamps, thick underbrush, and heavy, jungle-like vines. But, by far, the area's most puzzling occupants, unbelievable as it sounds, are a group of Yeti whose very existence threatens the "Darwinian" laws, and pose untold questions which may soon *have* to be answered.

At the time of the 1971 sighting, "Buz" Osbon's scientific group had built a camp on the site of an old Indian burial mound in the Everglades. They always had a fire for warmth and protection against wild animals.

"We had all gone to bed," Buz recalled, "when around three o'clock in the morning, one of the members of our expedition was startled awake by weird sounds coming from just beyond the perimeter of our camp.

"At first he thought it was a wild beast, and thinking the fire would eventuafly chase him off, he turned over and tried to go back to sleep. All of a sudden, there was a thundering noise which sounded as though a wild bull elephant was thrashing about amidst the thick trees and bushes. We all were

"Buz" Osbon with a cast of the Swampman's f

116

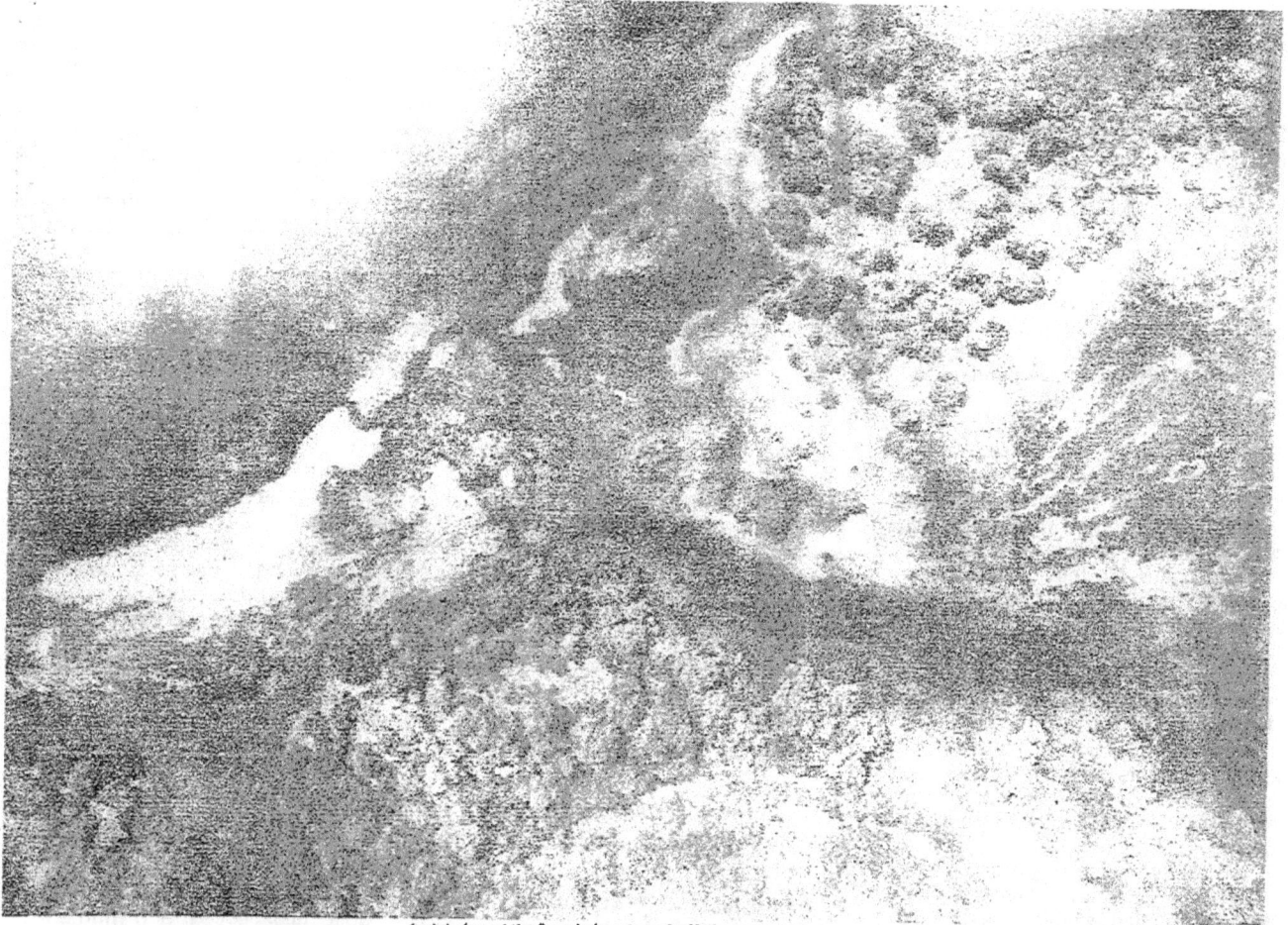

Aerial view of the Everglades where the Yeti was spotted.

awakened at this point and we were on our hands and knees trying to get ourselves together—enough at least to see what was causing the commotion,"

Peering into the light cast by their campfire and the full moon. the group received the biggest shock of their lives, Osbon recalls.

'There, directly in front of us, not more than 10 feet away, was a creature which was, to all intents and purposes, only rumored to exist. He stood in the middle of our camp looking back and forth as if searching for something. His huge seven foot frame was an awesome sight to behold, and was covered from head to toe with thick, matted white hair, and he Kept swinging his long, powerful arms from side to side It didn't take us long to realize that this was no bear in our midst, no escaped gorilla, nor any other known animal To think it was any of these would have been sheer folly.''

The pungent odor that was given off by this creature was so overpowering that it caused the men to gag even after it finally vanished within the maze of thicket

Their immediate reaction was amazement coupled with panic When me shock subsided, they eventually managed to fall back to sleep after posting a guard and praying that whatever-it-was would decade not to pay another call.

"Our minds were going a mile a minute," Buz said. "What had we seen? What did all this mean? indeed, our scientific curiosity was more than slightly aroused,"

At dawn, the team of archaeologists started their search for evidence to prove that their nighttime visitor had not been the figment of a mass hallucination.

'We knew almost immediately that our minds had not played tricks with our senses because, along the maze of trail we had cleared leading us to the Indian burial grounds, were tracks which measured 17½ inches long and 11 inches wide. If they were made by a man, he had to be walking around wearing size 18 shoes," Buz said. Plaster of pans casts were immediately made of the imprints before the elements had a chance to change their form or alter their size.

''i couldn't accept what we had seen," Buz said earnestly. "But from what has happened since, i am convinced that an entire family of these creatures are living today somewhere in the Everglades."

Because of his strong desire to prove the reality of these creatures, Buz has adopted one goal in life—to capture one alive and bring it back for scientific scrutiny. "I want to prove that what I am saying is not a lie. These creatures come damned dose to being human, and I think to kill one would be an act of murder. They have their own life style; they walk on two legs like man, and their communication is a seemingly intelligent high speed chatter."

Variations in the size of the tracks, along with additional professional observations, have convinced Osbon that there are at least three Yeti lurking about the ares; a male. a female, and their young one. "But the largest—the male—is the one we have seen most of the time," he contends.

The second sighting of the creature was made exactly one week after the initial encounter when the group return& to the same area in an effort to continue their burial mound digging. Again the "Swampman" made a Sae night appearance.

This time, however, the group was equipped for a visit from the Yeti. "The first thing we did after setting up camp

(Continued '

117

THE SWAMPMAN

{Continued

was to "lay an electric wire around the camp's entire perimeter," Buz said. "This in turn was connected to an ultrasensitive electronic device which would immediately sound an alarm if anything crossed the wire. Needless to say, we had plenty of camera equipment with flash attachments and portable lighting.

"About midnight, we heard something with heavy, sluggish steps sloshing through the water in the nearby swamp and our instruments started beeping. Knowing that something had crossed the wire and was on the edge of our camp, we excitedly searched the area with heavy floodlights—but we saw nothing.

"Tile next morning, however, we again found large footprints around the outer edge of our site, and we knew then that we were being observed.

"A complete search of the area revealed footprints of three distinctively varied sizes, our first indication that a family truly existed and was not far away."

On another occasion, the group had returned to the area to resume their digging. They had been out in the bright sun at the burial mound for only an hour when they caught a glimpse of the male watching from a distance. He was well concealed under a tree whose drooping branches provided nature! cover. Again, the air became foul from the stench given off by the enigmatic creature.

Thinking this time that the "Swampman" might respond to friendly calls, the men tried this. Instead of coming closer, however, the Yeti turned and fled back into the murky depths of the swamp. The team tried searching the area but its tracks disappeared in the surrounding mire.

To date, the creature has "dropped in" to scan the group's activities eight times. The most recent sighting occurred when he was seen running across a shallow lake. "He was really cutting loose, going through the bushes so silently that it was unbelievable for something his size and weight," Buz said.

"In fad. it has gotten to the point

★ SAGA

where the team can actually smell him before he actually shows himself," Buz casualty remarked in a recent interview- "One time, I got wind of him and returned to camp just in time to see a shadowy figure disappear down the path. Checking out the area. I discovered he had moved a good bit of our supplies and equipment, including shovels, plows, cameras, and he had even thrown two rakes into a nearby pit."

Skeptics who question the validity of these reports usually raise the question: why, if these beings exist, hasn't anyone else besides Osbon and his party seen them?

An examination of the news files from several small newspapers throughout the southern region of Florida indicate that a number of sightings of the creature have indeed occurred in past years.

> "...'From the prints we now have, we can tell that this "Skunk Man" is definitely not a member of the ape family, but closer to human than anything else in the animal kingdom—if indeed it can be considered an animal'..."

In addition, other professional men have seen the "Yeti of the Everglades," but have remained silent until Osbon's account was publicized in newspapers, radio, and TV.

Among the individuals who support Osbon in his quest is Norman Altman, the custodian of the South Florida Museum.

Altman says that his first encounter with the "Skunk Man" goes back more than 10 years when he was exploring Big Cypress Swamp with another group of scientists- "At sunset, we chose a parcel of solid ground on which to pitch camp," Altman said. "Looking for a place to set the poles for our tents, I spotted a set of strange tracks in the soil. I also took notice almost immediately of the fact that some of the nearby mangroves, which were four

inches in diameter, had been unaccountably snapped in two by some powerful force. Whatever had done it had simply grabbed the trunks and twisted them into several sections, causing the mangroves to splinter into many large pieces."

At this point, Altman admits that he was puzzled, but that he didn't dwell on the mangroves or the tracks for very long. Then, several nights later an incident occurred which completely unnerved him. "I had become separated from the rest of our party and had begun to backtrack down to our boat to get some fresh water for drinking.

"It was already getting pretty late, and so I was walking rather fast, hoping to complete my chore before nightfall- As I went along, I began to hear a thrashing in the bushes behind me. At first, I thought that one of our group was coming after me, perhaps to help me."

What Altman soon noticed was that the sound was much louder than that naturally made by an average-sized man. "I was becoming more bewildered by the minute, and finally decided I'd pick up a large limb from a fallen tree and throw it in the general direction of the thrashing to see what reaction it would bring."

Altman insists that the reaction was fast, quite unexpected, and frightening- "A spirt second after I tossed the limb I heard this grunting noise that nearly shook the ground. Then, whatever had been keeping close tabs on my movements began edging off and eventually I could hear him trudging off into the distance."

Returning to the main camp, Altman asked if anyone had been out of camp for any reason. When everyone answered no. Altman decided not to make an issue of the matter.

Years later, he read about Buz Osbon's experiences in the Everglades and decided to contact him to perhaps join forces on a forthcoming trip to the swamp area.

"I saw the tracks all right," Altman says. "And from the size of the piaster casts Buz has, and the ones along the trait, I definitely agree that there has to be a family of them. The largest prints discovered so far are the ones which measure approximately 17½ inches from the tip of the big toe to the end of

(Continued

the heel, **and** about 11 inches across. From the prints we now have, **we** can tell that this 'Skunk Man' is definitely not a member of *the* ape family, **but** closer to a human than anything else in the animal kingdom—if indeed it **can be considered** an animal."

The point of disagreement **Norman** Altman has with Buz Osbon's findings is the size of the creature. "Buz has told me that he believes its size to be somewhere between 7½ to eight feet in height. From the stride **pattern** of the tracks I would say that it's closer to nine feet tall," Altman says, and adds that the creature's weight is difficult to esti-*mate*, but that it must be well over 800 pounds. "I'd really **hate** to **meet** *this* thing **face** to **face and** find out it's not friendly. The chances though are that it has no hostile intent as it has gotten pretty close to humans a number of times without hurting anyone."

More confirmation about the creature comes from Frank Hudson, **head of** Artifacts International, an independent firm **in** St. Petersburg, **Fla.** Hudson says he has been on expeditions several times when an overwhelming foul odor prevented his party from continuing their work. He has also seen *the* tracks left by the creatures in question, and has talked with witnesses outside of his own **group** who **vouch** for the existence of the elusive Everglades Yeti.

After their own experiences, Frank **Hudson** and Buz Osbon began re-searching the history of similar sight-ings in Florida, and have managed to compile an impressive file of observa-tions dating back more than 30 years.

An abridged summary follows:

• *1941-Brandon, Fla.:* A teen-ager visiting his girl friend in this rural area reported that "something" jumped out of the woods as he was driving along a back **road,** and it hopped onto the running board of his vehicle. After several minutes of riding along and watching the youth through the rolled-up window, **it stepped** onto the **road and** ran off.

• *1948–New* Port *Richey, Fla.:* A white-haired creature approached a man who had stopped his automobile to examine the remains of a dead animal on the **road.** The mysterious **Yeti** walked to within 20 feet of the witness, and began chattering at him **before** it turned and fled.

• *1950–New* Port *Richey, Fla.:* A huge beast terrified a young housewife as she was attempting to **hang** her wash and chased her around her yard. The frightened woman managed to **lock** herself inside her house, and the *crea-*ture **disappeared.**

• *1952–North of Brooksville,* Fla.: A group of hunters were exploring a limestone cave when they suddenly saw something "resembling an ape" standing on a ledge directly above

them. They shot at it, but had the impression their bullets merely bounced off. No blood **nor body** was found.

• *1958–Brooksville, Fla.:* A driver of a large semitrailer pulled off the road north of Brooksville on Route 41 and climbed into his bunk to get **some** rest. He had barely stretched out when something **with** long arms **reached** in, grabbed him, **and** pulled him out of the cab. His clothes were nearly torn to **shreds** while he screamed for help. **Some** nearby dogs heard the commo-tion and **came** running, barking fiercely. The "thing" promptly ran off into the **nearby** woods.

From all indications, there seems to have been an increase of sightings in recent **years** in this same area, intimat-ing, at least to Osbon. that "civilization is moving in on **these** creatures, and they **are getting** acclimated to us."

Osbon **asserted:** "For **the most** part, he probably lives off **fish** and small lobster caught in the brackish waters around its home, but small animals **and** other **edibles** may occasionally bring

> "... To add more **mystery to** the Yeti phenomenon, *the* night watchman testified *'the* creature vanished **as** though **into** thin air, right in front of **my** *eyes.'* The evidence left behind: *'a* smell, like that of burning sulphur'..."

him **out** into the open for brief periods,"

Among the most recent reports com-piled **by** Artifacts International, is the first known confrontation with a three-foot-tall **baby** Yeti. According to Allan Carter of Brooksville, his five-year-old **son** was frightened **by** an adult Yeti which was accompanied **by** its **young.** **as** Carter's **son was** tricycling near his home. **The** young humanoid creature vaulted over the fence surrounding the Carter property "as though the fence wasn't even there."

Carter's son ran into the house to tell his older brothers and sisters about what he had **seen.** They **all** returned with **him** to **the** spot in time to *see* the tricycle turned over on its side and the small Yeti **standing** next to the over-turned bike turning one of the **wheels.**

Catching sight of the children the tiny creature returned to the adult Yeti, who immediately put it **under a nearby bush and** stood in front of it as if protecting it After a short standoff both **creatures** disappeared into the woods.

Returning home from work later that day, Allen Carter was told of his chil-

dren~experience. Though his reaction was tinged with skepticism, he **found tracks** in the woods near his home suggesting that **the** youngsters had told the truth.

Carter also remembered that just a few nights before, "something" had gotten into **his** garden and **had** stolen some vegetables.

A night **watchman** from Bradenton, Fla., *(whose* name is being withheld at his **request) reported** to Frank Hudson **that** he came across an eight-foot-tall Yeti standing in the middle of an open telephone company truck. The **creature** appeared to be covered *with* hair and *was* like "nothing I had ever seen."

To add more mystery to the Yeti phenomenon, the **night** watchmen tes-tified *"the* creature vanished as though into thin air, right in front of my eyes." The evidence left behind: "a smell, like that of burning sulphur."

In keeping a careful log on other sightings, this writer has **been** collecting news stories and other accounts sub-mitted by correspondents throughout the country. I have also talked with dozens of eyewitnesses **who** are abso-lutely certain they have seen "some **type** of creature" which **they** said was 'definitely not any animal known *to* **exist,** but **a** combination of **ape and human being."**

Regardless of **where these** stories originate, witnesses tend to confirm that the creature **is** very close **to** being humanoid, except for two distinct characteristics: its head lies directly on its shoulders, and **its** arms **are** elon-gated.

Other corresponding details which are frequently tied to **the** Yeti are: a **forehead** which **slopes backward nearly** to a point; **and** that its face is almost entirely free of hair.

Some witnesses refuse to speculate upon what they think the creature is, while others ultimately state that it has to be a "missing link" which time and civilization has totally forgotten.

There is almost unanimous agree-ment that the Yeti possesses a high degree of intelligence, which **is** vastly superior to that of any other mammal excluding man. From all indications, they seem to *have a* language all their own, and **for** the most part try to keep human contact at a minimum.

Of the many **reports** this researcher has investigated, the following warrant mention.

Donna Sikes had been listening to her two German shepherd dogs howl-ing and crying intermittently for half an hour before she decided to investigate. The 13-year-old Loma Linda, Calif., girl had tried to ignore their whinings, but the continuous sounds finally drove her out into the late night air.

As she approached the animals, which were tied to a fence near the (Continued

(Continued

back of her house, Donna heard a **rustling** noise among **the** *trees.* At first she attributed this to **the wind** but **suddenly,** the branches began to thrash back and forth more violently. In just a **few seconds,** *the* girl found herself facing a nightmare.

Donna let out a scream which carried back to the house **where** her mother, Mrs. Barbara Sikes, was getting ready for bed.

"I was **alarmed, to say the least,**" admitted **Mrs.** Sikes during a long distance telephone conversation with me. "At first I didn't know what **was** happening, *but* I **headed** *for* **the back** porch where my daughter's cries were coming from. "Upon reaching the rear of the house, I switched on the outside lights which we **used to illuminate** the **back** yard. I froze in **my tracks because** of the sight before me."

Mrs. Sikes went **on to** describe **a story** similar to those I have been **hearing for the** past few years while **attempting** to **track** down **and** gather as **much** evidence as possible as to the **existence** of these strange creatures.

'My immediate reaction was that a wild bear had wandered into the yard **and** was rummaging through our garbage for food, scaring the daylights out of our dogs in the process," she said. "But I realized, almost at once, that this 'bear' (if that was what it truly **was**) **had** to be enormous. I'm a little over four-feet-11-inches **tall, and the** fence *it* stood in front of is a few inches taller. its head was looming **up** well above this structure."

What did it **took** like? "Well," Mrs. **Sikes said,** ". . .all I can really say is that he was covered from the top of *his* **head, down** *to* his **feet,** with a coat of rough, matted hair.

"Within about 15 **seconds of** Donna's screams, and my turning on the back porch lights, he was off and running, though previously he had been standing there as puzzled over our reaction to him **as** he was to our presence."

After **recovering** sufficiently from her initial shock, Mrs. Sikes calmed down her frightened daughter and then called the local sheriff's office. The officer answering the call spent the rest of the **night** patrolling the neighborhood, but without results. Similar accounts told by bewildered and jittery **neighbors backed** Mrs. Sikes in every detail.

Her closest neighbor, 29-year-old Kenneth Corbin, a husky, former Army officer, told San *Bernardino* Sun reporters that he had caught the creature in the bright headlights of his truck. "I've seen **every** kind of animal you'd ever want to see between Fort Worth, and Great Falls, Mont. I'm over six-feet-two, and **that thing** is taller than I am." Corbin first spotted the creature shortly after three a.m., while leaving **for** his **job.** He insists that it has **made** return

★ **SAGA**

visits on at least five different occasions-

"I don't think it's hungry **enough to hurt** anyone," **he said.** "but it sure **in hell** harasses the animals." He pointed out that his horses and his Doberman pinscher have a "fit" every time it *comes* near.

Other Wallace County residents reported sighting **the creature at** about the same time. One woman, who *refused* to give her name, claimed that her prize horse had to receive medical treatment for an unexplained gash across **the neck. On** the same night two heavy bales of hay simply vanished from her property.

An endless barrage of frantic telephone calls **prompted the Wallace County Sheriff's Department to send** a helicopter over the area. Equipped with powerful floodlights the copter's **broad** beacon scanned the ground in search of anything unusual in the darkness.

According *to* Mrs. *Sikes,* one of the neighbors later told her that she had seen something run across a field at "high speed" as the helicopter's lights

> ". . After fours days of **being** *sighted* at **various points** in the **area, the creature** mysteriously disappeared. **Those responsible for what** the authorities termed 'near **mass hysteria'** insisted **that what they saw** was **not an ordinary animal nor the product of their imaginations.. .**"

swept the ground. "**She** told me that it *was off into* the *bushes* quicker **than** a jackrabbit," she reported.

After four days of being sighted at various points in the area, the creature mysteriously disappeared. Those *responsible* for what the authorities termed "near mass hysteria" insisted that *what* they saw *was* not an ordinary animal nor the product of their imaginations. "I am insulted **by** people who say what **my** daughter and I saw was a large animal," Mrs. Sikes reiterated several times during our conversation.

Of all the states in which the Yeti **has** been spotted in the past years, Oregon, with its vast wilderness and remote and inaccessible regions, has been a continuing hotbed of sightings. In fact, ?972 alone produced a number of **exceptional** cases.

On the night of August 24th, police were called to **the** Conser Lake home of Mrs. Burkhart who told them that **a** six-foot three-inch **tall** "man," covered with hair, had been prowling around her farm. Two workmen chased the thing, firing several rounds from a shotgun at

"**something** moving in **the blackness.**" Investigating the **disturbance,** police uncovered **a** fresh pool of blood, indicating that something or **someone** had been hit. Whatever it **was, didn't seem** to be looking for medical assistance.

Leonard Boekelman found the head-**fights** of *his* **car** bouncing off a "seven-foot ape" standing upright in a ditch alongside the **road,** at four in the morning, on September 30th. It happened on busy Highway **42. just** outside Lee Valley as Boekelman was returning home "Completely sober." **The** *Myrtle Point Herald* **printed** a plea the following day calling on readers who might have been out at that hour and driving along this main highway, to call the newspaper and report anything **odd** they might have **seen.**

Dozens **of** other, fully documented reports have recently **come** to my attention, many of them from outside this western wilderness region. In fact, a good portion of the more up-to-date sightings have come from such seemingly unlikely places as Defiance **and** Cleveland, Ohio, Wayne County, Mich , Fouke, Ark., (home of the **famous** Fouke River **Monster),** Edmonton, Ky., and Lander, Wyo. Here are the details:

• Defiance, Ohio: Three people living on the outskirts of town are among those **who testified** that **they had** *spotted* a large **eight-foot-tall** "**beast.**" A **train** crewman, while switching trains, said that **he** was hit from behind by the **creature,** with a piece of lumber. Ted Davis **and** Thomas **Jones,** crewmen **on** the N & W local **fright** train **which** serves **Defiance,** claim they saw a large figure resembling a **man "but not a** man" under a full moon—*twice.*

In *another* incident, **police** received a report stating that a motorist stopped his automobile at four a.m., "to let a strange creature pass."

◦ Cleveland, Ohio: **A** monster animal at least seven feel tall and weighing in **the vicinity** of 350 pounds, was **seen** in the neighborhood of Brookside **Park.** Patrolman Richard Brindza of **the** Cleveland Police **Department,** reported that a clump of bushes behind a fence **in this area** had **been crushed** "as though a large animal had trudged clumsily through it."

Wayne Lewis, a witness, told *Toledo Blade* reporters that upon seeing **the** creature, he ran into his house to get a shotgun, but **when** he **returned** it had **vanished.**

• Lander, **Wyo.:** Two teen-agers, Curt Laninger and Tom Hernandez, reported their **sighting** of "**Bigfoot.**" They told sheriff's office representatives that it had **chased them** while they were riding horses near *the* Wind River Indian Reservation. They claimed that the creature took five-foot-long strides, and had one hand tucked underneath his arm as though it were broken. The

(Continued

(Continued . . .)

reservation's chief of police, Bill King, confirmed that prints of **"a large** beast with a higher than normal instep, and two toes" **had been discovered, and** that *other* telephoned reports indicated that the "**man** or animal" was seen wandering near water.

• *Edmonton,* Ky.: Dozens of residents heard the sounds of an unknown "varmint" which was like "the bellowing of a bull or the **trumpeting** of an elephant." Those who chanced to go near **where** the sounds were coming **from said** whatever **was making the noise was** moving extremely fast, because when they approached this spot they heard them again, only this time they were farther away.

One of those who feel the beast was using the area for its home, Vernon Fancher, **says that his two boys** found unusual prints in the earth *near* their house. "I can't **say for sure what it was,"** he reported, "but it **wasn't** a bear. it *was* much too large to be any animal that I know **exists** around here—or anywhere **else** for that matter." **As** in most cases, the creature **disappeared** mysteriously, **without** leaving any trace, with the exception of a few footprints.

Despite this overwhelming documentation, few people with **scientific** credentials have bothered to look at **the mass of reports** or **tried** to **evaluate the existing evidence.** The few who have taken advantage of this opportunity, have come away thoroughly convinced that a serious study of the American Yeti should be undertaken—at once.

Credibility to this field of investigation **has** been added recently with the announcement by Colorado University professor, Dr. Edward Killian, that he has obtained a federal grant to **continue studies of these strange creatures.** "I haven't **made up my** mind **either** way, but I now **hope** with the **help** of some funding something solid can be yielded once and for all relating to any positive identification of what we have in our midst."

More academic credence has come from a confirmed believer, **Dr.** Grover Krantz, who has made his position clear concerning Bigfoot's **existence. The** Washington State University professor who specializes in human evolution, declared that his two-year, independent field expeditions into remote parts of California, Oregon, and Washington have convinced him **such** a creature does in fact roam desolate parts of the American wilderness.

Florida's Buz Osbon also has been trying to interest as many scientists and scientific groups *as* possible in the existence of his own area's "Swampman." "I believe that capturing this creature *would* prove to be one of the *greatest* achievements and discoveries science could possibly make at this time, and could very well teach

★ **SAGA**

us a lot about our own past civilization."

One of the biggest unanswered questions now is, just **where does the Yeti belong on our** evolutionary **scale?** "At present we just do not know," Buz admits, and **adds that such a finding could very well** foster a reevaluation of Darwin's theory.

Osbon, recently recuperated from heart surgery, has resumed his **search** for the elusive Yeti. This time he hopes to return from his quest with a captured creature.

"It has **been suggested we use** a stun gun to capture a Yeti," Buz said. "Then the question arises, what would we do with him if **we** had him in captivity? *I'm* thoroughly against **putting** him in a zoo, and no laboratory is **equipped** to **tackle** the situation should it *arise."*

What then? Buz **would like** to raise enough **money so he** can construct a specially equipped area for the Yeti in order for science to make a thorough study and determine just how **close** to us the Swampman really is.

"I've already gone to the U.S. Government," he said, "but they will never get around to **providing the necessary money,** with all the red tape you have to go through. I'm also asking for private support, perhaps from some wealthy individual who would like to see a new field of science opened up, or, excluding this, a foundation grant would be suitable. We are sorting out all kinds of data **now and as yet** we just don't know what to do with what we **have. We would certainly welcome any help."**

Asked to comment on **why** at least one family of Yeti has settled in the Everglades, Buz told a rather lengthy, **but** fascinating story. "**The swamps here abound** with strange **stones and** legends **of lost cities, hidden treasures, UFO bases, and so** forth. Many of those who had wandered into this area have come out of it with incredible tales.

"For **years,** pyramid-like **structures** have **been** found, **and** then lost again—ad in the area known **as Big Cypress Swamp, where** we have been carrying out **our archaeological** activities.

"It **is said that some years ago,** an **escaped** convict from a Florida chain gang made his way into this swamp to avoid being captured. While wandering **through the** murky mud, thick foliage, and dense underbrush, **the** fugitive came across a pyramid-like structure. Within it, *he* found a secret room where he hid, and in the silence and **darkness** plotted his future, which at the time didn't look very bright.

"Why he finally left his well-hidden sanctuary is not known, but the convict turned himself in, telling authorities that 'something very odd forced him to abandon his refuge'."

Osbon's **close** relationship, with the "Swampman," came about when his

organization decided *to* check out the claims that such a pyramid-like structure really existed.

"We found two such pyramids after **searching** for a number of **weeks."** Buz told me. "The more complete of the pair is a 12½-foot-tall structure, and for the life of **me it's** impossible to tell how **the** blocks were fitted together since they're so tightly **packed.** The pyramid has **a** fantastic amount of writing on its surface in what I can **best** describe as symbols, or hieroglyphics.

The second pyramid. Buz revealed, "remains covered by a good 10 *feet* of water, but its upper portion is jutting out of the swamp."

. Speculation has it that **these** structures were built by a **civilization** long **gone** from the face of this planet. "This could well be **part** of Atlantis, the Lost Continent we have heard so much **about**," Buz speculated. "But we have no positive proof nor are we offering any conclusion at this *time."*

In addition to the pyramids, a "waif" with a **hard, smooth surface,** six to eight *feet* high. has also been uncovered approximately five miles from **the** site of *the* pyramids, running along for about six miles. **This poses** a real challenge.

'We are **keeping** the exact location closely guarded." Buz says. "It's **known** only to a handful of **people now and we want** to keep it that way **so** the area will not be trampled on by curiosity seekers or by those not equipped to help us in our work."

Although he can't prove it, Buz believes "the Everglades Yeti and his **family,** are using **the** region around the ruins as *their* home," **and** says "the **entire locale** is dotted with old Indian Mounds and **the remains of** structures dating back to—we *can* only guess how long. The digging we do always *seems,* for some reason, to attract the creature. Perhaps it's-the physical activity. We've seen them eight times during the past three years while working here. Sometimes, it takes four or five trips before we see one, *but* other times they turn up every trip. One of our men spent four weeks out near **the diggings and saw**

him more than that."

And so the search continues for the Yeti, leaving many unanswered **questions.** Tune, hopefully, will **provide a scientific solution to these riddles.**

Osbon and a small team of explorers and archaeologists are convinced that a Yeti *can* be captured, and they hope this incredible event will take **place soon.**

Until it **does, frightened** and bewildered residents in remote areas **all** over

the country will **be encountering** "Bigfoot," **and the** possibility always exists that **someone may be** hurt.

THE UFO BASE 40 MILES FROM THE WHITE HOUSE

By Timothy Green Beckley

May 1978

The setting sun loomed ahead like a gigantic fireball on *the* horizon, *as* Captain C.S. Wilson prepared to land his Eastern Airlines jumbo jet at Washington's National Airport during the early evening hours of Nov. 19, *1975.* The veteran pilot, with more than 10,000 flight hours to his credit, had descended from 24,000 to 15,000 feet, when he caught *sight* of several cylindrical-shaped objects crossing from east to west in front *of* his plane at *a* distance of *five* miles.

"At first I thought them to be a formation of three or four aircraft above us," Wilson told *his* superiors upon landing· "As I looked closer, all I could make out were short vapor traits." The idea crossed Wilson's mind that the rapidly moving devices might be missiles. This upset him momentarily, when he realized they might be capable of changing course and striking *his* plane. "I have never watched a salvo of missiles being fired before, *but* from pictures I've seen, these were very similar."

The commercial airliner, with 85 passengers aboard, was en route from West Palm Beach, Fla., *to* Washington, when the incident occurred. Wilson says the weather was perfectly clear and visibility unlimited. Because of the speed and trajectory at which the UFOs traveled, he was unable to point them out to his co-pilot.

Attempts to identify the aerial denizens were futile. NASA, which maintains a fully staffed base near Richmond, from which rockets are launched for atmospheric research, denied that any missiles had been fired at the time of the sighting· Due to the serious nature of Captain Wilson's report and *the* fact that it took place inside highly-restricted military airspace, a Defense Department spokesman admitted that his agency *was* anxious to investigate the matter *further.*

The following night a multitude of highly

luminous "fireballs" were spotted up and down the east coast. Sightings were particularly heavy in the Washington, D.C., area· Robert Hitt, director *of* the Chesapeake (Va.) Planetarium had just finished delivering a lecture and was setting up a telescope on the *roof* of the planetarium, when a UFO streaked by overhead. "I was talking to a visitor," said Hitt, "when I saw it and grabbed him (the visitor) and spun him around. It appeared brilliant green and *was* falling straight down. it turned deep orange and finally bright red before it dropped below the horizon. I held my breath, because I really expected to hear a crash and rumble as it landed. The impression I got was that it—whatever the thing was—should have made *a* loud noise. If someone painted a picture of it, as it changed from bright green to red, you wouldn't believe it. It was the *most* incredible night *of* my life?"

Many readers are probably aware that during the summer of 1952, UFOs buzzed the nation's capitol on several occasions, causing near panic in military circles. The UFOs were tracked as blips on radar, seen simultaneously from both the ground and air, and chased by our fastest military planes* But what most Americans do *not* realize *is* that sightings of unidentified flying objects over the district are not rare at all. In fact, they are quite common.

Since the late 1940's government employees, high-ranking military personnel, and police officers, as well as a host of other responsible individuals, have spotted strange pulsating craft soaring about over such historic landmarks as the Pentagon, the Washington Monument and the White House. Although *to* the public, the military brass has repeatedly tried to dismiss these sightings as nothing more esoteric than "meteorite showers" or "temperature inversions," officially a large percentage of the *cases* remain on the books as *UN-SOLVED'*

As difficult as it might *be* to believe, my own files contain adequate testimony which **suggests** that UFO witnesses have been threatened with instant dismissal from their government-related jobs if they dared to break the cloud of secrecy that **hangs** ominously over the Capitol Hill UFO cover-up. Apparently, it has become routine procedure to go so far as to transfer those in the Armed Forces who have been among the observers of UFOs over D.C. One such incident, involving the CIA, **Navy** Intelligence and an admiral? **was** reported on by **this write-** in a pre-**vious issue** of UFO REPORT. Quite obviously the **"powers** that **be"** will go to great lengths to prevent what they consider to be "essential" information from leaking out.

One individual, who under the prevailing circumstances might be considered to "know too much about flying saucers,' but who hasn't been silenced, contends that an unearthly power **has** establishes a stronghold in *the* hills of Virginia just forty miles from the hallowed halls of Congress. Here, where eyes cannot pry, an alien race from the **stars has** constructed a secret **base** from which they are keeping a constant vigil on our seat of Government.

Martha Lang has been aware of their presence for almost **twenty-five** years. At **the** age of ten, in 1953, the attractive, brown-haired **young** woman saw her first UFO.

Residents of Warrenton, Va., and surrounding communities have come to take these metallic, sometimes glowing

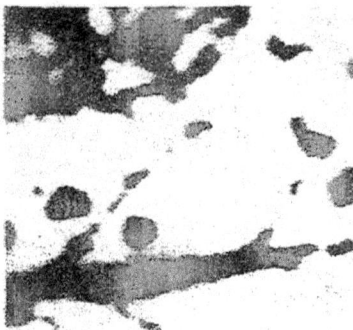

ships for granted, "They come in and out of here *so* often," Martha informed **me** at our first meeting, "that nobody bothers to get excited any longer. I've personally seen these UFOs hover within a few feet of the ground so many times that I've long since lost count.'

After talking with **Martha** for long periods over the last two years, I **feel confident** that she is not the type of **person** to fabricate or deliberately embellish any part of what she **has** experienced. Born and raised in a rural setting, she adheres to the old belief that "honesty is the best policy." Indeed, *for* many years she hesitated telling anyone her story.

And it is a fascinating one!

"The first time I saw them, it *was* all pretty much undeveloped **land** around these parts," **Martha begins,** *as* .we drove along in her Ford stationwagon taking in the better part of what *is* geographically Loudon County. "Back when I was growing up, around **the** time of my initial sighting, our telephone directory **consisted** of a page and a half, and **we** didn't even have yellow pages."

As far *as* the **eye** is able to scan there **is** beautiful, fertile farmland. "People in the city might think **we're** *a* little backward," Martha confided, **"but** in realty **we're** just **as** aware as anyone living in New York, Boston or Washington. After all," she laughed, **"we** have TV down here, too!"

It is difficult to mistrust Martha. She has a warm and vibrant personality that **is** contagious

"I remember *that* afternoon clearly," Martha began reminiscing, turning back the calendar to the summer of 1953. "I

was sitting on the front porch talking to my lather, **while** my mother **was** inside doing her household chores. Suddenly, out of the corner of my eye, toward the northwest, I noticed something glittering **in** the air over a **wooded** area adjacent to our house. There, hovering motionless in the bright sunlight, were three gold-colored, **disc-shaped objects**, 30 *feet* in diameter. Quickly, I pointed them out to my dad and we *watched* as they began to move **slowly** over the **tops of** the *trees*. **Dad** went into the house shortly thereafter leaving me **alone**. Within **seconds** they came to **a** complete hault, hovered for 15 minutes and then fully reversed their position and drifted back over the **Held**." At this point Martha became frightened when the **center** *object began* **moving** *away* from **the** other two toward *her*. She ran *into* the *house and* peeked *through the* screen *door* as it remained in this position *for a* **short period**. Eventually, the trio **moved** off towards the southwest.

Reliving the events of that afternoon, Martha says the three objects remained **in** sight for **some** time, but that her mother and father quickly lost interest. She **didn't**! "Even at the age of ten I knew they couldn't be airplanes, because of their shape and the fact that they moved without making **any** noise. Looking back, I guess I was really excited. Something told me they weren't from this planet. I **tried** to **get Mom** and **Dad** to **pay special** attention, **but** they were busy elsewhere. Often, in the years since, I've attempted to bring up the issue of our sighting, only to have **my folks** change **the subject.** I guess it's just something too heavy for them to cope with, and so they've pushed it to the back of their minds."

Several years passed before she had her next **experience**. *On* this **occasion**, *Martha* did *not observe* anything unusual in the sky, but instead **came** face-to-face with a silver-clad creature, the likes of which admittedly **frightened** her half **to death**.

"I'll never forget that night **and what I saw as long as** I live! How could you?" Martha asks. "**After all**, it's not **every** day you nearly run over a strange man standing in the **road**, dressed in a space suit right out of They Came From Outer **Space**.'"

As Martha tells it, she had just turned fourteen, *and as* part *of* her 'grown-up' responsibilities, *she* was helping **her brother**, Roger, deliver papers. Every Saturday after midnight they **would load** up the **back** seat of his car and **head** out into the hills to deliver the *Washington Star*, **so that those on** their route would be assured of having **ample reading** material as **they** sat down to Sunday breakfast.

"We *had* what *they* call the milk run,

which means we had to make deliveries 20 miles **back** in the boondocks, in the pitch black of **night**. Martha **also points** out that **in** those days there **were** no such *things* as *street* lights. "For most of the route, it **was so** dark that you couldn't **see** your hand in front of your face.'

"I don't **know exactly** how long we were driving, **but** I would **estimate** that it was about two a.m., when from a wooded area, all of a **sudden** out pops this luminous figure **It** was on **my** brother's side of the road **and** so he **saw** it first, yelling, 'What's that?' Roger **slowed** the car **and** stopped All I can definitely **remember** is coming face to face with this 'man'—if you **could call him that—standing** there on **the** road, our **headlights** reflecting off his silvery suit."

In appearance, *Martha* claims, the *being was* a little **bit tailer** than average height, "maybe around six feet, **eleven**," and heavy-set, "more muscular than fat." While she can't be **positive, she** thinks the **humanoid's head was covered with a helmet** or hood She definitely saw its face, but something prevents Martha from recalling what it **looked like**.

I was anxious to get as **many details** *as* possible, so I quizzed Martha at length on her encounter with this alien being. Through the process of repeated questioning, I was able **to** extract important information regarding the witnesses' impressions which otherwise would not have surfaced:

"Was *the* suit *he was* wearing **self-illuminating** or **did** *it* merely shine when struck by the beams from your headlights?"

"It was **like** light **shining on** silver or aluminum foil. but the material his suit was made out of **was** very brilliant, much more brilliant than the **reflection** you might **expect** to get *from* any type of metal or foil."

"What did you think this was?"

"My first impression was it was something substantial—we didn't have astronauts then, but it **looked so** solid that I knew it had to be real."

'You **mention** a **helmet or** hood of sorts; **could** you tell whether he seemed to **be** wearing a **multi-pieced** suit, or **was** his outfit **one** piece?"

"I **would** say **that** it was probably all one piece. It was very much like **he had** a **kind** of hood that went up over his **head** *in the* back, *just* like we have built into our winter ski parkas. I'd also say he **probably had** on gloves."

"Did he finally disappear, or just walk away?"

"**My** memory **eludes me. The last** thing I can clearly recollect is that he seemed about to step into the path **of our** *auto*. He **walked** *onto* the road and then paused **in front of** our car, as my brother started to hit **the** brakes. That's when I saw the belt. . ."

Of all the **things she** can remember about this figure, Martha's mind keeps flashing back to a glowing belt buckle. From what I can ascertain from interviewing the witness, it was almost as **if** the **buckle had** a hypnotic effect on her, preventing Martha from getting a better **look** *at* the rest of the alien's features, and perhaps from even recalling additional details of her experience. "My eyes focussed on this belt buckle and I found it impossible to turn away. It was as if it were pulling me toward it,"

Being familiar as I am with the cases in which individuals have undergone a mysterious lapse of time after encountering ufonauts, I was curious **to know** if it took longer than usual for them to complete their newspaper **deliveries**. As willing as she was to cooperate, Martha could **not supply** me with a satisfactory **answer**. "That's as much as I can remember about **that night**. I **don't know** if we got home early or late. I never thought to check. **It was** an all-night job anyway. so **there** was no reason to be **finished** before **five or** six a.m., give or **take** an hour."

CONTINUED **ON PAGE 56**

Martha is convinced that the occupants of UFOs have been *keeping* tabs on her over the years, and that at times they may even be *reading* her mind. After she got married and had children of her own, Martha claims UFOs would often pace her automobile in the late afternoon and **evening** hours as she returned home from the grocery store or post office.

Several of Martha's sightings have been of a routine nature—lights in the sky—while others have been quite spectacular. On numerous occasions she's seen them hovering just above the ground. One place where she's ob-

served UFOs is over *a* rock and gravel quarry **located** less than five miles from **Martha's** home. "It was during the winter of 1967," she states. "I was *at* home *at* eight p.m., when an uncontrollable **urge came** over me to hop into the car and take a ride. I proceeded toward Route 50, planning to **stop** to *get* a pack of cigarettes at a local store *that* **was open late.** Instead, I turned left—to this day I don't know why—and **continued driving** for approximately two miles, until I noticed **three bright lights** which kind of **resembled arc** lights, **the** type they **use** *to* **light up a baseball field** at night."

As she drove along, Martha began *to* **realize** that *the* road was totally deserted. "Usually you *see* one or two **cars** going in either **direction**. This evening, however, nobody was out." Little by **little the lights** continued to grow in

CONTINUED ON

thing drew Martha **back into the** cold, alone. And this is where her **experience** takes on all **the** elements of a classic UFO contact, *except,* **as before,** recall of what actually transpired has been erased from her memory.

"I **left the house,** making a mental note to return in time to catch the beginning of **the Jerry Lewis** movie. The half hour until **the** show *started* should have *left* me enough time to drive out to *the* quarry, *see* if *anything* was around, and **then** return home."

Following her hunch that **they would be** there **when she got back to the** quarry, Martha drove **along** the old dirt road once more. "Sure enough, **the** three UFOs were hovering in **tire sky,** just **like I knew they would be,** *in* the same *exact* spot as a **short** white before." As far as Martha can remember, nothing else unusual happened *that* evening. "Finally I just got tired of *staring* at them, **and** started back *to* the house." Expecting to arrive in time to catch the beginning of **the** Jerry Lewis movie, Martha received **Ole** **biggest** shock of her life when she discovered that the film was already half over. "It was a 90 *minute* picture and as far as I'm concerned, I shouldn't have missed more than five minutes at me very most, but here was my husband asking me where I'd been for the last hour or so. Frankly, I couldn't *answer* him. To this day I can't figure it out in **my** own head. Apparently, I was down at **the** quarry watching for UFOs, but I can't **be sure!"**

It may just be that, **like** in so many other cases that *follow* **this** pattern, **Martha** not **only** saw UFOs, **but** contacted the crew members of these **Ships** and possibly—just possibly— went on **board** one of **them.**

In 1952 UFOs Buzzed The Capitol *On* Several Occasions...Were These Events Significant of a New UFO Wave?

CONTINUED FROM r

size until they were **the** size of a **house. Then** *it* happened! "Looking up. *at* about **forty** *feet* above the ground I saw three **huge** silver **discs,** each appearing like two saucers, one inverted on top of **the** other. At first I thought they were airplanes **about** to crash. After *a* few minutes of being absolutely stunned, however, I put two **and** two **together,** and it finally struck **me** *that* they *were* flying saucers."

Too stunned to drive **any** further, **Martha** braked to a complete standstill. "I thought. 'I **wish** Mack was here right now to see **this!"** Her husband had retained a healthy **skepticism** toward the subject, "They were so **eerie looking** that I knew they couldn't **possibly have** been **any type** of device built here on Earth." What made these UFOs so unusual, as compared to the others she'd *seen,* was that directly in the *center* of each disc, painted on their silvery metal bodies, was the letter "S," followed by a zig-zagging lightning bolt. **The** letter *"S"* was black in color, the bolt of lightning a deep, dark red. "For all intents and purposes, if *they had been* airplanes, **the** markings could have either read TWA, Eastern **or** some *other* line—that's how clearly the insignia *stood* out to me."

Seated behind **the** steering wheel of *her* car, Martha continued to watch the sky for *a* full fifteen minutes. Finally the

objects slowly moved away. As they vanished over the trees. Martha felt totally *frustrated,* as she *had* never felt before. "It's as if I were sitting here, and they were there, each not *knowing* what to do next. Mentally, something told me *they* wanted to establish contact but didn't know how to go about doing it We had a sort *of* telepathic link between us. but I can't tell you what was said. because it was more *a* sense of feeling than the transmission of actual words."

In an **excited** frame of mind. Martha turned the key in the car's ignition and sped straight for **home .** Arriving, **she** rushed into the house and excitedly told her husband what she'd just seen. To **Martha's** way of thinking it *was* one of her best sightings to *date,* and *she* felt confident that if Mack would only return with her to the quarry, he **would** have all **the** evidence he'd been demanding. "I thought they **might still** be in the vicinity and that they **would** come back if I **wished** them too." However, instead of rustling out into the night. her husband seemed **comfortable** *staying* right where he was in front of the TV set. "There was a Jerry Lewis movie due **on** in another half hour. and he didn't want to miss **it.**"

Despite Mack's reluctance to **leave** the confines of the **living room,** some-

Probing deeper during **fay many** talks with **Martha,** I was able to draw her out **on several** subjects. Like *so* many other silent **contactees,** Martha is also fascinated with the occult, and has had several psychic experiences going back to when she was young. She seems to have a natural *extrasensory* ability, and several times has stunned me with her insights, which I **believe could only** have been obtained by paranormal means. I've even seen her demonstrate what could have been **psychokinetic** powers. It *happened the night* she telepathically **read my** mind. As she hit upon one important factor about a recent dream I'd had (which I'd told absolutely no one about), the ceiling light above us blew out. Coincidence? Maybe—but there's always a chance it wasn't!

To *this* day Martha hasn't any explanation for what **she saw.** What struck me was **the** fact that in **both** this inci-

CONTINUED ON PAGE 63

CONTINUED FROM PAGE 80

dent and the episode involving the silver-suited beings on the highway, Martha was *not* able to recall seeing the facial features of either entity. This is a truly amazing aspect of the case that I find hard-put to understand, unless it's because the face wouldbe easily recognizable to her—the face of someone she's met on the street or at work. Whatever the explanation it seems like an important puzzle to ponder.

Because of the continuing intensity of UFO waves across the country, there are many additional witnesses besides Martha who have come forward to tell of their sightings.

On Friday, December 28, 1973, *Sheriffs* Deputy John Payne was leaving his brother's house in Marshall, Va., at around 4:30 a.m., when he had stopped for a cup of coffee before going back on duty patrolling the streets of Warrenton. As he pulled out of the driveway, he noticed a bright object blinking on and off in the sky to the north.

Stepping on the gas peddle, Payne began to pursue the craft. He followed it till he climbed a hill oft Rt. 55 where he was able to get a clearer look at it.

"It was something—what, I don't know," he declared, admitting that from what he could see, it might well have been a "spaceship." The deputy took a pair of binoculars out of the glove compartment, and peering through them, was able to see that the UFO had "red, blue and green lights in streamer form from top to bottom." According to the *Fauquier Democrat,* residents listening to the police radio band heard several officers excitedly commenting that "all heft is breaking loose" and that UFOs were all over the country. Concluded the *democrat:* "Flickering lights were spotted winging over Prince William, Loudon, Fairfax and Culpepper counties. but *no one is sure whether* it was a fleet of UFOs or only one covering a lot of territory."

At about the same time *as* Deputy Payne's sighting, Manassas Park Policeman Joseph Scalici reported that he saw two UFOs hovering over the southwestern portion of Prince William, Va. According to his field reports, one of the UFOs dropped down to tree-top level while the other remained high in the sky. The sightings occurred only a few miles from the Manassas police station.

None of *the* sightings made on that morning have everbeen explained, and it doesn't seem likely they ever will be!

I'm not afraid to admit I've seen UFOs around here. and so have others." These are the words of Linda Bernhardt, residing in Remington, Va.,

Passing by Peter Genovese

Brunswick man mixes business with UFOs, holy water

Jesus' mother has appeared over 209 times this century to issue a terrifying warning! New miracles and prophecies of the Virgin Mary: Do they foretell of World War III? The End of the World?

For the first time offered in America: Authentic water from the shrine of Fatima. The world's most beautiful crystal rosary. Fatima good luck medallion.

Space Brothers Warn. Time is Running Out for People of Earth! Count St. Germain may still be alive at age 323! By Following Simple Instructions Everything You Desire Will Materialize Instantly. Just Snap Your Fingers and Count One, Two, Three. You Can Become a ... SUPER-BEING!

Tim Beckley writes good copy.

Beckley is the man behind UFO Review, Inner Light magazine, Global Communications and all those medallions, crystal rosaries, holy water and UFO books mentioned above.

He's made a living — apparently a good one, if he can afford full-page ads in the National Enquirer and Star — supplying the remaining, metaphysical, cosmic and just-plain-curious needs of people around the world. His classmates from New Brunswick High School, Class of '65, chose accounting, law and engineering, but Tim Beckley decided to try something different.

"I'm an inquisitive-type person," he says, sitting in his tiny office in the basement of his Cortland Street home. "I don't believe anyone has all the answers to God; the universe, UFOs; I think we should keep an open

mind. I don't have any particular ax to grind

Many of the items he offers through the mail are a bit unusual. You can get Fatima holy water (one ounce is $10; Beckley says it comes from "an order or something of brothers in Portugal"), crystal rosaries ($49.95 each), a Space Medallion in Honor of the Ashtar Command ($3.95), an Ark of the Covenant Charm (free with purchase of "God's Secret Weapon").

There are scores of books and tapes — "Alien Bases on the Moon," "Strange and Unknown Facts about the Life of Jesus," "Flying Saucerama," "How to Become an Interplanetary Traveler.

"It's not your run-of-the-mill business," Beckley says.

A UFO sighting got him started in all this. As a youngster of 10, he was sitting one summer evening on the front porch of his parents' New Brunswick home when something flew right over the house. The authorities, he says, called them weather balloons. Beckley's not sure what the objects were, but says they weren't weather balloons.

At 14, he started publishing a UFO newsletter. The Interplanetary News Service. He became managing editor of The Saucer News out of New York. He became a free-lance writer, doing stories for Moped

Action, National Enquirer and other publications.

In 1975, Beckley started UFO Review. Circulation is 40,000, with subscribers, he says, in all 50 states and 37 countries, including the Soviet Union. He says between 20 and 25 percent of his readers have seen UFOs, while the rest "would like to." He believes aliens exist and that there are three kinds; Alien No.1, "little people, 3½ to 4 feet high, tall, high foreheads, wrap-around eyes; Alien No. 2, "people who look so human they can walk among us and no one would know the difference," and Alien No. 3, "the really strange type — giant, hairy, winged flying creatures."

With Inner Light, Beckley deals with the religious and occult. The magazine mixes stories — "The Day a Priest Performed the Rites of Exorcism for Ann Miller" — with ads for religious items, books, pamphlets.

Inner Light, UFO Review and Beckley's UFO News Service are all part of his Global Communications, which has an office in midtown Manhattan. If Beckley's not there, he's in New Brunswick. If he's not there, he's somewhere appearing on a talk show or trying to nail down a distribution deal. He's just started a record company and is thinking about making horror movies. This is a guy who never lacks for ideas.

"Global is a good name," he says. "I can go anywhere with it."

What will he be doing in five years?

"Hopefully, circulation (of The UFO Review) will double and we'll be putting out more books and sending out more holy water," he laughs.

"Maybe it'll be alien holy water. From the canals of Mars or something.

Tim Beckley peruses a copy of UFO Review, one of his out-of-this-world offerings.

Her sightings out of this world
Woman claims she was *abducted* by *aliens*

By JAM RAK
Sentinel Staff

At age six she encountered a golden-haired man from outer space "... not dissimilar from me," recalled Diane Tessman. "The only thing different about him was a light in his eyes – a feeling of advancement"

Tessman said she was taken to a space ship for a brief period, one of three times as a child she was abducted from her family's farm in Iowa

Tessman is now 36 years old and does not lent like the stereotype of a wild-eyed person claiming to have friends in outer space. She lives in a modest home in Mira Mesa, is a mother, and has been a school teacher for 11 years

Under hypnosis administered by Dr. Leo Sprinkle of the University of Wyoming, Tessman has been able to recall as early as age three, contacts with aliens

Over the years she estimates that she has seen five UFOs (unidentified flying objects) – including one over Penasquitos Canyon in northern Mira Mesa Five other objects she has sighted she is not sure about, and the remaining she s ruled out as being IFOs (identified flying objects)

Tessman has also served as an investigator through MUFON (Mutual UFO Network), an organization comprised of nuclear physicists, NASA employees and other scientists attempting to document or explain sightings. About 90 to 95 percent of the cases they investigate torn out to be IFOs, such as balloons, airplanes, lights, etc, Tessman said.

While some people might consider Tessman and others like her a crackpot. "At this point I don't care anymore," she said.

Tessman recently authored "The Transformation," a story about how UFOs transformed her life and how they will transform civilization The book is expected to be released in a few months, and is published by Tim Beckley, himself an author of several books on UFOs, and the editor of the magazine, "UFO Review."

It was in 1979 that the Florida teacher (now on a one-year leave of absence) was visiting a friend in San Diego. They' were on Black Mountain Road when they saw a star aver the canyon.

"I soon realized it was flying," Tessman retailed Then she watched it move toward a larger star or light, toping the two objects wouldn't collide. Then the smaller star merged into the bigger light and it took off. a lighted, flying triangle

"I was familiar with Miramar (the nearby Navy jet air station) and it didn't fit," said Tessman. "I could come up with no earthly explanation for that "

Whether you believe the story or not, millions of Americans have seen UFOs. According to Beckley, who once went by the nickname "Mr UFO "

"California is probably the hotbed of sightings and encounters." he said. One theory is that the land contains a special material which re-energizes space craft

Beckley, who had his first sighting of a UFO when he was a youngster in New Jersey, says he is convinced that outer space creatures are more developed than humans and they want to share their knowledge with us. Only until earthlings acknowledge them and show them we would not use knowledge to destroy ourselves will they help. he says

Neither he nor Tessman fears the alien creatures, however. and Beckley characterizes them as benevolent.

The space creatures are particularly *concerned* with our abuse of nuclear energy. Beckley says: he is not active in the anti-nuclear movement. though.

Beckley. a walking encyclopedia replete with stories about UFO sightings and encounters around the world, is also the author of " Riddle of Hangar 18," a book about a special site at Wright-Patterson Air Force Base where allegedly dead aliens killed in space ship crashes have been stored He has also written about UFOs and other stories for the National Enquirer *and* similar magazines

He is critical of the scientific community and government for not spending more money on research of UFOs. The existence of life more intelligent than ours would change the power structure in the world. Beckley says,

Tessman is quick to agree that the implications are enormous. To acknowledge a greater intelligence would be "humbling" for mankind and a tremendous chance tor advancement, she said

Tessman, who also does "past life" readings, believes it is "highly likely" that the world will end in her lifetime. Like Beckley, she believes a certain number of people will be evacuated *from* this planet by space creatures

"Not that we think 'Oh. we're the chosen ones,' " she is quick to say

The skies over Penasquitos Canyon, as viewed from Block Mountain Road, once yielded a UFO, says Diane Tessman. With the Mira Mesa woman is Tim Beckley, who is known in some circles as "Mr. UFO."

---

only 12 miles from Warrenton. "Over the years, I've seen all kinds of odd shapes in the sky, so that you could never convince me they were anything but spaceships." Linda isn't a person to cut corners when she talks to you, nor is she one for beating around the bush. "Of course they're from other planets," she openly states. "Where else could they possibly come from? t mean they travel so gracefully, yet upon occasions can reach supersonic speeds without creating a ripple in the air. None of out own aircraft can do that."

To date. the best multiple witness sighting was made in April, 1973, fay a group of children playing touch football. Knowing of Martha Long's interest in the subject, the group led by sixteen-year old Teresa Smith ran to her house and pounded repeatedly on the front door until she came outside. The children wanted her to witness what they had seen, to prove to themselves (and their parents later on) that it was *not* their imagination tricking them.

"Looking up in the clear blue autumn sky, I counted seven disc-shaped UFOs. Quickly two disappeared to the southwest and two toward the northwest Of the three that remained, one of them—the center object—appeared to be in trouble. It started tilting, and turned from a bluish gray to a silver color. It seemed as if it couldn't get its speed up, and that the other two objects were watching out for it."

Suddenly, Martha says, there was a loud commotion in the sky as a formation of jets appeared. "Andrews Air Force Base must have picked them up on radar. Meanwhile, a piper cub pilot, apparently about to land at our local private airfield, spotted the UFOs and nearly crashed into a tree trying to get a better look at the objects. it was quite a spectacle. People in cars on the road were cutting each other off trying to see better."

According to Martha, the "troubled" UFO wobbled slowly off toward the south, flanked by the other two craft. our military jets powerless to do anything.

Bull Run Mountain, for those readers who don't immediately recognize the name, is the exact same mountain which caused such a great controversy a few years ago. Investigative columnist Drew Pearson had uncovered the fact that a secret military installation had been tunneled out in the base of a mountain—Bull Run Mountain—where, in case of nuclear attack, important military and political "bigwigs" could be taken safely underground, while the rest of the country fended for itself. What had caused a particularly loud stir was that those to be admitted were almost entirely personal friends of the president.

And while the underground facilities at Bull Run Mountain were designed to be "top secret"—its very existence denied—almost everyone in Washington seemed to know about it. Pearson even appeared on the Johnny Carson show, where he and the talk-show host joked about not being on the list of the "special" few who would be permitted underground in the *event* of a holocaust. Needless to say, once the cat was out of the bag, the base was shut tight, though rumor has it that the underground caverns still contain enough food and supplies to comfortably take care of several hundred "key individuals", should the occasion arise.

One of the reasons Bull Run Mountain was selected for such an honor in the first place is because its natural caverns are said to be among *the* largest in the United States. Huge "rooms" carved out by nature's own hand, millions of years ago, are nearly perfect for the intended purpose. High ceilings and a wide expanse would make it almost unnecessary to do any "retouching." Millions of dollars could be saved by not having to dig or tunnel with machinery.

Needless to say, if Uncle Sam and the Pentagon brass knew of Bull Run Mountain's natural cavern formations in

UFO REPORT

128

tire 1950's, no doubt the occupants of UFOs could have discovered them eons ago and used them to their own advantage. If flying saucers are coming here from other worlds, the most practical thing for any alien race to do would be to construct bases right here on our own planet so that they wouldn't have to travel senselessly back and forth the vast distance to their home planet. Time and energy could be saved and a lot more accomplished.

Naturally, since the United States is among the most powerful nations on the face of the globe and Washington our capital, the UFOs would want to be as close as possible to our seat of government. It is interesting to note that most of the UFOs seen in the Washington area have been sighted low, just above tree-top level. This would stand to reason, since the air space around the capital probably has more radar per square foot than anywhere else in the country. Any craft flying in over the Potomac would have to zoom in and out as rapidly as possible and as close to the ground as feasible. If they didn't, they would be "sitting ducks," susceptible to discovery and possibly aerial attack by our mightiest military jets.

Martha Long admits that she is as puzzled as can be. Although she has had all sorts of experiences, she doesn't profess to understand all of what is going on. Has she been "chosen" as a representative of the saucerians? Or does her psychic background merely make her an "open channel,"

able to receive messages and data through no "fault of her own?" Will they continue to utilize her "services" if indeed that is what they have been doing all along? The questions are many, answers few.

In recent months Martha has begun to have a series of dreams, in which it seems she is actually on board a vehicle from another galaxy. After awakening, she can remember speaking in strange foreign languages and conversing with people she has never seen before. To tier, the "dreams" are all too vivid, and she senses that they could be very important. After discussing the matter with her, she admits they could possibly be placed in the category of astral projections. if she is traveling "out-of-the-bow at night and boarding UFOs in her "dreams," this would only tend to verify the research of Ufologists like Brad Steiger (see the article *Beam Me Aboard—UFOs and Astral Travel,* UFO REPORT , Dec., '76,) who have long contended that the flying saucer enigma *can* be linked with psychic phenomena, and what a lot of percipients actually experience can be classified as parapsychological in origin.

Martha has also expressed an interest in Bigfoot, the tall, hairy creature seen around the world which has of late become more and more often associated with UFOs. Though Martha has never seen such a creature, she has heard loud, high-pitched screams

coming from the woods behind her home. Upon investigation, heavy tree branches have been found broken off at heights which, under normal conditions, would be difficult for anyone human to reach. A Mrs. Higgins, who lives with her husband in a house situated further back in the woods, has told Martha that she and her sister have heard the cries several times, and, "they scared me so badly they made my hair stand on end." The screams are heard only at night.

On this same line, as of late her twelve-year-old daughter Teresa (who had never heard or seen pictures of Bigfoot before) says the half-animal-like creature has been turning up during her sleeping hours· In her dreams the hairy humanoid is always seen standing in the same spot, in their back yard pointing in the direction of a fallen tree.

Maybe with Jimmy Carter in the White House (an admitted UFO believer and observer) the mysterious aliens based inside Bull Run Mountain won't be so afraid to surface once in a while. In the past, the UFOs have kept a close watch on our nation's capital, and if Martha's "vision" is prophetic, we might see a re-run of the 1952 Washington, D.C. flap. This time, however, maybe our enlightened government officials won't tell us we've all been fooled by temperature inversions or swamp gas! ●

John - "Mothman Prophecies" - Keel presents Tim Beckley with the NY Fortean Society Of The Year Award, it's mascot (rubber) frog. Frogs represent the strange fall or "teleportation" of mysterious objects from the sky as first described by historian Chariest Fort in his book, "Lo."

DR. J. ALLEN HYNEK *Director, Center For UFO Studies*

August 1976

By Timothy **Green Beckley**

The name Dr. J. Allen Hynek is, in many quarters, synonymous with UFO research. As a scientist and a former consultant to the U.S. Air Force on the matter of unidentified flying objects, the bearded scholar **has** been involved with this worldwide phenomenon for more than 25 years.

Indeed, his personal biography is both lengthy and impressive.

Currently, Dr. Hynek is Professor of Astronomy at Northwestern University (Evanston, Ill.). He obtained this position in 1960 after retiring from his job as Associate Director of the Smithsonian Astrophysical Observatory in Cambridge, Mass., where he was in charge of the U.S. Optical Satellite Tracking Program. While there, Dr. Hynek was responsible for *the* precise tracking of man's first space satellites, as well as for some 270 volunteer "Moonwatch" stations in various countries.

A native of Chicago, Dr Hynek has had many illustrious posts in his scientific career. After receiving his doctorate in astronomy from the University of Chicago, he became, in turn, Professor of Astronomy and Director of the McMillin Observatory at Ohio State University, supervisor of technical **reports** at the Applied Physics Laboratory of John Hopkins University, Assistant Dean of the Graduate School at Ohio State, and Professor of Astronomy and lecturer in Astronomy at Harvard University during the four years he was affiliated with the Smithsonian's Observatory in Cambridge, Mass.

Most important of all, for more than two decades Professor Hynek served as astronomical consultant to the U.S. Air **Force** on *Projects Sign* and *Blue Book,* which processed and studied reports of UFO sightings from somewhat cramped quarters at Wright-Patterson Air Force Base in **Dayton,** Ohio. As part of *his* job, Dr. Hynek had access to more than 10,000 sighting report ——any of which he admits the government did not have any logical explanation for.

In addition, since ending his association with the Air Force—after the government closed down Project*Blue* Book in 1969—Dr Hynek has continued to **actively** pursue the subject. Working with other scientists, it is his aim to investigate the UFO phenomenon from a scientific viewpoint and to provide a public source of reliable and authoritative information on the subject. To this

end he has set up the Center for UFO Studies, enlisting the aid of established scientists from various universities in this country and **abroad.**

"The Center for UFO Studies came into **existence."** Dr. Hynek **says,** "largely because a growing number of qualified scientists, engineers, and other professionals have long believed the UFO phenomenon to be worthy of investigation, and decided that positive action should be taken to end a quarter-century of misunderstanding and misrepresentation. **More** than 15 million Americans believe that they have sighted UFOs, **and these** essentially similar reports persist year after year. With the cooperation of the police, the FBI, and the Civil Defense Agency, the Center now provides the organization and the personnel to study the problem."

Among the projects undertaken by the Center is a comprehensive computer analysis. To date, more than 80,000 cases have been fed into a data bank. The **Center** also enlists the help of several dozen trained field investigators, who, when a report comes in on the UFO "Hot Line" [maintained on a 24-hour basis), are immediately dispatched to the area to interrogate wit **nesses,** check out any physical evidence, and file a detailed report. The Center also publishes technical papers, issues frequent "special reports," **and a** newsletter which prints the results of their research.

"We try to be as thorough as is humanly possible," Dr. Hynek told *UFO* REPORT. "The Center approaches the matter seriously. We are not a bunch of 'gung ho' amateurs chasing around the countryside. Nor are we interested in producing sensational copy. We adhere to a strict, scientific formula for our work. The facts are facts! We don't alter them to suit our own purpose. '

Dr Hynek's attitude on the origin of UFOs has changed over the years—"I think that's a pretty healthy approach" From arch-debunker to an advocate of the interplanetary hypothesis, he now leans toward a psychic explanation. His latest **book,** *The Edge of Reality* (Henry Regnery Co.), written in collaboration with Jacques Vallee, approaches this aspect gingerly. In this exclusive interview, Dr. **Hynek** seemed to have quite a lot to get off his chest. He selected our audience—"for obvious reasons," he says—to air his controversial views.

UFO REPORT: In 1948 you became an official advisor tw the U.S. Air Force on the matter of UFOs. What are your earliest recollections—did you feel there was a legitimate mystery to solve, or did you dismiss the entire phenomenon as just so much nonsense?

DR. HYNEK: In retrospect, I was a complete jerk. When I got into this business I was teaching **astronomy** at Ohio State University in Columbus, which is not far from Dayton, Ohio, where Wright-Patterson Air Force Base—the home of the now defunct Project *Blue Book*—is located. At the time, the government was trying like mad to determine whether it was the Martians or the Russians who were responsible for the elusive discs being tracked in our atmosphere. To put it bluntly, they needed a competent astronomer to tell them which cases **arose** out of the misidentification of planets, stars, meteors, and so forth. Personally+I was dead sure that the entire affair could be accounted for in mundane terms—that it was a cut-and-dried case of post-war nerves, and people had to have something to occupy their minds. I likened it to swallowing goldfish or seeing how many people could cram themselves into a phone booth. It's fantastic how many of these early sight i n g actually could be accounted for by the planet Venus sighted low on the horizon or a plane's fuselage glistening in the early dawn. In all honesty, however, looking back there were several **dozen** hard core episodes which I'm sorry to say I neglected on the general hypothesis **that** it cannot be—therefore it isn't.

Certainly when I started getting involved, I would have **taken bets** that by 1952, at the very latest, the whole **mess** would have been forgotten. I was convinced it w a s a phase that **would** quickly pass. Of course, I was dead wrong!

On top of this, just like everyone else, I felt positive flying saucers were an acute American fad. Never did I suspect in my wildest dreams that it would turn out to be a global phenomenon·

UFO REPORT: **Can** you pinpoint when you began to realize there might be a lot more to the UFO mystery than you had originally figured?

HYNEK: As early as 1953, I wrote an article for the Journal of *the Optical Society of America,* hinting that there was a good possibility we were bypassing some pretty important data. By then I realized that UFO reports were not just confined to this country. We were starting to get reports on a more or less regular basis from all over the world. Allowing for translation, I would challenge anyone to distinguish between a French UFO sighting, a Japanese report, or one from South America. As a practical scientist, it took a number of years for the fact to sink in that there was a serious problem confronting us. Later, around 1956, I went to the Smithsonian Institution in Washington, D.C., and talked them into establishing a satellite-tracking network, which I became completely immersed in for approximately five years. I had hoped we would be able to zero in on UFOs sailing high above the earth. We never did!

UFO REPORT: Among UFO buffs you were typecast from the outset as an Air Force "flunky."

HYNEK: I suppose that's correct, and in a sense I was *Blue Book's* tame professor. Nobody enjoyed busting holes in a wild story and showing off more than I did. It was a game and it was a heck of a lot of fun. The famous sightings of April 1967 which took place in and around Ann Arbor, Mich. really planted me firmly on the front pages. But, for the first time, I was beginning to feel a backlash of public sentiment. The tide was slowly turning.

UFO **REPORT:** Once and for all, if we can, let's set the record straight as to what happened during this controversial, historic UFO sighting. You were quoted in the media as having said that law enforcement officials and other seemingly reliable individuals had seen nothing more unusual than swamp gas. A national furor erupted following your statements* Rep. Gerald Ford of Michigan—now President Ford—even went so far as to suggest Congress look into the reports. Were you being honest with the public and the press when you explained the cause of those sightings as gas fumes coming from a swampy bog—or were you acting under orders?

HYNEK: The Center *for* UFO Studies is still distributing my original press release in which I specifically say that if we confine our attention solely to the faint lights that the college girls in Hillsdale saw from their dormitory window, then the most likely explanation is that they saw swamp gas rising from the marsh in back of their school. Although I could not prove it in a court of law, this seemed to be a perfectly logical solution. If you review the case carefully, you will find that the students only saw the dim glow when the ceiling lights in their room were shut off completely. Never once did they describe a physical vehicle of any type. They saw flickering lights. Nothing else! Of course, before I could finish talking, the reporters covering this rather ill-fated

press conference were dashing off down the hall to telephone their editors who, in turn, blew this one quote out of proportion. I wish I could have yelled at them, "Hey fellows, come back here, I'm not finished yet." But it didn't happen that way, and so "swamp gas" it was, and is.

UFO REPORT: Obviously, if you had it to do over, you would handle the situation differently.

HYNEK: Being more mature today, I would have probably said, "Gentlemen, you simply cannot conduct a serious, scientific inquiry in an atmosphere of hullabaloo. We'll just have to have open hearings. Call witnesses one by one, until everybody's had his day in court." That's what I wish I'd done! But I didn't.

There was a positive *side*. Now, if anybody starts giving me the raspberry about believing in little green men or being a gullible believer, I can always tell them, "Listen, buddy, who the hell do you think started the swamp gas routine?"

UFO REPORT: From an insider's point of view, can you reveal what was really going on behind the scenes during the era of *Project Sign* and its successor *Project Blue book?*

No less a source than the late Capt. Edward J. Ruppelt—an outspoken Air Force critic, who for several years in the mid-1950s headed the Air Force's UFO program—projected a picture of utter confusion and lack of communication among the top brass. He said that there was always a vast difference in opinion as to what flying saucers actually were, even among the Pentagon big-wigs. Some of our military leaders supposedly dismissed the entire affair as rubbish, while other senior officers were strong believers in the interplanetary theory.

HYNEK: Two factions definitely existed. There were those individuals who were extremely concerned over the radar trackings and the close approaches made by UFOs to civilian and military aircraft. They conjectured that their pilots were being truthful and were not concocting far-out tales. They wanted to check all the possibilities Hopefully, clues could be gathered which would lead to an eventual solution as to how UFOs accomplished such drastic right-angle turns and accelerations without apparent harm t either craft or occupants. The possible method of propulsion also intrigued them.

Most of the top brass, however, thought of themselves as being down-to-earth. They couldn't understand for a split second why any of their colleagues would bother to take the subject seriously.

UFO REPORT: Didn't the sightings and radar reports of UFOs over Washington, D.C., during July and August of 1952 shake up the Pentagon hierarchy? Radar units at National Airport verified the fact that "unknowns" were flying near the White House and Capitol.

HYNEK: Their reaction was typical. Not being a scientific body, the Joint Chiefs of Staff immediately put the problem squarely to their board of technical advisors. These men were rigid, establishment-oriented. They "knew" there had to be a logical explanation. Since, in their minds, flying saucers did not exist, a rational solution was mandatory. They chose what—to them—seemed to be the most logical theory: *Temperature Inversion.* Boom! Officialdom had what they were eagerly seeking—a scientific scapegoat. In order to get themselves off the hook, they jumped at the first crumb thrown at them. Otherwise, the fixed thinking pattern was that the problem would have been very embarrassing to all concerned.

Let's get one item perfectly clear. In working with the Air Force, I discovered a rule of thumb: four-fifths of the raw reports were of what I define as IFOs (Identified Flying Objects) and not UFOs. Because the general public is *(Continued*

HYNEK INTERVIEW

(Continued)

untutored in what is visible in the sky, competent people have frequently mistaken planets and stars for UFOs. During both world wars, countless rounds of ammunition were wasted an Venus. Allied forces thought the "evening star" was a spy device launched by the enemy. So, when I talk about UFOs, I am not referring to birds, balloons, or aircraft, but to reports from responsible people, often in concert. I always give additional credence to reports from several witnesses rather than just me. The scientific advisory board utilized by Project Blue Book did not take this into consideration when evaluating a sighting. That radar had verified the presence of glowing lights seen independently by airline pilots over the Capitol meant absolutely nothing.

UFO REPORT: In most instances, wasn't Blue Book's panel of select "experts" doing merely what was expected of them?

HYNEK: I tend to believe they were more honest than that. As an example of their attitude, if the Academy of Science were to be asked about ghosts and witches, they would laugh, anc .. the long run not even bother to investigate these topics. They would say, "Everybody knows there are no such things," and leave it at that. In turn, the military would rub its hands gleefully. They could always point to their technical people and say, "See, see, our scientists have figured it all out. Didn't we tell you there was nothing to it all along?" Serious scientific discussion was absolutely discouraged. Not once in my years at Blue Book was I able to get a dialogue going. The attitude of the board members was absolutely adamant. There were personnel in high places who really won-

---

Daniel Boone's New Age pioneers

Expo, Palm Springs
June 1996
Article from Desert Sun

BLUEPRINT FROM ABOVE: 67-year-old Daniel Boone (right) and his son Matthew are keeping the legend of the Integratron alive. The idea for the structure came to Daniel's father-in-law, George Van Tassle, after an extraterrestrial experience near Landers in 1953.

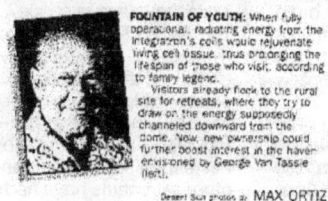

EN ARRIVAL:
) dynasty camps on
ders' Giant Rock, wait-
for word from Venus.

ON YATES
Desert Sun

's the kind of story that's best told over beers, and at 10 a.m. with the nearest bank clock already flashing 99 degrees, Matthew Boone cracks open his first 12-ounce can

here's a small patch of shade er a group of young trees in his l, and as the day progresses foldout chairs move with the lows.

tant Rock, the seven-story boulwhere Boone's tale begins, is n three miles from his doorstep. Integratron, where it ends, is yards away.

the bright desert sun, the domed e building looks more like a ipe than a fountain of youth and iow, Boone admits, it is. After 35 rs of sweat and toil, his grandfa-George Van Tassle, was never to finish the project. But his famas yet to give up hope.

oon, the Integratron will have owners — a group interested in irbishing the aging building — if all goes well, the aliens who inspired its construction will rn.

there are still a lot of people y who think we're friggin' out of minds, says Boone, his beer can ssting in the oppressive heat and dad kind of made a pact. I tell the truth, and if people t to believe us, it's up to them.

aniel Boone, 67, is in the folding ir next to his son. He was there, says, when the flying saucer ne down in 1953, and he helped fleet in Santa Monica, left the state for health reasons in 1929 and stumbled into Giant Rock soon after. Convinced there was gold in the nearby hills, Critzer decided to move to the area, but had no money. He met Van Tassle by chance. They both lived in Santa Monica at the time, and when Critzer's car broke down, Van Tassle offered to help. Talk soon turned to gold mining and Giant Rock — topics that fascinated the 20-year-old aviation buff. Van Tassle agreed to "grubstake" Critzer — providing him with food and money for a cut of the action — but never expected to hear from him again.

Critzer moved to the desert and built a home under Giant Rock, digging deep under the boulder, then reinforcing his underground dwelling with iron rods.

A year later, he sent Van Tassle a postcard showing how to get to the big boulder. Van Tassle made the trip and fell in love with the area.

It's here that accounts tend to vary. The Boones, who have passed the story through three generations, swear theirs is accurate. But even they admit what happened to Critzer is somewhat hazy.

One thing is clear: By the early 1940s, rumors about Critzer took on a life of their own. With World War II raging in Europe, many thought Critzer, an American of German

was almost 20 miles to the south. There Van Tassle met a woman who held seances. After just one meeting, he said he began "channeling" other beings, serving as a conduit for extra-terrestrial and extradimensional messages.

"The first actual "encounter" with
— Aug 2, 1953

FOUNTAIN OF YOUTH: When fully operational, radiating energy from the Integratron's coils would rejuvenate living cell tissue, thus prolonging the lifespan of those who visit, according to family legend.

Visitors already flock to the rural site for retreats, where they try to draw on the energy supposedly channeled downward from the dome. Now, new ownership could further boost interest in the haven envisioned by George Van Tassle (left).

Desert Sun photos by MAX ORTIZ

Each forearm bears a small green, indiscernible tattoo on each forearm — one for each love of his life. He sits back and listens as his son talks, sipping his own beer.

It was about 10 minutes before 2 a.m. when the landed

gift to mankind" — the formula for the Integratron.

An alien Fountain of Youth

The idea was to create a machine ...d rejuvenate l... ...l tis-

LANDERS

For more information
Landers Chamber of Commerce,
364-3824

old him yet."

Van Tassle died in 1978 at the age of 66. At the time, he estimated the Integratron to be 82 percent complete. His wife sold the building shortly after his death for $13,000, later reclaimed the structure, then sold it again for $25,000. Little work has been done on it since, but the Integratron remains an imposing structure.

Humans, heal thyself

Built entirely with wood, the 38-foot-high dome is split into two floors. On the top floor, the Integratron is an acoustic wonder. From the center of the floor, small whispers are amplified like a rock concert.

A coil in the ceiling is designed to have healing powers. Similar coils are placed in the hollow column that runs through the middle of the building and in the floor. Curved ribs of lumber scale the walls in beautiful symmetry.

Outside, metal poles jut like spokes from the structure's midriff. In the 1970s, when it was still partially operational, pressurized air pushed a wooden ram, causing the poles to spin around the building Integratron to keep vandals out. Matthew Boone still gives tours of the dome when people knock on his door, and business is picking up.

On a given week, 10-20 people stop here, but there are no formal hours.

"It just sounds so fascinating," said Linda Muller, librarian at the Twentynine Palms public library, about 40 miles away. There, she keeps a small manila envelope full of press clippings about Giant Rock and the Integratron.

"It's always out," she said. "People want to believe."

Generally, though, it's people from outside the area who show the most interest.

"I get calls from everywhere," said Mary Sunderlage who runs the Landers Chamber of Commerce out of her home. "We get maybe four or five a week, which is amazing, I think. We didn't get that many when we had the biggest earthquake in the world in 1992."

ET, phone Landers

In fact, other than the 7.2 quake that shook the area four years ago, this unincorporated community of about 8,000 is mostly just a bl... the rur... ...mar ho..

from their neighbors. Van Tassle's three daughters went to school in Twentynine Palms, where children teased them about their father.

"George w...
... his

dered and appeared troubled by what was going on, but, goddammit, **they** couldn't admit it. Not **publicly!**

UFO REPORT: Out of curiosity, what happened to those individuals who believed the subject warranted **serious** study?

HYNEK: The procedure was just about always the same—they were usually transferred *to* another line *of* work. Dewey Fournet is a typical example of "company policy." Soon after he came out with a pretty solid pro-UFO statement, he was eased out of **any** official involvement with the Air Force's flying saucer project. I saw this happen time after time.

UFO REPORT: At any time during your long tenure with the Air Force, did you ever get the feeling that orders may **have** originated higher up than with *Blue* Book personnel?

HYNEK: Very definitely, I knew this all along. Orders were passed down from the top office in the Pentagom—the **Secretary of the Air Force.** On several occasions, I was called in to see *Secretary* Harold Brown. Never once was I asked **my** opinion as an astronomer. I was always *told*, "That was a balloon," or "That was a flock of geese!" It was clear that *Project Blue Book* was a finger exercise. **Of** course, you **might** very **well** ask me, "Why, as a scientist, did you stay with **it?** Why didn't you tell them to go stick it?" Well, to be frank, I was interested in collecting the data for later *use* of my own. I knew from experience that the Air Force **wasn't** going to do a blessed thing with what they had **gathered.**

UFO REPORT: *Over* the years, we've *heard* all sorts of rumors to the effect that the CIA was behind the so-called "wall of silence." Just how were they **actually** involved?

HYNEK: We know they organized the **Robertson Panel.** This was a hand-picked group, composed of scientists **and** various technically-oriented people. The job **of the** committee was to determine what effect UFOs **might** have on the public if one morning John **Doe** awoke to find aliens had landed in spaceships during the night. How **much** further the CIA went, I have absolutely no way of **knowing.** However, I would not be surprised to discover **that** they **were** operating very heavily behind the scenes, shaping **much** of *Blue Book* and earlier *Project Sign's* policy.

UFO REPORT: What could have been **their** motivation? The CIA is supposed to *be* involved only with foreign matters. Their **intelligence specialists** must have been smart enough to realize even in the opening stages of the drama that UFOs **were** not secret **weapons** under construction by the **Russians or** by any other foreign power.

HYNEK: Who can say what is **behind** anything the CIA does? Their position has become increasingly difficult to

fathom in recent years. They might have been afraid of another Pearl Harbor. All this country would need is **to** have a foreign agent start a whole **burst** of UFO reports. **They'd** have a field day. The military wires would be **so** jammed with bogus flying saucer reports that a legitimate red alert couldn't be quickly ascertained. In July 1952 this actually **happened. A genuine** bombing or some other overt act of espionage could be mixed in with all the UFO reports, and go undetected. *The CIA was* concerned about this. I'm sure this was uppermost in their minds when they decided that the whole mess should be debunked and downgraded* and the public's attention diverted. Basically, **their** attitude was drawn up for **purposes** of defense. As I say in my book, The **UFO** *Experience,* no **mention** was ever made of or explanations offered for the many "Unidentified" cases in the **files** at Wright-Patterson. The committee members **were shown** only cases that had been satisfactorily solved.

". . . The close encounter of the third **kind** -- type six -- involves humanoid occupants. Currently we have an estimated 800 sightings of this sort on file. **These** encounters constitute what is probably the most incredibly bizarre aspect of the UFO enigma. . ."

UFO REPORT: The Air Force **had a** long-standing regulation known as AFR 200-2, which governed the **release** of information on sightings made by servicemen. **This** regulation called for **a** fine **of** $10,000 and a lengthy prison sentence for those military men who spoke out and dared to tell the media of their experiences. Were any convictions ever handed down?

HYNEK: I couldn't give you a definite answer, but no such incident was ever brought to my attention. When **you're in** the military, you're pretty scared **most** of the time. You know that the noose can be **slipped around** your neck in nothing flat. Therefore, you tend to watch your step. From a **public relations** standpoint, however, it would have been a fatal mistake to carry out such a threat. After all, why **take** such extreme measures over **something** that officially doesn't *exist?*

UFO **REPORT:** In 1969 *Project Blue Book* **was** shut down. The decision to close their files was based **on the** negative findings of Prof. Edward Condon of the University of Colorado following an 18-month-long study of the UFO phenomenon. Branded a **whitewash** by just about every civilian UFO organi-

zation, the Condon Committee concluded that flying saucers did not exist, and therefore government funds **should** no longer **be** appropriated to study future cases. This, at a cost to taxpayers of more than a million dollars. Since then, **do** you know if **the** government is continuing its investigation of UFOs secretly?

HYNEK: I only wish I knew. Why don't you find out and let me know? I could make a lot of money writing potboilers based on **pure** speculation, but I couldn't look myself in the mirror any more.

UFO REPORT: As a trusted confidante of *Blue Book,* did you ever see any hardware which might possibly have been built by an extraterrestrial civilization?

HYNEK: Let's see, **I guess you** already know about the bodies of the little men in the freezers at Wright-Patterson, and **the UFO** that was captured on a runway at Edwards Air Force **Base** in California. All joking aside, I've **never** been able to substantiate **any** of these fanciful yarns—and we certainly have **had** a fair number of them. **Every** time I hear such stories, I cringe! Where, I ask, is the evidence? Almost inevitably, the witnesses have been hushed up or their names are being kept confidential. Even if the Air Force had such physical **evidence** or the remains of humanoid creatures, they would not necessarily take me **into** their confidence. Remember, *Project Blue Book* was pretty much a public relations operation.

UFO REPORT: In essence you're saying there were probably a lot of matters that you were not privileged to know about or consulted on?

HYNEK: Absolutely I'd be the first to admit it. What it gets down to is this: the Air Force was playing m y **with me,** and I was playing coy with **them. I** was privileged to bits and pieces of information that I knew one day would be useful to me in my own attempts to unravel this riddle.

UFO REPORT: Several of our astronauts have either had **sightings,** or expressed a fascination with UFOs. Do **you think, as** a person with former close ties with the government, that NASA has a "secret dossier" containing photos and **unedited** transcripts of conversations made with our astronauts while **they were** in space?

HYNEK: The only **astronaut** who has repeatedly admitted **having** seen **a** UFO, had taken motion pictures of the object—**which** were never **shown** to anyone, not even him—IS James McDivitt. I understand Gordon Cooper has expressed a belief, and one or two other astronauts have had sightings out of the service. As for **the** space administration **knowing** more then they admit, wouldn't it be a huge joke if

NASA were spending our hard earned tax dollars in the search *for* extraterrestrial life, when that life *might* be right under their noses? If this turns out to be the case, I think a lot of people are going to be angry. If they really knew anything at all, it would seem to me that their attitude would—should—be quite different.

UFO REPORT: Before we leave the area of physical evidence, what are your opinions on the mysterious 20 pound sphere—the "Betz Ball"—that was found several years ago in Florida? News reports claimed that it was of non-Earthly origin and moved about oddly on its own, as if controlled by an outside force. Didn't you investigate these claims for *the* Betz family on whose property the strange device was found?

HYNEK: Not only that, but I slept with the ball when I stayed at the Betz home for several days. It never acted funny around me. I took shavings from it and had a spectrographic analysis done. It turns out that the ball is constructed of the same components as number 646 stainless steel. If they're not manufacturing this metal on Mars, then it's probably man-made.

UFO REPORT: Isn't it possible that this element could be obtained universally?

HYNEK: Sure. There's also a possibility that the Sun won't rise tomorrow.

UFO REPORT: If we lack physical hardware, what then is the best evidence for the existence of UFOs?

HYNEK: We have a significant number of physical trace cases in which UFOs seem to land or hover mere inches from the ground. These are the most fascinating, bemuse *the* traces can be photographed, and soil samples subjected to laboratory analysis. A number of years ago, I began breaking down UFO reports into six major classifications.

UFO REPORT: Can you list these?

HYNEK: The majority of cases are what we call *nocturnal lights.* These are generally colored globes that maneuver about the sky as no conventional aircraft can. They have been known to move slowly at first, or sometimes they're seen coming in rapidly. People have told me, "initially we thought it was a shooting star," or, "I thought it was an accident on the road, bemuse the *red* lights were flashing." Another popular description is that an aircraft flying low ts going to crash-landi. Observers have tried to explain the phenomena themselves and, failing to do so, they frequently find themselves in a state of shock. They have come up against something that really puzzles *the* daylights out *of* them.

In the second category, we have *day-*

k UFO REPORT

light discs. In the majority of these cases, the objects appear metallic, oval or elongated. They range in size anywhere from five feet *to* 30 feet in diameter. Can be tracked on radar. Frequently leave physical traces behind. Give off a humming noise, often described to me as (something like) a dentist's drill or a high-pitched sewing machine. Suddenly they take off with tremendous speed after having hovered for an indefinite period. We have many photos of these craft. They all look remarkably alike.

Next, we have a very special classification—*radar* cases. My categorization here is one of convenience. Radar cases may overlap into the other five areas. The ones I like the best are the incidents that involve "radar visuals." That is, cases in which radar trackings are verified by sightings from me ground or by airplane pilots. Just recently, I returned from Mexico, where I talked to 23-year-old Carlos Santos Montiel, who maintains that on May 3, 1975, three dark gray-colored discs circled his aircraft at 15,000 feet, sub-

---

" . . . We *have* a significant number of physical trace cases in which UFOs seem to land or hover mere inches from the ground. These are the most fascinating, *because* the traces can *be* photographed and the soil samples subjected to laboratory analysis. . ."

---

sequently taking control of his plane and forcing it to gain altitude. He was panic stricken. His voice was filled with fear. Tears frightfully swelled in his eyes. While he was undergoing this traumatic experience, radar technicians at Mexico City Airport were watcing the cat and mouse game on their scopes. *So* here we *have a case* where radar provided independent confirmation of a very exciting aerial confrontation.

Categories four, five and six, I have designated Close *Encounters.*

Type four is a near approach, with no physical effects.

Type five is a close encounter with physical evidence, the nature of which is often quite impressive. As I mentioned earlier, bum marks may be found at the site of a landing. Or the branches of nearby trees may have been snapped off high above the ground, where no lone individual could have accomplished the deed. Investigators arriving at the scene are often confronted with valuable scientific evidence—something that can be studied. The close encounter of the third kind—type six—involves humanoid oc-

cupants. Currently we have an estimated 800 sightings of this sort on file. These encounters constitute what is probably the most incredibly bizarre aspect of the UFO enigma. When I first heard of such episodes, my own natural prejudices told me to throw them out. The "little green men syndrome," as I call it, has never ceased to exist. I've since come to believe that no scientist should discard data simply because he doesn't like it.

UFO REPORT: Was there a particular case involving humanoids which swayed your opinion?

HYNEK: I had been building toward a positive attitude for a number of years when John Fuller, the well-known writer and then columnist for the Saturday *Review,* told me the fascinating story of Betty and Barney Hill. I listened with open ears. Editor's *Note:* "The Hills' encounter with a UFO is one of the most popularly cited contact cases. It involves their being taken aboard a strange vehicle and given a physical examination by aliens. A Boston psychiatrist, Dr. Benjamin Simon, later hypnotized them separately, and extracted a full account of the abduction.

My thinking was altered completely when I was called in along with Dr. James Harder of the University of California to interrogate two Mississippi fisherman, Calvin Parker and Charles Hickson, who insist they were literally "kidnapped" and forced to go on board a spacecraft, *where* they were subjected—just as in the case of the Hills—to a physical examination. The tale told by these two rugged shipyard workers held up under grueling cross-examination. They were even hypnotized by Dr. Harder, who pulled from their subconscious additional details. What really struck me was the fact that the local Sheriff, in an attempt to get to the bottom of the mystery, had placed the two men inside a jail cell and walked out of listening range, The Sheriff had hidden a microphone inside their quarters in order to eavesdrop on their private conversation. He wanted to see if they would talk freely amongst themselves and admit they were in collusion on a hoax. From the tone of their voices, and what they said, the Sheriff was convinced Hickson and Parker were telling the truth.

I don't know what makes me want to automatically look down upon these creature cases. Maybe this involves an atavistic fear of the unknown, or of rivalry with another species. There is, upon closer scrutiny, another factor which I find difficult to sort out. It is odd that the creatures seen coming from these craft should resemble our own

135

homo sapiens race so closely. It is also peculiar that *they* would be able to *adjust to our* gravitational pull or breathe our air so easily. This could only mean *that* they are mechanical creatures—robots—or they originate from a habitat whose environment is very similar to ours here on Earth.

In recent times I have come to support less and less the idea that UFOs are "nuts-and-bolts" *spacecraft* from other worlds. There are just *too* many things going against this theory. To me—and please understand this is only my opinion—it seems ridiculous that super intelligence would travel great distances to do relatively stupid things like stop cars, collect soil samples, and frighten people. I think we must begin to re-examine the evidence. We must begin to look closer to home.

UFO REPORT; Is it your opinion that UFOs *originate from* another time-space continuum or dimension. as has recently been suggested by a growing number of UFOlogists?

HYNEK: I would have to say that the extraterrestrial theory is *a* naive one. It's the simplest of all hypotheses, but not a very likely explanation for the phenomenon we have seen manifesting *itself over* centuries. In Toronto, Canada, not *too* long ago, I spoke be-*fore a group* of liberal-thinking scientists who had gathered for a serious discussion on the latest discoveries in the field of parapsychology. The *conference* was sponsored by the New Horizons Research Foundation, which is ably presided over by Dr. George Owen, a Former Fellow of Trinity College, Cambridge, England. I told these astute men *of* learning—including a respected Nobel Prize winner in physics—that we should *lake* into consideration the various factors which strongly suggest a linkage, or at least a parallelism with occurrences of *a* paranormal nature. Among *the* factors which belie the interplanetary theory is the proneness of certain individuals to have repeated UFO experiences.

Another peculiarity is the alleged ability *of* certain UFOs to dematerialize. A plasma is said to envelope the object in *many cases*. Then the "cloud" *becomes* more and more opaque, until it completely obscures the UFO. Finally, the whole cloud vanishes as though going into another *dimension*. There are quite a few reported instances where two distinctly different UFOs hovering in a clear sky will converge and eventually fuse into one object. These are the types of *psychic* phenomena that are confronting us in the UFO mystery.

UFO REPORT: I guess you are familiar with the cases where UFO witnesses claim that at the time of their experience they were overcome with a

A Ringing UFO Appeal:
Believer Sets Up Hot Line

By BOB GROVES
Courier-Express Staff Reporter

HERE'S A TELEPHONE number to mark on the wall next to the ones for fires or the family physician. It's the UFO Hotline:

Anytime you sight an Unidentified Flying Object and you don't get invited aboard. yan can report them on the UFO Ho**G.**

The hotline is connected with the New York City office of Timothy Green Beckley, founder and editor of the UFO Review, a bimonthly flying saucer magazine, circulation, about 30,000 worldwide.

When you call the UFO Hotline, somebody in Beckley's office—maybe even Beckley himself—will take down all *your* information, so try to be (tact.

The people at the UFO Hotline are dead serious about this, so they *didn't* put in a toll-free number. They figure that if you think you saw a real UFO, you won't mind paying for the call.

FROM 9 TO MIDNIGHT Sunday. Beckley, 32, will be a *guest* on the Steve Church Show on WBUF Radio. (Too bad it wasn't WUFO.) Beckley will briefly discuss the state of the art, such as the filming of two UFOs over New Zealand last Dec. 30. and then answer telephone calls.

Saturday *evening*, he will *address* the Northeastern UFO Organization, a private group meeting in *a* North Tonawanda home.

Beckley's Global Communications firm in New York is the American sales agent for the New Zealand UFO movie taken by an A̶u̶s̶t̶r̶a̶l̶i̶a̶n̶ TV crew. The American print of *the* film is owned by Dr. Brace Maccabee, a Navy physicist *in* Washington- D.C.

"I believe in UFOs. I've seen them myself. I've interviewed hundreds of witnesses, I'm not really out to convince *anyone*. I'm not an evangelist on a soapbox," Beckley said during a recent interview over (be UFO Hotline.

WHEN HE WAS 12 YEARS old. Beckley and his family in New Brunswick. N.J. saw two circular-shaped objects in the sky above them one night. Their neighbors also saw the objects. When *newspapers* the next day dismissed these UFOs as searchlight beams bouncing off the clouds, Beckley, *even* at that tender age, lost faith in their ability to deal with the subject.

"There's *a* wealth of information being kept from the public," he says. "not through secrecy, but because the media isn't interested or thinks it's all too sensationalized."

Although the federal government concluded its *Project Bluebook* study of UFOs 10 years ago without any substantial results, Beckley believes "there is some indication the government is continuing *its* investigation on 'a confidential *level*.' "

"...YES SIR... YOU SAY YOU'VE SPOTTED A FLYING SAUCER WHERE?

BECKLEY SAYS he has written articles on UFOs for 150 journals including the National Enquirer and the National Star, and in countries ranging from Japan to Africa. His *interviews* with UFO witnesses included former astronaut Gordon Cooper who, Beckley said, sent a taped statement *about* bus dose encounters to *a* UFO convention at the United Nations last November.

The current issue of UFO *Review*, he says. contains photos taken by Malcolm Williams of Niagara Falls of an orange object spotted over the Niagara Frontier Halloween Night, 1973. Williams was asked to photograph the object, Beckley says, by then weekend WGR-TV sportscaster Joe Pope who had received half a dozen calls from viewers reporting the UFO.

"Ninety percent of the calls we get are from people who sincerely believe they saw a UFO. People are seeing something, there's no doubt about that. You can't get thousands of *people* and say they are lying. These sightings *take* place all over the world."

136

feeling of tranquility and peacefulness. Many contactees claim to have communicated telepathically with the crew of *these* craft. Have you taken into consideration these psychic elements?

HYNEK: Let me relate to you a fascinating story. I originally told it to the attending members of the New Horizons Foundation and they were visibly awed. The witnesses in this episode swear their account is legitimate.

Two brothers were driving along a lonely road in the state of Nevada. If was a clear evening and the stars shone brightly. Four bluish lights appeared from out of nowhere and began following their automobile. After a few minutes, one of the objects crossed over the hood of the car and took up a position on the driver's side. Almost immediately the engine conked out, causing the vehicle to come to a complete halt. At this point an additional UFO appeared farther up the road. One of the men shone a flashlight at it, whereupon the object appeared to move slowly toward them. Both witnesses reported being frightened and anxious to get out of there. Suddenly, the car was given a tremendous push as if by unseen hands, causing the axle to break. A typical close encounter was turned into a virtual psychic occurrence when the mother of the two brothers reported that at the exact moment her sons were being scared witless, she, from her home in Buhl, Ida., felt the presence of one of them in her bedroom, and heard him call her by name. Here we have a classical case of telepathic communicaton with a loved one or close family member at the *precise* time of persona; discomfort or need. Only this time the incident was coupled with the dramatic approach of a UFO. Is it mere coincidence, or something more?

UFO REPORT: Well, all right, that's certainly fascinating, but still, you can't dismiss the entire incident as just a psychic manifestation. After all, something very real caused the pushing of the car and the axle to break.

HYNEK: You're so right. I prefer not to conjecture beyond a certain point. A trained mechanic examined the broken axle and the car for the Center, and said to him there seemed to be a rational explanation: The broken axle looked identical to the way a broken axle should look when it is not properly lubricated at regular intervals. What do I make of this fact? I don't. Did it happen "by chance," or what?

Of course, there are several other uncanny psychic aspects we have to contend with. Quite a number of UFO witnesses have been healed of serious

ailments or injuries following a close encounter with a flying saucer. As an example, I personally interviewed a sheriff's deputy in Texas who claimed that a giant UFO about 100 feet in diameter hovered over his patrol car late one evening, white he was making his rounds with another law officer. His hand was resting outside the car window when the glowing sphere beamed down a powerful ray of Sight. Earlier that day the officer had been severely bitten by his *son's* pet alligator. The finger had become infected and was badly swollen. It was painful and should have required medicat attention. Almost immediately following the near approach of the UFO. the deputy's wound had healed, miraculously.

UFO REPORT: One thing that stands out in UFO literature is the paranoid attitude of many witnesses. Flying saucer tore is rife with accounts of mysterious "agents" who verbally threaten observers, warning them not to discuss their experience with anyone. Several years ago, you mentioned in a published article how on numerous occasions you were being told what seemed to be a straightforward story, when suddenly the witness would lapse into a highly confidential mood and reveal how he was sure his phone was being tapped or that he was being watched, sometimes on a regular basis, either by the "government" or by occupants of the craft itself. Have reports of this type persisted, and how do you account for them?

HYNEK: The appearance of the "Men In Black" — named primarily because these individuals usually wear dark clothing and act sinisterly toward witnesses—are a recurring aspect, and a mighty big puzzle. Researchers have for the most part tried, as a matter of

convenience, to sweep these incidents under the UFOlogical *rug*. They had a good reason: these experiences are damn hard to relate to.

h e most recent "Men in Black" case I am familiar with concerns Carlos Montiel, the young man whose plane was trailed by three UFOs near Mexico City in May. Several weeks after his encounter, Montiel was supposed to appear on a TV show to talk about what had happened. He never showed up at the studio. The witness later claimed that his car had been forced off the road while driving to the station A strange-looking man dressed in dark clothing approached him and said it would be wise if he did not go on the show. The following Saturday, I interviewed Montiel for two hours in my hotel room. As we concluded our conversation, Carlos promised to have breakfast with me on Monday morning. Again he pulled a "no show." Over the telephone later that afternoon he explained how the same individual had again "requested" he not meet with me. It was a "better not, or *else*" sort of veiled threat.

Another thing we've noted at the Center for UFO Studies, is how unmarked helicopters sometimes appear, immediately, over the site where a UFO has been seen, and *then* they, too, disappear. No one has been able lo trace them. All these items apparently tie together. As for an explanation, we really don't know what the nature of these "silencers" might be. It seems to belong, in many cases, in the category of a psychic occurrence. as some of these "Men In Black" seem to be able to read the minds of witnesses, thus knowing what course of action they plan to take following their UFO encounter. Again, you're seeking answers, and all I can give you is the problem

UFO REPORT: Since you seem to believe that UFOs present at least as much of a psychic problem as a matter of interplanetary vehicles, the next question would seem to be a logical one. Have you ever had a psychic experience of your own—an experience that may or may not be related to UFOs?

HYNEK: I'm about the most unpsychic individual in the world. I've never even had a precognitive dream. Even as far as UFO sightings go. I can only admit to the sighting of nocturnal tights which didn't amount to much

Getting back to this psychic bit, I'm still at the stage of simply learning the facts. We don't know to whom—which field—the subject belongs. Does it belong to the physicist, the astronomer, the psychiatrist, the anthropologist, or the parapsychologist? It would appear to be an interdisciplinary problem. My principal question *has* always been, "Did the witnesses see what they claimed to?" When someone tells me their car was stalled and their headlights doused, I'm interested in finding out if this is so. I *want an investigation* to commence immediately. I want an investigator to be on the scene as soon *after* the incident as is humanly possible. We **need field equipment,** including **fully-equipped vans** which will **enable** us to move around quickly from place to place.

UFO REPORT: Obviously, you've long ago concluded *that* **something** is taking place, otherwise you wouldn't have **set up the Center for UFO** Studies.

HYNEK: The Center *was* started because *the* **subject** of UFOs is significantly intriguing, and **because** there was no established organization where scientists could share their independent findings. Let's use the Northern *Lights* in our **analogy.** In **1875 someone might ask what caused** this colored aerial display, and the *best* **scientists** in the world would be mystified. "Hells-bells, you could have said they were the souls of the dead and gotten people to believe you. When a scientific explanation was finally forthcoming, no doubt those **who believed the spirits** theory cried "cover-up." What I'm saying is not to jump to any premature conclusion. **We have no** *way* **of knowing what** the **right answers are.** All I assert is that the UFO problem is a tot more complex than we have given it credit for.

UFO REPORT: When did you first contemplate starting such a group?

HYNEK: Actually, the Center *was* begun **several years ago.** when a **number** of my scientific colleagues at Northwestern University and elsewhere would meet secretly to *discuss the* **phenomenon. Because** it was dangerous to associate **oneself with UFOs,** we jokingly called our group "The Invisible College." This name has an **honorable** and historic **precedent.** Way **back in** *the* **early 1600s,** when scientists in England **talked** to each **other,** they couldn't do it openly, as they **were** afraid *of* being accused *of* being in league with the devil. To **offset this** they met in back **rooms, taverns,** and down dark alleys and called **themselves** "The Invisible College," which is where we got our **name.**

UFO REPORT: Why did you decide to surface—come out in **the open?**

HYNEK: In late 7973 we saw quite a flap of UFO sightings in the Northern Hemisphere. **Nobody was doing** anything **about** it—no **one was** "minding **the** store"—and our "College" got a little mad and decided **we had better become at least partially** visible. **Part of** us still wants to operate **behind the scenes and** retain **anonymity. We have** members who **are** affiliated with **prominent** government laboratories, Los Alamos, Oak Ridge. **and** the Jet Propulsion Laboratory.

Other scientists and scholars associated with the Center, who are willing to **let their identities be known, include** : Dr. Paul Davies, University of London; Dr. Claude Poher, director **rocket division, French National Center** for Space **Studies;** Dr. Douglas Price-Williams, anthropologist, University of California **at Los Angeles;** Fred **Beckman, chief** scientist, **Argonne Cancer Laboratory,** Chicago; **and Dr.** David Saunders, **Industrial** Relations, University of Chicago.

We operate the **Center as a clearing-**house, to which persons **can** report **UFO experiences without fear of** ridicule **or** unwanted **publicity, and** with the **knowledge** that their sightings will be **given** *serous* **attention. More** *than* 15 million Americans believe **they** have observed UFOs—according to a **recent Gallup Poll**—and these essentially similar reports persist year **after** *year.* With **the cooperation** of **the police,** the **Federal** Bureau of **Investigation,** and the **Civil Defense Agency,** the Center now provides **the organization and the** personnel to **study the problem.**

UFO REPORT: Wasn't it difficult obtaining **the** assistance of law **enforcement agencies?**

HYNEK: In the beginning it was **slow.** but then, *in an* **unprecedented move,** the FBI printed an article of mine in **their** monthly **bulletin.** We **furnished them** with **a** special toll-free **number** which they **can** call 24 hours a day, seven days a week. **Every night we get at least** one call. The number isn't **made** available to **the** general **public—can you** imagine what kind **of** response we would get on **April Foot's Day?**

UFO REPORT: What happens after *a* report is phoned in?

HYNEK: The **next day we contact** one **of** our **300** regional **representatives,** and they go and interview the witnesses. **If a** close encounter has transpired, our area investigator will take Geiger counter **readings of the ground,** collect **soil** samples for analysis, and **take** depth measurements if **the** object appears to have landed. Furthermore, if the witnesses **are** suffering from **any** after effects, such as blindness, headaches, **or** nausea, we **take an** interest in subsequent medical studies. If a contact has taken place **and** the witness is **agreeable,** we will subject him to **hypnosis** to **try and extract from his** **subconscious** as much detail as possible. Amnesia **attacks** are **common** to those individuals who have had **face-to-face** encounters with UFOnauts.

Finally, (tie reports are fed **into a** central **data** bank under the guidance of Dr. **David Saunders of** the **University of** Chicago. **This** data bank is invaluable. Eventually it will tell us a tot about **the** phenomenon that we might **now** be overlooking. Already when we plot the time **of** day of all the sightings, a pattern begins to **emerge.** There's **quite a host of reports between** nine and 10 **p.m., and a secondary jump** between two and three **in** the morning.

UFO REPORT: Because of your work, wouldn't you **say there is less of a stigma attached** to reporting a UFO today *than* **previously?**

HYNEK: That is **quite** an important **point.** I can **only** *state* that one **of** the major reasons we opened **the Center** for UFO **Studies is to** act as a repository **for** reports from **people who have been reluctant to tell** anyone else about their experience. During *the era of Project Blue Book,* **if** you **called your** local Air Force Base, *one* **of** two **things** were **likely to happen: you** were immediately dismissed **as** a crackpot: or, **a team of high pressure military** men were apt to show up at your front door with **a bunch of forms to fill out.** Quite often, the observer **would** be openly ridiculed in **the** press. Many witnesses lost their jobs and their self-esteem. Several **invididuals** even found that their **family** could **not** tolerate **the abuse heaped upon** them, **and** subsequently filed for divorce. Today the climate has cleared somewhat.

Interestingly enough, **the** situation is **different in other** parts of the world. For **years** the Brazilian government has studied the problem. **In fact,** I **have just returned from addressing the members** of both their **houses of Congress.** I gave a lecture about what has **been taking** place **on a global basis. The Brazilian** government was very **impressed.** They **have** shown their willingness to work **with me.** Last year, the **head of the**

French Department of Defense made a very pro-saucer statement on nation-wide television. His *statement* came shortly after (crewmen aboard) the Concorde (the world's first supersonic jet), photographed a gigantic object near the sun, during the course of filming the eclipse.

UFO REPORT: Have you made overtures to the U.S. government, seeking advice and assistance?

HYNEK: We have. Just recently I went to the White House, where I met with Mr. Donald Rumsfeld (currently Secretary of Defense), whom I have known since he was our representative in Evanston, Ill. The main purpose of my visit was to tell the President's (former) chief assistant about the kinds of scientists we are associated with, and to let him know that, if and when the subject gets to a Congressional or Executive level, the Center will be able to go into full action. I think that's all I should say about our meeting. Any other statement should come from Mr. Rumsfeld's office. Otherwise, there does seem to be a reversal taking place high up in the *military.* We've even received several reports from the Department of Defense. That would seem to give the Center a "Good Housekeeping Seal of Approval."

UFO REPORT: How can readers who wish to report a sighting reach the Center?

HYNEK: They may write to *us* at the Center for UFO *Studies,* 924 Chicago Ave., Evanston, Ill. 60201. And remember it *is* explicitly understood that their names will not be used in any published paper without their prior consent In every case. we *take* great pains to separate the names from *the* event.

UFO REPORT: Finally, what recent case has intrigued you the most?

HYNEK: Change the question, to what recent case has been most perplexing. and I'll tell you a whopper! Someone called the *"Hot Line"* in the middle of the night—got me out of bed. It was a police officer from a small town in Minnesota, where a focal flap has been going on since November 1975. What he told me fits *in* with these paranormal elements.

It seems that a couple were riding down a highway toward town, when the man remembered he had to make a phone call. He swung his car into the driveway of a motel and proceeded to walk toward an outdoor phone booth. Just as he was about to open the door to the booth, a big black Cadillac pulled up in front of him, blocking his path. An ordinary looking man hopped out of the front seat and literally pushed the gentleman out of the way in an effort to get to the phone first. Miffed by this uncourteous action, the man drove down

the *highway a* little while longer until he came to a second roadside telephone. This time the mysterious black car nearly drove the fellow and his wife *into* a ditch. They narrowly escaped injury. *As* before, the big "Caddy" came to a screeching halt, the front door flew *open* and *out* raced the same individual. His destination was the telephone. "He just about took the dime out of my hand!" was the way the incident was reported.

The story isn't over . . .

According to the police officer who called the Center, the identical routine was followed a third time. By now the couple were burning mad. They chased *the car down* the highway trying *to* copy down *the* license plate number, which *they* were successful in doing. Suddenly—and this is where *the* whole episode takes on an eerie quality— before their eyes. *the vehicle in front of them lifted up* into the *air and disappeared "as if* I *had flown into* another *dimension?"* (emphasis added)

Immediately, *the* confused couple contacted *the* police. The investigating officer—the policeman who placed the call *to* me—said his department verified *the* fact that this particular license plate number *bad* been issued to a man residing in a nearby town. When questioned, this individual refused to say whether or not he was involved *in* the episode. Eventually the officer impressed him with the fact that he might be charged with reckless driving if he didn't cooperate. With this, the man stated that he was a Jehova's Witness and therefore could not tell a lie. Though he was rather ambiguous, the outcome was that *he* did not see *the* episode in a UFO context but accepted it *as a religious* miracle. Normally we wouldn't bother to investigate this sort of thing, but somehow it just seems to fit *in.* I *know* there are many unanswered questions here, but we will just have *to* leave *it* as a cliff-hanger until a later date.

UFO REPORT: What do you think the future holds for us as far as UFOs are concerned? Will there ever come a time when they will openly establish contact with the human race?

HYNEK: I'm anxiously waiting for the curtain to rise and the next act *to* begin. I do not know what they have in store for us, but it should be interesting. We have behaved quite foolishly in the past. For several decades, there has been a tremendous amount of buffoonery. We've been party to a three-ring circus. Anything that is as farfetched as flying saucers will always be laughed at, *out* of hand. What we really need to do is change our whole attitude and manner of thinking. Remember what George Bernard Shaw once said, "All great ideas begin as heresies!" ★

Last year, there was an unusual concentration of
sightings along the Calaveras fault line in the
Santa Cruz Mountains. Some researchers say they are
studying the massive shifts in the Earth's crust—
while others claim they may be triggering the tremors

UFOs SPOTTED ALONG CALIFORNIA'S

By Timothy Beckley & **Harold** Salkin

The usually quiet atmosphere of the Stockton (Calif.) Municipal Airport was unexpectedly shattered on August 14, **1975.** The **time** was 9:35 p.m., and the night was hot and clear. The unforgettable conversation between Army National Guard helicopter pilot Maj. **Claude** Riddle **and FAA** flight control operator Dan Long broke the drawn-out monotonous routine:

Tower: **There seems to be** a **bright** light tailing **you** . . .

Copter: Can you tell what it is?

Tower We do not have an identification. **Why** don't you turn around **and try** to **identify** it for **us?**

With these words. Major Riddle swung **his** helicopter around, only to be confronted by "a **diamond** shimmering **in** the night."

Major Riddle was obviously puzzled and openly voiced his bewilderment to the flight control operator:

Copter: It's certainly strange . . . I can't make out what it is . . . The damn thing keeps moving closer . . . I hope it doesn't decide to do anything foolish!

For more than a week in mid-August. dozens of residents in several northern California **towns** were perplexed by strange aerial intruders which appeared daily in the sky over their communities, hovering and darting about at fantastic

speeds Investigators from **a** national UFO research organization later pointed **out** that this same area had been a hotbed for UFO-related events for several decades, **emphasizing** that **at least** two incidents involving encounters between earthlings **and** humanoids have **taken** place in the vicinity

FAA flight control operator Dan Long was keeping á routine watch on the sky over Stockton Airport when *he* caught sight of the unusual light hovering in the south 20 degrees above the horizon. Something about the strange light bothered him What was it doing there. bobbing up and down in one spot **like** a "sparkling jewel"? He realized that the only aircraft in the area at the time was the helicopter piloted by Maj **Claude** Riddle **The** National Guard uses Stockton's field as a **base, keeping** a small force on duty there around the clock.

Without hesitation, Dan Long radioed the chopper, which was circling the airport about to land The unidentified object appeared to be closing in on the helicopter—and fast! The *air trafficcontroller* was worried *that* the two *might collide*

Standing beside Long within the glass enclosure of the Stockton flight tower were two other FAA men, Joe

Savage. and John-Paul Ammirata All three are Vietnam veterans and have had extensive experience The object they saw on this occasion had all the earmarks of not being man-made. Passing around a pair of binoculars the trio watched the UFO intently

"Through the field glasses I was **able** *to* make out a definite form, Long said The object appeared to be circular in shape—like a flying saucer—and was giving off an intense orange glow.'

Leaving **the** glass **enclosed** tower, Long **and** Savage walked out onto a narrow catwalk that circled the 50-foot-high structure for a better view of the "thing in the sky The object was now flashing a powerful red fighton **and** Off at intermittent intervals

Dan Long says the UFO then **began** moving slowly in an easterly direction. Suddenly it stopped, and remained hovering for approximately five minutes before shooting straight up into the starry night

'It was completely silent for the entire period we had it in view,' Long later told me Then. without warning, it took off! I mean this thing really traveled One second it was there **and** the next— poof!—it was gone, up into **the** heavens '

As **the** object took off". Lung says it

Dec 1976

EARTHQUAKE LINES

emitted a **large puff** of *green* **smoke** which **hung** *in* **the** air well after the UFO **vanished.**

"The whole affair **freaked me** out," Long **admitted.** "I *got the* **surprise** of my life out **there** *on* the catwalk. Not in a million years had I **expected to witness** a phenomenon **like** that!"

While Long and the others were carefully **watching** the UFO from their relatively safe position, pilot Riddle was trying to maintain visual contact with it To **this** day the major holds strong convictions about what he **saw.** He is *positive* that nothing comparable *to* **this** object **exists** on our planet.

During an exclusive interview conducted *for UFO Report* the experienced pilot—who has **more than** *5,000* hours *of* flying **time** to his credit — managed to **recall** in dramatic details his hair-raising encounter with this **"bogie."** Though he is still in the service, the helicopter pilot sees **no reason** why he should mince **words.** To Major Riddle his eerie **experience was all** *too* vivid—and frightening.

Because of *the* peculiarity of the object, coupled with the usual **human** fear of **the** unknown, **he decided** to **keep** a **safe distance** from the UFO *and* no; **"close in."**

"From where I **was,** it **seemed** to hover for a **brief instant** and **then** move away from me — sort of ambling along—in a westerly direction. All **at** once it turned a bright red—lit up like a neon sign—and blasted off I wouldn't dare guess how fast it was traveling But I've observed enough missile launchings in my military **career** to **know** we have nothing that can compare in speed or maneuverability with that thing I tell you its speed was absolutely astronomical!"

Perhaps the most unusual aspect of the sighting concerns a strange "cloud" which appeared to **envelop** the UFO **as** it **rocketed** toward space.

"Seconds before the object zoomed upward, a gray mist—something like **a** cloud—began to form around its surface. This was followed immediately **by** a **blast** of green exhaust that penetrated the cloud-going right through A **like** you might **poke your finger** through a ring of cigarette **smoke.** I mean it **moved** out smartly "

When questioned about the objects size, Major Riddle responded, 'I'm a pilot and I've been around military aircraft of all types To me it looked about the size of a DC-6 "

At its closes; point, the major claims the UFO **was** within a mile of his own aircraft "I wasn't really interested in getting too much closer, **because—to** put it bluntly—it **scared the** hell **out of** me Nor **was** I about *to* slay around and become a sitting duck if **anyone had** told me to go after it, I'd *have* probably told **them** to go after it **themselves!'**

As to what the object *"night* have **been.** Major Riddle also has **definite** opinions "I'm not going to **sit here and** tell you it was a flying saucer, because I've never seen a flying saucer **before** But I'll tell you what it *wasn t.* It **was** no reflection' No balloon! No **planet** or **star!** Nor was it a conventional aircraft, **because** I've seen **every** type of **plane** there **is** to **see** In fact, I've got to be **honest and** tell *you* I've *never* **seen** anything **even closely resembling this before'**

Another eyewitness air traffic *controller* Joe Savage was carefully **watching** the air corridor **around** Stockton Airport, when his. **friend and co-worker** Dan Long pointed out the **object** to him Savage **sucked** in his breath when he saw the bobbing light The helicopter with Major Riddle a? the controls and the glowing orb appeared to be **headed** straight for each other Savage was worried At the time he wasn't thinking of UFOs but instead thought it might **be** a jet airliner or private plane that had strayed from its intended flight **path**

"I *saw* those flashing lights closing in on the National Guard 'copter. Although they were' a considerable **distance** sway, **my** calculations **showed** they **were** on *a* direct collision course. To **head** of a **possible** smashup, I go! on *the* horn **and began** issuing evasive-action orders As I did. *the* object turned a bright reddish-orange and zipped up to **5,000** fee?, where it appeared to hover. I asked *fie* 'copter pilot if he would make a 180-degree turn to see if he could get a **bead** on **it**. Major Riddle responded accordingly He had it in view. The object **was** now starting to move from east to **west** in level flight.

At first Joe Savage confessed he thought the UFO looked spherical— "like a basketball"—but as it climbed higher, he **could** make out **its shape** *more* clearly. "It was disc-shaped, distinctly **round."**

Like the others, Joe Savage watched the object move away slowly until it was almost due south of the tower "**As** it hovered, some sort of green mist came out of it, creating a smoke **screen** It seemed to completely envelop **the** UFO and then **a** few seconds **later** the object blasted **out** *of* view." Savage **says** that in the past he has watched a good many rocket launchings. "I've been down *at* Vandenberg **Air** Force Base, and **this** object appeared to be traveling quite a bit faster than any rocket shot I've **seen** there. **The** sighting remains a puzzler to me."

John-Paul Ammirata, the third FAA air traffic controller on **duty** that night **added** his description of the cloud-like effect that developed around *the* UFO.

"**As** the object leveled off, a cloud **began** to form around **its** outer **edges**, giving the appearance **of** *a* halo. Then the **object** shot straight **up.** In a matter of five or **six** seconds, it want to **60.000 feel** and faded completely from **view. However**, this 'cloud' remained visible in the **sky** for some time after Eventually it spread out and **disappeared**"

At the precise moment that the three FAA flight controllers were watching *the* UFO put **on its** aerial display, the strange antics of this same craft were also **being observed** by 27-year-old Gary Duran of nearby French Camp, Calif., who **was** out walking not far from the airport with two teenaged girls, Carrie and Edie Gallego Reached **at** home, Duran *was* **positive he** had seen something "**mighty** peculiar." What he thought was a "**twinkling star**" gradually

grew larger and turned into a disc. Duran and his companions also saw the UFO emit a large puff of green smoke. He described it as "a vaporous mist that was visible around it almost all the time." Duran says that he and the two girls hurriedly telephoned the airport only to be told the control tower already had the UFO in clear view.

There can be little doubt but that what we call a "flying saucer" was hovering up there above Stockton Airport, and the UFOnauts didn't seem to care who noticed.

For all intents and purposes, the flap, which was concentrated primarily within a radius of 100 square miles, began on August 10, 1975, in Gilroy, Calif., a community located in the Santa Cruz Mountains, roughly 45 miles to the northwest of Stockton, and 80 miles south of San Francisco.

The first to notice anything out of the ordinary was 19-year-old Terry Smith. The teenager was fighting a slight case of drowsiness as she drove her younger cousin, Imelda Lugo, home around midnight. They were returning from a party, which had lasted longer than they had expected. Peering out into a crystal-clear night, Ms. Smith noticed an unusually bright object high in the skies. In an attempt to get a better look, and perhaps identify it, the teenager leaned over the steering wheel of her VW van, while at the same time putting her foot on the brake to slow down. Her first reaction was that the object was a low-flying plane, perhaps in trouble and about to crash into the nearby mountains.

As they rounded a bend onto Kelton Street, the object swooped down and began pacing their van. The girls quickly realized that their new-found companion was no conventional aircraft, but instead appeared to be something out of a science fiction movie.

"**Suddenly, it was right** there in front of us," Terry exclaimed, "It was jumping up and down, just a few feet away from the van. Neither one of us knew what *to* **expect** mainly because we had never **seen** anything like **this** before We were really scared!"

According *to* the witnesses the UFO **was shaped** "like a ball." dark-gray in color, **and** had antenna-like protrusions jutting out from the top In addition, a row of four high-intensity lights circled the outer rim of the object Terry and Imelda both agreed that the craft itself was engulfed in a pale blue-green haze.

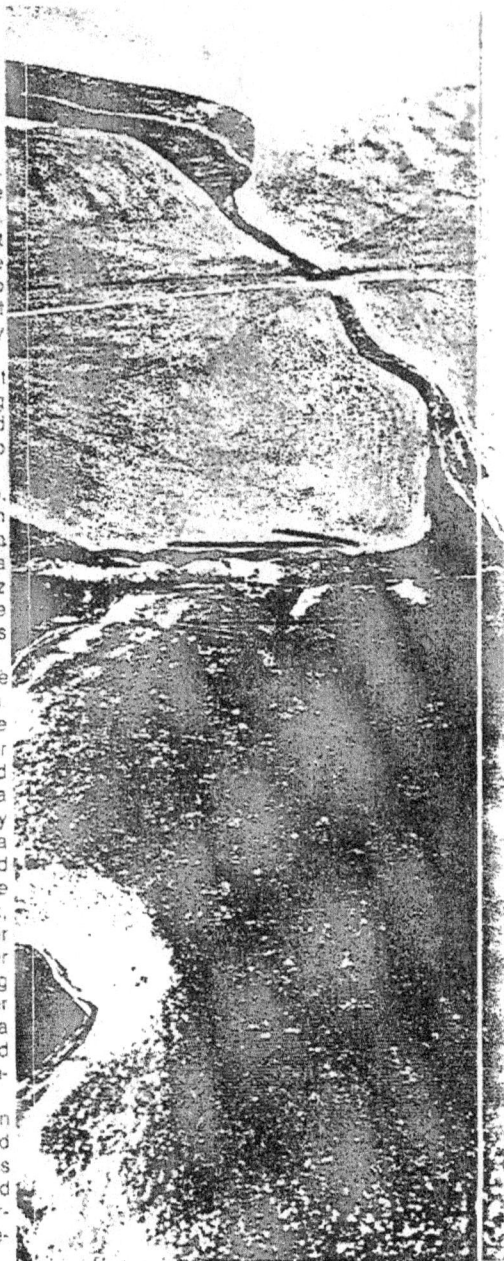

This same "haze" was quite similar to the cloud **observed** around the UFO at Stockton

Her heart pounding. Terry floored the accelerator and roared along **the streets** of Gilroy until she came to **her** cousin's house The van screeched to a **stop** with the object directly behind. and **the two** hysterics! girls ran to the Lugos' front porch. They **just** leaned on the bell **and hammered** on the **door** until they were let in

Imelda Lugo's father, Herman, gave this firsthand account of *what* happened shortly after midnight that **Sunday.**

UFOs have shown unusual interest in California's earthquake zones, including notorious San Andreas fault (pinpointed here by wavy line). Notice how far crust has shifted: stream has made virtual 90 degree turn along fault line.

My wife, Frances, *out* on her housecoat and went to the front door to see what the commotion was all about. I heard one of the girls scream, 'Don't go out there—they're going to catch you!' I didn't know what was happening, but I assumed that someone perhaps a mugger, had been chasing them. I jumped out of **bed**, put *on* my **pants** and rushed out."

On **the** lawn, Herman Lugo got the jolt *of* his life "The three of them—my wife, daughter, and niece—were staring up a the **sky. There**, about 100 **fee? above** *the* electrical wires near our

home, *was* **this** strange device with lots of blinking lights—red, white **and** blue ones—circling its **central portion,"**

Lugo **says** the object **was** huge, "twice as big as an automobile," **and** had what looked like three "suction cups" coming out *of* the bottom,

I t just hung there in mid-air," Mrs. Lugo explained. "The object **was** *so* low that I could **see** two square windows on top and Sanding gear similar to the tripod that photographers use. As for' the tights circling the craft. **Mrs.** Lugo *says* they reminded her of "a string of twinkling **bulbs"** on a Christmas tree. She **added** that she also saw *a* row of metal panels that reflected the light, giving it a gem-like quality. When asked what she thought it might have *been* Mrs Lugo was emphatic "This thing wasn't an airplane or helicopter, or anything else I ve **seen** before in all likelihood. it was probably a craft from another world!"

Terrified **by** what they saw, **the** Lugo family and Terry Smith decided to **keep** silent about their sightings. It was only later, after similar resorts **started** appearing in the local newspaper, that they decided to **share** their eerie experience

The majority of sightings in the vicinity of Gilroy took place on Tuesday August 12th, and Wednesday, August 73th. and **again** later *in* the **week A sizable** percentage of the reports came **from** *the* area of the Santa **Cruz** Mountain **range** and **the** Santa Theresa foothills on the west side of the valley

According to police records, **Mrs** Lynn Lance, the wife of a Gilroy high school teacher, was the next one to **encounter** the area's strange intruder "I was standing in my **back** yard," she stated, "sometime after 8 p m (Tuesday, August 12th), when I happened *to* glance toward the Santa Cruz **Mountains There.** maneuvering **above** *the* distant ridges was a brilliant beacon of light, like **She headlights** of a car,"

Calling to **her** family, Mrs Lance was soon **joined** by **her seven children**, who **range in age** from five to 17 Together they **watched** the phenomenon. "I **was** just south and in back of Gavilan College, which is tucked away in the foothills near a point known **as** Sargent's Pass Hovering there. was this extremely bright light It was glowing with tremendous brilliance all **the** time."

Initially. Mrs Lance **believed** the object *was* an automobile She quickly abandoned this idea as the UFO zig-

zagged down the mountain in **an erratic** pattern.

"I pointed it *out* So **my** children," she said. "All of us **saw** it at the **same** moment. **There was** little question **about** what **we** *were* watching. **We just stood** there, not **uttering** a word," Mrs. Lance said the glowing sphere was in *an area* where there are **no** roads. "There's no way a car could **get** back in there. **Besides, this** thing *was* **definitely** in the **air,** not on the ground!"

At one point, the UFO **seemed** *to* be moving toward them. "My oldest girl saw it coming down the mountain, heading our way. *it's* simply too difficult to estimate how close it got. because at night there's nothing but black sky and the outline of **the** mountains, and no visible landmarks to compare it to '

The Lance family do not have a logical explanation for what they saw "We've thought about it **since then** it *was* traveling much too close to the mountain to have **been** an airplane, and a helicopter would have no reason to **spend** *so* much time in **w e** position

Mrs Lanes and her seven children observed the UFO for approximately 15 minutes before giving up and **returning** indoors. It didn t **seem** to be **doing** much, **so at** that point, realizing **there** was nothing we could do **about** the situation. we just retired to the **living** room to talk some more about what we d **seen** I can tell **you** this " she **added** firmly. "it was *very* strange— something **we d** definitely never **seen** before!'

What was this brilliant light doing cruising *above* the **Santa Cruz** Mountains?

Robert Bluemmer, a **prater** employed by the *Santa Cruz Sentinel*, offered a plausible explanation. "From what my **wife** and I *saw*, I d say it was photographing **the area** up there During the **20 minutes** we watched it. **there** would be occasional bright **flashes, as** if they **were** taking pictures of something in the **dark.** One of **the flashes was** *so* bright it lit up a water **storage tank** on the **side** of a hill "

Interestingly enough, Bluemmer's sighting, was later pinpointed as **having** occurred at the same **time** the **Lance** family was watching the UFO perform its aerial **acrobatics** over the Santa Cruz Mountain range Because **he** was nearer to **the** foothills than Mrs Lance, Bluemmer was able to make out additional details He said the **object** had "an eerie red center." was round "like a ball," and had several "twinkling lights" on the bottom.

During his observation, Bluemmer maintains that the UFO repeatedly "ducked back and forth behind the trees" near Gavilan College. He and his wife, Claire, watched in awe as the craft "literally beamed down into the valley." The object finally disappeared, but only after it seemingly landed in a crevice. Though the Bluemmers watched the rest of the night, they both declared it never emerged from its landing place.

Not surprisingly, Robert Bluemmer has grown tired of discussing the incident. "I've gotten too many crank calls," he contends. Before ending our conversation, however, he did admit the sighting "troubled" him for several days, until finally he felt he just had to report what he'd seen.

More anxious to talk about his experience was Chick Bambino, a meat-cutter by profession. Bambino, in an exclusive interview with UFO Report, said he had just gotten out of his car and was walking across the lawn toward his house when something "mighty peculiar" caught his attention.

"There was this orange glow in the sky. It was oval shaped and larger than a full moon."

Bambino says he couldn't take his eyes off it. "I was glued to the spot, not able to make out what was going on."

After watching the UFO for several minutes, he saw it suddenly disappear. "It just blinked out. All at once the night sky was black again."

Rushing across the lawn, Chick called for his wife, Wanda, and his 16-year-old son, Freddy, to come outside and take a look at the strange light in the sky. "They didn't know what I was talking about. I suppose I was pretty excited. Finally we all went out on the lawn to see if it would reappear."

'Sure enough," Chick said, "about 100 yards to the north of where I first saw it, was the same object. I believe the glowing sphere was no more than a couple of miles away, hovering somewhere up in the Santa Cruz Mountains." Again, after a couple of minutes, the UFO "blinked out." This time it did not return.

Nonetheless, the flap was not over. Though the center of activity shifted briefly to Stockton, the UFOs returned to Gilroy on Friday, August 15th, when Leonard and Vincent Murray (16 and 18 years old, respectively) of nearby Modest~sighted a UFO which flew right over their home, about 15 feet above the rooftop. It lit up the entire area, including a barn on their neighbor's property a short distance away.

'We live on a ranch, a few miles from town," young Leonard explained. "I was up late with my brother watching television, when the living room lit up as if the sun had come up early. immediately, we went to the window and saw this

THE TATE PR   M GAZINE / Septembe 19 1

SPACING OUT
A group of other wordly-minded people bring stories of aliens, ufos and other strange goings-on in hopes to be taken seriously

Do you ever wonder if your human sexuality teacher is really an alien?

He could be, according to a group of people who believe in extraterrestrial life and otherwordly goings-on.

A veritable mass of people who claim to have proof of UFOs, aliens on Earth and corrupt, cove&up governmental experiment; will be converging on Phoenix this Friday, Saturday, Sunday and Monday, Sept. 6-9, for me 3rd Annual National New Age and Alien Agenda Conference.

The weekend's events will be held at the Airport Holiday Inn located at 4300 E. Washington St and will include eight informational sessions, 23 depth workshops and the Pleiadian Starship Experience

One of the speakers at the conference is former NASA space scientist Fred Bell, who will give a lecture on Extraterrestrial Holistic Survival Techniques.

Bell, who wholly believes in the other world, is discouraged by the current medium for information regaining UFOs and extraterrestrials — the tabloids He feels most college students arc aware only of what is read on the covers of the infamous supermarket papers, making it difficult for any mention of UFOs to be taken seriously.

"The stuff in the tabloids is trash," he said, explaining that people need to rise above the misinformation in such publications and give the serious researchers an honest chance

"I would encourage them (students) lo do some open-minded research and become familiar with the basic material and concepts before making any misinformed or premature judgements. Once you have a good understanflingof the real information, then you can choose to believe whatever you want."

According to Bell, there is much that goes on behind closed government doors that the public isn't made aware of. He said that there are had ETs working with key government figureheads in undertakings that are potentially harmful Is society.

The Majestic 12, said Bell, is made up of elite governmem officials who hold membership in Yale's secret society, the skull and bones and several high level fraternities. These 12 leaders, Bell continued, one of whom is President George Bush (member of the skull and bones society) are the one's that work with the bad ETs.

"They have done a lot of damage to humanity," Bell said. "One example is AIDS Most people don't realize it, but the AIDS virus was mar.-made.the result of a careless experiment by the American government The list of blatant wrongdoings is a long one."

However, Bell also stated that there are good ETs that he and others are working with in opposition lo the bad forces. Without elaborating, he said that Japan is presently a key aria in these communications

"The President Bush) is in the middle of 2 very touchy situation right now," explained Bell. "If he doesn'tcome out to the public with the information he has, he'll be basically condemning his political future.

The public is going to find out one way or another, and if they have to find out from a source outside the government, they won't be happy"

In addition to the above information, Bell will be presenting a Pleidian laser concert which is a "laser light rock music concert" featuring "authentic" sounds of UFOs. The concert takes place an Saturday at 10 p.m. and will be conducted by Bell Featured will be the Moody Blues' keyboardist, who is a [personal friend of Bell's

"I think the Saturday concert will be a big interest for college students especially," Bell said. "It's going to be an interesting evening"

Another presenter coming to the Valley this weekend is independent filmmaker/producer Joseph Randazzo.

Randazzo was skeptical about the concept of bad ETs working in tandem with the government, but said that he is now convinced that there is extraterrestrial life.

At the conference, the Californian film producer will share what he has experienced aver the past five years during his world tour. The tour was a project to gather solid information on actual UFO contacts for use in a TV miniseries.

"Actually, the original plan was to make a one-hour TV special, but the number of good cases that we found ended up being almost 200." Randazzo said

He said that he went into the project somewhat skeptically. "It was really tough. we ran into a lot of false claims, but the work paid off because we came up with some high quality information."

Randazzo said he worked with well-known UFO researchers in the project. He said that he is anxious to inform the general public of his findings in hopes of nurturing an understanding of this oft-misunderstood phenomena.

The independent producer helped in establishing The UFO Library, a body formed "to advance UFO and extraterrestrial research and brine the results to the attentar of the public." Randazzo donated al: of his research to the library.

Peter Wehinger, an astronomy professor with ASU, is not affiliated with the conference but said that from his scientific point of view, astronomers are always looking for the possibility of life somewhere else in the solar system. He believes, however, that evidence of UFOs and extraterrestrial life has been scarce.

"There is very little hard evidence of UFOs, so it is difficult to speculate." Wehinger said

Paul Schmidtke, also an astronomy professor at ASU, had only one comment on this weekend's activities

"A UFO is an unidentified flying object," he said. "If it's anything else, it's not a UFO"

In addition lo tile talk of flying saucers and such, a has! of Arizonans will be giving lectures of other goings-on at tile weekend's conference.

Jack Stephens and Calvin Vanness represent the Phoenix-based House of Dawn, an organization that, among other things helps in the rehabilitation of ex-convicts.

The two Valley residents are known for their ability tc 'channel' messages from the now deceased Nikola Tesla. Channeling essentially means relaying messages from a dead person through a living person.

When he was alive, Tesla was a well-known scientist and researcher He invented the fluorescent bulb and many claim that he, not Marconi, was the true inventor of radio.

Stephens will be the means of transmission, white Vanness will aid in hypnotizing his partner into a state of relaxation and mental openness.

"In order for Be channeling to work, my mind has to be completely free from distraction," Stephens sari.

"By the way, they're starting to use hypnotism in courts now because it's been proven that when you are hypnotized you can only tell the truth," added Vanness

Recent messages channeled through Stephens by Tesla have been focused on the present state of overall disorder in our world, saying that if we don't take drastic action the world will be ruined environmentally.

Also, according to Stephens, Tesla has said that in his voyages through space he has learned that there are

millions (bother populated planets out there, and all of these Itie forms are human

Stephens subsequently doesn't buy into Bell's description of good and bad ETs, saying that not only are the supposed 'aliens' all human, they are all good.

"They come to earth regularly to visit, but we are so wrapped up in our own world that we don't notice." Stephens said

He continued, explaining that the outer-space humans are stared by our lack of concern for what lies outside of our own worlds.

Another Phoenix resident, Alfred Bielek claims la have worked with Tesla or. the highly controversial Philadelphia Experiment which was made into a movie in the 1980s dealing with time warps, radiation and a huge government cover-up. Tesla is believed to be the original project director in the early 1940s.

The navy denies that any experiment ever took place, but Bielek said that their actions to control and/or destroy any conflicting information prove otherwise.

He said that as the result of a 1343 navy testing disaster, he was propelled into 1983 and then, shortly thereafter, came back to 1943.

He will speak on Saturday during session four of the conference as well as giving a more detailed workshop on Sunday, discussing other classified government projects dealing with time travel and other phenomena

The other motioned Arizona resident presenting this weekend. William Cooper, will be talking about a supposed conspiracy by the government/CIA to control the way we think about UFOs and alien life.

Also, he will conduct a workshop discussing other CIA conspiracies such as Kennedy's assasination

Cooper is one who at least partially concurs with Bell in saying that there are underground aliens working with the U S government

Conference passes cost $130 and are good for admission to all of the sessions and the laser concert Individual tickets to any one of the eight sessions cost $20, and admission to the Saturday evening laser and music spectacular is $15. Workshop entrance is not included in the pass: the price is $40 per workshop.

For further information call 230-5361, 223-0533 or, beginning September 5, the Holiday inn UFO Conference Desk at 273-7778,

(Continued from page 70)

shiny **object** passing by outside. It was sort of floating. It traveled across the yay until it got over our neighbor's barn. It stayed there for a minute or so, just going down and then going up—like a yo-yo." Leonard added that at its closest approach it came to within 10 **feet** of the roof of their ranch-style house. "I got the shakes," he later admitted.

A few nights later, Pura Garza of Gilroy called the *Hollister* Free *Lance* and said that her daughter, Tina, was home at about one a.m., talking to her boyfriend on the telephone, **when** she heard a "roaring, buzzing" sound coming from outside. Thinking that a car might have pulled into their driveway, the teenager went outside and looked around. **She** saw no one, and as she was about to re-enter the **house** she suddenly spotted a beam of white light shining from the roof of her house into a nearby orchard. The **beam** then blinked out **and** as soon **as** it vanished the strange noise faded into the distance.

Independent confirmation of the **UFOs** that harassed Gilroy came when several heat-sensitive fire alarms **went** off as the strange objects passed nearby. "I can't explain how this happened," noted Capt. Kenneth Higgins, of the Gilroy Rural Fire Department, 'but we have to take the reports of UFOs seriously. At least half-a-dozen fire alarms went off, and at each location we found no sign of a fire or that the alarms had been tampered with in any way." As far as is known, this is the first time that a fire department has become involved in a UFO flap.

Even police officials were refusing to dismiss the reports coming in Gilroy police officer George Steer issued a statement to the effect that "I know all the people who saw the UFO, **and** they just aren't the kind to be pulling something to get publicity. In fact, they'd rather not have it at all."

After the wave of sightings dwindled, civilian researchers probing the flap over northern California began to admit they were baffled.

Paul **Cerney,** a representative of the Center for UFO Studies in Illinois (the organization headed by Professor J. Allen Hynek) who is also regional director for the Mutual **UFO** Network, studied the reports closely. He interviewed many of the witnesses within hours of their original sightings. "We are quite impressed with the caliber of the witnesses," said Cerney "To date we've rounded up a total of 24 individuals who we believe saw something strange and unexplainable in the sky. All the sighting seem to he together, it is apparent that there was a vehicle of unknown origin maneuvering in the area for a period of several days."

Cerney, who has studied the phenomenon for nearly 10 years, says

he is particularly intrigued by the Lugo family's sighting. "I would give anything to have been in Mrs. Logo's shoes, because **she observed** the thing about 200 feet from her. She said it was the most beautiful display she'd ever **seen!**"

Elaborating on his investigation. Cerney said that **matters** got "hairy" during the peak of *the* flap. "It **seemed** like everyone was seeing something. One night I even got a call about two **a.m.,** from the San Jose sheriff's office. They wanted to meet me *right away.* It seems that several of their men were **watching** a UFO hover over an intersection just north of Gilroy, out in the country." Unfortunately, Cerney got there too late to see the UFO.

Thumbing through his files, Paul **Cerney** pulled out a **thick** folder. "UFO sightings are nothing really **new** around these parts" he emphasized. "I've been checking into several cases involving close encounters."

He said that one such incident took place a decade ago, up in the hills adjacent to Mount Madonna Park, eight miles west of Gilroy. "It **was** broad daylight, **and** several park rangers and maintenance men saw this large disc—200 feet in diameter, glassy **blue** and with an icy sheen to it—hovevering

'out of its way,' Donald climbed a *tree* to hide. There was silence for the next hour or so, and finally feeling he was safe, the man came down from his perch and built a signal fire to let his hunting companions know where he was. As if in response to his fire, a bright 'blaze' **appeared** on the horizon. As it got **closer,** he realized that the 'light' did not belong to any hunting party at all, but was something completely different—eerie

Cerney says that because of this, Donald climbed back up into the **same** tree. Then, from out of nowhere, came a small **circular device,** several feet in diameter, which dived at him. "Several minutes passed, and suddenly from the nearby thickets, two strange creatures **emerged.** They were **humanoids,** outfitted in a gray, shiny material, and had **some** sort of helmets or visors over **their** heads, so I couldn't make out any facial features," Donald said.

Even more **bizarre** was a third entity, more robot-like in appearance than the first two creatures. The entities appeared to become hostile when all three began climbing the tree as if to get at Donald. "Unable to get a good grip on the tree trunk, the third creature floated up to the now-terrified man, and began

There is **every** indication that the UFOnauts are trying *to* warn us that a catastrophe is in the offing. **Or maybe** if **they originate** from another dimension, they might have cause to worry, for what transpires here on our planet could indeed affect their own "parallel" world

over their heads at about 1.500 feet. It just hung there in one spot for three or four minutes, then it suddenly swung around in a large circle and moved out **over the** park. It was only four o'clock in the afternoon, so they felt it was impossible for them to have mistaken the object because of **any** lack of daylight. They absolutely refused to allow their names to be disclosed. Some of the men have since taken other jobs, while others **are still** employed as park rangers. It was a really good, solid, close encounter, with the kind of verifications **and** testimony we like to get whenever possible."

As is to be expected, the Gilroy area had also had its share of encounters with alien beings.

"There is one very famous case," notes Cerney, "which took place during the Labor Day weekend in 1964. The witness, who will only let us identify him by **the** code name Donald K, claims he was bow-and-arrow **hunting** with a number of companions, when he became separated from the group. As he pushed his way through the underbrush, he believed he heard something following close behind. Thinking it might be a bear, and that he was better off

billowing smoke from its **mouth.**" In defense, Cerney says. Donald took his bow and began shooting arrows at the floating UFOnaut. "The witness claims he was hitting a metallic surface, because he heard a 'ping' every time an arrow struck its mark."

Rescued at daybreak by his friends, **Donald's** hunting companions later told investigators they **had** seen a "brilliant light on the horizon' and had simply followed it until they found their missing friend.

Cerney says at first he thought the story was a hoax. "We're **now** convinced it wasn't. Donald has been hypnotized and still tells the same story. There are no **signs** that he is tying in any way The witness is a very quiet type of person and doesn't want any publicity" Cerney added that the case has been thoroughly investigated. "You could tell quite readily that whatever it was that happened affected **him** enormously. He was really shook up. His wife told **me** he woke up screaming every night for a month after going through his ordeal."

Reflecting on the many sightings in the Gilroy **area,** Paul Cerney **pointed** out that there was another case very similar to what has become known as the "bow-and-arrow incident," which has received absolutely no publicity and is known only to a *handful* of people. "In Nolan, Calif., an ex-deputy sheriff and his sister came face-to-face with a UFOnaut out in the woods. He was also bow-and-arrow hunting when the incident took place. The former deputy told me that he was going through a thicket, his sister about 150 feet behind him, when he encountered a strange creature coming straight toward him. They stood there, almost eyeball *to* eyeball, glaring at one another for practically a minute. The ex-deputy *said the being was only four feet high, very human in appearance, and dressed in a red suit with yellow lapels and a big white belt around his waist. After the confrontation — which ended in a standoff — was over, the little man, who *looked* to be no more than 30 or 40 years old, bounded up the mountain in 20-foot Sorg leaps."

So much for a brief *history* of UFO sightings around Gilroy.

Sifting through all the documentation, one question emerges above all *the others*: why the obvious concentration of UFO sightings in this one particular area?

Is *there* something "different" of unique about the community of Gilroy *which* would prompt attention from space beings?

White a superficial *review* of the many reports might prove fruitless, a deeper, more penetrating study of all the bits and pieces of information is bound to shed some additional light on why the UFOnauts have selected Gilroy as one of their prime targets *for* continual harassment.

In previous issues of *UFO Report*, authors such as the late Otto Binder wrote about the sizable percentage of UFO appearances that seemed to originate along the world's major fault lines. In Binder's definitive article, "Are UFOs Here To *Save* the Earth?" (*UFO Report*, Summer 1974), he has collected an impressive amount of data to prove his theory — that many times UFO sightings occur just prior to major tremore or earthquakes. According to Binder, approximately 40 percent of all flying saucer sightings are made along known stress lines in *our* planet's crust.

What has *this* to do with the Gilroy sightings?

Apparently a lot!

According to a recent report released by the U.S. Department of the Interior, there have been more than 25 tremors in northern California in the last 16 years. The Department lists the following *quakes* as taking place in the vicinity of Gilroy. Each of the four tremors registered an intensity of five or above on the Richter Scale, the highly sensitive seismographic instrument used to measure earthquake activity:

December 28, 1959;
January 19, 1960;
October 27, 1969;
March 30. 1970.

Interestingly enough, the Santa Cruz Mountains lie directly on top of the Calaveras fault zone, which has been unusually active in recent years. The Calaveras fault is merely one of some 20 active faults which exist in California. The best known, the San Andreas fault, runs the entire length of the stale. it was this fault that the "Sleeping Prophet," Edgar Cayce, saw cracking wide open just prior to his vision of California slipping into the sea.

What "hard" scientific evidence *is* there that California is due for a massively destructive earthquake? Plenty, according to geophysicist James H. Whitcomb, who has predicted that a sizable tremor — which could cause enormous property damage and loss of lives — will occur at any time between now and the summer of 1977. Whitcomb, a senior research fellow in the seismological laboratory at the *California* Institute of Technology, believes the earthquake could reach a magnitude of 5.5 to 6.5 on *the* Richter Scale — and that is cause for ample concern.

There is every indication that the UFOnauts are attempting to warn us such a catastrophe is in the offing. Or maybe, if *they* originate from another dimension, as several top-flight researchers now believe — they might have cause to worry themselves, for what transpires here on our physical *planet* could indeed, in some way, affect their own "parallel" world.

"The bright flashes of light and the searchlight beacon which residents have seen scanning the Santa Cruz Mountains has a definite *meaning* when taken in this context Several observers reportedly watched a UFO *direct* a beam of light or ray of some kind which swept the entire mountainside "as if taking photos or looking for something." One witness told *the* press that he felt the UFO was actually surveying the area.

For what possible reason? The UFOnauts could be trying to discover where the faults lie and maybe even repair the cracks in our planet's crust. The "beam of light" could be some sort of scanner which is able to X-ray the earth and "see" below the ground,

Verification of such a theory is, *of* course, hard to *come* by, but there are certain parallels in other UFO flaps to which we can point to support such a hypothesis.

Recently, for example, there was a massive wave of UFO sightings in northern New Jersey, directly across the Hudson River from New York City. Several residents of Bergen County claim to have seen "little men" in coveralls digging up soil samples in

North ... n Park. After placing the *effected* dirt in pouches slung over their shoulders, it was reported *the* UFOnauts walked back up a ladder and disappeared inside a circular craft that had windows and rotating lights. White the first *such* incident dates back to January 1975, there were three similar cases reported in the same park during the months of January and February of this year, lending support to the *theory* that they are returning to the exact spot — with a definite mission in mind.

Where's the earthquake-saucer connection? One newspaper, *The* Elizabeth *Daily Journal*, printed a front-page story on April 13, 1976, which told of a slight earth tremor that had jarred and had broken windows in nearby suburban communities, including North Bergen, site of the UFO landings.

Is all *this* a coincidence, or were the UFOs hovering over the park to provide us with dues, *trying* to alert us to something? Perhaps that a much bigger earthquake is due on the East Coast, as predicted by many seers.

By themselves, each one of these individual cases may lack sufficient meaning, but taken *together*, a pattern may be starting to emerge.

Many researchers around the world are taking the correlation between earthquakes and UFO sightings seriously.

Gordon Creighton of England, a distinguished UFOlogist and past editor of the *Flying Saucer* Review, said: "I regret to have to say that I think the most probable reason for at least some — if not all — of the current activities of alien beings in the sky and in the sea and on the surface of our planet, is that they are watching some

process that is now taking place within the bowels of Planet Earth."

Australia's Stan Seers, Director of the Queensland flying Saucer Research Bureau in Brisbane, subscribes to a similar theory. "There is," he says, "more than enough evidence to suggest a link between UFOs and seismic activity. Indeed, if one cares to plot all authentic reports on a map of the world, you will find that there is a noticeable concentration of sightings along the earth's main fault lines."

Every effort should be made to carefully study all future UFO flaps for fragments of information that lend themselves to such research. Such a careful probing of 1975's most extensive and highly dramatic UFO flap was a beginning to what may well be one solution to the *enigma* of the flying saucers.

Speakers voice fears, hopes for man at UFO meet

By Hal McKenzie
and James H. Robinson
News World staff

Last weekend the Christ Church Auditorium at 60th St. and Park Ave. was filled with UFOlogists, interested observers and perhaps a few extraterrestrials (some say they have been known to frequent UFO conferences), to hear speakers talk about a subject which changed their lives and will perhaps change the lives of everyone on earth in the near future.

Some of the speakers told of dark and dangerous forces connected with UFOs, such as the mysterious "Men in Black" who are said to threaten UFO researchers who know too much. But on the whole, the speakers at the National UFO and New Age Conference gave a message of hope and love — that benevolent entities from beyond the earth are concerned about us and watching over our development.

Timothy Green Beckley, editor of the UFO Review newspaper which sponsored the program, urged the audience on Saturday to "Approach the whole subject with an open mind." And, quoting from a message he and some of the other speakers had tried to communicate telepathically to UFOs on top of the Empire State building the previous Thursday, said to the extraterrestrials, "We ask that you show yourselves. Feel free to appear over our city. We hope that you will share your knowledge and hope for mankind."

Beckley then introduced a "charming young lady" whose "specialty is witchcraft and psychic phenomena — Witch Hazel."

The attractive Ms. Hazel, wearing a green robe and black cape, reminded the audience that UFO sightings go back some 5,000 years to the age of the Egyptian pharoahs. "No one knows what they are but they've been around a long time," she said.

Introducing the first scheduled speaker, Gray Barker on the mysterious "men in black," Witch Hazel said that her own experiences confirmed what Barker was about to say. "I have seen the men in black," she said — three men in black suits and hats, riding in a big black car, who shadowed her soon after she had a close encounter with a UFO which landed in her back yard, and then as mysteriously disappeared just as she made up her mind to confront them.

She urged all those people who had seen UFOs to report them, because "if everyone that had sightings reported en masse there would be millions. Then the government would have to do something to study these phenomena. Then we would get some answers."

The strangers among us

Gray Barker began his speech by greeting the FBI agent in the audience, any extraterrestrials traveling incognito, and "the two men in black in the audience."

Barker, one of the earliest writers about UFOs, was an associate of Albert K. Bender, head of the International Flying Saucer Bureau, one of the earliest civilian-run UFO groups. However, the activities of the group suddenly ceased, Barker said, after Bender was "hushed up" by three men in black suits who had paid a visit to his headquarters. Bender subsequently wrote a cryptic message in the organization's newsletter implying that he had stumbled upon the "secret" of UFOs, but could not reveal what it was out of fear of serious "consequences."

Barker related another story about a physician in New England who had taped

a hypnotic session with a man who claimed to have been disturbed by a UFO sighting. Barker said the doctor was threatened by the men in black who demanded that he turn the tapes over to them. To illustrate what would happen to him if he didn't comply, the stranger made a coin disappear before his eyes. Naturally, Barker said, he gave them the tapes.

Barker said the men in black also pose as Air Force researchers, policemen or even telephone repairmen. Some accounts depict them acting in a mechanical manner indicating they may be androids or robots.

Barker accompanied his talk with a film which showed no actual photographs of men in black, but showed a man in a trance transmitting an alleged telepathic message from some entity telling earthlings to stay out of space because it was their territory.

Case of the teleported warship

In a similar vein, Ann Genzlinger spoke about Dr. Morris K. Jessup, an early UFO researcher whose death in 1959 she said was staged to look like suicide. He was silenced, Genzlinger believes, because of his knowledge of a secret naval experiment in 1943 in which an entire ship was teleported from its dock in Philadelphia to its dock in the Norfolk area and back again. The experiment was revealed in a series of letters sent by a mysterious Carlos Allende.

The Allende Letters, as they are called, are still a source of controversy among UFO buffs although the original Allende is said to have confessed to Jim Lorenzen, international director of the Aerial Phenomena Research Organization (APRO) that he had made up the entire story as a hoax, according to the Encyclopedia of UFOs.

Genzlinger, however, will propound further on her theories concerning Jessup in a soon-to-be-released book, "The Jessup Dimension."

Next on Saturday's program was Pam Miller and Jean Ortiz, long-time UFO researchers who said that communications from extraterrestrials through radio, light beams and telepathy as well as personal contact is, had revealed the "secret" of UFO propulsion. They said that the craft follow the laws of quantum mechanics and relativity theory to transport themselves at the speed of light. A special force field enables the vehicles to assume the nature of photons, or light energy particles, while protecting the crew inside, they said.

They predicted that in the near future, this knowledge would become well known and a new golden age would dawn upon the earth.

Lynn and Anthony Volpe, who say they are soulmates from another galaxy who chose to re-incarnate on earth, concluded Saturday's program telling about the messages they say they have received from numerous extraterrestrials from a variety of distant planets.

The Volpes warn that the East Coast will suffer a destructive flood in the near future. "For the past seven years I have had visionary dreams of the flooding out of the eastern seaboard," states Lynn. Anthony also predicted many changes in *(continued elsewhere)*

Photos by Victoria Shaw

Kitty Steele, a psychic who said she began to receive messages from a Venusian ship in 1956, says she believes the space people are concerned about earth.

Bill Cox describes the amazing healing powers of "space people" he had met.

Jane Allyson, a New York psychic healer, said she received her healing power in a close encounter with a UFO on the roof of her Manhattan apartment building.

Gray Barker spoke about mysterious "men in black" who are said to threaten UFO researchers when they get too close to the truth.

ON THE COVER: This is one of a series of color photos taken in Yungay, Peru, in March 1967, by Augusto Arranda while he was trekking in the mountains near Yungay, located about 11,000 feet above sea level. Photo courtesy Colman Vonkeviczky, ICUFON.

THE NEWS WORLD, NEW YORK CITY, OCTOBER 3, 1981

www.ingramcontent.com/pod-product-compliance
Lightning Source LLC
Chambersburg PA
CBHW081631040426
42449CB00014B/3262